2003 SUPPLEMENT

CASES AND MATERIALS

CORPORATIONS AND OTHER BUSINESS ORGANIZATIONS

EIGHTH EDITION—UNABRIDGED AND CONCISE

by

MELVIN ARON EISENBERG
Koret Professor of Law
University of California at Berkeley

FOUNDATION PRESS

NEW YORK, NEW YORK

2003

THOMSON

WEST

COPYRIGHT © 2001, 2002 FOUNDATION PRESS
COPYRIGHT © 2003 By FOUNDATION PRESS
     395 Hudson Street
     New York, NY 10014
     Phone Toll Free 1–877–888–1330
     Fax (212) 367–6799
     fdpress.com
Printed in the United States of America

ISBN 1–58778–548–X

 TEXT IS PRINTED ON 10% POST CONSUMER RECYCLED PAPER

ANALYTICAL TABLE OF CONTENTS

TABLE OF CASES

Principal cases are in bold type. Non-principal cases are in roman type. References are to Pages.

2003 SUPPLEMENT

CASES AND MATERIALS

CORPORATIONS AND OTHER BUSINESS ORGANIZATIONS

*

CHAPTER II

PARTNERSHIP

SECTION 3. THE ONGOING OPERATION OF PARTNERSHIPS

(a) Management

Insert the following Note at p. 43 of the Unabridged Edition and p. 35 of the Concise Edition, after Summers v. Dooley:

SANCHEZ v. SAYLOR, 129 N.M. 742, 13 P.3d 960 (2000). Sanchez and Saylor were partners. A third party was considering lending money to the partnership to finance a proposed restructuring of the partnership's debt, but it required Sanchez to provide his personal financial statements as a condition to granting the loan. Sanchez refused to furnish the statements that the potential lender required. Saylor brought suit against Sanchez on the ground that Sanchez's refusal to provide his financial statements to the potential lender violated his fiduciary obligations. Held, for Sanchez:

> ... We turn to *Covalt v. High*, 100 N.M. 700, 675 P.2d 999 (Ct.App.1983) ... Covalt and High formed an oral partnership which owned and rented an office to a corporation, CSI, in which Covalt owned 25 percent of the corporate stock and High owned 75 percent.... After resigning from CSI, Covalt demanded that the partnership increase CSI's rent, but High took no action. See *id.* The increase in rent would benefit the partnership, but it was detrimental to High. The district court found that CSI could afford the rent increase and High had breached his fiduciary duty. See *id.*

> In reversing, this Court stated that "all partners have equal rights in the management and conduct of the business of the partnership," that Covalt therefore "was legally invested with an equal voice in the management of the partnership affairs," and that "neither partner had the right to impose his will or decision concerning the operation of the partnership business upon the other." *Id.* at 703, 675 P.2d at 1002. The fact that a proposal benefitted the partnership did not require High to agree. See id. As authority for its decision, *Covalt* cited UPA, Section 54–1–

18(H), stating "any difference arising as to ordinary matters connected with the partnership business may be decided by a majority of the partners." Further, the Court relied on the interpretation of the UPA language by the Idaho Supreme Court in *Summers v. Dooley*, 94 Idaho 87, 481 P.2d 318 (1971) that the language is mandatory rather than permissive in nature and means that business differences must be decided by a majority, not by one of two equal partners when the other objects. *See Summers*, 481 P.2d at 320–21.

Simply stated, *Covalt* says that, absent an enforceable agreement covering such circumstances of disagreement, when both partners in a two-partner partnership disagree on an advantageous prospective business transaction, it is dissolution, not an action for breach of fiduciary duty, that is the appropriate avenue of relief. . . .

. . . Without [the *Covalt*] rule, virtually each instance in which one partner for personal reasons does not agree with a proposed transaction that will benefit the partnership can result in a claim for breach of his or her partnership or fiduciary duty. Absent an enforceable contractual duty to agree, if the two partners cannot agree and do not want to (or cannot) continue their partnership, under *Covalt* the remedy is dissolution. . . .

SECTION 4.   THE AUTHORITY OF A PARTNER

Insert the following case at p. 54 of the Unabridged Edition, and p. 39 of the Concise Edition, preceding the Note on the Authority of Partners under RUPA:

RNR Investments Limited Partnership v. Peoples First Community Bank

District Court of Appeal of Florida, First District, 2002
812 So.2d 561

■ VAN NORTWICK, J. . . .

Factual and Procedural History

RNR is a Florida limited partnership formed pursuant to chapter 620, Florida Statutes, to purchase vacant land in Destin, Florida, and to construct a house on the land for resale. Bernard Roeger was RNR's general partner and Heinz Rapp, Claus North, and S.E. Waltz, Inc., were limited partners. The agreement of limited partnership provides for various restrictions on the authority of the general partner. Paragraph 4.1 of the agreement required the general partner to prepare a budget covering the cost of acquisition and construction of the project (defined as the "Approved Budget") and further provided, in pertinent part, as follows:

> The Approved Budget for the Partnership is attached hereto as Exhibit "C" and is approved by evidence of the signatures of the Partners on the signature pages of this Agreement.... In no event, without Limited Partner Consent, shall the Approved Budget be exceeded by more than five percent (5%), nor shall any line item thereof be exceeded by more than ten percent (10%), ...

Paragraph 4.3 restricted the general partner's ability to borrow, spend partnership funds and encumber partnership assets, if not specifically provided for in the Approved Budget. Finally, with respect to the development of the partnership project, paragraph 2.2(b) provided:

> The General Partner shall not incur debts, liabilities or obligations of the Partnership which will cause any line item in the Approved Budget to be exceeded by more than ten percent (10%) or which will cause the aggregate Approved Budget to be exceed by more than five percent (5%) unless the General Partner shall receive the prior written consent of the Limited Partner.

In June 1998, RNR, through its general partner, entered into a construction loan agreement, note and mortgage in the principal amount of $990,000. From June 25, 1998 through Mar. 13, 2000, the bank disbursed the aggregate sum of $952,699, by transfers into RNR's bank account. All draws were approved by an architect, who certified that the work had progressed as indicated and that the quality of the work was in accordance with the construction contract. No representative of RNR objected to any draw of funds or asserted that the amounts disbursed were not associated with the construction of the house.

RNR defaulted under the terms of the note and mortgage by failing to make payments due in July 2000 and all monthly payments due thereafter. The Bank filed a complaint seeking foreclosure. RNR filed an answer and affirmative defenses. In its first affirmative defense, RNR alleged that the Bank had failed to review the limitations on the general partner's authority in RNR's limited partnership agreement. RNR asserted that the Bank had negligently failed to investigate and to realize that the general partner had no authority to execute notes, a mortgage and a construction loan agreement and was estopped from foreclosing. The Bank filed a motion for summary judgment with supporting affidavits attesting to the amounts due and owing and the amount of disbursements under the loan.

In opposition to the summary judgment motion, RNR filed the affidavit of Stephen E. Waltz, the president one of RNR's limited partners, S.E. Waltz, Inc. In that affidavit, Mr. Waltz stated that the partners anticipated that RNR would need to finance the construction of the residence, but that paragraph 2.2(b) of the partnership agreement limited the amount of any loan the general partner could obtain on behalf of RNR to an amount that would not exceed by more than 10% the approved budget on any one line item or exceed the aggregate approved budget by more than 5%, unless the general partner received the prior written consent of the limited partners. Waltz alleged that the limited partners understood and orally agreed that the general partner would seek financing in the approximate amount of $650,000. Further, Waltz stated:

> Even though the limited partners had orally agreed to this amount, a written consent was never memorialized, and to my surprise, the [Bank], either through its employees or attorney, . . . never requested the same from any of the limited partners at any time prior to [or] after the closing on the loan from the [Bank] to RNR.

> Waltz alleged that the partners learned in the spring of 2000 that, instead of obtaining a loan for $650,000, Roeger had obtained a loan for $990,000, which was secured by RNR's property. He stated that the limited partners did not consent to Roeger obtaining a loan from the Bank in the amount of $990,000 either orally or in writing and that the limited partners were never contacted by the Bank as to whether they had consented to a loan amount of $990,000.

RNR asserts that a copy of the limited partnership agreement was maintained at its offices. Nevertheless, the record contains no copy of an Approved Budget of the partnership or any evidence that would show that a copy of RNR's partnership agreement or any partnership budget was given to the Bank or that any notice of the general partner's restricted authority was provided to the Bank.

    . . . [T]he trial court entered a summary final judgment of foreclosure in favor of the Bank. The foreclosure sale has been stayed pending the outcome of this appeal. . . .

Apparent Authority of the General Partner

Although the agency concept of apparent authority was applied to partnerships under the common law, see, e.g., *Taylor v. Cummer Lumber Co.*, 59 Fla. 638, 52 So. 614, 616 (1910), in Florida the extent to which the partnership is bound by the acts of a partner acting within the apparent authority is now governed by statute. Section 620.8301(1), Florida Statutes (2000),[1] a part of the Florida Revised Uniform Partnership Act (FRUPA), provides:

> Each partner is an agent of the partnership for the purpose of its business. An act of a partner, including the execution of an

---

1. RNR mistakenly argues that section 620.8301(1) has no application to a limited partnership because that section is part of the Florida Revised Uniform Partnership Act, not the Florida Revised Uniform Limited Partnership Act. Section 620.186, however, provides, as follows:

In any case not provided for in this act, the provisions of the Uniform Partnership Act or the Revised Uniform Partnership Act of 1995, as applicable, and the rules of law and equity shall govern.

instrument in the partnership name, for apparently carrying on in the ordinary scope of partnership business or business of the kind carried on by the partnership, in the geographic area in which the partnership operates, binds the partnership unless the partner had no authority to act for the partnership in the particular manner and the person with whom the partner was dealing knew or had received notification that the partner lacked authority.

Thus, even if a general partner's actual authority is restricted by the terms of the partnership agreement, the general partner possesses the apparent authority to bind the partnership in the ordinary course of partnership business or in the business of the kind carried on by the partnership, unless the third party "knew or had received a notification that the partner lacked authority." Id. "Knowledge" and "notice" under FRUPA are defined in section 620.8102. That section provides that "[a] person knows a fact if the person has actual knowledge of the fact." § 620.8102(1), Fla. Stat. (2000). Further, a third party has notice of a fact if that party "(a) [k]nows of the fact; (b) [h]as received notification of the fact; or (c) [h]as reason to know the fact exists from all other facts known to the person at the time in question." § 620.8102(2), Fla. Stat. (2000). Finally, under section 620.8303 a partnership may file a statement of partnership authority setting forth any restrictions in a general partner's authority.

Commentators have described the purpose of these knowledge and notice provisions, as follows:

> Under RUPA, the term knew is confined to actual knowledge, which is cognitive awareness. . . . Therefore, despite the similarity in language, RUPA provides greater protection [than the Uniform Partnership Act (UPA)] to third persons dealing with partners, who may rely on the partner's apparent authority absent actual knowledge or notification of a restriction in this regard. RUPA effects a slight reallocation of the risk of unauthorized agency power in favor of third parties. That is consistent with notions of the expanded liability of principals since the UPA was drafted.

> RUPA attempts to balance its shift toward greater protection of third parties by providing several new ways for partners to protect themselves against unauthorized actions by a rogue partner. First, the partnership may notify a third party of a partner's lack of authority. Such notification is effective upon receipt, whether or not the third party actually learns of it. More significantly, the partnership may file a statement of partnership authority restricting a partner's authority.

Donald J. Weidner & John W. Larson, *The Revised Uniform Partnership Act: The Reporters' Overview*, 49 BUS. LAW 1, 31–32 (1993) (footnotes omitted). "Absent actual knowledge, third parties have no duty to inspect the partnership agreement or inquire otherwise to ascertain the extent of a partner's actual authority in the ordinary course of business, . . . even if they have some reason to question it."

Id. at 32 n. 200. The apparent authority provisions of section 620.8301(1), reflect a policy by the drafters that "the risk of loss from partner misconduct more appropriately belongs on the partnership than on third parties who do not knowingly participate in or take advantage of the misconduct ..." J. Dennis [Hynes], *Notice and Notification Under the Revised Uniform Partnership Act: Some Suggested Changes*, 2 J. SMALL & EMERGING BUS. L. 299, 308 (1998).

Analysis

Under section 620.8301(1), the determination of whether a partner is acting with authority to bind the partnership involves a two-step analysis. The first step is to determine whether the partner purporting to bind the partnership apparently is carrying on the partnership business in the usual way or a business of the kind carried on by the partnership. An affirmative answer on this step ends the inquiry, unless it is shown that the person with whom the partner is dealing actually knew or had received a notification that the partner lacked authority. See *Kristerin Dev. Co. v. Granson Inv.*, 394 N.W.2d 325, 330 (Iowa 1986) (applying Iowa version of UPA). Here, it is undisputed that, in entering into the loan, the general partner was carrying on the business of RNR in the usual way. The dispositive question in this appeal is whether there are issues of material fact as to whether the Bank had actual knowledge or notice of restrictions on the general partner's authority.

RNR argues that, as a result of the restrictions on the general partner's authority in the partnership agreement, the Bank had constructive knowledge of the restrictions and was obligated to inquire as to the general partner's specific authority to bind RNR in the construction loan. We cannot agree. Under section 620.8301, the Bank could rely on the general partner's apparent authority, unless it had actual knowledge or notice of restrictions on that authority. While the RNR partners may have agreed upon restrictions that would limit the general partner to borrowing no more than $650,000 on behalf of the partnership, RNR does not contend and nothing before us would show that the Bank had actual knowledge or notice of any restrictions on the general partner's authority. Here, the partnership could have protected itself by filing a statement pursuant to section 620.8303 or by providing notice to the Bank of the specific restrictions on the authority of the general partner.

RNR relies on *Green River Assocs. v. Mark Twain Kansas City Bank*, 808 S.W.2d 894 (Mo.Ct.App.1991), as authority for its argument that the Bank was negligent in providing financing in reliance upon the apparent authority of the general partner. RNR's reliance is misplaced. In *Green River*, the express language of the partnership agreement, known to the bank, required that the proceeds of the loan be deposited in the partnership bank account. The court found that, when the bank wired partnership money to an account of an entity other than the partnership, the bank knew that its actions were contrary to the partnership agreement. Therefore, the court reasoned, the bank could not argue that the general partner had apparent authority to direct the bank to disburse the funds to a non-partnership account. Id. at 897. As a result, because the bank paid the loan proceeds to an entity other than the borrower, the court concluded that the partnership's note was void for lack of consideration. Id. at 898. Interestingly, Green River rejected the partnership's claim based upon the bank's alleged negligence. Id. at 899. Here, unlike *Green River*, all funds advanced by the Bank were paid into RNR's account. There is no basis for arguing a failure of consideration. Further, there is no fact in the record that would show that the Bank had actual knowledge or notice of restrictions on the general partner's authority.

Because there is no disputed issue of fact concerning whether the Bank had actual knowledge or notice of restrictions on the general partner's authority to borrow, summary judgment was proper.

AFFIRMED.

■ Miner and Wolf, JJ, concur.

SECTION 5. LIABILITY FOR PARTNERSHIP OBLIGATIONS

Insert the following Note at p. 55 of the Unabridged Edition, and p. 40 of the Concise Edition, following the cross-references to the UPA and RUPA:

DAVIS v. LOFTUS, 334 Ill. App.3d 761, 778 N.E.2d 1144 (Ill. App. 2002). Davis claimed that two lawyers, Loftus and Engel, at the law firm of Gottlieb & Schwartz had committed malpractice in connection with a real estate transaction that Davis had engaged in. Davis sued all the partners of the firm for damages. Some of the partners of the firm, including Frink, were denominated "income partners," as opposed to "equity partners." According to the partnership agreement, the firm paid each income partner a fixed level of compensation determined on an annual basis by the Executive Committee, plus a bonus. The partnership agreement added that: "Income Partners will not share in Partnership Net Profit or Loss." Each income partner made a "capital contribution" of $10,000 to the firm. If an income partner withdrew from the firm, or upon dissolution of the firm, the firm would return the $10,000 capital contribution to the income partner without any adjustment for the growth or profits of the firm from the time of the capital contribution. Income partners also had no voting rights and were not eligible to serve on the executive committee.

Held, the "income partners" were not partners with the meaning of the liability provisions of the Uniform Partnership Act:

Section 13 of the Uniform Partnership Act (the Act) (805 ILCS 205/13 (West 1992)) provides that a partnership is liable for any wrongful act of any partner acting in the course of partnership business. Section 15 makes all partners liable for any such acts. 805 ILCS 205/15 (West 1992). The trial court found Frink and others not liable for the acts of Loftus and Engel based on its finding that the income partners of Gottlieb & Schwartz are not "partners" within the meaning of the Act.

The substance and not the form of a business relationship determines whether the relationship qualifies as a partnership. *Koestner v. Wease & Koestner Jewelers, Inc.*, 63 Ill.App.3d 1047, 1050–51, 21 Ill.Dec. 76, 381 N.E.2d 11 (1978). Thus, we must decide whether the provisions of the partnership agreement pertaining to "Income Partners" make them partners within the meaning of the Act.

Cook v. Lauten, 1 Ill.App.2d 255, 117 N.E.2d 414 (1954), controls our disposition of this appeal. In that case the plaintiff and the defendant signed an "agreement for junior partnership." *Cook*, 1 Ill.App.2d at 258, 117 N.E.2d 414. The agreement named the plaintiff as the managing partner and sole owner of the firm's assets, and established the defendant's compensation as a fixed annual salary plus a bonus. While the defendant could advance money to the firm, the firm would only return the same amount later. The defendant, as a junior partner, had no right to participate in the firm's profits or losses. The court held:

> "[T]he agreement for a 'junior partnership' negatives every one of the elements essential to constitute a partnership relation. * * * Defendant's salary is fixed regardless of profits or losses of the alleged partnership and plaintiff as managing partner may by unilateral action alter defendant's share of the profit at will. * * * In short, defendant was to have no interest in the so-called 'partnership' except his unpaid salary and one month's bonus." *Cook*, 1 Ill.App.2d at 259, 117 N.E.2d 414.

Here, too, the agreement established that income partners, including Frink, received a fixed salary plus a bonus, and the income partners took no share of the partnership's profit or loss. While income partners paid a "capital contribution" to the firm, the firm would repay the same amount, without regard to the firm's profit or loss from the time of the "capital contribution." The executive committee, like the managing partner in *Cook*, set the level of compensation for all income partners. Moreover, the income partners had no right to vote on the management or conduct of the partnership business. See 805 ILCS 205/18(e) (West 1992). Following *Cook*, we find that income partners under Gottlieb & Schwartz' partnership agreement do not qualify as partners within the meaning of the Act, and therefore the Act provides no basis for holding income partners liable for the acts of Loftus and Engel.

———

CHAPTER IV

CORPORATE STRUCTURE

SECTION 2. THE ALLOCATION OF POWER BETWEEN MANAGEMENT AND SHAREHOLDERS

Insert the following case at p. 203 of the Unabridged Edition, and p. 146 of the Concise Edition, at the end of Section 2:

MM Companies, Inc. v. Liquid Audio, Inc.
Supreme Court of Delaware, 2003
813 A.2d 1118

■ Before: HOLLAND, BERGER, and STEELE, JUSTICES.

■ HOLLAND, JUSTICE:

This is an expedited appeal from a final judgment entered by the Court of Chancery. That final judgment permitted an incumbent board of directors to adopt defense measures which changed the size and composition of the board's membership. The record reflects that those defensive actions were taken for the primary purpose of impeding the shareholders' right to vote effectively in an impending election for successor directors. We have concluded that the judgment of the Court of Chancery must be reversed. This matter is remanded for further proceedings in accordance with this opinion.

Procedural Background

On August 26, 2002, MM Companies, Inc. ("MM") filed its original complaint in this action in the Court of Chancery against Liquid Audio, Inc. ("Liquid Audio"), as well as Raymond A. Doig, Gerald W. Kearby, Robert G. Flynn, Stephen V. Imbler and Ann Winblad (the "Director Defendants"). The original complaint sought injunctive relief against the August 22, 2002 action taken by the board of directors of Liquid Audio ("Board") to expand from five to seven members, and the purported effects that expansion might have on Liquid Audio's 2002 annual meeting that was scheduled for September 26, 2002. MM alleged that the Director Defendants' decision to expand the Board violated the principles established by the decision of the Court of Chancery in *Blasius*[1] and the decision of this Court in *Unocal*.[2] ...

1. *Blasius Indus., Inc. v. Atlas Corp.*, 564 A.2d 651 (Del.Ch.1988).

Chancery Court Denies Relief

... [A] trial was held on October 21, 2002. At the conclusion of the trial, the Court of Chancery ruled in favor of the defendants, holding that the Board expansion did not violate Delaware law under either *Blasius* or *Unocal*. The Court of Chancery rejected the plaintiff's independent *Blasius* claim on the basis that the addition of two new directors "did not impact the shareholder vote or the shareholder choices in any significant way." The Court of Chancery rejected the plaintiff's *Unocal* claim, on the basis that: plaintiff did "not contend that the board expansion was coercive," the expansion was not "preclusive," because the "choices that the shareholders had before the board action was taken were the same as they had after," and the plaintiff failed to make a showing that "the action that the board took falls outside a range of reasonable responses."

Following the entry of the final judgment, MM filed a Notice of Appeal and a Motion for Expedited Scheduling. The motion was granted by this Court. Oral argument was held on December 3, 2002.

Issues on Appeal

MM has raised two issues on appeal. First, it contends that the Court of Chancery erred in ruling that the "compelling justification" standard, as enunciated in *Blasius*, was not applicable to the Board's action. In support of that argument, MM relies upon the finding by the Court of Chancery that the Director Defendants manipulated the size and composition of the Liquid Audio board during a contested election for directors *primarily* to interfere with and impede the success of MM's ability to gain two-of-five directorships on the Board, and, thus, to diminish the influence of MM's nominees on the Board.

Second, MM argues that the Court of Chancery erred in ruling that the precepts of this Court's holding in *Unocal* and its progeny were not violated by the Board's defensive action. According to MM, the Director Defendants never identified a legally cognizable threat to the corporate policy and effectiveness of Liquid Audio and, to the extent that a threat existed, never demonstrated that the "manipulation of the size and composition" of the Liquid Audio board was a reasonable response in relation to such threat. Based upon that asserted lack of record evidence, MM submits the Court of Chancery erred in concluding that this Court's holding in *Unocal* was not violated.

Background Facts

Liquid Audio is a publicly traded Delaware corporation, with its principal place of business in Redwood City, California. Liquid Audio's primary business consists of providing software and services for the digital transmission of music over the Internet. MM is a publicly traded Delaware corporation with its principal place of business in New York,

2. *Unocal Corp. v. Mesa Petroleum Co.,*
493 A.2d 946 (Del.1985).

New York. As of October 2002, MM was part of a group that collectively held slightly over 7% of Liquid Audio's common stock.

For more than a year, MM has sought to obtain control of Liquid Audio. On October 26, 2001, MM sent a letter to the Liquid Audio board of directors indicating its willingness to acquire the company at approximately $3 per share. Liquid Audio's board rejected MM's offer as inadequate, after an analysis of the offer and consultation with its investment banker, Broadview International LLC ("Broadview").

Liquid Audio's bylaws provide for a staggered board of directors that is divided into three classes. Only one class of directors is up for election in any given year. The effect is to prevent an insurgent from obtaining control of the company in under two years.[3]

From November 2001, until August 2002, the Liquid Audio board of directors consisted of five members divided into three classes. Class I had two members (defendants Flynn and Imbler), whose terms expire in 2003; Class II had one member (defendant Winblad), whose term expires in 2004; and Class III had two members (defendants Kearby and Doig), whose terms expired in 2002. Defendants Flynn, Doig and Imbler were not elected to the Board by the stockholders of Liquid Auido. They were appointed to the Board by the directors of Liquid Audio to fill vacancies on the Board.

In October 2001, prior to the appointment of defendants Doig and Imbler to the Board, MM requested the Liquid Audio board to call a special meeting of the company's stockholders to consider filling the existing vacancies on the Board and to consider other proposals to be presented to the stockholders. On October 24, 2001, the Liquid Audio board issued a press release which stated that it had denied MM's request to call a special meeting because the Board believed that under the Liquid Audio bylaws stockholders are not permitted to call special meetings. Thereafter, the Board appointed defendants Doig and Imbler to the Liquid Audio board of directors.

MM's Various Actions

On November 13, 2001, MM announced its intention to nominate its own candidates for the two seats on Liquid Audio's board of directors that were up for election at the next annual meeting. On December 18, 2001, MM delivered a formal notice to Liquid Audio stating that it intended to nominate Seymour Holtzman and James Mitarotonda as directors to fill the two seats on the Board then held by the individuals designated as Class III directors whose terms expired at the next annual meeting. The December 18, 2001 notice also requested that the Board adopt resolutions declaring certain amendments to the certificate of incorporation and bylaws advisable and that such amendments be submitted to the stockholders.

---

3. *See* Lucian Arye Bebchuk, John C. Coates, IV & Guhan Subramanian, *The Powerful Antitakeover Force of Staggered Boards:* *Theory, Evidence, and Policy,* 54 Stanford L.Rev. 887 (2002).

On December 20, 2001, MM sent notice to Liquid Audio informing the Board of its intention to bring before the annual meeting a proposal that would amend the bylaws and increase the size of the Board by four members. The December 20, 2001 notice also informed the Board of MM's intention to nominate four individuals as directors to fill those four newly created directorships. MM subsequently demanded that the Board commit to fixing an annual meeting date by February 22, 2002.

On February 22, 2002, MM renewed its October 2001 offer to acquire Liquid Audio. That offer, however, was at the reduced price of $2.50 per share. The Liquid Audio board rejected that offer as inadequate.

On May 17, 2002, MM forwarded a written demand to Liquid Audio under Section 220, which requested a list of stockholders of Liquid Audio and related materials. Liquid Audio did not respond to the demand letter. On May 30, 2002, MM filed an action under Section 220 seeking, among other things, an order of the Court of Chancery directing that Liquid Audio forward to MM the information identified in the demand letter. A hearing before the Court of Chancery with respect to the Section 220 complaint was scheduled to be held on June 14, 2002.

On June 10, 2002, MM filed proxy materials with the Securities and Exchange Commission ("SEC") and commenced soliciting proxies for a shareholder meeting Liquid Audio planned to have on July 1, 2002. In addition to proposing two nominees for the Board, MM's proxy statement included a takeover proposal to increase the size of the Board by an additional four directors and to fill those positions with its nominees. As outlined in its initial proxy materials, MM's takeover proposal sought to expand the Board from five members to nine. If MM's two directors were elected and its four proposed directors were also placed on the Board, MM would control a majority of the Board.

Alliance Merger

On June 13, 2002, Liquid Audio announced a stock-for-stock merger transaction with Alliance Entertainment Corp. ("Alliance"). This announcement came three days after MM mailed its proxy statement and other materials to the stockholders of Liquid Audio, and one day before the scheduled Court of Chancery hearing in connection with the Section 220 complaint. In addition to announcing the merger, the Liquid Audio board also announced that: the July 1, 2002 meeting would be postponed; a special meeting of stockholders of Liquid Audio would be held sometime in the future to vote upon the merger; and, if the merger received the requisite stockholder and regulatory approval, the merger would "close in the Fall of 2002." Based upon this announcement, the annual meeting was postponed indefinitely by the Liquid Audio board.

The merger with Alliance that was announced to the stockholders of Liquid Audio on June 13, 2002 and the merger agreement executed by Liquid Audio and Alliance in connection therewith were not approved unanimously by the Board. The record reflects that at a meeting of the Board held to vote upon the merger and the merger agreement, defendants Kearby, Flynn, Imbler and Doig voted for the merger and the merger agreement and defendant Winblad voted against the merger and the merger agreement.

After Liquid Audio announced that the annual meeting would be postponed indefinitely, MM filed an amended complaint, seeking an order of the Court of Chancery directing Liquid Audio to hold the annual meeting as soon as possible, and a motion for expedited and summary proceedings. On June 20, 2002, the Court of Chancery granted MM's motion for expedited and summary proceedings and directed that a trial in connection with MM's application for relief be held on July 15, 2002.

Shortly, before that trial took place, the Liquid Audio board announced that certain terms of the merger agreement had been modified to permit Liquid Audio to conduct a self-tender offer under which Liquid would acquire up to 10 million shares of its common stock at $3.00 per share in cash, if the merger was approved by the stockholders of Liquid Audio. Upon consummation of the merger and a fully subscribed self-tender offer, Liquid Audio's stockholders would own 26% and Alliance stockholders would own 74% of the combined enterprise. The Liquid Audio board also announced that certain senior officers of Liquid Audio committed not to tender their shares in the self-tender offer. Finally, the Liquid Audio board announced that the Director Defendants reduced the "trigger" of Liquid Audio's shareholders rights plan or "poison pill" to 10% from 15%. The modified merger agreement was approved unanimously by the Board at a meeting held on July 14, 2002.

After expedited discovery, a trial was held on July 15, 2002. The Court of Chancery ordered that the annual meeting of Liquid Audio's shareholders occur on September 26, 2002. The record date for the meeting was August 12, 2002.

Board Adds Two Directors

By the middle of August 2002, it was apparent that MM's nominees, Holtzman and Mitarotonda, would be elected at the annual meeting, to serve in place of the two incumbent nominees, as members of the Liquid Audio board. On August 23, 2002, Liquid Audio announced that the Board had amended the bylaws to increase the size of the Board to seven members from five members. The Board also announced that defendants James D. Somes and Judith N. Frank had been appointed to fill the newly created directorships. Defendant Somes was appointed to serve as a Class II member of the Board and defendant Frank was appointed to serve as a Class I member of the Board. After the Board expanded from five directors to seven, MM revised its proxy statement to note that its proposal to add four directors, if successful, would have resulted in a board with eleven directors, instead of nine.

MM Challenges Board Expansion

On August 26, 2002, MM filed its initial lawsuit challenging the Board's decision to add two directors. In the initial complaint, MM alleged that the Board expansion interfered with MM's ability to solicit proxies in favor of its two nominees for election to the Liquid Audio board at the annual meeting. In support of this claim, MM alleged that "some stockholders would believe that electing two members of a seven-member board, rather than two members of a five-member board, would not be worthwhile, and, thus, such stockholders simply would not vote."

At the September 26, 2002 annual meeting, the two directors proposed by MM, Holtzman and Mitarotonda, were elected to serve as directors of the Board. Liquid Audio's stockholders, however, did not approve MM's takeover proposals that would have expanded the Board and placed MM's four nominees on the Board. The stockholders' vote on both issues was consistent with the recommendation of Institutional Investor Services ("ISS"), a proxy voting advisory service, which had recommended that the stockholders vote in favor of MM's two nominees, but recommended against stockholders voting to give MM outright and immediate control of the Board.

Following the election of MM's two nominees to the Liquid Audio board of directors at the annual meeting, MM filed an amended lawsuit, challenging the Board's appointment of directors Somes and Frank. In the amended complaint, MM alleged that the expansion of the Liquid Audio board, its timing, and the Board's appointment of two new directors violated the principles of *Blasius* and *Unocal*. According to MM, that action frustrated MM's attempt to gain a "substantial presence" on the Board for at least one year and guaranteed that Liquid Audio's management will have control of, or a substantial presence on, the Board for at least two years.

Board's Primary Purpose: Impede Effective Vote

The expedited trial was held by the Court of Chancery, as scheduled. During pretrial discovery, the Director Defendants identified the primary purpose of their action in expanding the Liquid Audio board from five to seven members. Their response to the following interrogatory request is illustrative:

> 6. Summarize the complete reasons that support the decision of the Board to amend the Bylaws or to approve the Bylaw Amendment.

> *Response:* Subject to and without waiving the General Objections stated above, Defendants state that the Board of Directors, after receiving legal advice regarding their fiduciary duties, voted to expand the size of the board after a thorough and deliberate

evaluation of the qualifications and expected contributions of Judith N. Frank and James D. Somes to Liquid's current operations and business plans. Furthermore, the Board of Directors believed that the Company would benefit from having seven directors instead of only five directors. In particular, the Company believed that it would benefit from creating new directorships and placing two additional outside directors on the board in light of the potential difficulties that may result from the addition of MM's nominees on the Board and in light of the possibility that one or more directors would decide to resign for a variety of reasons including, but not limited to, a reluctance to serve alongside a slate of directors proposed by MM. . . .

When defendant Doig was asked to elaborate upon this response to the interrogatory request, he testified:

There was concern that if the MM slate won and then it did become too acrimonious and that Ms. Winblad and Mr. Imbler decided to resign, that ran an undue risk to the shareholders by giving MM the ability to control the company.

The testimony of each other member of the Board also reflects that the Director Defendants were concerned that incumbent directors Winblad and Imbler would resign from the Liquid Audio board if MM's nominees were elected to the board at the annual meeting, which would result in MM gaining control of the Board. The record also reflects that the timing of the Director Defendants' decision to expand the Board was to accomplish its primary purpose: to minimize the impact of the election of MM's nominees to the Board. The Court of Chancery's post-trial ruling from the bench states:

The board's concern was that given the past acrimonious relationship between MM and Liquid Audio, a relationship characterized by litigation, if MM's two nominees were elected, the possibility of continued acrimony might cause one or more of the current board members to resign. If one director resigned, that would deadlock the board two-to-two; and if two directors resigned, then MM would gain control on a two-to-one basis. Either scenario could jeopardize the pending merger, which the incumbent board favored. That was the *primary* reason. (emphasis added).

After making that factual determination, the Court of Chancery recognized the effect of the Board's action in changing the size and composition of its membership immediately prior to the election of directors at the annual meeting:

By adding two additional directors, the board foreclosed the result that it feared: The possibility of a deadlock or of MM taking control of the board. The reason is that even if MM's two nominees were elected at the 2002 annual meeting, the current directors would still constitute a majority of five. The result of the board's action was to *diminish the influence of any nominees of MM* that were elected, at least in numerical terms.

Thus, based upon the evidence presented at trial, including an assessment of the witnesses' credibility, the Court of Chancery concluded that the Director Defendants amended the bylaws to expand the Board from five to seven, appointed two additional members of the Board, and timed those actions for the *primary purpose* of diminishing the influence of MM's nominees, if they were elected at the annual meeting.

Corporate Governance Principles

The most fundamental principles of corporate governance are a function of the allocation of power within a corporation between its stockholders and its board of directors. The stockholders' power is the right to vote on specific matters, in particular, in an election of directors. The power of managing the corporate enterprise is vested in the shareholders' duly elected board representatives. Accordingly, while these "fundamental tenets of Delaware corporate law provide for a separation of control and ownership,"[7] the stockholder franchise has been characterized as the "ideological underpinning" upon which the legitimacy of the directors managerial power rests.[8]

Maintaining a proper balance in the allocation of power between the stockholders' right to elect directors and the board of directors' right to manage the corporation is dependent upon the stockholders' unimpeded right to vote effectively in an election of directors. This Court has repeatedly stated that, if the stockholders are not satisfied with the management or actions of their elected representatives on the board of directors, the power of corporate democracy is available to the stockholders to replace the incumbent directors when they stand for re-election. Consequently, two decades ago, this Court held:

> The Courts of this State will not allow the wrongful subversion of corporate democracy by manipulation of the corporate machinery or by machinations under the cloak of Delaware law. Accordingly, careful judicial scrutiny will be given a situation in which the right to vote for the election of successor directors has been *effectively frustrated* and denied.[10]

This Court and the Court of Chancery have remained assiduous in carefully reviewing any board actions designed to interfere with or impede the effective exercise of corporate democracy by shareholders, especially in an election of directors.

Corporate Governance Review Standards

The "defining tension" in corporate governance today has been characterized as "the tension between deference to directors' deci-

7. *Malone v. Brincat,* 722 A.2d 5, 9 (Del.1998).

8. *Blasius Indus., Inc. v. Atlas Corp.,* 564 A.2d 651, 659 (Del.Ch.1988).

10. *Giuricich v. Emtrol Corp.,* 449 A.2d 232, 239 (Del.1982).

sions and the scope of judicial review.''[12] The appropriate standard of judicial review is dispositive of which party has the burden of proof as any litigation proceeds from stage to stage until there is a substantive determination on the merits. Accordingly, identification of the correct analytical framework is essential to a proper judicial review of challenges to the decision-making process of a corporation's board of directors.

The business judgment rule, as a standard of judicial review, is a common-law recognition of the statutory authority to manage a corporation that is vested in the board of directors. The business judgment rule is a "presumption that in making a business decision the directors of a corporation acted on an informed basis, in good faith and in the honest belief that the action taken was in the best interests of the company.''[15] An application of the traditional business judgment rule places the burden on the "party challenging the [board's] decision to establish facts rebutting the presumption.''[16] The effect of a proper invocation of the business judgment rule, as a standard of judicial review, is powerful because it operates deferentially. If the business judgment rule is not rebutted, a "court will not substitute its judgment for that of the board if the [board's] decision can be 'attributed to any rational business purpose.' ''[17]

In *Blasius,* Chancellor Allen set forth a cogent explanation of why judicial review under the deferential traditional business judgment rule standard is inappropriate when a board of directors acts for the *primary* purpose of impeding or interfering with the effectiveness of a shareholder vote, especially in the specific context presented in *Blasius* of a contested election for directors:

> [T]he ordinary considerations to which the business judgment rule originally responded are simply not present in the shareholder voting context. That is, a decision by the board to act for the primary purpose of preventing the effectiveness of a shareholder vote inevitably involves the question who, as between the principal and the agent, has authority with respect to a matter of internal corporate governance. That, of course, is true in a very specific way in this case which deals with the question who should constitute the board of directors of the corporation, but it will be true in every instance in which an incumbent board seeks to thwart a shareholder majority. A board's decision to act to prevent the shareholders from creating a majority of new board positions and filling them does not involve the exercise of the corporation's power over its property, or with respect to its rights

---

12. E. Norman Veasey, *The Defining Tension in Corporate Governance in America,* 52 Bus. Law. 393 (1997).

15. *Unitrin, Inc. v. American Gen. Corp.,* 651 A.2d at 1373 quoting *Aronson v. Lewis,* 473 A.2d 805, 811 (Del.1984).

16. *Id.*

17. *Id.,* quoting *Unocal Corp. v. Mesa Petroleum Co.,* 493 A.2d 946, 954 (Del.1985) (citation omitted).

or obligations; rather, it involves allocation, between shareholders as a class and the board, of effective power with respect to governance of the corporation. . . . Action designed principally to interfere with the effectiveness of a vote inevitably involves a conflict between the board and shareholder majority. Judicial review of such action involves a determination of the legal and equitable obligations of an agent towards his principal. This is not, in my opinion, a question that a court may leave to the agent finally to decide so long as he does so honestly and competently; that is, it may not be left to the agent's business judgment.[18]

In *Blasius,* the Chancellor did not adopt a rule of *per se* invalidity once a plaintiff has established that a board of directors has acted for the primary purpose of interfering with or impeding the effective exercise of a shareholder vote. Instead, the Chancellor concluded that such situations required enhanced judicial scrutiny, pursuant to which the board of directors "bears the heavy burden of demonstrating a compelling justification for such action."

In *Blasius,* the Chancellor then applied that compelling justification standard of enhanced judicial review in examining a board's action to expand its size in the context of a contested election of directors, exactly what the Liquid Audio board did in this case. In *Blasius,* notwithstanding the fact that the incumbent board of directors believed in good faith that the leveraged recapitalization proposed by the plaintiff was ill-advised and less valuable than the company's business plan, Chancellor Allen explained why the incumbent board of directors' good faith beliefs were not a proper basis for interfering with the stockholder franchise in a contested election for successor directors.

> The only justification that can be offered for the action taken is that the board knows better than do the shareholders what is in the corporation's best interest. While that premise is no doubt true for any number of matters, it is irrelevant (except insofar as the shareholders wish to be guided by the board's recommendation) when the question is who should comprise the board. . . . It may be that the Blasius restructuring proposal was or is unrealistic and would lead to injury to the corporation and its shareholders if pursued. . . . The board certainly viewed it in that way, and that view, held in good faith, entitled the board to take certain steps to evade the risk it perceived. It could, for example, expend corporate funds to inform shareholders and seek to bring them to a similar point of view. But there is a vast difference between expending corporate funds to inform the electorate and exercising power for the primary purpose of foreclosing effective shareholder action. A majority of shareholders, who were not dominated in any respect, could view the matter differently than did the board. If they do, or did, they are entitled to employ the mechanisms

18. *Blasius Indus., Inc. v. Atlas Corp.,* 564 A.2d 651, 659–60 (Del.Ch.1988).

provided by the corporation law and the Atlas certificate of incorporation to advance that view.[21]

In *Blasius,* the Chancellor set aside the board's action to expand the size of its membership for the primary purpose of impeding and interfering with the effectiveness of a shareholder vote in a contested election for directors. In this case, not only did the Liquid Audio board of directors take similar action in expanding the size of its membership and appointing two new directors to fill those positions, but it took that action for the same *primary* purpose.

Compelling Justification Within Unocal

The *Blasius* compelling justification standard of enhanced judicial review is based upon accepted and well-established legal tenets. This Court and the Court of Chancery have recognized the substantial degree of congruence between the rationale that led to the *Blasius* "compelling justification" enhanced standard of judicial review and the logical extension of that rationale *within* the context of the *Unocal* enhanced standard of judicial review.[23] Both standards recognize the inherent conflicts of interest that arise when a board of directors acts to prevent shareholders from effectively exercising their right to vote either contrary to the will of the incumbent board members generally or to replace the incumbent board members in a contested election.

In *Gilbert,* we held that a reviewing court must apply the *Unocal* standard of review whenever a board of directors adopts any defensive measure "in response to some threat to corporate policy and effectiveness which touches upon issues of control."[24] Later, in *Stroud,* this Court acknowledged that board action interfering with the exercise of the shareholder franchise often arises during a hostile contest for control when an acquiror launches both a proxy fight and a tender offer.[25] Accordingly, in *Stroud,* we held that "such action necessarily invoked both *Unocal* and *Blasius.*"[26]

In *Stroud,* we emphasized, however, that the *Blasius* and *Unocal* standards of enhanced judicial review ("tests") are *not* mutually exclusive.[27] In *Stroud,* we then explained why our holding in *Gilbert* did not render *Blasius* and its progeny meaningless:

> In certain circumstances, a court must recognize the special import of protecting the shareholders' franchise within *Unocal's* requirement that any defensive measure be proportionate and "reasonable in relation to the threat posed." A board's unilateral decision to adopt a defensive measure touching "upon issues of

21. *Id.* at 663.

23. *Id.* at 91. *Chesapeake Corp. v. Shore,* 771 A.2d 293, 320 (Del.Ch.2000). *See also* David C. McBride and Danielle Gibbs,*Voting Rights: The Metaphysics of Blasius Industries v. Atlas Corp.,* 26 Del. J. Corp. L. 927 (2001).

24. *Gilbert v. El Paso Co.,* 575 A.2d 1131, 1144 (Del.1990).

25. *Stroud v. Grace,* 606 A.2d at 92 n. 3.

26. *Id.*

27. *Id.*

control" that purposefully disenfranchises its shareholders is strongly suspect under *Unocal,* and cannot be sustained without a "compelling justification."[28]

Thus, the same circumstances must be extant before the *Blasius* compelling justification enhanced standard of judicial review is required to sustain a board's action either independently, in the absence of a hostile contest for control, or within the *Unocal* standard of review when the board's action is taken as a defensive measure. The "compelling justification" standard set forth in *Blasius* is applied independently or within the *Unocal* standard only where "the primary purpose of the board's action is to interfere with or impede exercise of the shareholder franchise and the shareholders are not given a full and fair opportunity to vote" effectively.[29] Accordingly, this Court has noted that the non-deferential *Blasius* standard of enhanced judicial review, which imposes upon a board of directors the burden of demonstrating a compelling justification for such actions, is rarely applied either independently or within the *Unocal* standard of review.

In *Unitrin,* for example, although the board's action in adopting a repurchase program was a defensive measure that implicated the shareholders' franchise and called for an application of the *Unocal* standard of review, it did not require the board to demonstrate a compelling justification for that action.[31] In *Unitrin,* the primary purpose of the repurchase program was not to interfere with or impede the shareholders' right to vote; the shareholders' right to vote effectively remained extant; and, in particular, we noted that the shareholders retained sufficient voting power to challenge the incumbent board by electing new directors with a successful proxy contest.

In this case, however, the Court of Chancery was presented with the ultimate defensive measure touching upon an issue of control. It was a defensive action taken by an incumbent board of directors for the primary purpose of interfering with and impeding the effectiveness of the shareholder franchise in electing successor directors. Accordingly, the incumbent board of directors had the burden of demonstrating a compelling justification for that action to withstand enhanced judicial scrutiny *within* the *Unocal* standard of reasonableness and proportionality.

Unocal Required Compelling Justification

This case presents a paragon of when the compelling justification standard of *Blasius* must be applied within *Unocal* 's requirement that any defensive measure be proportionate and reasonable in relation to the threat posed. The *Unocal* standard of review applies because the Liquid Audio board's action was a "defensive measure taken in re-

28. *Id.*

29. *Williams v. Geier,* 671 A.2d 1368, 1376 (Del.1996) quoting *Stroud v. Grace,* 606 A.2d 75, 92 (Del.1992).

31. *Unitrin, Inc. v. American Gen. Corp.,* 651 A.2d 1361 (Del.1995).

sponse to some threat to corporate policy and effectiveness which touches upon issues of control."[33] The compelling justification standard of *Blasius* also had to be applied *within* an application of the *Unocal* standard to that specific defensive measure because the primary purpose of the Board's action was to interfere with or impede the effective exercise of the shareholder franchise in a contested election for directors.

The Court of Chancery properly decided to examine the Board's defensive action to expand from five to seven members and to appoint two new members in accordance with the *Unocal* standard of enhanced judicial review. Initially, the Court of Chancery concluded that defensive action was not preclusive or coercive. If a defensive measure is not draconian, because it is neither coercive nor preclusive, proportionality review under *Unocal* requires the focus of enhanced judicial scrutiny to shift to the range of reasonableness.[35]

After the Court of Chancery determined that the Board's action was not preclusive or coercive, it properly proceeded to determine whether the Board's action was reasonable and proportionate in relation to the threat posed.[36] Under the circumstances presented in this case, however, the Court of Chancery did not "recognize the special [importance] of protecting the shareholder's franchise within *Unocal*'s requirement that any defensive measure be proportionate and reasonable in relation to the threat posed."[37] Since the Court of Chancery had already concluded that the *primary* purpose of the Liquid Audio board's defensive measure was to interfere with or impede an effective exercise of the shareholder's franchise in a contested election of directors, the Board had the burden of demonstrating a compelling justification for that action.

When the *primary purpose* of a board of directors' defensive measure is to interfere with or impede the effective exercise of the shareholder franchise in a contested election for directors, the board must first demonstrate a compelling justification for such action as a condition precedent to any judicial consideration of reasonableness and proportionately. As this case illustrates, such defensive actions by a board need not actually prevent the shareholders from attaining any success in seating one or more nominees in a contested election for directors and the election contest need not involve a challenge for outright control of the board of directors. To invoke the *Blasius* compelling justification standard of review *within* an application of the *Unocal* standard of review, the defensive actions of the board only need to be taken for the primary purpose of interfering with or

33. *Gilbert v. El Paso Co.*, 575 A.2d 1131, 1144 (Del.1990).

35. *Unitrin, Inc. v. American Gen. Corp.*, 651 A.2d 1361, 1387–88 (Del.1995).

36. In our review of the Court of Chancery's *Unocal* analysis, we have assumed

without deciding that the Board was independent and had reasonable grounds for believing that there was a danger to corporate policy.

37. *Stroud v. Grace*, 606 A.2d at 92 n. 3.

impeding the effectiveness of the stockholder vote in a contested election for directors.

Board Expansion Invalid

The record reflects that the primary purpose of the Director Defendants' action was to interfere with and impede the effective exercise of the stockholder franchise in a contested election for directors. The Court of Chancery concluded that the Director Defendants amended the bylaws to provide for a board of seven and appointed two additional members of the Board for the primary purpose of diminishing the influence of MM's two nominees on a five-member Board by eliminating either the possibility of a deadlock on the board or of MM controlling the Board, if one or two Director Defendants resigned from the Board. That defensive action by the Director Defendants compromised the essential role of corporate democracy in maintaining the proper allocation of power between the shareholders and the Board, because that action was taken in the context of a contested election for successor directors. Since the Director Defendants did not demonstrate a compelling justification for that defensive action, the bylaw amendment that expanded the size of the Liquid Audio board, and permitted the appointment of two new members on the eve of a contested election, should have been invalidated by the Court of Chancery.

One of the most venerable precepts of Delaware's common law corporate jurisprudence is the principle that "inequitable action does not become permissible simply because it is legally possible."[40] At issue in this case is not the validity generally of either a bylaw that permits a board of directors to expand the size of its membership or a board's power to appoint successor members to fill board vacancies. In this case, however, the incumbent Board timed its utilization of these otherwise valid powers to expand the size and composition of the Liquid Audio board for the primary purpose of impeding and interfering with the efforts of the stockholders' power to effectively exercise their voting rights in a contested election for directors. As this Court held more than three decades ago, "these are inequitable purposes, contrary to established principles of corporate democracy . . . and may not be permitted to stand."[41]

Conclusion

The judgment of the Court of Chancery is reversed. This matter is remanded for further proceedings in accordance with this opinion.[42]

40. *Schnell v. Chris–Craft, Indus., Inc.,* 285 A.2d 437, 439 (Del.1971).

41. *Id.*

42. Supr. Ct. R. 4(f).

CHAPTER V

SHAREHOLDER INFORMATIONAL RIGHTS AND PROXY VOTING

SECTION 1. SHAREHOLDER INFORMATIONAL RIGHTS UNDER STATE LAW

(a) INSPECTION OF BOOKS AND RECORDS

Insert the following case at p. 264 of the Unabridged Edition, and p. 189 of the Concise Edition, in place of Security First Corp. v. U.S. Die Casting and Development Corp.:

Saito v. McKesson HBOC, Inc.

Supreme Court of Delaware, 2002
806 A.2d 113

■ Before VEASEY, CHIEF JUSTICE, WALSH, HOLLAND, BERGER, JUSTICES and HARTNETT, JUSTICE (Retired), constituting the Court en Banc.

■ BERGER, JUSTICE.

In this appeal, we consider the limitations on a stockholder's statutory right to inspect corporate books and records. The statute, 8 Del.C. § 220, enables stockholders to investigate matters "reasonably related to [their] interest as [stockholders]" including, among other things, possible corporate wrongdoing. It does not open the door to the wide ranging discovery that would be available in support of litigation. For this statutory tool to be meaningful, however, it cannot be read narrowly to deprive a stockholder of necessary documents solely because the documents were prepared by third parties or because the documents predate the stockholder's first investment in the corporation. A stockholder who demands inspection for a proper purpose should be given access to all of the documents in the corporation's possession, custody or control, that are necessary to satisfy that proper purpose. Thus, where a § 220 claim is based on alleged corporate wrongdoing, and assuming the allegation is meritorious, the stockholder should be given enough information to effectively address the problem, either through derivative litigation or through direct contact with the corporation's directors and/or stockholders.

Factual and Procedural Background

On October 17, 1998, McKesson Corporation entered into a stock-for-stock merger agreement with HBO & Company ("HBOC"). On October 20, 1998, appellant, Noel Saito, purchased McKesson stock. The merger was consummated in January 1999 and the combined company was renamed McKesson HBOC, Incorporated. HBOC continued its separate corporate existence as a wholly-owned subsidiary of McKesson HBOC.

Starting in April and continuing through July 1999, McKesson HBOC announced a series of financial restatements triggered by its year-end audit process. During that four month period, McKesson HBOC reduced its revenues by $327.4 million for the three prior fiscal years. The restatements all were attributed to HBOC accounting irregularities. The first announcement precipitated several lawsuits, including a derivative action pending in the Court of Chancery, captioned *Ash v. McCall*, Civil Action No. 17132. Saito was one of four plaintiffs in the *Ash* complaint, which alleged that: (i) McKesson's directors breached their duty of care by failing to discover the HBOC accounting irregularities before the merger; (ii) McKesson's directors committed corporate waste by entering into the merger with HBOC; (iii) HBOC's directors breached their fiduciary duties by failing to monitor the company's compliance with financial reporting requirements prior to the merger; and (iv) McKesson HBOC's directors failed in the same respect during the three months following the merger. Although the Court of Chancery granted defendants' motion to dismiss the complaint, the dismissal was without prejudice as to the pre-merger and post-merger oversight claims.

In its decision on the motion to dismiss, the Court of Chancery specifically suggested that Saito and the other plaintiffs "use the 'tools at hand,' most prominently § 220 books and records actions, to obtain information necessary to sue derivatively."[2] Saito was the only Ash plaintiff to follow that advice. The stated purpose of Saito's demand was:

> (1) to further investigate breaches of fiduciary duties by the boards of directors of HBO & Co., Inc., McKesson, Inc., and/or McKesson HBOC, Inc. related to their oversight of their respective company's accounting procedures and financial reporting; (2) to investigate potential claims against advisors engaged by McKesson, Inc. and HBO & Co., Inc. to the acquisition of HBO & Co., Inc. by McKesson, Inc.; and (3) to gather information relating to the above in order to supplement the complaint in *Ash v. McCall*, et al., . . . in accordance with the September 15, 2000 Opinion of the Court of Chancery.

2. Ash v. McCall, 2000 WL 1370341, *15 (Del.Ch.).

Saito demanded access to eleven categories of documents, including those relating to Arthur Andersen's pre-merger review and verification of HBOC's financial condition; communications between or among HBOC, McKesson, and their investment bankers and accountants concerning HBOC's accounting practices; and discussions among members of the Boards of Directors of HBOC, McKesson, and/or McKesson HBOC concerning reports published in April 1997 and thereafter about HBOC's accounting practices or financial condition.

After trial, the Court of Chancery found that Saito stated a proper purpose for the inspection of books and records—to ferret out possible wrongdoing in connection with the merger of HBOC and McKesson. But the court held that Saito's proper purpose only extended to potential wrongdoing after the date on which Saito acquired his McKesson stock. The court also held that Saito did not have a proper purpose to inspect documents relating to potential claims against third party advisors who counseled the boards in connection with the merger. Finally, the court held that Saito was not entitled to HBOC documents because Saito was not a stockholder of pre-merger HBOC, and, with respect to post-merger HBOC, he did not establish a basis on which to disregard the separate existence of the wholly-owned subsidiary.

DISCUSSION

Stockholders of Delaware corporations enjoy a qualified common law and statutory right to inspect the corporation's books and records.[3] Inspection rights were recognized at common law because, "[a]s a matter of self-protection, the stockholder was entitled to know how his agents were conducting the affairs of the corporation of which he or she was a part owner."[4] The common law right is codified in 8 Del.C. § 220, which provides in relevant part:

(b) Any stockholder ... shall, upon written demand under oath stating the purpose thereof, have the right ... to inspect for any proper purpose the corporation's stock ledger, a list of its stockholders, and its other books and records, and to make copies or extracts therefrom. A proper purpose shall mean a purpose reasonably related to such person's interest as a stockholder.

Once a stockholder establishes a proper purpose under § 220, the right to relief will not be defeated by the fact that the stockholder may have secondary purposes that are improper. The scope of a stockholder's inspection, however, is limited to those books and records that are necessary and essential to accomplish the stated, proper purpose.

After trial, the Court of Chancery found "credible evidence of possible wrongdoing," which satisfied Saito's burden of establishing a

3. Shaw v. Agri–Mark, Inc., 663 A.2d   **4.** Id. at 467.
464 (Del.1995).

proper purpose for the inspection of corporate books and records. But the Court of Chancery limited Saito's access to relevant documents in three respects. First, it held that, since Saito would not have standing to bring an action challenging actions that occurred before he purchased McKesson stock, Saito could not obtain documents created before October 20, 1998. Second, the court concluded that Saito was not entitled to documents relating to possible wrongdoing by the financial advisors to the merging companies. Third, the court denied Saito access to any HBOC documents, since Saito never was a stockholder of HBOC. We will consider each of these rulings in turn.

A.   *The Standing Limitation*

By statute, stockholders who bring derivative suits must allege that they were stockholders of the corporation "at the time of the transaction of which such stockholder complains...." The Court of Chancery decided that this limitation on Saito's ability to maintain a derivative suit controlled the scope of his inspection rights. As a result, the court held that Saito was "effectively limited to examining conduct of McKesson and McKesson HBOC's boards following the negotiation and public announcement of the merger agreement."

Although we recognize that there may be some interplay between the two statutes, we do not read § 327 as defining the temporal scope of a stockholder's inspection rights under § 220. The books and records statute requires that a stockholder's purpose be one that is "reasonably related" to his or her interest as a stockholder. The standing statute, § 327, bars a stockholder from bringing a derivative action unless the stockholder owned the corporation's stock at the time of the alleged wrong. If a stockholder wanted to investigate alleged wrongdoing that substantially predated his or her stock ownership, there could be a question as to whether the stockholder's purpose was reasonably related to his or her interest as a stockholder, especially if the stockholder's only purpose was to institute derivative litigation. But stockholders may use information about corporate mismanagement in other ways, as well. They may seek an audience with the board to discuss proposed reforms or, failing in that, they may prepare a stockholder resolution for the next annual meeting, or mount a proxy fight to elect new directors. None of those activities would be prohibited by § 327.

Even where a stockholder's only purpose is to gather information for a derivative suit, the date of his or her stock purchase should not be used as an automatic "cut-off" date in a § 220 action. First, the potential derivative claim may involve a continuing wrong that both predates and postdates the stockholder's purchase date. In such a case, books and records from the inception of the alleged wrongdoing could be necessary and essential to the stockholder's purpose. Second, the alleged post-purchase date wrongs may have their foundation in events that transpired earlier. In this case, for example, Saito wants to investigate McKesson's apparent failure to learn of HBOC's accounting irregularities until months after the merger was consummated. Due diligence documents generated before the merger agreement was signed may be essential to that investigation. In sum, the date on which a stockholder first acquired the corporation's stock does not control the scope of records available under § 220. If activities that occurred before the purchase date are "reasonably related" to the stockholder's interest as a stockholder, then the stockholder should be given access to records necessary to an understanding of those activities.[10]

B.   *The Financial Advisors' Documents*

The Court of Chancery denied Saito access to documents in McKesson–HBOC's possession that the corporation obtained from financial and accounting advisors, on the ground that Saito could not use § 220 to develop potential claims against third parties. On appeal, Saito argues that he is seeking third party documents for the same reason he is seeking McKesson HBOC documents—to investigate possible wrongdoing by McKesson and McKesson HBOC. Since the trial court found that to be a proper purpose, Saito argues that he should not be precluded from seeing documents that are necessary to his purpose, and in McKesson HBOC's possession, simply because the documents were prepared by third party advisors.

We agree that, generally, the source of the documents in a corporation's possession should not control a stockholder's right to inspection under § 220. It is not entirely clear, however, that the trial court restricted Saito's access on that basis. The Court of Chancery decided that Saito's interest in pursuing claims against McKesson HBOC's advisors was not a proper purpose. It recognized that a secondary improper purpose usually is irrelevant if the stockholder establishes his need for the same documents to support a proper purpose. But the court apparently concluded that the categories of third party documents that Saito demanded did not support the proper purpose of investigating possible wrongdoing by McKesson and McKesson HBOC.

We cannot determine from the present record whether the Court of Chancery intended to exclude all third party documents, but such a blanket exclusion would be improper. The source of the documents and the manner in which they were obtained by the corporation have little or no bearing on a stockholder's inspection rights. The issue is whether the documents are necessary and essential to satisfy the stockholder's proper purpose. In this case, Saito wants to investigate possible wrongdoing relating to McKesson and McKesson HBOC's failure to discover HBOC's accounting irregularities. Since McKesson

---

10. As noted ... above, a Section 220 proceeding does not open the door to wide ranging discovery. See *Brehm v. Eisner,* 746 A.2d 244, 266–67 (Del.2000) (Plaintiffs "bear the burden of showing a proper purpose and [must] make specific and discrete identification, with rifled precision ... [to] establish that each category of books and records is essential to the accomplishment of their articulated purpose ..."); *Security First Corp. v. U.S. Die Casting and Dev. Co.,* 687 A.2d 563, 568, 570 (Del.1997) ("mere curiosity or desire for a fishing expedition" is insufficient.).

and McKesson HBOC relied on financial and accounting advisors to evaluate HBOC's financial condition and reporting, those advisors' reports and correspondence would be critical to Saito's investigation.

C. *HBOC Documents*

Finally, the Court of Chancery held that Saito was not entitled to any HBOC documents because he was not a stockholder of HBOC before or after the merger. Although Saito is a stockholder of HBOC's parent, McKesson HBOC, stockholders of a parent corporation are not entitled to inspect a subsidiary's books and records, "[a]bsent a showing of a fraud or that a subsidiary is in fact the mere alter ego of the parent...."[11] The Court of Chancery found no basis to disregard HBOC's separate existence and, therefore, denied access to its records.

We reaffirm this settled principle, which applies to those HBOC books and records that were never provided to McKesson or McKesson HBOC. But it does not apply to relevant documents that HBOC gave to McKesson before the merger, or to McKesson HBOC after the merger. We assume that HBOC provided financial and accounting information to its proposed merger partner and, later, to its parent company. As with the third party advisors' documents, Saito would need access to relevant HBOC documents in order to understand what his company's directors knew and why they failed to recognize HBOC's accounting irregularities.

Conclusion

Based on the foregoing, the decision of the Court of Chancery is AFFIRMED in part and REVERSED in part, and this matter is REMANDED for further action in accordance with this decision. Jurisdiction is not retained.

SECTION 5.   THE PROXY RULES (III): SHAREHOLDER PROPOSALS

Insert the following material at p. 314 of the Unabridged Edition, and p. 226 of the Concise Edition, after the Aon Corporation No–Action Letter:

DIVISION OF CORPORATION FINANCE: STAFF LEGAL BULLETIN NO. 14A

SHAREHOLDER PROPOSALS

Date: July 12, 2002

Rule 14a–8 provides an opportunity for a shareholder owning a relatively small amount of a company's securities to have his or her

---

11. *Skouras v. Admiralty Enterprises, Inc.,* 386 A.2d 674, 681 (Del.Ch.1978).

proposal placed alongside management's proposals in that company's proxy materials for presentation to a vote at an annual or special meeting of shareholders. The rule generally requires the company to include the proposal unless the shareholder has not complied with the rule's procedural requirements or the proposal falls within one of the rule's 13 substantive bases for exclusion.

Rule 14a–8(i)(7) is one of the substantive bases for exclusion in rule 14a–8. It provides a basis for excluding a proposal that deals with a matter relating to the company's ordinary business operations. The fact that a proposal relates to ordinary business matters does not conclusively establish that a company may exclude the proposal from its proxy materials. As the Commission stated in Exchange Act Release No. 40018, proposals that relate to ordinary business matters but that focus on "sufficiently significant social policy issues ... would not be considered to be excludable because the proposals would transcend the day-to-day business matters."

In the 2001–2002 proxy season, shareholders submitted proposals to several companies relating to equity compensation plans. Some of these proposals requested that the companies submit for shareholder approval all equity compensation plans that potentially would result in material dilution to existing shareholders. We received four no-action requests from companies seeking to exclude these proposals from their proxy materials in reliance on rule 14a–8(i)(7). In each instance, we took the view that the proposal could be excluded in reliance on rule 14a–8(i)(7) because the proposal related to general employee compensation, an ordinary business matter.

The Commission has stated that proposals involving "the management of the workforce, such as the hiring, promotion, and termination of employees," relate to ordinary business matters. Our position to date with respect to equity compensation proposals is consistent with this guidance and the Division's historical approach to compensation proposals. Since 1992, we have applied a bright-line analysis to proposals concerning equity or cash compensation:

- We agree with the view of companies that they may exclude proposals that relate to general employee compensation matters in reliance on rule 14a–8(i)(7); and

- We do not agree with the view of companies that they may exclude proposals that concern only senior executive and director compensation in reliance on rule 14a–8(i)(7).

The Commission has previously taken the position that proposals relating to ordinary business matters "but focusing on sufficiently significant social policy issues ... generally would not be considered to be excludable, because the proposals would transcend the day-to-day business matters and raise policy issues so significant that it would be appropriate for a shareholder vote." The Division has noted many times that the presence of widespread public debate regarding an issue is among the factors to be considered in determining whether proposals concerning that issue "transcend the day-to-day business matters."

We believe that the public debate regarding shareholder approval of equity compensation plans has become significant in recent months. Consequently, in view of the widespread public debate regarding shareholder approval of equity compensation plans and consistent with our historical analysis of the "ordinary business" exclusion, we are modifying our treatment of proposals relating to this topic. Going forward, we will take the following approach to rule 14a–8(i)(7) submissions concerning proposals that relate to shareholder approval of equity compensation plans:

- *Proposals that focus on equity compensation plans that may be used to compensate only senior executive officers and directors.* As has been our position since 1992, companies may not rely on rule 14a–8(i)(7) to omit these proposals from their proxy materials.

- *Proposals that focus on equity compensation plans that may be used to compensate senior executive officers, directors and the general workforce.* If the proposal seeks to obtain shareholder approval of all such equity compensation plans, without regard to their potential dilutive effect, a company may rely on rule 14a–8(i)(7) to omit the proposal from its proxy materials. If the proposal seeks to obtain shareholder approval of all such equity compensation plans that potentially would result in material dilution to existing shareholders, a company may not rely on rule 14a–8(i)(7) to omit the proposal from its proxy materials.

- *Proposals that focus on equity compensation plans that may be used to compensate the general workforce only, with no senior executive officer or director participation.* If the proposal seeks to obtain shareholder approval of all such equity compensation plans, without regard to their potential dilutive effect, a company may rely on rule 14a–8(i)(7) to omit the proposal from its proxy materials. If the proposal seeks to obtain shareholder approval of all such equity compensation plans that potentially would result in material dilution to existing shareholders, a company may not rely on rule 14a–8(i)(7) to omit the proposal from its proxy materials. . . .

CHAPTER VI

THE SPECIAL PROBLEMS OF CLOSE CORPORATIONS

SECTION 5. FIDUCIARY OBLIGATIONS OF SHAREHOLDERS IN CLOSE CORPORATIONS

Insert the following Note at p. 400 of the Unabridged Edition, and p. 292 of the Concise Edition, following Smith v. Atlantic Properties:

SLETTELAND v. ROBERTS, 304 Mont. 21, 16 P.3d 1062 (2000). Sletteland was a shareholder in Billings Generation, Inc. (BGI), a closely held Montana corporation. The four other shareholders in BGI were Smith, Blendu, Orndorff and Roberts. BGI and Exxon Billings Cogeneration, Inc. were partners in Yellowstone Energy Limited Partnership (YELP). YELP owned and operated a cogeneration plant in Billings, Montana which generated steam and electric power. Sletteland had been removed as an officer of BGI by a vote of 60 percent of the shareholders, comprised of Orndorff, Roberts, and Smith. Thereafter, Sletteland brought a derivative action against Orndorff and Roberts, requesting a return of excessive legal fees that they had charged BGI, and removal of Orndorff and Roberts as directors. Orndorff and Roberts counterclaimed, alleging that Sletteland brought the suit in bad faith, causing damage to the company and to the other shareholders.

At the time Sletteland's lawsuit was filed, YELP's project was in financial trouble due to high-interest debts and technical problems with the plant. YELP was attempting to refinance the high-interest debt with lower-interest financing. The window of opportunity for the financing was short, and the lawsuit became an issue hampering the refinancing. Ultimately, the refinancing fell through, and Sletteland's suit was a substantial factor in causing this result. Orndorff and Roberts claimed that the timing of the lawsuit by Sletteland was specifically intended to derail the financing. The District Court found that Sletteland was negligent and breached his fiduciary duties to BGI and his fellow shareholders by the timing of his filing of his action, and found Sletteland liable to Orndorff, Roberts, and Smith for $3,027,939. Affirmed:

There was clearly animosity in the relationship between the business partners. . . . Ultimately, in June of 1996, Sletteland was removed as an officer of BGI. According to Roberts and Orndorff, Sletteland and Blendu wanted the other three shareholders to purchase their interests, and warned that "unpleasant things would happen" if their demands were not met.

It appears that the suit was brought specifically to derail refinancing of the project. Sletteland admitted at trial that the timing of the suit was up to him and that he was not faced with any statute of limitations problem. The initial law suit was filed by Sletteland on October 2, 1996. This was immediately before the individuals involved in the refinancing were to meet to discuss the refinancing. He did no investigation to see what the effect of the lawsuit would be on the refinancing. The court concluded that "it only makes sense that he would be expected to know that the filing of his suit alleging director fraud would delay or derail the refinancing . . . there was no particular reason to file this suit when he did." He was asked to withdraw the suit so that the refinancing could conclude, but he refused to do so.

CHAPTER VII

ALTERNATIVE FORMS OF BUSINESS ORGANIZATION: LIMITED PARTNERSHIPS, LIMITED LIABILITY COMPANIES, AND LIMITED LIABILITY PARTNERSHIPS

SECTION 1.   LIMITED PARTNERSHIPS

(e) FIDUCIARY OBLIGATIONS

Insert the following case at p. 497 of the Unabridged Edition, and p. 354 of the Concise Edition, at the end of section 1(d):

Gotham Partners, L.P. v. Hallwood Realty Partners, L.P.

Supreme Court of Delaware, 2002
817 A.2d 160

■ Before: VEASEY, CHIEF JUSTICE, WALSH, HOLLAND and BERGER, JUSTICES and HARTNETT, JUSTICE (Retired), constituting the Court en Banc.

■ VEASEY, CHIEF JUSTICE:

In this appeal, we hold that a limited partnership agreement may provide for contractually created fiduciary duties substantially mirroring traditional fiduciary duties that apply in the corporation law. The Court of Chancery held that the limited partnership agreement here provided for such fiduciary duties by requiring the general partner and its controlling entity to treat the limited partners in accordance with the entire fairness standard. We agree with this holding and also agree with the trial court that the defendants are jointly and severally liable because the challenged transaction breached the entire fairness provisions of the partnership agreement.

With respect to remedies for that breach, the plaintiff limited partner had demanded rescission or an adequate damage award and sterilization of the voting rights attached to the partnership units involved in the challenged transaction. The Court of Chancery refused to order rescission and awarded damages. We affirm the holding of the Vice Chancellor that he was not necessarily required to order rescission by the limited partnership contract or the application of equitable principles. Such a decision is properly within the discretion of a court of equity, but here the Court of Chancery did not fashion a remedy that is an appropriate substitute for rescission under the circumstances.

As the Court of Chancery noted, one effect of the challenged transaction was that the general partner and its corporate parent gained control of the limited partnership as a result of wrongdoing. In our view, the value of the control thus achieved was not properly compensated for by the award of damages because the trial court did not account properly for a control premium in its remedy calculation.

Consequently, we reverse the damages award and remand for such proceedings as may be necessary and appropriate: (1) to quantify how the challenged transaction would have been consummated had the defendants adhered to the entire fairness standards and procedures of the limited partnership agreement; and (2) to consider and award one or more of the various equitable remedies available to the limited partnership, including rescission, rescissory damages, sterilization of voting rights, or other appropriate methods of accounting for the control premium.

Facts

Hallwood Realty Partners, L.P. ("the Partnership") is a Delaware limited partnership that owns commercial office buildings and industrial parks in several locations in the United States and lists its partnership units on the American Stock Exchange. Gotham Partners, L.P. ("Gotham") is a hedge fund, the investments of which include real estate. It is the largest independent limited partner in the Partnership with approximately 14.8 percent of the outstanding partnership units. Hallwood Realty Corporation ("the General Partner") is the sole general partner and is a wholly-owned subsidiary of Hallwood Group Incorporated ("HGI"), which owned 5.1 percent of the outstanding partnership units before the transactions challenged in this case. Anthony Gumbiner and William Guzzetti were members of the board of directors of the General Partner. They were also officers of HGI at the time of the challenged transaction.[1]

---

1. Gumbiner, a corporate lawyer, owned 30 percent of HGI's shares between 1994 and 1995 and was the chairman of the board of directors and chief executive officer of the General Partner at the time of the challenged transactions. Guzzetti, a former lawyer, is an executive vice-president of HGI and was the president of the Partnership and a member of the General Partner's board of directors at the time of the challenged transactions.

In 1994, the Partnership's units were trading at a low price because of the ongoing economic recession in real estate. On October 12, 1994, Guzzetti proposed to the Partnership's board of directors that it approve a reverse split,[2] a unit option plan,[3] and an odd lot tender offer[4] subject to HGI's willingness to finance the transactions by buying any fractional units generated by a reverse split and any units purchased by the Partnership in an odd lot tender offer. At the time, more than half of the Partnership's units were held in odd lots and could be resold to HGI. Guzzetti told the board that HGI was the only source of financing available and that the transactions would, among other things, raise the trading price of the Partnership's units, reduce the Partnership's administrative costs, and give odd lot holders the chance to sell at market price without incurring brokerage fees. The Partnership's board approved the transactions, citing Guzzetti's reasons.

At first, HGI declined to provide funding for the reverse split and odd lot offer. But, by March 1995, HGI was willing to fund the Reverse Split and Option Plan, which were approved by the non-HGI directors on the General Partner's board. HGI purchased 30,000 units, approximately 1.6 percent of the Partnership's equity, through the Reverse Split. The Option Plan resulted in officers and employees of the General Partner purchasing 86,000 units or 4.7 percent of the Partnership's equity. Through these two transactions, HGI increased its ownership of outstanding Partnership units from 5.1 percent to approximately 11.4 percent.

By May 1995, HGI was willing to fund an odd lot tender offer. Guzzetti called a special meeting of the General Partner's board of directors after circulating a memorandum indicating that 55 percent of the Partnership's units were held in odd lots and thus could be tendered in the odd lot offer. The non-HGI directors voted as a "special committee" to approve the Odd Lot Offer. The purchase price of an odd lot was putatively set at the five-day market average referenced in Section 9.01(b) of the Partnership Agreement.[5] No valuation information was shared with the board.

The Odd Lot Offer began on June 5, 1995. The accompanying press release indicated that the Partnership would resell any tendered

---

2. A reverse split reduces the number of outstanding units and consequently increases the per unit value of each unit. Reverse splits usually create odd lots.

3. In this case, the option plan would sell post-reverse split units to officers and employees of the General Partner, including Gumbiner and Guzzetti.

4. An odd lot offer is a tender offer by the issuer for blocks of fewer than one hundred outstanding units or shares. Such "odd lots" are considered small and thus create inefficient administrative costs for issuers and may be difficult to sell at an attractive

price. Odd lot offers are designed to provide liquidity to small holders and to reduce issuer costs.

5. Section 9.01(b) of the Partnership Agreement states: "Except as set forth above, the number of Units issued to the General Partners or any such Affiliate in exchange for any Capital Contribution shall not exceed the Net Agreed Value of the contributed property or amount of cash, as the case may be, divided by the Unit Price of a Unit as of the day of such issuance."

odd lot units to HGI, affiliates of HGI, or other institutional investors. The Odd Lot Offer and Resale was pitched to the public and the American Stock Exchange as a resale to HGI of existing, listed Partnership units, not as an issuance of new, unlisted units. Consequently, the Partnership never filed a listing application with the American Stock Exchange for the units sold to HGI, and the Partnership's accounting books did not treat the Odd Lot Resale to HGI as an issuance of units.

From June 9 to July 25, 1995, when the Odd Lot Offer closed, the Partnership purchased 293,539 units from odd lot holders and placed them in a holding account. The Partnership then resold the units to HGI at the same price the Partnership paid for them, approximately $4.1 million. The Odd Lot Resale resulted in HGI purchasing approximately 23.4 percent of the Partnership's outstanding units. Thus, HGI increased its stake in the outstanding Partnership units from 11.4 percent to 29.7 percent and solidified its control over the Partnership. The Partnership Agreement requires the written consent or affirmative vote by at least 66 and 1/3 percent of the limited partners to remove a general partner.

Gotham began purchasing Partnership units in 1994 and owned 14.8 percent of the outstanding units as of September 1996. Gotham was aware of the Odd Lot Offer and Resale but did not complain to the Partnership until January 1997 when it requested access to the Partnership's books and records. The Partnership denied the request.

Preliminary Proceedings in the Court of Chancery

Gotham filed a books and records action in the Court of Chancery in February 1997. On June 20, 1997, Gotham filed another action in the Court of Chancery alleging derivative claims in connection with the Odd Lot Offer and Resale, the Reverse Split, and the Option Plan. Gotham alleged that these transactions were unfair to the Partnership's unitholders because HGI paid an unfairly low price to acquire control over the Partnership. Gotham's claims included breaches by the General Partner of traditional fiduciary duties and contractually based fiduciary duties. The claims also charged Gumbiner and Guzzetti, the General Partner's HGI-affiliated directors, and HGI itself with aiding and abetting those breaches. Gotham and the Partnership negotiated a settlement of the books and records action but the derivative action continued.

On summary judgment, the Court of Chancery sustained the contractual fiduciary duty claims and dismissed the traditional fiduciary duty claims on the ground that the Partnership Agreement supplanted traditional fiduciary duties and provided for contractual fiduciary duties by which the defendants' conduct would be measured.[7] The

---

7. *Gotham Partners, L.P. v. Hallwood Realty Partners, L.P.* ("*Gotham S.J. Op.*"), Del. Ch., C.A. No. 15754, 2000 WL 1476663 (Sept. 27, 2000), at 23–29.

Vice Chancellor found that Sections 7.05[8] and 7.10(a)[9] of the Partnership Agreement operate together as a contractual statement of the entire fairness standard, with Section 7.05 substantively requiring fair price and Section 7.10(a) substantively requiring fair dealing. No appeal has been taken from this ruling.

The Vice Chancellor's summary judgment opinion in this case, however, creates a separate problem. We refer to one aspect of the Vice Chancellor's discussion of the Delaware Revised Uniform Limited Partnership Act ("DRULPA") in his summary judgment opinion in this case where he stated that [DRULPA] section 17–1101(d)(2) "expressly authorizes the elimination, modification or enhancement of . . . fiduciary duties in the written agreement governing the limited partnership." It is at least the second time the Court of Chancery has stated in dicta that DRULPA . . . § 17–1101(d)(2) permits a limited partnership agreement to eliminate fiduciary duties.[12]

Because the Vice Chancellor's summary judgment order in this matter has not been appealed, his opinion on this point is not before us for review on this appeal. In our view, however, this dictum should not be ignored because it could be misinterpreted in future cases as a correct rule of law. Accordingly, in the interest of avoiding the perpetuation of a questionable statutory interpretation that could be relied upon adversely by courts, commentators and practitioners in the future, we are constrained to draw attention to the statutory language and the underlying general principle in our jurisprudence that scrupulous adherence to fiduciary duties is normally expected.

[DRULPA] § 17–1101(d)(2) states: "the partner's or other person's duties and liabilities may be expanded or restricted by provisions in the partnership agreement." There is no mention in § 17–1101(d)(2), or elsewhere in DRULPA . . . that a limited partnership agreement may eliminate the fiduciary duties or liabilities of a general partner.

Finally, we note the historic cautionary approach of the courts of Delaware that efforts by a fiduciary to escape a fiduciary duty, whether by a corporate director or officer or other type of trustee, should be scrutinized searchingly. Accordingly, although it is not appropriate for

---

8. Section 7.05 of the Partnership Agreement states: "Transactions with General Partner or Affiliates. The Partnership is expressly permitted to enter into transactions with the General Partner or any Affiliate thereof provided that the terms of any such transaction are substantially equivalent to terms obtainable by the Partnership from a comparable unaffiliated third party."

9. Section 7.10(a) of the Partnership Agreement states in relevant part: "Audit Committee; Resolution of Conflicts of Interest. (a) The General Partner shall form an Audit Committee (the 'Audit Committee') to

be comprised of two members of the board of directors of the General Partner who are not affiliated with the General Partner or its Affiliates except by reason of such directorship. The functions of the Audit Committee shall be to review and approve . . . (ii) transactions between the Partnership and the General Partner and any of its Affiliates."

12. Id. See also *Sonet v. Timber Co.*, 722 A.2d 319, 323 (Del.Ch.1998) (stating that § 17–1101(d) "apparently [allows] broad license to enhance, reform, or *even eliminate* fiduciary duty protections . . .") (emphasis added).

us to express an advisory opinion on a matter not before us, we simply raise a note of concern and caution relating to this dubious dictum in the Vice Chancellor's summary judgment opinion.

Decision After Trial

After trial, the Court of Chancery found the defendants liable for their conduct associated with the Odd Lot Resale to HGI, but upheld their conduct connected with the Reverse Split and the Option Plan. The Vice Chancellor found that the Odd Lot Resale, unlike the other two transactions, did not involve an issuance of units, but rather a resale of existing units to HGI. As a result, the Vice Chancellor found "inapplicable" the protections of Section 9.01 of the Partnership Agreement, which authorizes the General Partner to issue Partnership Units of any kind to any person without the consent or approval of the Limited Partners. Instead, the Vice Chancellor continued, the Odd Lot Resale was subject to Partnership Agreement Sections 7.05 and 7.10(a), which provide for the contractually created fiduciary duties of entire fairness.

The Vice Chancellor found that the General Partner breached the contractual fiduciary duties of entire fairness because (1) the General Partner never formed the Audit Committee as required by Section 7.10(a) to review and approve the Odd Lot Offer and Resale, and (2) the General Partner failed to perform a market check or obtain any reliable financial analysis indicating that the Odd Lot Resale would be conducted on the same terms obtainable from a third party. The Court of Chancery thus held the General Partner liable for breach of the contractually created fiduciary duties of entire fairness contained in the Partnership Agreement and found HGI, Gumbiner, and Guzzetti jointly and severally liable with the General Partner for aiding and abetting its breach.

Gotham requested rescission, or money damages and sterilization of voting rights. The Court of Chancery awarded money damages plus compound interest instead of rescission, in part because it found that Gotham delayed challenging the transaction "for nearly two years, and then filed suit to rescind only after it was clear that the market price [of the Partnership units] was up substantially and on a sustainable basis." The Vice Chancellor then went on to find that the challenged transactions were not "conceived of as a conscious scheme to entrench the General Partner's control and enrich HGI" improperly. He stated that if he had been convinced otherwise, "I might be inclined to grant rescission despite Gotham's torpid pace."

Gotham then filed a direct appeal in this Court contesting the remedy. The General Partner, HGI, Gumbiner, and Guzzetti filed cross appeals asserting that the Court of Chancery erred by finding Section 9.01(a) of the Partnership Agreement inapplicable to the Odd Lot Offer and Resale or, alternatively, by holding HGI, Gumbiner, and Guzzetti liable for aiding and abetting the General Partner's breach of its contractually created fiduciary duties and by awarding compound interest on a damages award.

Issues on Appeal

On appeal, Gotham argues that the Court of Chancery was required to award rescission as a matter of law and, even if an award of monetary damages were appropriate, the Court of Chancery erred in its calculation of the damages by failing to account for a control premium. Gotham seeks reversal in part of the judgment of the Court of Chancery and a remand to the court with instructions to order rescission of the Odd Lot Resale to HGI. Alternatively, Gotham seeks an award of rescissory damages or sterilization of HGI's voting rights connected to the Odd Lot Resale units, or both.

The General Partner, HGI, Gumbiner, and Guzzetti, contend in their cross appeal that the Court of Chancery erred: (1) by finding the Odd Lot Resale to HGI subject to Sections 7.05 and 7.10(a) of the Partnership Agreement, which provide for contractual fiduciary duties of entire fairness, instead of Section 9.01, which authorizes the General Partner to issue Partnership Units of any kind to any person without the consent or approval of the Limited Partners; [and] (2) by finding HGI, Gumbiner, and Guzzetti jointly and severally liable with the General Partner for aiding and abetting a breach of a contractually created fiduciary duty.... We will address the cross appeals first.

Whether the Court of Chancery Erred By Ruling That the Odd Lot Resale to HGI Was a Resale of Partnership Units

This Court reviews de novo the Court of Chancery's interpretation of written agreements and Delaware law.

As the Vice Chancellor noted at summary judgment, a general partner owes the traditional fiduciary duties of loyalty and care to the limited partnership and its partners, but DRULPA § 17–1101(d)(2) "expressly authorizes the ... modification, or enhancement of these fiduciary duties in the written agreement governing the limited partnership."[31] Indeed, we have recognized that, by statute, the parties to a Delaware limited partnership have the power and discretion to form and operate a limited partnership "in an environment of private ordering" according to the provisions in the limited partnership agreement.[32] We have noted that DRULPA embodies "the policy of freedom of contract"[33] and "maximum flexibility."[34] DRULPA's "basic approach is to permit partners to have the broadest possible discretion

---

31. *Gotham S.J. Op.*, at 24, 2000 WL 1476663 at *10. DRULPA § 17–1101(d)(2), codified at 6 Del. C. § 17–1101(d)(2), reads: "To the extent that, at law or equity, a partner or other person has duties (including fiduciary duties) and liabilities relating thereto to a limited partnership or to another partner or to another person that is a party to or is otherwise bound by a partnership agreement, ... (2) the partner's or other person's duties and liabilities may be expanded or restricted by provisions in the partnership agreement."

32. *Elf Atochem North America, Inc. v. Jaffari*, 727 A.2d 286, 287 (Del.1999).

33. Id at 290....

34. *Elf Atochem*, 727 A.2d at 291 n. 27.

in drafting their partnership agreements and to furnish answers only in situations where the partners have not expressly made provisions in their partnership agreement"[35] or "where the agreement is inconsistent with mandatory statutory provisions."[36] In those situations, a court will "look for guidance from the statutory default rules, traditional notions of fiduciary duties, or other extrinsic evidence."[37] But, if the limited partnership agreement unambiguously provides for fiduciary duties, any claim of a breach of a fiduciary duty must be analyzed generally in terms of the partnership agreement.[38]

The Vice Chancellor found, and the parties do not contest, that Partnership Agreement Sections 7.05 and 7.10(a) set forth fiduciary duties of entire fairness owed by the General Partner to its partners generally in self-dealing transactions, such as the Odd Lot Resale. Section 7.05 expressly permits the Partnership to enter into self-dealing transactions with the General Partner or its affiliate "provided that the terms of any such transaction are substantially equivalent to terms obtainable by the Partnership from a comparable unaffiliated third party."[39] Section 7.10(a) requires the General Partner to form an independent Audit Committee that shall review and approve self-dealing transactions between the Partnership and the General Partner and any of its affiliates.[40] The Vice Chancellor found, and the parties do not contest, that Sections 7.05 and 7.10(a) "operate together as a contractual statement of the traditional entire fairness standard [of fair price and fair dealing], with § 7.05 reflecting the substantive aspect of that standard and § 7.10 reflecting the procedural aspect of that standard."

Because the Partnership Agreement provided for fiduciary duties, the Vice Chancellor properly held that the Partnership Agreement, as a contract, provides the standard for determining whether the General Partner breached its duty to the Partnership through its execution of the Odd Lot Resale. As the Vice Chancellor stated, the Partnership Agreement "leaves no room for the application of common law

---

35. Id. at 291.

36. Id. at 292.

37. *Sonet*, 722 A.2d at 324.

38. See id. ("[U]nder Delaware limited partnership law a claim of breach of fiduciary duty must first be analyzed in terms of the operating governing instrument—the partnership agreement—and only where that document is silent or ambiguous, or where the principles of equity are implicated, will a Court begin to look for guidance from the statutory default rules, traditional notions of fiduciary duties, or other extrinsic evidence.")....

39. Section 7.05 of the Partnership Agreement states in its entirety: "The Partnership is expressly permitted to enter into transactions with the General Partner or any Affiliate thereof provided that the terms of

any such transaction are substantially equivalent to terms obtainable by the Partnership from a comparable unaffiliated third party."

40. Section 7.10(a) states in its entirety: "The General Partner shall form an Audit Committee ("the Audit Committee") to be comprised of two members of the board of directors of the General Partner who are not affiliated with the General Partner or its Affiliates except by reason of such directorship. The functions of the Audit Committee shall be to review and approve (i) the expense reimbursements and compensation paid by the Partnership to the General Partner or any of its Affiliates and (ii) transactions between the Partnership and the General Partner and any of its Affiliates."

fiduciary duty principles to measure the General Partner's conduct'' because the Partnership Agreement "supplanted fiduciary duty and became the sole source of protection for the public unitholders of the Partnership." Thus, "the General Partner was subject, by contract, to a fairness standard akin to the common law one applicable to self-dealing transactions by fiduciaries."

The General Partner, HGI, Gumbiner, and Guzzetti apparently concede: (1) the General Partner's conduct associated with the Odd Lot Resale did not comply with Sections 7.05 and 7.10(a) of the Partnership Agreement because, as the Vice Chancellor found; (2) the Audit Committee never reviewed or approved the Odd Lot Resale to HGI; and (3) the General Partner never obtained a reliable financial analysis indicating that the Odd Lot Resale would be conducted on the same terms obtainable from an independent third party. Nonetheless, they argue that they are not liable for failing to comply with Sections 7.05 and 7.10(a) because Section 9.01 alone governed the Odd Lot Resale. They assert that the Odd Lot Resale was an issuance rather than a resale of Partnership units to HGI. The defendants seek the protection of Section 9.01, which gives the General Partner absolute and independent authority to issue additional Partnership units to any person or entity, including affiliates such as HGI.

The Vice Chancellor properly found that the Odd Lot Resale was a resale of Partnership units to HGI and thus Section 9.01 is inapplicable. It is undisputed that the Partnership's accounting books did not treat the sale of odd lots to HGI as an issuance of units. Furthermore, the Partnership units from the Odd Lot Resale were listed on the American Stock Exchange, but the Resale was presented to the Exchange as a resale, not as an issuance. The Vice Chancellor properly found that the Odd Lot Resale was structured as a resale, in part to avoid American Stock Exchange Rule 713, which requires that holders approve additional issuances as a prerequisite to the shares or units' listing on the Exchange. Thus, the General Partner is liable for breaching the contractually created fiduciary duties of entire fairness provided by Sections 7.05 and 7.10(a) of the Partnership Agreement.

Whether the Court of Chancery Erred by Holding HGI, Gumbiner, and Guzzetti Jointly and Severally Liable with the General Partner for Aiding and Abetting

HGI, Gumbiner, and Guzzetti argue that only the General Partner was a party to the Partnership Agreement, and therefore they cannot be held liable for breach of the Agreement. They also assert that there is no cause of action under Delaware law for aiding and abetting a breach of contract. This Court reviews de novo the Court of Chancery's interpretation of Delaware law.

HGI, Gumbiner, and Guzzetti are correct that they cannot be held liable for breach of the Partnership Agreement because they were not parties to it. "It is a general principle of contract law that only a party to a contract may be sued for breach of that contract."[46] But, the Court of Chancery properly held HGI, Gumbiner, and Guzzetti jointly and severally liable with the General Partner for aiding and abetting the General Partner's breach of fiduciary duties created by the Partnership Agreement. "The elements of a claim for aiding and abetting a breach of a fiduciary duty are: (1) the existence of a fiduciary relationship, (2) the fiduciary breached its duty, (3) a defendant, who is not a fiduciary, knowingly participated in a breach, and (4) damages to the plaintiff resulted from the concerted action of the fiduciary and the non-fiduciary."[47]

In this case, the General Partner had a fiduciary relationship with the Partnership and its limited partners as defined by the Partnership Agreement. The General Partner breached Sections 7.05 and 7.10(a), which impose the fiduciary duties of entire fairness. HGI, Gumbiner, and Guzzetti knowingly participated in the breach of fiduciary duties, and the limited partners consequently were injured. The Vice Chancellor correctly noted that "where a corporate General Partner fails to comply with a contractual standard [of fiduciary duty] that supplants traditional fiduciary duties and the General Partner's failure is caused by its directors and controlling stockholder, the directors and controlling stockholders remain liable."[48] The Court of Chancery thus properly held HGI, Gumbiner, and Guzzetti jointly and severally liable with the General Partner for the General Partner's breach of the Partnership Agreement's fiduciary duties of entire fairness....

Whether the Court of Chancery Had Discretion Not to Grant Recission in This Case ...

... Because Gotham unjustifiably delayed challenging the Odd Lot Resale and the defendants did not intend to entrench the General Partner or improperly enrich HGI, we find that the Vice Chancellor was within his discretion in refusing to grant rescission in this case, even though the result of the challenged transaction was to secure control by the defendants. Given the result of control and the defendants' conduct, however, an adequate, rationally-articulated substitute remedy must be awarded.

Whether the Court of Chancery Abused Its Discretion by Failing to Account for a Control Premium

The Court of Chancery awarded money damages of approximately $3.4 million based on a per unit value of $25.84 for each Partnership unit resold to HGI. The court gave equal weight to four factors: book value, Gotham's comparables for minority stakes in other limited partnerships, the per unit price of an unrelated Spring 1996 repurchase of Partnership units, and the average price paid by the Partner-

46. *Wallace v. Wood*, 752 A.2d 1175, 1180 (Del.Ch.1999) (citation omitted).

47. *Fitzgerald v. Cantor*, 1999 WL 182573 (Del.Ch.), at *1.

48. *Gotham Partners*, 795 A.2d at 34.

ship during the Odd Lot Offer. Gotham notes that none of the four factors "takes account of the lock on control that HGI obtained in the Resale." Gotham emphasizes that, at trial, Gumbiner valued control of the Partnership at $50 to $55 million and that only a mere $3.4 million was awarded as monetary damages. Gotham argues that this Court should reverse on this issue and remand to the Court of Chancery for a new remedy calculation that accounts for the value of control of the Partnership. This Court reviews the Court of Chancery's fashioning of remedies for abuse of discretion.

The Partnership Agreement provides for contractual fiduciary duties of entire fairness. Although the contract could have limited the damage remedy for breach of these duties to contract damages, it did not do so. The Court of Chancery is not precluded from awarding equitable relief as provided by the entire fairness standard where, as here, the general partner breached its contractually created fiduciary duty to meet the entire fairness standard and the partnership agreement is silent regarding damages. The Court of Chancery in this case may award equitable relief as provided by the entire fairness standard and is not limited to contract damages for two reasons: (1) this case involves a breach of the duty of loyalty and such a breach permits broad, discretionary, and equitable remedies; and (2) courts will not construe a contract as taking away other forms of appropriate relief, including equitable relief, unless the contract explicitly provides for an exclusive remedy.

In this case, as the Vice Chancellor properly found, the fiduciary duties provided for by the Partnership Agreement supplanted common law fiduciary duty principles, but "some of the agreement's provisions were 'in some sense . . . an explicit acceptance of the default duty of loyalty and fair dealing.' " The General Partner breached its duty of loyalty by failing to comply with the contractually created entire fairness standard during the Odd Lot Resale, which resulted in the General Partner and its corporate parent solidifying their control over the Partnership. Where there is "a breach of the duty of loyalty, as here, 'potentially harsher rules come into play' and 'the scope of recovery for a breach of the duty of loyalty is not to be determined narrowly [because t]he strict imposition of penalties under Delaware law are designed to discourage disloyalty.' "[70] Therefore, the Court of Chancery's "powers are complete to fashion any form of equitable and monetary relief as may be appropriate."[71] . . .

---

70. *Cantor Fitzgerald, L.P. v. Cantor,* 2001 WL 536911 (Del.Ch.), at *3 (quoting *Int'l Telecharge,* 766 A.2d at 441 (quoting *Thorpe v. CERBCO, Inc.,* 676 A.2d 436, 445 (Del.1996))).

71. *Weinberger,* 457 A.2d at 714. See also *Int'l Telecharge,* 766 A.2d at 440 (stating that "the powers of the Court of Chancery are very broad in fashioning equitable and

monetary relief under the entire fairness standard as may be appropriate"); *Cantor Fitzgerald, L.P. v. Cantor,* 2000 WL 307370 (Del.Ch.), at *29–*30 (stating that "equity must try to right the wrongs with adequate remedies" and awarding a declaratory judgement and money damages for a breach of a contractually created fiduciary duty).

... Although the Vice Chancellor found that the defendants did not intend for the General Partner to become entrenched or HGI to be unjustly enriched, the Odd Lot Resale had that effect. The Court of Chancery was thus required to remedy that effect by compensating the limited partners for a control premium. As the Vice Chancellor recognized, the Audit Committee—whose contractually-mandated functions were not implemented—conceivably would have "taken into account the fact that the Odd Lot resales were of particular advantage to HGI and demanded value for that advantage in exchange" because "the Odd Lot resales solidified HGI's control." Consequently, we find that the Vice Chancellor abused his discretion in fashioning the remedy in this case by failing (1) to address and decide the applicability of rescissory damages, and (2) to include in the damages calculation a premium for the control acquired by HGI through the Odd Lot Resale.

The Partnership is entitled to receive, at a minimum, what the Partnership units sold to HGI would have been worth at the time of the Odd Lot Resale if the General Partner had complied with the Partnership Agreement. We thus reverse the judgment of the Court of Chancery regarding the remedy in this case, and we remand for procedures, such as expansion of the record, as may be necessary and appropriate to accomplish two objectives. First, the Court of Chancery should seek to quantify how the challenged transaction would have been consummated had the defendants adhered to the Partnership Agreement's contractual entire fairness provisions. Specifically, the court should determine and consider what price the Audit Committee would have approved for the Odd Lot Offer resales to HGI if the Audit Committee had been aware that the transaction would result in HGI solidifying control over the Partnership. Second, the Court of Chancery should reconsider and award some form or combination of the various equitable remedies available to the limited partnership, including rescissory damages, sterilization of voting rights, and other appropriate methods of accounting for a control premium. We note that the Court of Chancery has the discretion to consider afresh in light of the above analysis whether or not to order rescission.

Conclusion

We affirm the judgment of the Court of Chancery that (1) the contractual fiduciary duties of entire fairness contained in the Partnership Agreement applied to the disputed transaction in this case; (2) defendants HGI, Gumbiner, and Guzzetti are jointly and severally liable with the General Partner because they aided and abetted the General Partner's breach of the contractually created fiduciary duties of entire fairness; [and] (3) the Court of Chancery has the discretion not to grant rescission where the plaintiff unjustifiably delays seeking that remedy, provided that the court articulates and orders a reasonable alternative remedy. . . .

We reverse the judgment of the Court of Chancery regarding the calculation of damages. We remand, as discussed above, for the court to fashion a remedy according to its discretion that accounts for a control premium. . . .

SECTION 2.   LIMITED LIABILITY COMPANIES

Insert the following case at p. 506 of the Unabridged Edition, and page 359 of the Concise Edition, in place of Hollowell v. Orleans Regional Hospital:

Bastan v. RJM & Associates, LLC

Superior Court of Connecticut, 2001.
29 Conn. L. Rptr. 646.

■ BEACH, J.

This action seeks primarily to recover a deposit paid to a builder. The defendant Robert J. Moravek, Sr., allegedly was the sole member of RJM & Associates, LLC, the limited liability company which contracted with the plaintiff to build the house. The fourth count of the complaint seeks to impose personal liability upon Moravek individually; the count alleges that Moravek is the controlling member of the LLC, that he treated LLC funds as his own by paying virtually all of his personal expenses from the account of the LLC, thus draining the LLC's assets such that they are insufficient to meet its obligations, that by his conduct Moravek "caused the independence of said LLC to cease", and that adherence to the fiction of separate identity would defeat the interests of justice.

The defendant Moravek has moved to strike the fourth count. Although he expressly does not concede that the allegations would be sufficient to "pierce the veil" of corporate protection against individual liability, the thrust of his argument is that in the context of a member-operated limited liability company, there can be no piercing of the LLC veil. Recognizing that there is no binding Connecticut authority precisely on point, Moravek argues that the statutory scheme expressly allows the individual to manage the LLC; he also refers to several law review articles which note the difficulty with which the veil ought to be allowed to be pierced in the context of member-operated LLC's.

Having reviewed the authorities cited by both sides,[1] I am not persuaded that the legislature intended the limitation on member

---

1. The plaintiff specifically refers to a Superior Court case, *Litchfield Asset Manag-* *ment v. Howell*, 2000 WL 1785122 (Gill, J.)(2000), in which Judge Gill applied princi-

liability to be absolute. Section 34–133(a) of the General Statutes provides that "[except as provided in (b)], a person who is a member or manager of a limited liability company is not liable, *solely* by reason of being a member or manager . . . for a debt, obligation or liability [of the LLC]." (Emphasis added). Subsection (b) provides, inter alia, that the personal liability of a member "shall be no greater than that of a shareholder who is an employee of a corporation formed under Chapter 601." The legislature is deemed to have been aware of our deeply rooted common law remedy of imposing personal liability upon a shareholder of a corporation where the corporate shield has been used to promote injustice, and the legislature surely could have expressly created a blanket limitation of member liability had it so chosen. Not much imagination is required to hypothesize all sorts of pernicious uses of such a blanket limitation.

I hold, then, that the traditional notions of imposing boundaries on the limitation of individual liability apply to limited liability companies. See, e.g., *Litchfield Asset Management,* supra. The defendant suggests that even if that is so, individual liability ought not be imposed on the so-called "identity" theory where the LLC is member-managed.

There have been at least two theories suggested as specific ways of piercing the corporate veil, the instrumentality rule and the identity rule. "The instrumentality rule requires, in any case but an express agency, proof of three elements:(1) Control, not mere majority or complete stock control, but complete domination, not only of finances but of policy and business practice in respect to the transaction attacked so that the corporate entity as to this transaction had at the time no separate mind, will or existence of its own; (2) that such control must have been used by the defendant to commit fraud or wrong, to perpetrate the violation of a statutory or other positive legal duty, or a dishonest or unjust act in contravention of plaintiff's legal rights; and (3) that the aforesaid control and breach of duty must proximately cause the injury or unjust loss complained of." *Tomasso v. Armor Construction & Paving, Inc.*, 187 Conn. 544 (1982). Under the identity theory, the proponent must " 'show that there was such a unity of interest and ownership that the independence of the corporation had in effect ceased or had never begun, [such that] an adherence to the fiction of separate identity would serve only to defeat justice and equity by permitting the economic entity to escape liability arising out of an operation conducted by one corporation for the benefit of the whole enterprise.' . . .[2] . . . . The identity rule primarily applies to prevent injustice in the situation where two corporate entities are, in reality, controlled as one enterprise because of the existence of common owners, officers, directors or shareholders and because of the lack of observance of corporate formalities between the two

---

ples of corporate veil-piercing in the context of the LLC.

2. *Saphir v. Neustadt,* 177 Conn. 191 (1979).

entities. See *Zaist v. Olson,*[3] . . . (and cases cited therein)." *Tomasso,* supra, 559–60 (footnotes omitted).

Although the narrowly defined identity theory would not appear to apply on the facts alleged in this case in any event, the narrow definitions may not be overwhelmingly significant. As stated by Justice Borden, the principle underlying the identity theory was applied to an individual in *Saphir,* and in any event:

> As a matter of policy I see no reason to permit recovery against a controlling individual under the instrumentality theory but to deny it under the identity theory. They are simply slightly different roads to the same destination. They both derive from the same principle: "Courts will . . . disregard the fiction of a separate legal entity to pierce the shield of immunity afforded by the corporate structure in a situation in which the corporate entity has been so controlled and dominated that justice requires liability to be imposed on the real actor." Saphir v. Neustadt, supra, 209. And they both require uniquely factual determinations by the trial court, in which "each case in which the issue is raised should be regarded as sui generis, to be decided in accordance with its own underlying facts." 1 Fletcher, op. cit., 41.3.

Tomasso, supra, 577–78 (dissenting opinion) (footnotes omitted).

As stated by Judge Gill in *Litchfield Asset Management,* supra:

> "The rationale behind the alter ego theory is that if the shareholders themselves, or the corporations themselves, disregard the legal separation, distinct properties, or proper formalities of the different corporate enterprises, then the law will likewise disregard them so far as is necessary to protect individual and corporate creditors." 1 W. Fletcher, Cyclopedia of the Law of Private Corporations (1990) § CT Page 13765 41.10, p. 614. The same theory applies in the case of a limited liability company. See, e.g., New England National, LLC v. Kabro, Superior Court, judicial district of New London. Docket No. 550014 (Feb. 16, 2000, Martin, J.); see also M. Pruner, supra, § § 3.1.1.4, 7.14, pp. 10, 106–07.

The defendant argues that because the statutory scheme allows members to manage LLC's; see *§ 34–140 of the General Statutes,* there can be no equitable piercing of the veil because members are allowed to act as individuals. This argument overlooks the consideration that considerable structure is required in the formation and operation of LLC's; see, e.g., § § 34–119 to 124 and indeed all of Chapter 613 of the General Statutes; and a person who ignores the intended separation between the individual and the company ought to be no better off than the sole shareholder who ignores corporate obligations.

---

3. *Zaist v. Olson,* 154 Conn. 563 (1967).

The plaintiffs have alleged facts which, if true, can support a conclusion that the limitation contemplated in *§ 34–133* does not apply. The motion to strike, then, is denied.

———

Insert the following case at p. 518 of the Unabridged Edition, and p. 371 of the Concise Edition, at the end of Section 2:

VGS, Inc. v. Castiel

Court of Chancery of Delaware, 2000.
2000 WL 1277372.

■ STEELE, V.C.

One entity controlled by a single individual forms a one "member" limited liability company. Shortly thereafter, two other entities, one of which is controlled by the owner of the original member, become members of the LLC. The LLC Agreement creates a three-member Board of Managers with sweeping authority to govern the LLC. The individual owning the original member has the authority to name and remove two of the three managers. He also acts as CEO. The unaffiliated third member becomes disenchanted with the original member's leadership. Ultimately the third member's owner, also the third manager, convinces the original member's owner's appointed manager to join him in a clandestine strategic move to merge the LLC into a Delaware corporation. The appointed manager and the disaffected third member do not give the original member's owner, still a member of the LLC's board of managers, notice of their strategic move. After the merger, the original member finds himself relegated to a minority position in the surviving corporation. While a majority of the board acted by written consent, as all involved surely knew, had the original member's manager received notice beforehand that his appointed manager contemplated action against his interests he would have promptly attempted to remove him. Because the two managers acted without notice to the third manager under circumstances where they knew that with notice that he could have acted to protect his majority interest, they breached their duty of loyalty to the original member and their fellow manager by failing to act in good faith. The purported merger must therefore be declared invalid.

The parties tried this case from June 15, 2000 through June 23, 2000. In further detail below, I describe the case's relevant facts and explain the rationale for my ruling.

I. Facts

David Castiel formed Virtual Geosatellite LLC (the "LLC") on January 6, 1999 in order to pursue a Federal Communications Commission ("FCC") license to build and operate a satellite system which its proponents claim could dramatically increase the "real estate" in outer space capable of transmitting high speed internet traffic and other communications. When originally formed, it had only one Member—Virtual Geosatellite Holdings, Inc. ("Holdings"). On January 8, 1999, Ellipso, Inc. ("Ellipso") joined the LLC as its second Member. Several weeks later, on January 29, 1999, Sahagen Satellite Technology Group LLC ("Sahagen Satellite") became the third Member of the LLC.

David Castiel controls both Holdings and Ellipso. Peter Sahagen, an aggressive and apparently successful venture capitalist, controls Sahagen Satellite.

Pursuant to the LLC Agreement, Holdings received 660 units (representing 63.46% of the total equity in the LLC), Sahagen Satellite received 260 units (representing 25%), and Ellipso received 120 units (representing 11.54%). The founders vested management of the LLC in a Board of Managers. As the majority unitholder, Castiel had the power to appoint, remove, and replace two of the three members of the Board of Managers. Castiel, therefore, had the power to prevent any Board decision with which he disagreed. Castiel named himself and Tom Quinn to the Board of Managers. Sahagen named himself as the third member of the Board.

Not long after the formation of the LLC, Castiel and Sahagen were at odds. Castiel contends that Sahagen wanted to control the LLC ever since he became involved, and that Sahagen repeatedly offered, unsuccessfully, to buy control of the LLC. Sahagen maintains that Castiel ran the LLC so poorly that its mission had become untracked, additional necessary capital could not be raised, and competent managers could not be attracted to join the enterprise. Further, Sahagen claims that Castiel directed LLC assets to Ellipso in order to prop up a failing, cash-strapped Ellipso. At trial, these issues and other similar accusations from both sides were explored in great detail. For our purposes here, all that need be concluded is the unarguable fact that Castiel and Sahagen had very different ideas about how the LLC should be managed and operated.

Sahagen ultimately convinced Quinn that Castiel must be ousted from leadership in order for the LLC to prosper. As a result, Quinn (Castiel's nominee) covertly "defected" to Sahagen's camp, and he and Sahagen decided to wrest control of the LLC from Castiel. Many LLC employees and even some of Castiel's lieutenants testified that they believed it to be in the LLC's best interest to take control from Castiel.

On April 14, 2000, without notice to Castiel, Quinn and Sahagen acted by written consent to merge the LLC under Delaware law into VGS, Inc. ("VGS"), a Delaware corporation. Accordingly, the LLC ceased to exist, its assets and liabilities passed to VGS, and VGS became the LLC's legal successor-in-interest. VGS's Board of Directors is comprised of Sahagen, Quinn, and Neel Howard. Of course, the incorporators did not name Castiel to VGS's Board.

On the day of the merger, Sahagen executed a promissory note to VGS in the amount of $10 million plus interest. In return, he received two million shares of VGS Series A Preferred Stock. VGS also issued 1,269,200 shares of common stock to Holdings, 230,800 shares of common stock to Ellipso, and 500,000 shares of common stock to Sahagen Satellite. Once one does the math, it is apparent that Holdings and Ellipso went from having a 75% controlling combined ownership interest in the LLC to having only a 37.5% interest in VGS. On the other hand, Sahagen and Sahagen Satellite went from owning 25% of the LLC to owning 62.5% of VGS.

There can be no doubt why Sahagen and Quinn, acting as a majority of the LLC's board of managers did not notify Castiel of the merger plan. Notice to Castiel would have immediately resulted in Quinn's removal from the board and a newly constituted majority which would thwart the effort to strip Castiel of control. Had he known in advance, Castiel surely would have attempted to replace Quinn with someone loyal to Castiel who would agree with his views. Clandestine machinations were, therefore, essential to the success of Quinn and Sahagen's plan.

II. Analysis

A. The Board of Managers did have authority to act by majority vote.

The LLC Agreement does not expressly state whether the Board of Managers must act unanimously or by majority vote. Sahagen and Quinn contend that because a number of provisions would be rendered meaningless if a unanimous vote was required, a majority vote is implied. Castiel, however, maintains that a unanimous vote must be implied when the majority owner has blocking power.

Section 8.01(b)(i) of the LLC Agreement states that, "the Board of Managers shall initially be composed of three (3) Managers." Sahagen Satellite has the right to designate one member of the initial board, and if the Board of Managers increased in number, Sahagen Satellite could "designate a number of representatives on the Board of Managers that is less than Sahagen's then current Percentage Interest." If unanimity were required, the number of managers would be irrelevant—Sahagen, and his minority interest, would have veto power in any event. The existence of language in the LLC Agreement discussing expansion of the Board is therefore quite telling.

Also persuasive is the fact that Section 8.01(c) of the LLC Agreement, entitled "Matters Requiring Consent of Sahagen," provides that Sahagen's approval is needed for a merger, consolidation, or reorganization of the LLC. If a unanimity requirement indeed existed, there would have been no need to expressly list matters on which Sahagen's minority interest had veto power.

Section 12.01(a)(i) of the LLC Agreement also supports Sahagen's argument. This section provides that the LLC may be dissolved by written consent by either the Board of Managers or by Members holding two-thirds of the Common Units. The effect of this Section is to allow any combination of Holdings and Sahagen Satellite, or Holdings and Ellipso, as Members, to dissolve the LLC. It seems unlikely that the Members designed the LLC Agreement to permit Members holding two-thirds of the Common Units to dissolve the LLC but denied their appointed Managers the power to reach the same result unless the minority manager agreed.

Castiel takes the position that while the Members can act by majority vote, the Board of Managers can act only by unanimous vote. He maintains that if the Board fails to agree unanimously on an issue the issue should be put to an LLC Members' vote with the majority controlling. The practical effect of Castiel's interpretation would be that whenever Castiel and Sahagen disagreed, Castiel would prevail because the issue would be submitted to the Members where Castiel's controlling interest would carry the vote. If that were the case, both Sahagen's Board position and Quinn's Board position would be superfluous. I am confident that the parties never intended that result, or if they had so intended, that they would have included plain and simple language in the agreement spelling it out clearly.

B. By failing to give notice of their proposed action, Sahagen and Quinn failed to discharge their duty of Loyalty to Castiel in good faith

Section 18–404(d) of the LLC Act states in pertinent part:

> Unless otherwise provided in a limited liability company agreement, on any matter that is to be voted on by managers, the managers may take such action without a meeting, *without prior notice* and without a vote if a consent or consents in writing, setting forth the action so taken, shall be signed by the managers having not less than the minimum number of votes that would be necessary to authorize such action at a meeting (emphasis added).

Therefore, the LLC Act, read literally, does not require notice to Castiel before Sahagen and Quinn could act by written consent. The LLC Agreement does not purport to modify the statute in this regard.

Those observations cannot complete the analysis of Sahagen and Quinn's actions, however. Sahagen and Quinn knew what would happen if they notified Castiel of their intention to act by written consent to merge the LLC into VGS, Inc. Castiel would have attempted to remove Quinn, and block the planned action. Regardless of his motivation in doing so, removal of Quinn in that circumstance would have been within Castiel's rights as the LLC's controlling owner under the Agreement.

Section 18–404(d) has yet to be interpreted by this Court or the Supreme Court. Nonetheless, it seems clear that the purpose of permitting action by written consent without notice is to enable LLC managers to take quick, efficient action in situations where a minority of managers could not block or adversely affect the course set by the majority even if they were notified of the proposed action and objected to it. The General Assembly never intended, I am quite confident, to enable two managers to deprive, clandestinely and surreptitiously, a third manager representing the majority interest in the LLC of an opportunity to protect that interest by taking an action that the third manager's member would surely have opposed if he had knowledge of it. My reading of Section 18–404(d) is grounded in a classic maxim of equity—"Equity looks to the intent rather than to the form."[3] In this hopefully unique situation, this application of the maxim requires construction of the statute to allow action without notice only by a *constant or fixed majority*. It can not apply to an illusory, will-of-the wisp majority which would implode should notice be given. Nothing in the statute suggests that this court of equity should blind its eyes to a shallow, too clever by half, manipulative attempt to restructure an enterprise through an action taken by a "majority" that existed only so long as it could act in secrecy.

Sahagen and Quinn each owed a duty of loyalty to the LLC, its investors and Castiel, their fellow manager. Castiel or his entities owned a majority interest in the LLC and he sat as a member of the board representing entities and interests empowered by the Agreement to control the majority membership of the board. The majority investor protected his equity interest in the LLC through the mechanism of appointment to the board rather than by the statutorily sanctioned mechanism of approval by members owning a majority of the LLC's equity interests. It may seem somewhat incongruous, but this Agreement allows the action to merge, dissolve or change to corporate status to be taken by a simple majority vote of the board of managers rather than rely upon the default position of the statute which requires a majority vote of the equity interest. Instead the drafters made the critical assumption, known to all the players here, that the holder of the majority equity interest has the right to appoint and remove two managers, ostensibly guaranteeing control over a three member board. When Sahagen and Quinn, fully recognizing that this was Castiel's protection against actions adverse to his majority interest, acted in secret, without notice, they failed to discharge their duty of loyalty to him in good faith. They owed Castiel a duty to give him prior notice even if he would have interfered with a plan that they conscientiously believed to be in the best interest of the LLC.[4] Instead,

3. Donald J. Wolfe, Jr. & Michael A. Pittenger, Corporate and Commercial Practice in the Delaware Court of Chancery, at vii (1998) (listing the maxims of equity)....

4. I make no ruling here as to whether I believe the merger and the resulting recapitalization of the LLC was in the LLC's best interests, nor do I rule here regarding the

they launched a preemptive strike that furtively converted Castiel's controlling interest in the LLC to a minority interest in VGS without affording Castiel a level playing field on which to defend his interest. "[Another] traditional maxim of equity holds that equity regards and treats that as done which in good conscience ought to be done."[5] In good conscience, under these circumstances, Sahagen and Quinn should have given Castiel prior notice.

Many hours were spent at trial focusing on contentions that Castiel has proved to be an ineffective leader in whom employees and investors have lost confidence. I listened to testimony regarding delayed FCC licensing, a suggested new management team for the LLC, and the alleged unlocked value of the LLC. A substantial record exists fully flushing out the rancorous relationships of the members and their wildly disparate views on the existing state of affairs as well as the LLC's prospects for the future. But the issue of who is best suited to run the LLC should not be resolved here but in board meetings where all managers are present and all members appropriately represented, and/or in future litigation, if it unfortunately becomes necessary.

Likewise, the parties spent much time and effort arguing over the standard to be applied to the actions taken by Sahagen and Quinn. Specifically, the parties debated whether the standard should be entire fairness or the business judgment rule. It should be clear that the actions of Sahagen and Quinn, in their capacity as managers constituted a breach of their duty of loyalty and that those actions do not, therefore, entitle them to the benefit or protection of the business judgment rule. They intentionally used a flawed process to merge the LLC into VGS, Inc., in an attempt to prevent the member with majority equity interest in the LLC from protecting his interests in the manner contemplated by the very LLC Agreement under which they purported to act. Analysis beyond a look at the process is clearly unnecessary. Perhaps, had notice been given and an attempt then made to block Castiel's anticipated action to replace Quinn, the allegedly disinterested and independent member that Castiel himself had appointed, the analysis might be different. However, this, as all cases must be reviewed as it is presented, not as it might have been.

III. Conclusion

For the reasons stated above, I find that a majority vote of the LLC's Board of Managers could properly effect a merger. But, I also find that Sahagen and Quinn failed to discharge their duty of loyalty to Castiel in good faith by failing to give him advance notice of their merger plans under the unique circumstances of this case and the

---

wisdom of Castiel's actions had he in fact been able to remove Quinn before the merger.

5. Wolfe & Pittenger, *supra,* at § 2-3(B)(1)(I), *citing* 2 John Norton Pomeroy, . . . A Treatise on Equity Jurisprudence § 363 Et Seq. (5th Ed. (1941)).

structure of this LLC Agreement. Accordingly, I declare that the acts taken to merge the LLC into VGS, Inc. to be invalid and the merger is ordered rescinded....

SECTION 3.   THE LIMITED LIABILITY PARTNERSHIP

Insert the following materials at p. 519 of the Unabridged Edition, and p. 372 of the Concise Edition, at the end of section 3:

MEGADYNE INFORMATION SYSTEMS v. ROSNER, OWENS & NUNZIATO, L.L.P., 2002 WL 31112563 (Cal. App. 2002).* In October 1995, Megadyne entered into a two-year contract with the Orange County Transportation Authority (OCTA). By November 1995, Megadyne learned that it had based its successful contract bid on misinformation that OCTA had furnished to Megadyne in March 1995. In December, Megadyne retained the law firm of Irell & Manella to negotiate a settlement with OCTA. In November 1996, the one-year Statute of Limitations period, within which Megadyne had to file a claim against OCTA, expired. In November 1997, the Rosner firm served OCTA with a statutory claim for $500,000 damages. By that time, however, the one-year Statute of Limitations on the claim had run out. The Rosner firm nevertheless worked on the case and billed Megadyne. In January 1998, OCTA returned the claim because it had not been presented within one year of the accrual of the cause of action.

Megadyne claimed that the Rosner firm had breached its fiduciary duty by falsely informing Megadyne that it had a viable claim; that in reliance upon that misrepresentation Megadyne retained the Rosner firm to pursue an action that was doomed to failure; and that Megadyne was damaged to the extent that it had paid for worthless legal representation. Megadyne's suit had been handled by Andrew Owens, one of the partners in the Rosner firm. One of the issues was whether, if Megadyne established liability, all three partners in the Rosner firm would be liable, or only Owens, who was directly responsible. The court stated that all three partners might be liable even though the firm was a limited liability partnership:

> ... Pursuant to Corporations Code section 16306, subdivision (c), an individual partner of a registered limited liability partnership such as the Rosner firm has no vicarious liability for the tort(s) of another partner. Only the partnership and the individual partner are liable. (See Corp.Code, § 16306, subd. (e).) Consequently, Megadyne can only hold Nunziato and Rosner liable if they were involved in the handling of its matter. All three

---

* Unpublished opinion.

partners offered declarations averring Owens was "the sole attorney" who handled the Megadyne matter and that neither of the other two had "any involvement" in the case. To contradict that showing, Megadyne offered Owens's testimony that "there might have been discussions" with his two partners that Megadyne had a viable legal malpractice claim against Irell & Manella. This is sufficient to create a triable issue of fact as to whether the partners were personally involved in the firm's breach of fiduciary duties. If the partners had *discussions* that Megadyne could sue Irell & Manella for malpractice, it is reasonable to infer that they knew Megadyne's claim against OCTA was time-barred and that they participated in the decision to not disclose this fact to Megadyne while the firm continued to represent it. In addition, the fact Nunziato's name was on the caption page of the claim filed with OCTA suggests his involvement in the case.

Jonathan D. Glater
FEARING LIABILITY, LAW FIRMS CHANGE PARTNERSHIP STATUS
The New York Times, January 10, 2003.*

Two of New York's most prominent law firms have quietly converted to a type of partnership that shields members from personal liability if the firms collapse under devastating lawsuits by clients or investors. Several other large firms are weighing similar steps.

The moves by Sullivan & Cromwell and Paul, Weiss, Rifkind, Wharton & Garrison, reported yesterday in The New York Law Journal, come in the wake of widespread corporate fraud at several public companies last year and a rising number of shareholder lawsuits, some aimed at law firms that had advised the companies.

Becoming a limited liability partnership, or L.L.P., is simply a smart business move, lawyers said, pointing out that partners at the accounting firm Arthur Andersen—which was such a partnership—would have been far worse off if their homes and cars had been vulnerable to Enron investors seeking to recover billions.

"It seems like a prudent thing to consider in light of all the litigation against professionals that has been going on in the last several years," said Robert D. Joffe, managing partner at Cravath, Swaine & Moore, which is a general partnership. He said his firm's partners were considering conversion, too.

Partners at Shearman & Sterling, another large New York firm, are also considering it, said Kenneth J. Laverriere, a Shearman partner. "I expect that we will decide to convert," he said.

Lawyers at large firms said they did not anticipate a wave of successful shareholder lawsuits and noted that in most cases such suits were settled. The size of settlements might even fall, some lawyers said, because plaintiffs would realize there was less money available. Plaintiffs would be limited to the firm's assets—operating capital, leases, furniture, computers and other office supplies.

"We were obviously aware of the current business climate, but we have considered doing this for many years," said Alfred D. Youngwood, a partner at Paul, Weiss. The firm's partners decided to convert now, he said, after determining that the move would not adversely affect the firm's image, its client relationships or its internal workings and culture.

Each state has its own laws on limited liability partnerships; before 1994, when New York adopted its law, it was not possible for law firms to use the structure. Lawyers—like accountants, doctors and some consultants—usually belonged to general partnerships.

Each partner's personal assets are at risk if a general partnership fails, said Jennifer H. Arlen, a law professor at New York University. If one partner commits fraud, for example, and resulting litigation bankrupts the firm, claimants can pursue the personal wealth of all partners, she said.

"The benefit of the L.L.P. is that if a law firm gets hit with sufficient liability to bankrupt it, then the partners of an L.L.P. are probably not personally liable for the debts of the partnership," she said. Of course, she added, partners who commit fraud may still be personally liable.

How much protection L.L.P. status provides has not been extensively tested, and lawyers are anxiously monitoring the progress of shareholder suits against Vinson & Elkins, an L.L.P. that is a defendant in Enron shareholder litigation. But L.L.P.'s do not afford as much protection as do publicly held companies, Professor Arlen said. (Law firms cannot be publicly held; if they were, lawyers would face potential conflicts of interest in serving both shareholders and clients.)

Despite the apparent advantages of L.L.P. status, the weight of tradition at law firms rests on the general partnership structure. There is a perception, several lawyers said, that firms' advice means more because all the partners ultimately put their own wealth behind it.

But as more and more firms have converted to L.L.P.'s and clients have not abandoned them, that concern has eased, lawyers said.

"Clients don't seem to care," one senior partner said.

The percentage of law firms using limited liability partnerships has increased steadily over the last five years, to 25 percent from 20 percent, according to a survey of law firm economics by Altman Weil, a consulting company that advises law firms. The study, which drew on responses from a group of fewer than 500 firms, is not comprehensive.

Two trends are causing lawyers to worry more about liability, said William G. Johnston, a director at Hildebrandt International, a consulting firm. First, as share prices have increased, the size of potential damage awards in shareholder lawsuits has grown to the point that a firm could potentially be destroyed.

Second, as firms have grown, chances have increased that a partner may not know how reliable or ethical other partners are, and so will not want to risk being liable for their actions, he said.

But lawyers at several large firms said they worried that becoming an L.L.P. could hamper their business in intangible ways. Lawyers who in a general partnership might have helped colleagues serving other clients might not do so in an L.L.P. to avoid taking on potential liability for the work, said one lawyer who insisted on anonymity.

At Weil, Gotshal & Manges, which converted to an L.L.P. several years ago, the partners decided to indemnify one another in such a situation, said Richard J. Davis, a partner at the firm. That way, he said, a partner who was not primarily involved in a transaction would still be willing to provide advice.

"We have had no problems, either with clients or internally," he said. "There was no reason not to do it."

———

CHAPTER VIII

THE DUTY OF CARE AND THE DUTY TO ACT LAWFULLY

SECTION 1. THE DUTY OF CARE

(d) Limits on Liability; Directors' and Officers' Liability Insurance

(1) Limits on Liability

Insert the following case and Note at p. 590 of the Unabridged Edition, and page 427 of the Concise Edition, following the Note on Emerald Partners v. Berlin (Del. 1999):

Malpiede v. Townson

Supreme Court of Delaware, 2001.
780 A.2d 1075.

■ VEASEY, CHIEF JUSTICE:

In this appeal, we affirm . . . the granting of a motion to dismiss the plaintiffs' due care claim on the ground that the exculpatory provision in the charter of the target corporation authorized by 8 Del. C. § 102(b)(7), bars any claim for money damages against the director defendants based solely on the board's alleged breach of its duty of care. Accordingly, we affirm the judgment of the Court of Chancery dismissing the amended complaint. . . .

Facts

Frederick's of Hollywood ("Frederick's") is a retailer of women's lingerie and apparel with its headquarters in Los Angeles, California. This case centers on the merger of Frederick's into Knightsbridge Capital Corporation ("Knightsbridge") under circumstances where it became a target in a bidding contest. Before the merger, Frederick's common stock was divided into Class A shares (each of which has one vote) and Class B shares (which have no vote). As of December 6, 1996, there were outstanding 2,995,309 Class A shares and 5,903,118 Class B shares. Two trusts created by the principal founders of Frederick's, Frederick and Harriet Mellinger (the "Trusts"), held a total of about 41% of the outstanding Class A voting shares and a total of about 51% of the outstanding Class B non-voting shares of Frederick's.

On June 14, 1996, the Frederick's board announced its decision to retain an investment bank, Janney Montgomery Scott, Inc. ("JMS"), to advise the board in its search for a suitable buyer for the company. In January 1997, JMS initiated talks with Knightsbridge. Four months later, in April 1997, Knightsbridge offered to purchase all of the outstanding shares of Frederick's for between $6.00 and $6.25 per share. At Knightsbridge's request, the Frederick's board granted Knightsbridge the exclusive right to conduct due diligence.

On June 13, 1997, the Frederick's board approved an offer from Knightsbridge to purchase all of Frederick's outstanding Class A and Class B shares for $6.14 per share in cash in a two-step merger transaction.[5] The terms of the merger agreement signed by the Frederick's board prohibited the board from soliciting additional bids from third parties, but the agreement permitted the board to negotiate with third party bidders when the board's fiduciary duties required it to do so.[6] The Frederick's board then sent to stockholders a Consent Solicitation Statement recommending that they approve the transaction, which was scheduled to close on August 27, 1997.

On August 21, 1997, Frederick's received a fully financed, unsolicited cash offer of $7.00 per share from a third-party bidder, Milton Partners ("Milton"). Four days after the board received the Milton offer, Knightsbridge entered into an agreement to purchase all of the Frederick's shares held by the Trusts for $6.90 per share. Under the stock purchase agreement, the Trusts granted Knightsbridge a proxy to vote the Trusts' shares, but the Trusts had the right to terminate the agreement if the Frederick's board rejected the Knightsbridge offer in favor of a higher bid.

On August 27, 1997, the Frederick's board received a fully financed, unsolicited $7.75 cash offer from Veritas Capital Fund ("Veritas"). In light of these developments, the board postponed the Knightsbridge merger in order to arrange a meeting with the two new bidders. On September 2, 1997, the board sent a memorandum to Milton and Veritas outlining the conditions for participation in the

---

5. Shortly before the board approved the merger on June 13, 1997, two directors, Sylvan Lefcor and Morton Fields, resigned from the board. The remaining five directors approved the merger agreement unanimously.

6. In the event that the Frederick's board terminated the merger agreement in order to accept a superior proposal by a third party bidder, the agreement entitled Knightsbridge to liquidated damages of $1.8 million.

bidding process. The memorandum required that the bidders each deposit $2.5 million in an escrow account and submit, before September 4, 1997, a marked-up merger agreement with the same basic terms as the Knightsbridge merger agreement. Veritas submitted a merger agreement and the $2.5 million escrow payment in accordance with these conditions. Milton did not.[9]

On September 3, 1997, the Frederick's board met with representatives of Veritas to discuss the terms of the Veritas offer. According to the plaintiffs, the board asserts that, at this meeting, it orally informed Veritas that it was required to produce its "final, best offer" by September 4, 1997. The plaintiffs further allege that that board did not, in fact, inform Veritas of this requirement.

The same day that the board met with Veritas, Knightsbridge and the Trusts amended their stock purchase agreement to eliminate the Trusts' termination rights and other conditions on the sale of the Trusts' shares. On September 4, 1997, Knightsbridge exercised its rights under the agreement and purchased the Trusts' shares. Knightsbridge immediately informed the board of its acquisition of the Trusts' shares and repeated its intention to vote the shares against any competing third party bids.

One day after Knightsbridge acquired the Trusts' shares, the Frederick's board participated in a conference call with Veritas to discuss further the terms of the proposed merger. During this conference call, Veritas representatives suggested that, if the board elected to accept the Veritas offer, the board could issue an option to Veritas to purchase authorized but unissued Frederick's shares as a means to circumvent the 41% block of voting shares that Knightsbridge had acquired from the Trusts. Frederick's representatives also expressed some concern that Knightsbridge would sue the board if it decided to terminate the June 15, 1997 merger agreement. In response, Veritas agreed to indemnify the directors in the event of such litigation.

On September 6, 1997, Knightsbridge increased its bid to match the $7.75 Veritas offer, but on the condition that the board accept a variety of terms designed to restrict its ability to pursue superior offers.[10] On the same day, the Frederick's board approved this agreement and effectively ended the bidding process. Two days later, Knightsbridge purchased additional Frederick's Class A shares on the open market, at an average price of $8.21 per share, thereby acquiring a majority of both classes of Frederick's shares.

---

9. Milton apparently discontinued its efforts to acquire Frederick's after Veritas submitted its higher bid.

10. The terms included: a provision prohibiting any Frederick's representative from speaking to third party bidders concerning the acquisition of the company (the "no-talk" provision); a termination fee of $4.5 million (about 7% of the value of the transaction); the appointment of a non-voting Knightsbridge observer at Frederick's board meetings; and an obligation to grant Knightsbridge any stock option that Frederick's granted to a competing bidder. The revised merger agreement did not expressly permit the Frederick's board to pursue negotiations with third parties where its fiduciary duties required it to do so.

On September 11, 1997, Veritas increased its cash offer to $9.00 per share. Relying on (1) the "no-talk" provision in the merger agreement, (2) Knightsbridge's stated intention to vote its shares against third party bids, and (3) Veritas' request for an option to dilute Knightsbridge's interest, the board rejected the revised Veritas bid. On September 18, 1997, the board amended its earlier Consent Solicitation Statement to include the events that had transpired since July 1997. The deadline for responses to the consent solicitation was September 29, 1997, the scheduled closing date for the merger.

Before the merger closed, the plaintiffs filed in the Court of Chancery the purported class action complaint that is the predecessor of the amended complaint before us. The plaintiffs also moved for a temporary restraining order enjoining the merger. The Court of Chancery denied the requested injunctive relief.

The plaintiffs then amended their complaint to include a class action claim for damages caused by the termination of the auction in favor of Knightsbridge and the rejection of the higher Veritas offer. The amended complaint alleged that the Frederick's board had breached its fiduciary duties in connection with the sale of the company. . . .

The Court of Chancery granted the directors' motion to dismiss the amended complaint under Chancery Rule 12(b)(6), concluding that: (1) the complaint did not support a claim of breach of the board's duty of loyalty, [and] (2) the exculpatory provision in the Fredrick's charter precluded money damages against the directors for any breach of the board's duty of care. . . .

Standard of Review

We review de novo the dismissal by the Court of Chancery of a complaint under Rule 12(b)(6). . . .

The Duty of Loyalty Claim

The central claim in the amended complaint is that the sale of Frederick's to Knightsbridge "constituted a breach of [the Frederick's board's] fiduciary obligation to maximize shareholder value" because the board did not "conduct an auction with a 'level playing field' " as required by Revlon, Inc. v. MacAndrews & Forbes Holdings, Inc.[20] The plaintiffs contend that this sort of allegation cannot be neatly divided into duty of care claims and duty of loyalty claims.

In our view, *Revlon* neither creates a new type of fiduciary duty in the sale-of-control context nor alters the nature of the fiduciary duties that generally apply. Rather, *Revlon* emphasizes that the board must perform its fiduciary duties in the service of a specific objective: maximizing the sale price of the enterprise. Although the *Revlon* doctrine imposes enhanced judicial scrutiny of certain transactions involving a sale of control, it does not eliminate the requirement that

---

20. Del. Supr., 506 A.2d 173, 182–83 (1985).

plaintiffs plead sufficient facts to support the underlying claims for a breach of fiduciary duties in conducting the sale. Accordingly, we proceed to analyze the amended complaint to determine whether it alleges sufficient facts to support a claim that the board breached any of its fiduciary duties.

The Court of Chancery concluded, and the plaintiffs do not appear to contest on appeal, that the amended complaint adequately alleges a conflict of interest with respect to only one of the directors who approved the Knightsbridge merger.[24] The amended complaint does not allege that the lone conflicted director dominated the three other directors who approved the merger on September 6, 1997. The Court of Chancery therefore correctly held that the Knightsbridge merger was approved by a majority of disinterested directors....

The Due Care Claim

The primary due care issue is whether the board was grossly negligent, and therefore breached its duty of due care, in failing to implement a routine defensive strategy that could enable the board to negotiate for a higher bid or otherwise create a tactical advantage to enhance stockholder value.

In this case, that routine strategy would have been for the directors to use a poison pill to ward off Knightsbridge's advances and thus to prevent Knightsbridge from stopping the auction process. Had they done so, plaintiffs seem to allege that the directors could have preserved the appropriate options for an auction process designed to achieve the best value for the stockholders.

Construing the amended complaint most favorably to the plaintiffs, it can be read to allege that the board was grossly negligent in immediately accepting the Knightsbridge offer and agreeing to various restrictions on further negotiations without first determining whether Veritas would issue a counteroffer. Although the board had conducted a search for a buyer over one year, plaintiffs seem to contend that the board was imprudently hasty in agreeing to a restrictive merger agreement on the day it was proposed—particularly where other

---

24. See January 2000 Mem. Op., 2000 Del. Ch. LEXIS 19, *17. In particular, the complaint alleges that the Knightsbridge merger agreement provided for several cash payments to George Townson, who was the CEO, President, and Chairman of Frederick's during the relevant period. The personal benefits allegedly received by Townson as a result of the Knightsbridge merger included: (1) a payment of $.05 for each "under water" option held by Townson with an exercise price below the merger price, (2) a severance payment of $750,000 upon consummation of the merger, and (3) a payment of $250,000 on the date of the merger and sixteen quarterly payments of $100,000 under a noncompete and consulting agreement. The complaint also alleges that William Barrett, who was a Frederick's director and a vice president of JMS, the firm's financial advisor, had an interest in the merger transaction. Specifically, the complaint alleges that Barrett's firm received a $2 million fee upon consummation of the Knightsbridge merger. But because Barrett's firm was entitled to receive a fee upon the consummation of any merger and because the fee was proportional to the sale price, the Court of Chancery correctly concluded that the complaint was insufficient to establish a disabling conflict with respect to Barrett. See January 2000 Mem. Op., 2000 Del. Ch. LEXIS 19, *24....

bidders had recently expressed interest.[43] Although the board's haste, in itself, might not constitute a breach of the board's duty of care because the board had already conducted a lengthy sale process, the plaintiffs argue that the board's decision to accept allegedly extreme contractual restrictions impacted its ability to obtain a higher sale price. Recognizing that, at the end of the day, plaintiffs would have an uphill battle in overcoming the presumption of the business judgment rule, we must give plaintiffs the benefit of the doubt at this pleading stage to determine if they have stated a due care claim. Because of our ultimate decision, however, we need not finally decide this question in this case.

We assume, therefore, without deciding, that a claim for relief based on gross negligence during the board's auction process is stated by the inferences most favorable to plaintiffs that flow from these allegations. The issue then becomes whether the amended complaint may be dismissed upon a Rule 12(b)(6) motion by reason of the existence and the legal effect of the exculpatory provision of Article TWELFTH of Frederick's certificate of incorporation, adopted pursuant to 8 Del. C. § 102(b)(7). That provision would exempt directors from personal liability in damages with certain exceptions (e.g., breach of the duty of loyalty) that are not applicable here. . . .[45]

B.   Application of *Emerald Partners*

1.   The Court of Chancery Properly Dismissed Claims Based Solely on the Duty of Care

Plaintiffs here, while not conceding that the Section 102(b)(7) charter provision may be considered on this Rule 12(b)(6) motion nevertheless, in effect, conceded in oral argument in the Court of Chancery and similarly in oral argument in this Court that if a complaint unambiguously and solely asserted only a due care claim, the complaint is dismissible once the corporation's Section 102(b)(7) provision is invoked. . . .

Plaintiffs contended vigorously, however, that the Section 102(b)(7) charter provision does not apply to bar their claims in this case because the amended complaint alleges breaches of the duty of loyalty and other claims that are not barred by the charter provision. As a result, plaintiffs maintain, this case cannot be boiled down solely to a due care case. They argue, in effect, that their complaint is

---

43.   Relatedly, the plaintiffs also argue that the board breached its fiduciary duties by favoring Knightsbridge over Veritas in the bidding process.

45.   Article TWELFTH provides:

TWELFTH. A director of this Corporation shall not be personally liable to the Corporation or its shareholders for monetary damages for breach of fiduciary duty as a director, except for liability (i) for any breach of the director's duty of loyalty to the Corporation or its shareholders, (ii) for acts or omissions not in good faith or which involve intentional misconduct or a knowing violation of law (iii) under Section 174 of the Delaware General Corporation Law, or (iv) for any transaction for which the director derived an improper personal benefit.

sufficiently well-pleaded that—as a matter of law—the due care claims are so inextricably intertwined with loyalty and bad faith claims that Section 102(b)(7) is not a bar to recovery of damages against the directors.

We disagree. It is the plaintiffs who have a burden to set forth "a short and plain statement of the claim showing that the pleader is entitled to relief."[63] The plaintiffs are entitled to all reasonable inferences flowing from their pleadings, but if those inferences do not support a valid legal claim, the complaint should be dismissed without the need for the defendants to file an answer and without proceeding with discovery. Here we have assumed, without deciding, that the amended complaint on its face states a due care claim. Because we have determined that the complaint fails properly to invoke loyalty and bad faith claims, we are left with only a due care claim. Defendants had the obligation to raise the bar of Section 102(b)(7) as a defense, and they did. As plaintiffs conceded in oral argument before this Court, if there is only an unambiguous, residual due care claim and nothing else—as a matter of law—then Section 102(b)(7) would bar the claim. Accordingly, the Court of Chancery did not err in dismissing the plaintiffs due care claim in this case.

2. The Court of Chancery Correctly Applied the Parties' Respective Burdens of Proof

Plaintiffs also assert that the trial court in the case before us incorrectly placed on plaintiffs a pleading burden to negate the elements of the 102(b)(7) charter provision. Plaintiffs argue that this ruling is inconsistent with the statement in *Emerald Partners* that "The shield from liability provided by a certificate of incorporation provision adopted pursuant to 8 Del. C. § 102(b)(7) is in the nature of an affirmative defense. . . . Defendants seeking exculpation under such a provision will normally bear the burden of establishing each of its elements."

The procedural posture here is quite different from that in *Emerald Partners*. There the Court stated that it was incorrect for the trial court to grant summary judgment on the record in that case because the defendants had the burden at trial of demonstrating good faith if they were invoking the statutory exculpation provision. In this case, we focus not on trial burdens, but only on pleading issues. A plaintiff must allege well-pleaded facts stating a claim on which relief may be granted. Had plaintiff alleged such well-pleaded facts supporting a breach of loyalty or bad faith claim, the Section 102(b)(7) charter provision would have been unavailing as to such claims, and this case would have gone forward.

But we have held that the amended complaint here does not allege a loyalty violation or other violation falling within the exceptions to the Section 102(b)(7) exculpation provision. Likewise, we

---

63. Chancery Rule 8(a).

have held that, even if the plaintiffs had stated a claim for gross negligence, such a well-pleaded claim is unavailing because defendants have brought forth the Section 102(b)(7) charter provision that bars such claims. This is the end of the case.

And rightly so, as a matter of the public policy of this State. Section 102(b)(7) was adopted by the Delaware General Assembly in 1986 following a directors and officers insurance liability crisis and the 1985 Delaware Supreme Court decision in Smith v. Van Gorkom. The purpose of this statute was to permit stockholders to adopt a provision in the certificate of incorporation to free directors of personal liability in damages for due care violations, but not duty of loyalty violations, bad faith claims and certain other conduct. Such a charter provision, when adopted, would not affect injunctive proceedings based on gross negligence. Once the statute was adopted, stockholders usually approved charter amendments containing these provisions because it freed up directors to take business risks without worrying about negligence lawsuits.

Our jurisprudence since the adoption of the statute has consistently stood for the proposition that a Section 102(b)(7) charter provision bars a claim that is found to state only a due care violation.[69] Because we have assumed that the amended complaint here does state a due care claim, the exculpation afforded by the statute must affirmatively be raised by the defendant directors.[70] The directors have done so in this case, and the Court of Chancery properly applied the Frederick's charter provision to dismiss the plaintiffs' due care claim. . . .

Conclusion

We have concluded that: (1) the amended complaint does not adequately allege a breach of the Frederick's board's duty of loyalty or its disclosure duty; (2) the exculpatory provision in the Frederick's charter operates to bar claims for money damages against the directors caused by the alleged breach of the board's duty of care. . . . Accordingly, we affirm the judgment of the Court of Chancery dismissing the amended complaint against the Frederick's board. . . .

---

69. See, e.g., *Emerald Partners*, 726 A.2d at 1224; *Arnold v. Society for Savings Bancorp.*, Del. Supr., 650 A.2d 1270, 1288 (1994); *Zirn v. VLI Corp.*, Del. Supr., 681 A.2d 1050, 1061 (1996).

70. Although an exculpatory charter provision is in the nature of an affirmative defense under *Emerald Partners*, the board is not required to disprove claims based on alleged breaches of the duty of loyalty to gain the protection of the provision with respect to due care claims. Rather, proving the existence of a valid exculpatory provision in the corporate charter entitles directors to dismissal of any claims for money damages against them that are based solely on alleged breaches of the board's duty of care.

MCCALL v. SCOTT, 239 F.3d 808 (6th Cir.2001), as amended, 250 F.3d 997 (6th Cir.2001). "The contours of director liability for breach of the duty to care exercise appropriate attention to potentially illegal corporate activities were discussed in *In re Caremark International Inc. Derivative Litigation*, 698 A.2d 959 (Del.Ch.1996). There, the court explained that this was possibly the most difficult theory in corporation law upon which a plaintiff might hope to win a judgment. *Id.* at 967. Director liability for such a breach may arise (1) from a board decision that resulted in a loss because the decision was ill-advised, or (2) from 'an unconsidered failure of the board to act in circumstances in which due attention would, arguably, have prevented the loss.' *Id.* As discussed earlier, the duty of care claims in this case fall into the second category as they arise from the Board's failure to act under the circumstances. The court in *Caremark* held that when director liability is predicated upon ignorance of liability-creating activities, 'only a sustained or systematic failure of the board to exercise oversight—such as an utter failure to attempt to assure a reasonable information and reporting system exists—will establish the lack of good faith that is a necessary condition to liability.' *Id.* at 971.

"Unconsidered inaction can be the basis for director liability because, even though most corporate decisions are not subject to director attention, ordinary business decisions of officers and employees deeper in the corporation can significantly injure the corporation and make it subject to criminal sanctions. *Id.* This theory grew out of an earlier decision, in which the Delaware Supreme Court explained that

> the question whether a corporate director has become liable for losses to the corporation through neglect of duty is determined by the circumstances. If he has recklessly reposed confidence in an obviously untrustworthy employee, has refused or neglected cavalierly to perform his duty as a director, or has ignored either willfully or through inattention obvious danger signs of employee wrongdoing, the law will cast the burden of liability upon him.

Graham v. Allis–Chalmers Mfg. Co., 41 Del.Ch. 78, 188 A.2d 125, 130 (Del. 1963). Since then, the Delaware Supreme Court has specifically adopted gross negligence as the standard for measuring a director's liability for a breach of the duty of care. *See Aronson v.*, 473 A.2d 805, 812; *Smith v. Van Gorkom*, 488 A.2d 858, 872 (Del.1985).

"While defendants do not deny that allegations of gross negligence may state a claim for breach of the duty of care under *Caremark* they argue that they are protected against such claims under the waiver-of-liability provision contained in Columbia's corporate charter. Columbia's Restated Certificate of Incorporation provides:

> *TWELFTH:* A director of the Corporation shall not be personally liable to the Corporation or its stockholders for monetary damages for breach of fiduciary duty as a director, *provided, however, that* the foregoing shall not eliminate or limit the liability of a

director (i) for any breach of the director's duty of loyalty to the Corporation or its stockholders, (ii) for acts or omissions not in good faith or which involve intentional misconduct or a knowing violation of law, (iii) under Section 174 of the General Corporation Law of Delaware, or (iv) for any transaction from which the director derived an improper personal benefit.

"Columbia [the Corporation] adopted this provision pursuant to 8 DEL. CODE ANN. § 102(b)(7), which allows a corporation to amend its certificate of incorporation to protect its directors against claims for gross negligence. *See Rothenberg v. Santa Fe Pac. Corp.*, 1992 Del. Ch. LEVIS 106, Civ. A. No. 11749, 1992 WL 111206, at *4 (Del.Ch. May 18, 1992) ('Section 102(b)(7) permits a corporation, by so providing in its certificate of incorporation, "to protect its directors from monetary liability for duty of care violations, i.e., liability for gross negligence." ') . . . .

"Defendants contend that they must be held harmless under Columbia's waiver provision for claims based on breach of the duty of care. Plaintiffs argue that their duty of care claims are based not on gross negligence, but rather on reckless and intentional acts or omissions, and thus are not precluded by the waiver provision. Plaintiffs' claims of 'reckless or intentional breach of the duty of care' do not fit easily into the terminology of Delaware corporate law, however. Indeed, Delaware courts do not discuss a breach of the duty of care in terms of a mental state more culpable than gross negligence. Rather, allegations of intentional or reckless director misconduct are more commonly characterized as either a breach of the duty of loyalty or a breach of the duty of good faith. *See, e.g.*, Emerald Partners v. Berlin, 2001 Del. Ch. LEXIS 20, No. Civ. A. 9700, 2001 WL 115340, at *25 & n. 63 (Del, Ch. Feb 7, 2001) (discussing plaintiffs duty of good faith arguments based on allegations of reckless and intentional director misconduct). Thus, while it is true that duty of care claims alleging only grossly negligent conduct are precluded by a § 102(b)(7) waiver provision, it appears that duty of care claims based on reckless or intentional misconduct are not. As one treatise explained:

> Whether the statute would protect a director against reckless acts is not altogether clear. To the extent that recklessness involves a conscious disregard of a known risk, it could be argued that such an approach is not one taken in good faith and thus could not be liability exempted under the new statute. On the other hand, to the extent that the conduct alleged to be reckless is predicated solely on allegations of sustained inattention to the duty it is arguable whether such conduct is "grossly negligent," but not conduct amounting to bad faith.

Balotti & Finkelstein, Delaware Law of Corporations and Business Organizations § 4.29 at 4–116 to 4–116.1 (3d ed. Supp.2000).

"We construe plaintiffs' complaint as alleging a breach of the directors' duty of good faith for the purposes of determining whether plaintiffs' claims are precluded by Columbia's waiver-of-liability provision. Under Delaware law, the duty of good faith may be breached where a director consciously disregards his duties to the corporation, thereby causing its stockholders to suffer. *See Nagy v. Bistricer*, 770 A.2d 43, 2000 WL 1759860, at *3 n. 2 (de. Ch. 2000). Here, Plaintiffs accuse the directors not merely of 'sustained inattention' to their management obligations, but rather of 'intentional ignorance of' and 'willful blindness' to 'red flags' signaling fraudulent practices throughout Columbia. Accordingly, regardless of how plaintiffs style their duty of care claims, we find that they have alleged a conscious disregard of known risks, which conduct, if proven, cannot have been undertaken in good faith. Thus, we hold that plaintiffs' claims are not precluded by Columbia's § 102(b)(7) waiver provision. See 8 DEL. CODE ANN. § 102(b)(7)(ii) (exempting facts or omissions not in good faith or which involve intentional misconduct' from waiver provision's protection)."

(2) Directors' and Officers' Liability Insurance

Add the following case at p. 592 of the Unabridged Edition and p. 430 of the Concise Edition, at the end of Chapter VIII, Section 1(d)(2):

Level 3 Communications, Inc. v. Federal Insurance Co.

United States Court of Appeals, Seventh Circuit, 2001
272 F.2d 908

■ Before: BAUER, POSNER, and EVANS, CIRCUIT JUDGES.

■ POSNER, CIRCUIT JUDGE:

This appeal comes in a diversity suit [by Level 3 Communications, Inc.] seeking damages from a pair of insurance companies (a primary carrier, Federal, and an excess carrier that's no longer a party) that refused to pay on a policy of directors' and officers' liability insurance, a "D & O" policy, as it's known. Despite its name, such a policy insures not only officers and directors themselves but also their corporation if, as happened here, the corporation indemnifies them for their liability. This is known as "company reimbursement coverage," as distinct from "direct" coverage of the directors and officers. . . .

. . . [T]he district court determined that the amount of the settlement had been $11.8 million, that it was a loss within the meaning of the policy, that $1.8 million of the settlement [was not covered under a certain exclusion], and that Federal was therefore liable to its insured, Level 3, for $10 million.

Federal has appealed, arguing that the settlement, though an outlay by the insured, was not a "loss" within the meaning of the insurance policy, defined as "the total amount which any Insured Person becomes legally obligated to pay . . . including, but not limited to . . . settlements," because the relief sought in the suit against Level 3 was restitutionary in nature. The plaintiffs had sold shares in their corporation to Level 3 and charged that they had done so because of fraudulent representations that Level 3 had made. In effect, Level 3 was accused of having obtained the plaintiffs' company by false pretenses; and the plaintiffs' suit sought to rescind the transaction and recover their shares, or rather the monetary value of the shares because their company can no longer be reconstituted. It's as if, Federal argues, Level 3 had stolen cash from Pompliano and the other shareholders and had been forced to return it and were now asking the insurance company to pick up the tab. Federal continues that a D & O policy is designed to cover only losses that injure the insured, not ones that result from returning stolen property, and that if such an insurance policy did insure a thief against the cost to him of disgorging the proceeds of the theft it would be against public policy and so would be unenforceable. *Mortenson v. National Union Fire Ins. Co.*, 249 F.3d 667, 672 (7th Cir.2001); *Bank of the West v. Superior Court*, 2 Cal.4th 1254, 10 Cal.Rptr.2d 538, 833 P.2d 545, 554–55 (1992); *Central Dauphin School District v. American Casualty Co.*, 493 Pa. 254, 426 A.2d 94, 96 (1981).

The interpretive principle for which Federal contends—that a "loss" within the meaning of an insurance contract does not include the restoration of an ill-gotten gain—is clearly right. . . . The two cases on which Level 3 relies, *International Ins. Co. v. Johns*, 874 F.2d 1447, 1454–55 (11th Cir.1989), and *Limelight Productions, Inc. v. Limelite Studios, Inc.*, 60 F.3d 767, 769 (11th Cir.1995), are distinguishable, though *Limelight* only tenuously. The facts were similar to those in the present case, but the operative term in the insurance policy was "damages" rather than "loss," and so was broader. *In re Estate of Corriea*, 719 A.2d 1234, 1240–41 (D.C.App.1998), is similar.

As the interpretive principle controls this case, we need not consider the issue of enforceability, though the two issues are intertwined, since obviously an insurance policy wouldn't be presumed to have been drafted in such a way as to make it unenforceable. Cf. *Central Dauphin School District v. American Casualty Co., supra*, 426 A.2d at 96.

It is true, as Level 3 emphasizes, that the plaintiffs in the underlying suit were not seeking either the return of the shares that Level 3 had allegedly winkled them out of or the value of the shares on the date they were purchased. They were seeking the difference between the value of the stock at the time of trial and the price they had received for the stock from Level 3. That is standard damages relief in a securities-fraud case. But it is restitutionary in character. It seeks to divest the defendant of the present value of the property obtained by fraud, minus the cost to the defendant of obtaining the property. In other words, it seeks to deprive the defendant of the net benefit of the unlawful act, the value of the unlawfully obtained stock minus the cost to the defendant of obtaining the stock. It is equivalent to seeking to impress a constructive trust on the property in favor of the rightful owner. How the claim or judgment order or settlement is worded is irrelevant. An insured incurs no loss within the meaning of the insurance contract by being compelled to return property that it had stolen, even if a more polite word than "stolen" is used to character-ize the claim for the property's return.

We can imagine situations in which there would be a covered loss; this is important as showing that the D & O policy would not be rendered illusory by the acceptance of Federal's interpretation. An example would be a fraudulent statement by a corporate officer that inflated the price of the corporation's stock without conferring any measurable benefit on the corporation. Or suppose that unbeknownst to Level 3 the officer had stolen property for its benefit and, not knowing this, Level 3 defended against a suit seeking the return of the property and incurred heavy legal expenses in that defense. Those expenses would be a loss to the company not offset by any benefit to it, unlike the "expense" that consists simply of the value of the stolen property, a wash. *Safeway Stores, Inc. v. National Union Fire Ins. Co.*, 64 F.3d 1282, 1286–87 (9th Cir.1995). All that the plaintiffs in the underlying suit obtained was the amount they received in settlement of their claim against Level 3, and that amount was part of Level 3's gain from its officers' misbehavior. . . .

Level 3 acknowledges that if a judgment had been entered in the suit against it on the basis of a judicial determination that it had engaged in fraud, Federal would win; the policy so provides. It couples this acknowledgment with the inconsistent assertion that almost the entire purpose of D & O policies is to insure corporations and their officers and directors against claims of fraud. Pressed at argument concerning this inconsistency, it argued that the line runs between judgments and settlements. As long as the case is settled before entry of judgment, the insured is covered regardless of the nature of the claim against it. That can't be right. . . . It would mean, as Level 3's lawyer confirmed at argument, that if Level 3, seeing the handwriting on the wall, had agreed to pay the plaintiffs in the fraud suit all they were asking for (a very large amount—almost $70 mil-lion), which they surely would not have done had there been no evidence of fraud (no rational defendant settles a nuisance suit for the full amount demanded in the complaint, unless the amount is trivial), Federal would still be obligated to reimburse Level 3 for that amount. And that would enable Level 3 to retain the profit it had made from a fraud. In fact Level 3 settled with the plaintiffs in the fraud suit for the not inconsiderable amount of $12 million after the trial had begun and much of the expense of defending the suit had therefore already been incurred. It is not surprising, therefore, that Level 3 has made no attempt to show that the fraud suit was groundless and the settlement merely an effort to avoid the expense of defending a nuisance suit.

If Level 3 *had* shown that the fraud suit was groundless, that there was no ill-gotten gain that insurance would enable it to keep, would the $12 million be a "loss" within the meaning of the policy? Federal argues no, that all that matters is that the payment by the insured for which reimbursement is sought be in respect of a claim of fraudulent appropriation. Level 3 denies this. We need not decide; and prudence is definitely the better part of valor here, since we can find no guidance on the point from cases or other materials.

The judgment is reversed with instructions to enter judgment for the defendant.

CHAPTER IX

THE DUTY OF LOYALTY

SECTION 2. STATUTORY APPROACHES

*Insert the following Note and case at p. 637 of the Unabridged Edition following the
Note on the Effect of Approval by Disinterested Directors of Self-Interested
Transactions:*

In Cooke v. Oolie, 2000 WL 710199 (Del.Ch.2000), Chancellor
Chandler pulled back from the analysis of DGCL § 144 in his 1997
opinion in this case, as discussed in the prior Note. Instead, the
Chancellor said:

> To the extent that plaintiffs' oral argument suggested I revisit
> my decision regarding Oolie's and Salkind's loans to TNN, I refuse
> to reconsider my 1997 Opinion upholding those loans. Those
> loan transactions squarely fall within DGCL § 144 which governs
> interested director transactions. Under § 144, plaintiffs bear the
> burden of demonstrating that the defendants have engaged in an
> interested transaction. Clearly, the plaintiffs successfully carried
> this burden, demonstrating that the loan transaction between
> Oolie and Salkind and TNN was a "transaction between a corpora-
> tion and 1 or more of its directors." Once the plaintiffs demon-
> strate interest, the burden shifts to the defendants to show that
> one of § 144's safe harbor provisions protects them and the
> transaction. The defendants demonstrated to the Court that both
> disinterested directors, Janas and Wargo, negotiated and then
> ratified the loan transaction, which rendered § 144(1)(a)'s safe
> harbor applicable. Once the defendants demonstrate that a safe
> harbor protects the transaction, the plaintiffs can attempt to prove
> to the Court that the interested directors controlled or dominated
> the disinterested directors, which would destroy the disinterested
> ratification. The plaintiffs, however, failed to make such a show-
> ing. Oolie and Salkind were two directors of four on the board;
> therefore, they did not directly control the board's vote. More-
> over, the disinterested directors actions definitely demonstrate
> their independence. The disinterested directors obtained signifi-
> cant concessions through arms-length bargaining with Oolie and
> Salkind. For example, TNN would pay a reduced interest rate and
> deferred interest payments if it repaid the loan within six months

or if Oolie or Salkind converted the loan into equity. In addition, TNN maintained the right to terminate the loan entirely if it could find another lender within 10 days who would accept the same loan terms . As Oolie or Salkind neither maintained voting control of TNN at that time nor dominated or controlled the disinterested directors, the business judgment rule constitutes the appropriate standard of review for the loan transaction. (Had Oolie and Salkind been majority shareholders with voting control, as I inadvertently assumed in my 1997 Opinion, satisfying the requirements of the safe harbor provision would have merely shifted the burden of proving entire fairness to the plaintiffs.).

Emerald Partners v. Berlin

Supreme Court of Delaware, 2001.
787 A.2d 85.

■ Before WALSH, HOLLAND and BERGER, JUSTICES.

■ HOLLAND, JUSTICE.

This matter is before us for the third time. The present appeal is from a posttrial final judgment entered by the Court of Chancery. In the second appeal to this Court, we affirmed, in part, but reversed the entry of summary judgment in favor of the director defendants and remanded the case to the Court of Chancery for a trial.

In this appeal, the appellants contend that the Court of Chancery failed to follow the mandate of this Court upon remand and erred, as a matter of law, by not conducting an entire fairness analysis in its posttrial opinion. The director defendants contend that the Court of Chancery properly declined to address any issue in its posttrial decision except for the exculpatory provision in the corporate charter that was enacted pursuant to 8 *Del. C.* § 102(b)(7). We have concluded that the Court of Chancery was required to decide the issue of entire fairness at trial and that, once again, its consideration of the Section 102(b)(7) charter provision was premature. Accordingly, the judgment of the Court of Chancery must be vacated and this matter remanded.

Facts

The appellant, Emerald Partners, a New Jersey limited partnership, filed this action on March 1, 1988, to enjoin the consummation of a merger between May Petroleum, Inc. ("May"), a Delaware corporation and thirteen corporations owned by Craig Hall ("Hall"), the Chairman and Chief Executive Officer of May. Also joined as defendants were May's directors, Ronald P. Berlin, David L. Florence, Rex A. Sebastian, and Theodore H. Strauss (collectively the "director defendants"). Added later as a defendant was Hall Financial, the successor in interest to Hall Financial Group, Inc., the corporate defendant produced by the merger of May and the Hall corporations.

In October 1987, Hall, at that time a holder of 52.4% of May's common stock, proposed a merger of May and thirteen sub-chapter S corporations owned by Hall that were primarily engaged in the real estate service business. The board of directors of May consisted of Hall and Berlin, the inside directors, and Florence, Sebastian and Strauss, the outside directors,

The outside directors authorized the engagement of Bear Stearns & Company ("Bear Stearns") to act as investment advisor and render a fairness opinion to the board and the May stockholders. On the basis of company valuations and the Bear Stearns fairness letter, the transaction, as eventually crafted, contemplated that Hall would receive twenty-seven million May common shares in exchange for the merger of the Hall corporations with May, increasing Hall's shareholding to 73.5% of May's outstanding common stock as reflected in the post-merger entity.

May and the Hall corporations entered into a proposed merger agreement on November 30, 1987. On February 1, 1988, effective January 29, 1988, Hall reduced his beneficial interest in May to 25% of the outstanding common stock by transferring shares to independent irrevocable trusts created for the benefit of his children. This transfer took place before the record date and prior to the stockholder vote on the merger. The merger agreement was reaffirmed by the board on February 13, 1988 with the only change reflecting the reduction in Hall's ownership. On February 16, 1988, May issued a proxy statement to shareholders that described May, the Hall corporations and the proposed merger terms. The May shareholders approved the merger on March 11, 1988. . . .

. . . Thereafter, the merger was completed on August 15, 1988.

. . . [F]ollowing the consummation of the merger, Emerald Partners continued . . . class and derivative actions [they had initiated earlier to challenge the merger] . . . .

In [an] appeal to this Court, we reviewed the Court of Chancery's grant of summary judgment in favor of the defendant corporation and its directors. We concluded that "the entire fairness claim was fairly pleaded and [was] intertwined with disclosure violation claims." We affirmed the judgment in favor of the corporation but reversed the grant of summary judgment in favor of the director defendants. We remanded the matter to the Court of Chancery for a trial pursuant to the entire fairness standard of review.

Shareholder Litigation Review Standards

When shareholders challenge actions by a board of directors, generally one of three standards of judicial review is applied: the traditional business judgment rule, an intermediate standard of enhanced judicial scrutiny, or the entire fairness analysis. The applicable standard of judicial review often controls the outcome of the litigation on the merits. Similarly, the appropriate standard of judicial review determines the proper procedural posture for giving substantive effect to a charter provision that has been enacted pursuant to Section 102(b)(7).

Issue Presented

In this appeal, we must decide when it is appropriate procedurally to consider the substantive effect of a Section 102(b)(7) provision, in a shareholder challenge to a transaction that requires a trial pursuant to the entire fairness standard of judicial review. In *Malpiede v. Townson*,[16] we recently answered that question in a pretrial procedural context, when the applicable standard of judicial review was the business judgment rule. We begin, as in *Malpiede*, with a brief examination of the . . . operation of Section 102(b)(7). . . .

The statutory enactment of Section 102(b)(7) was a logical corollary to the common law principles of the business judgment rule. Since its enactment, Delaware courts have consistently held that the adoption of a charter provision, in accordance with Section 102(b)(7), bars the recovery of monetary damages from directors for a successful shareholder claim that is based exclusively upon establishing a violation of the duty of care. Accordingly, in *Malpiede*, this Court held that if a shareholder complaint unambiguously asserts *only* a due care claim, the complaint is dismissible once the corporation's Section 102(b)(7) provision is properly invoked. . . .[35]

The rationale of *Malpiede* constitutes judicial cognizance of a practical reality: unless there is a violation of the duty of loyalty or the duty of good faith, a trial on the issue of entire fairness is unnecessary because a Section 102(b)(7) provision will exculpate director defendants from paying monetary damages that are exclusively attributable to a violation of the duty of care. . . .

Entire Fairness and Section 102(b)(7)

In *Malpiede*, we noted that the procedural posture was "quite different" from the circumstances that were before this Court in the second appeal involving Emerald Partners. In *Malpiede*, the applicable pretrial standard for judicial review of the directors' actions *ab initio* was the business judgment rule. In *Emerald Partners*, however, we held that the complaint "made a sufficient showing through factual allegations that entire fairness should be the standard by which the directors' actions are reviewed" at trial.[43]

---

16. *Malpiede v. Townson*, Del.Supr., 780 A.2d 1075 (2001).

35. *Malpiede v. Townson*, 780 A.2d at 1093. . . .

43. *Emerald Partners v. Berlin*, Del. Supr., 726 A.2d 1215, 1222 (1999).

In *Malpiede,* we held that when the standard of review *ab initio* is the business judgment rule, properly raising the existence of a valid exculpatory Section 102(b)(7) provision in the corporate charter "entitles director [defendants] to dismissal of any claims for [monetary] damages against them that are based *solely* on alleged breaches of the board's duty of care."[44] The rationale of our holding in *Malpiede* explains why an entire fairness analysis can never be avoided in any challenged transaction that requires an application of the entire fairness standard of judicial review *ab initio* at trial—as we held in our last *Emerald Partners* opinion—notwithstanding the existence of a Section 102(b)(7) provision. The category of transactions that require judicial review pursuant to the entire fairness standard *ab initio* do so because, by definition, the inherently interested nature of those transactions are inextricably intertwined with issues of loyalty.[45]

In *Cinerama, Inc. v. Technicolor, Inc.,*[46] this Court held that evidence of how the board of directors discharged all three of its primary fiduciary duties has "probative substantive significance throughout an entire fairness analysis and, by necessity, must permeate that analysis, for two reasons." First, a substantive finding of entire fairness is only possible after examining and balancing the nature of the duty or duties that the board breached in a contextual comparison to how the board otherwise properly discharged its fiduciary responsibilities. Second, the determination that a board has failed to satisfy the entire fairness standard will constitute the basis for a finding of substantive liability.

A determination that a transaction must be subjected to an entire fairness analysis is not an implication of liability. Therefore, when entire fairness is the applicable standard of judicial review, this Court has held that injury or damages becomes a proper focus only *after* a transaction is determined *not* to be entirely fair.[51] *A fortiori,* the exculpatory effect of a Section 102(b)(7) provision only becomes a proper focus of judicial scrutiny after the directors' potential personal liability for the payment of monetary damages has been established. Accordingly, although a Section 102(b)(7) charter provision may provide exculpation for directors against the payment of monetary damages that is attributed exclusively to violating the duty of care, even in a transaction that requires the entire fairness review standard *ab initio,* it cannot eliminate an entire fairness analysis by the Court of Chancery.

44. *Malpiede v. Townson,* 780 A.2d at 1095–96 & n. 70.

45. *See Kahn v. Lynch Communication Sys., Inc.,* Del.Supr., 638 A.2d 1110, 1117 (1994), *accord Weinberger v. UOP, Inc.,* Del. Supr., 457 A.2d 701, 710–11 (1983); *Sterling v. Mayflower Hotel Corp.,* Del.Supr., 93 A.2d 107, 110 (1952).

46. *Cinerama, Inc. v. Technicolor, Inc.,* Del.Supr., 663 A.2d 1156 (1995).

51. *Cinerama, Inc. v. Technicolor, Inc.,* 663 A.2d at 1166 (citing *Cede & Co. v. Technicolor, Inc.,* Del.Supr., 634 A.2d 345, 371 (1993)).

If the board's actions do not withstand the judicial scrutiny of an entire fairness analysis, the breach or breaches of fiduciary duty upon which substantive liability for monetary damages is based become outcome determinative when the directors seek exculpation through a charter provision enacted in accordance with Section 102(b)(7). Such a provision bars any claim for monetary damages against director defendants based solely on the board's alleged breach of its duty of care but does not provide protection against violations of the fiduciary duties of either loyalty or good faith. Consequently, we have held that "[t]he Court of Chancery must identify the breach or breaches of fiduciary duty upon which liability [for damages] will be predicated in the *ratio decidendi* of its determination that entire fairness has not been established."[55] Accordingly, we hold that when entire fairness is the applicable standard of judicial review, a determination that the director defendants are exculpated from paying monetary damages can be made only *after the basis* for their liability has been decided.

Law of the Case

In the last appeal, we noted that, as a matter of substantive law, the circumstances attendant upon the events leading to the negotiation of the merger appear to implicate the entire fairness standard. Hall, as Chairman and Chief Executive Officer of both May and the Hall corporations and sole owner of the Hall corporations, "clearly stood on both sides of the transaction." Additionally, "at the time the parties entered the proposed merger agreement in November of 1987, Hall owned 52.4% of May common stock."

We expanded our observations in a footnote. We noted that "at the time of the merger, Hall had reduced his ownership interest to 25% of the outstanding common stock," We then recognized that "a shareholder who owns less than 50% of a corporation's outstanding stock, without some additional allegation of domination through actual control of corporat[e] conduct, is not a 'controlling stockholder' for fiduciary duty purposes. We specifically stated, however, that 'Hall's stance on both sides as a corporate fiduciary, *alone*, is sufficient to *require* the demonstration of entire fairness.'"

Consequently, we held that "Emerald Partners has made a sufficient showing through factual allegations that entire fairness should be the standard by which the directors' actions are reviewed. Such a showing shifts to the director defendants the burden to establish that the challenged transaction was entirely fair." Our last opinion acknowledged, however, that on remand the director defendants "may be able to secure the burden shifting benefit by demonstrating either sufficient independent director approval or fully informed shareholder approval."

55. *Cinerama, Inc. v. Technicolor, Inc.,* 663 A.2d at 1165.

The opening posttrial brief filed by the director defendants properly argued the first issue to be decided was entire fairness. The director defendants' opening posttrial brief then submitted "in the unlikely event the Court [of Chancery] finds that the merger was not entirely fair and May's shareholders were damaged as a result, judgment still must be entered in defendants' favor because of the Section 102(b)(7) provision in its charter." The shareholders' posttrial answering brief started by arguing that entire fairness had not been established. The shareholders then argued that the director defendants had also not sustained their burden of establishing exculpation by virtue of the Section 102(b)(7) charter provision.

Apparently, the Court of Chancery's decision not to conduct an entire fairness review in its posttrial opinion is attributable to the position asserted in director defendants' posttrial reply brief. In that reply brief, the director defendants argued that the Court of Chancery did not have to look at anything other than the Section 102(b)(7) charter provision. The Court of Chancery apparently accepted that argument because the posttrial opinion begins by stating: "it is unnecessary to address the plaintiffs claim that the merger fails the test of entire fairness." The posttrial opinion then continued, in part, as follows:

> As discussed below, the Court finds that the plaintiff's money damages claims cannot succeed because the defendants have carried their burden of showing that their affirmative defenses bar those claims. For that reason, the plaintiff's claims are evaluated within the analytical framework of those affirmative defenses, rather than independently as standalone claims.

The Court of Chancery should have rejected the erroneous legal argument in the director defendants' posttrial reply brief. It is not surprising that the director defendants wanted the Court of Chancery to start with their "bottom line" position: i.e., the shareholder plaintiffs could not collect monetary damages from them even if the transaction was unfair. When the entire fairness standard of review is applicable, however, judicial analysis must begin with an examination of the *process* by which the directors discharged their fiduciary responsibilities, notwithstanding the existence of a Section 102(b)(7) charter provision. The director defendants incorrectly asserted that they may avoid posttrial judicial scrutiny pursuant to the entire fairness standard of review, by asserting a Section 102(b)(7) provision as a defense to the payment of monetary damages, before a finding of unfairness had been made with a rationale for that determination. Such an assertion is not only unsupportable generally but contrary to the law of the case as defined by this Court.

Entire Fairness Analysis Required

When the General Assembly enacted Section 102(b)(7), three years after this Court's landmark decision in *Weinberger v. UOP, Inc.,*[70] it not only recognized but reinforced *Weinberger's* restatement of a venerable and fundamental principle of our common law corporate fiduciary jurisprudence: "there is no 'safe harbor' for ... divided loyalties in Delaware."[71] The fact that Section 102(b)(7) does not permit shareholders to exculpate directors for violations of loyalty or good faith reflects that the provision was a thoughtfully crafted legislative response to our holding in *Van Gorkom* and, simultaneously, reflected the General Assembly's own expression of support for our assertion in *Weinberger* that when the standard of review is entire fairness "the requirement of fairness is unflinching in its demand...."[72]

In this case, since Hall was on both sides of this transaction, the director defendants might ultimately be able to rely upon the Section 102(b)(7) charter provision to seek exculpation from paying monetary damages, but they cannot assert that provision to avoid the unflinching demand of demonstrating entire fairness. Once entire fairness is the applicable standard—as we held it was in our last *Emerald Partners* opinion—the director defendants, at least initially, bear the burden of proof. In our prior opinion, we acknowledged that the burden of proof on the issue of entire fairness might shift on remand. The Court of Chancery did not make a determination that the burden had shifted, either before or during the course of the trial in this matter, and that is now the law of this case. Nevertheless, even if the burden of proof had shifted, entire fairness would remain the proper standard of judicial review because the unchanging nature of the underlying inherently "interested" transaction requires that careful scrutiny.[76]

To demonstrate entire fairness, the board must present evidence of the cumulative manner by which it discharged all of its fiduciary duties.[78] An entire fairness analysis then requires the Court of Chancery "to consider carefully how the board of directors discharged all of its fiduciary duties with regard to each aspect of the non-bifurcated components of entire fairness: fair dealing and fair price." ...[79]

Second Remand Necessary

Upon remand, the Court of Chancery must analyze the factual circumstances, apply a disciplined balancing test to its findings on the issue of fair dealing and fair price, and articulate the basis upon which it decides the ultimate question of entire fairness.[81] If the Court of

70. *Weinberger v. UOP, Inc.*, Del.Supr., 457 A.2d 701 (1983).

71. *Id.* at 710.

72. *Id.*

76. *See Weinberger v. UOP, Inc.*, 457 A.2d at 710 (citing *Sterling v. Mayflower Hotel Corp.*, Del.Supr., 93 A.2d 107, 110 (1952)).

78. *Cinerama, Inc. v Technicolor, Inc.*, Del.Supr., 663 A.2d 1156, 1163 (1995).

79. *Id.* at 1172.

81. *Cinerama, Inc. v. Technicolor, Inc.*, Del.Supr., 663 A.2d 1156, 1179 (1995) (citing *Nixon v. Blackwell*, Del.Supr., 626 A.2d 1366, 1373, 1378(1993)).

Chancery determines that the transaction was entirely fair, the director defendants have no liability for monetary damages. The Court of Chancery should address the Section 102(b)(7) charter provision only if it makes a determination that the challenged transaction was not entirely fair. The director defendants' Section 102(b)(7) request for exculpation must then be examined in the context of the completed judicial analysis that resulted in a finding of unfairness. The director defendants can avoid personal liability for paying monetary damages only if they have established that their failure to withstand an entire fairness analysis is exclusively attributable to a violation of the duty of care.

Conclusion

The judgment of the Court of Chancery is vacated. This matter is remanded to the Court of Chancery for an initial analysis pursuant to the entire fairness standard of judicial review. If that standard is not satisfied, the Court of Chancery must decide if the director defendants have established that they are exculpated from liability for monetary damages because of the Section 102(b)(7) charter provision. . . .

[U]pon remand, the Court of Chancery's posttrial opinion must decide if the director defendants sustained their burden of proving entire fairness and, if not, whether the director defendants are exculpated by the Section 102(b)(7) charter provision.

This matter is remanded to the Court of Chancery. The mandate shall issue immediately.

SECTION 3.   COMPENSATION, THE WASTE DOCTRINE, AND THE EFFECT OF SHAREHOLDER RATIFICATION

Insert the following Note at p. 654 of the Unabridged Edition, following the note on Lewis v. Vogelstein:

HARBOR FINANCE PARTNERS v. HUIZENGA, 751 A.2d 879 (Del.Ch.1999). This case involved an acquisition of AutoNation, Inc. by Republic Industries, Inc., whose directors owned a substantial block of AutoNation shares. A majority of Republic's disinterested shareholders had ratified the transaction, after full disclosure in the proxy statement. Plaintiff, a Republic shareholder, brought suit on the ground that the transaction was unfair. Vice Chancellor Strine held that given the ratification, the transaction could be attacked only on the ground of waste. After holding that the plaintiff had not pleaded facts showing that the transaction constituted waste, the Vice Chancellor went on to discuss the rule that if a waste claim is adequately pleaded and proved, ratification is of no effect:

Although I recognize that our law has long afforded plaintiffs the vestigial right to prove that a transaction that a majority of fully informed, uncoerced independent stockholders approved by a non-unanimous vote was wasteful, I question the continued utility of this "equitable safety valve."

The origin of this rule is rooted in the distinction between voidable and void acts, a distinction that appears to have grown out of the now largely abolished *ultra vires* doctrine. Voidable acts are traditionally held to be ratifiable because the corporation can lawfully accomplish them if it does so in the appropriate manner. Thus if directors who could not lawfully effect a transaction without stockholder approval did so anyway, and the requisite approval of the stockholders was later attained, the transaction is deemed fully ratified because the subsequent approval of the stockholders cured the defect. . . .

In contrast, void acts are said to be non-ratifiable because the corporation cannot, in any case, lawfully accomplish them. Such void acts are often described in conclusory terms such as *"ultra vires"* or "fraudulent" or as "gifts or waste of corporate assets." Because at first blush it seems it would be a shocking, if not theoretically impossible, thing for stockholders to be able to sanction the directors in committing illegal acts or acts beyond the authority of the corporation, it is unsurprising that it has been held that stockholders cannot validate such action by the directors, even on an informed basis. . . .

One of the many practical problems with this seemingly sensible doctrine is that its actual application has no apparent modern day utility insofar as the doctrine covers claims of waste or gift, except as an opportunity for Delaware courts to second-guess stockholders. There are several reasons I believe this to be so.

First, the types of "void" acts susceptible to being styled as waste claims have little of the flavor of patent illegality about them, nor are they categorically *ultra vires*. Put another way, the oft-stated proposition that "waste cannot be ratified" is a tautology that, upon close examination, has little substantive meaning. I mean, what rational person would ratify "waste"? Stating the question that way, the answer is, of course, no one. But in the real world stockholders are not asked to ratify obviously wasteful transactions. Rather than lacking any plausible business rationale or being clearly prohibited by statutory or common law, the transactions attacked as waste in Delaware courts are ones that are quite ordinary in the modern business world. Thus a review of the Delaware cases reveals that our courts have reexamined the merits of stockholder votes approving such transactions as: stock option plans; the fee agreement between a mutual fund and its investment advisor; corporate mergers; the purchase of a business in the same industry as the acquiring corporation; and the repurchase of a corporate insider's shares in the company. These are all garden variety transactions that may be validly accomplished by a Delaware corporation if supported by sufficient consideration, and what is sufficient consideration is a question that fully informed stockholders seem as well positioned as courts to answer. That is, these transactions are neither *per se ultra vires* or illegal; they only become "void" upon a determination that the corporation received no fair consideration for entering upon them.

Second, the waste vestige is not necessary to protect stockholders and it has no other apparent purpose. While I would hesitate to permit stockholders to ratify a blatantly illegal act—such as a board's decision to indemnify itself against personal liability for intentionally violating applicable environmental laws or bribing government officials to benefit the corporation—the vestigial exception for waste has little to do with corporate integrity in the sense of the corporation's responsibility to society as a whole. Rather, if there is any benefit in the waste vestige, it must consist in protecting stockholders. And where disinterested stockholders are given the information necessary to decide whether a transaction is beneficial to the corporation or wasteful to it, I see little reason to leave the door open for a judicial reconsideration of the matter.

The fact that a plaintiff can challenge the adequacy of the disclosure is in itself a substantial safeguard against stockholder approval of waste. If the corporate board failed to provide the voters with material information undermining the integrity or financial fairness of the transaction subject to the vote, no ratification effect will be accorded to the vote and the plaintiffs may press all of their claims. As a result, it is difficult to imagine how elimination of the waste vestige will permit the accomplishment of unconscionable corporate transactions, unless one presumes that stockholders are, as a class, irrational and that they will rubber stamp outrageous transactions contrary to their own economic interests.

In this regard, it is noteworthy that Delaware law does not make it easy for a board of directors to obtain "ratification effect" from a stockholder vote. The burden to prove that the vote was fair, uncoerced, and fully informed falls squarely on the board. Given the fact that Delaware law imposes no heightened pleading standards on plaintiffs alleging material nondisclosures or voting coercion . . ., it is difficult for a board to prove ratification at the pleading stage. If the board cannot prevail on a motion to dismiss, the defendant directors will be required to submit to discovery and possibly to a trial.

Nor is the waste vestige necessary to protect minority stockholders from oppression by majority or controlling stockholders.

Chancellor Allen recently noted that the justification for the waste vestige is "apparently that a transaction that satisfies the high standard of waste constitutes a *gift* of corporate property and no one should be forced against their will to make a gift of their property."[77] This justification is inadequate to support continued application of the exception. As an initial matter, I note that property of the corporation is not typically thought of as personal property of the stockholders, and that it is common for corporations to undertake important value-affecting transactions over the objection of some of the voters or without a vote at all.

In any event, my larger point is that this solicitude for dissenters' property rights is already adequately accounted for elsewhere in our corporation law. Delaware fiduciary law ensures that a majority or controlling stockholder cannot use a stockholder vote to insulate a transaction benefiting that stockholder from judicial examination. Only votes controlled by stockholders who are not "interested" in the transaction at issue are eligible for ratification effect in the sense of invoking the business judgment rule rather than the entire fairness form of review. That is, only the votes of those stockholders with no economic incentive to approve a wasteful transaction count.

Indeed, it appears that a corporation with a controlling or majority stockholder may, under current Delaware law, never escape the exacting entire fairness standard through a stockholder vote, even one expressly conditioned on approval by a "majority of the minority." Because of sensitivity about the structural coercion that might be thought to exist in such circumstances, our law limits an otherwise fully informed, uncoerced vote in such circumstances to having the effect of making the plaintiffs prove that the transaction was unfair. Doubtless defendants appreciate this shift, but it still subjects them to a proceeding in which the substantive fairness of their actions comes under close scrutiny by the court— the type of scrutiny that is inappropriate when the business judgment rule's presumption attaches to a decision.

Third, I find it logically difficult to conceptualize how a plaintiff can ultimately prove a waste or gift claim in the face of a decision by fully informed, uncoerced, independent stockholders to ratify the transaction. The test for waste is whether any person of ordinary sound business judgment could view the transaction as fair.

If fully informed, uncoerced, independent stockholders have approved the transaction, they have, it seems to me, made the decision that the transaction is "a fair exchange." As such, it is difficult to see the utility of allowing litigation to proceed in which the plaintiffs are permitted discovery and a possible trial, at great

---

77. Lewis v. Vogelstein, 699 A.2d at 335–36.

expense to the corporate defendants, in order to prove to the court that the transaction was so devoid of merit that each and every one of the voters comprising the majority must be disregarded as too hopelessly misguided to be considered a "person of ordinary sound business judgment." In this day and age in which investors also have access to an abundance of information about corporate transactions from sources other than boards of directors, it seems presumptuous and paternalistic to assume that the court knows better in a particular instance than a fully informed corporate electorate with real money riding on the corporation's performance.

Finally, it is unclear why it is in the best interests of disinterested stockholders to subject their corporation to the substantial costs of litigation in a situation where they have approved the transaction under attack. Enabling a dissident who failed to get her way at the ballot box in a fair election to divert the corporation's resources to defending her claim on the battlefield of litigation seems, if anything, contrary to the economic well-being of the disinterested stockholders as a class. Why should the law give the dissenters the right to command the corporate treasury over the contrary will of a majority of the disinterested stockholders? The costs to corporations of litigating waste claims are not trifling.

Although there appears to be a trend in the other direction,[85] binding case law still emphasizes the ease with which a plaintiff may state a waste claim and the difficulty of resolving such a claim without a trial.[86] As in this case, proxy statements and other public filings often contain facts that, if true, would render waste claims wholly without merit. Plaintiffs' lawyers (for good reason) rarely put such facts in their complaints and it is doubtful that the court can look to them to resolve a motion to dismiss a waste claim even where the plaintiff has not pled that the facts in the public filings are not true. Given this reality and the teaching of prior cases, claims with no genuine likelihood of success can make it to discovery and perhaps to trial. To the extent that there is corporate waste in such cases, it appears to be some place other than in the corporate transactions under scrutiny.

For all these reasons, a reexamination of the waste vestige would seem to be in order. Although there may be valid reasons for its continuation, those reasons should be articulated and weighed against the costs the vestige imposes on stockholders and

85. Lewis v. Vogelstein, 699 A.2d at 339; Steiner v. Meyerson, mem. Op., 1995 Del. Ch. LEXIS 95; In re 3COM Corp. Shareholders Litig., mem. op. at 10–14.

86. Michelson v. Duncan, 407 A.2d at 223 ("[c]laims of gift or waste of corporate assets are seldom subject to disposition by summary judgement"); see also Haft v. Dart Group Corp., Del. Ch., 1994 WL 643185, at *3, C. (Nov. 14, 1994).

the judicial system. Otherwise, inertia alone may perpetuate an outdated rule fashioned in a very different time.

In re The Walt Disney Company Derivative Litigation

Delaware Court of Chancery, 2003
2003 WL 21267266 (Del.Ch.)

■ BEFORE: CHANDLER, CHIEF JUSTICE.

CHANDLER, J.

In this derivative action filed on behalf of nominal defendant Walt Disney Company, plaintiffs allege that the defendant directors breached their fiduciary duties when they blindly approved an employment agreement with defendant Michael Ovitz and then, again without any review or deliberation, ignored defendant Michael Eisner's dealings with Ovitz regarding his non-fault termination. Plaintiffs seek rescission and/or money damages from defendants and Ovitz, or compensation for damages allegedly sustained by Disney and disgorgement of Ovitz's unjust enrichment.

. . . Defendants moved to dismiss plaintiffs' second amended derivative complaint (hereinafter the "new complaint") pursuant to Court of Chancery Rules 12(b)(6) and 23.1. . . .

As will be explained in greater detail below, I conclude that plaintiffs' new complaint sufficiently pleads a breach of fiduciary duty by the Old and the New Disney Board of Directors[2] so as to withstand a motion to dismiss under Chancery Rules 23.1 and 12(b)(6). Stated briefly, plaintiffs' new allegations give rise to a cognizable question whether the defendant directors of the Walt Disney Company should be held personally liable to the corporation for a knowing or intentional lack of due care in the directors' decision-making process regarding Ovitz's employment and termination. It is rare when a court imposes liability on directors of a corporation for breach of the duty of care, and this Court is hesitant to second-guess the business judgment of a disinterested and independent board of directors. But the facts alleged in the new complaint do not implicate merely negligent or grossly negligent decision making by corporate directors. Quite the contrary; plaintiffs' new complaint suggests that the Disney directors failed to exercise *any* business judgment and failed to make *any* good faith attempt to fulfill their fiduciary duties to Disney and its stockholders. Allegations that Disney's directors abdicated all responsibility to consider appropriately an action of material importance to the corporation puts directly in question whether the board's decision-making processes were employed in a good faith effort to advance

---

2. The Disney Board of Directors changed from the time Ovitz was hired to the time of his non-fault termination. Therefore, the board at the time Ovitz was hired is referred to as the "Old Board," and the board at the time of the non-fault termination is the "New Board."

corporate interests. In short, the new complaint alleges facts implying that the Disney directors failed to "act in good faith and meet minimal proceduralist standards of attention."[3] Based on the facts asserted in the new complaint, therefore, I believe plaintiffs have stated cognizable claims for which demand is excused and on which a more complete factual record is necessary.

I.   PROCEDURAL AND FACTUAL BACKGROUND

As mentioned, this case involves an attack on decisions of the Walt Disney Company's board of directors, approving an executive compensation contract for Michael Ovitz, as well as impliedly approving a non-fault termination that resulted in an award to Ovitz (allegedly exceeding $140,000,000) after barely one year of employment. After the Supreme Court's remand regarding plaintiffs' first amended complaint,[4] plaintiffs used the "tools at hand," a request for books and records as authorized under 8 *Del. C.* § 220, to obtain information about the nature of the Disney Board's involvement in the decision to hire and, eventually, to terminate Ovitz. Using the information gained from that request, plaintiffs drafted and filed the new complaint, which is the subject of the pending motions. The facts, as alleged in the new complaint, portray a markedly different picture of the corporate processes that resulted in the Ovitz employment agreement than that portrayed in the first amended complaint.[5] For that reason, it is necessary to set forth the repleaded facts in some detail. The facts set forth hereafter are taken directly from the new complaint and, for purposes of the present motions, are accepted as true. Of course, I hold no opinion as to the actual truth of any of the allegations set forth in the new complaint; nor do I hold any view as to the likely ultimate outcome on the merits of claims based on these asserted facts. I determine here only that the facts, if true, arguably support all three of plaintiffs' claims for relief, as asserted in the new complaint, and are sufficient to excuse demand and to state claims that warrant development of a full record.

A.   *The Decision to Hire Ovitz*

Michael Eisner is the chief executive officer ("CEO") of the Walt Disney Company. In 1994, Eisner's second-in-command, Frank Wells, died in a helicopter crash. Two other key executives—Jeffrey Katzenberg and Richard Frank—left Disney shortly thereafter, allegedly because of Eisner's management style. Eisner began looking for a new

---

3. *Gagliardi v. TriFoods Int'l, Inc.*, 683 A.2d 1049, 1052 (Del.Ch.1996).

4. *Brehm v. Eisner*, 746 A.2d 244, 249 (Del.2000).

5. This case is yet another example where a books and records request in the first instance might have prevented expensive and time-consuming procedural machinations that too often occur in derivative litigation. The Supreme Court and this Court have repeatedly urged derivative plaintiffs to seek books and records before filing a complaint. *See, e.g., Guttman v. Nvidia Corp.*, Del. Ch., C.A. No. 19571–NC, at 1–2, Strine, V.C. (May 5, 2003). The amended pleading in this case is a perfect illustration of the benefit of such an approach.

president for Disney and chose Michael Ovitz. Ovitz was founder and head of CAA, a talent agency; he had never been an executive for a publicly owned entertainment company. He had, however, been Eisner's close friend for over twenty-five years.

Eisner decided unilaterally to hire Ovitz. On August 13, 1995, he informed three Old Board members—Stephen Bollenbach, Sanford Litvack, and Irwin Russell (Eisner's personal attorney)—of that fact. All three protested Eisner's decision to hire Ovitz. Nevertheless, Eisner persisted, sending Ovitz a letter on August 14, 1995, that set forth certain material terms of his prospective employment. Before this, neither the Old Board nor the compensation committee had ever discussed hiring Ovitz as president of Disney. No discussions or presentations were made to the compensation committee or to the Old Board regarding Ovitz's hiring as president of Walt Disney until September 26, 1995.

Before informing Bollenbach, Litvack, and Russell on August 13, 1995, Eisner collected information on his own, through his position as the Disney CEO, on the potential hiring of Ovitz. In an internal document created around July 7, 1995, concerns were raised about the number of stock options to be granted to Ovitz. The document warned that the number was far beyond the normal standards of both Disney and corporate America and would receive significant public criticism. Additionally, Graef Crystal, an executive compensation expert, informed board member Russell, via a letter dated August 12, 1995, that, generally speaking, a large signing bonus is hazardous because the full cost is borne immediately and completely even if the executive fails to serve the full term of employment.[6] Neither of these documents, however, were submitted to either the compensation committee or the Old Board before hiring Ovitz. Disney prepared a draft employment agreement on September 23, 1995. A copy of the draft was sent to Ovitz's lawyers, but was not provided to members of the compensation committee.

The compensation committee, consisting of defendants Ignacio Lozano, Jr., Sidney Poitier, Russell, and Raymond Watson, met on September 26, 1995, for just under an hour. Three subjects were discussed at the meeting, one of which was Ovitz's employment. According to the minutes, the committee spent the least amount of time during the meeting discussing Ovitz's hiring. In fact, it appears that more time was spent on discussions of paying $250,000 to Russell for his role in securing Ovitz's employment than was actually spent on discussions of Ovitz's employment. The minutes show that several issues were raised and discussed by the committee members concerning Russell's fee. All that occurred during the meeting regarding Ovitz's employment was that Russell reviewed the employment terms

---

6. Graef Crystal had been retained to advise Disney on Eisner's employment contract. Although not absolutely clear in the new complaint, it was apparently in this context that Crystal advised Russell of the dangers of a large signing bonus.

with the committee and answered a few questions. Immediately thereafter, the committee adopted a resolution of approval.

No copy of the September 23, 1995 draft employment agreement was actually given to the committee. Instead, the committee members received, at the meeting itself, a rough summary of the agreement. The summary, however, was incomplete. It stated that Ovitz was to receive options to purchase five million shares of stock, but did not state the exercise price. The committee also did not receive any of the materials already produced by Disney regarding Ovitz's possible employment. No spreadsheet or similar type of analytical document showing the potential payout to Ovitz throughout the contract, or the possible cost of his severance package upon a non-fault termination, was created or presented. Nor did the committee request or receive any information as to how the draft agreement compared with similar agreements throughout the entertainment industry, or information regarding other similarly situated executives in the same industry.

The committee also lacked the benefit of an expert to guide them through the process. Graef Crystal, an executive compensation expert, had been hired to provide advice to Disney on Eisner's new employment contract. Even though he had earlier told Russell that large signing bonuses, generally speaking, can be hazardous, neither he nor any other expert had been retained to assist Disney regarding Ovitz's hiring. Thus, no presentations, spreadsheets, written analyses, or opinions were given by any expert for the compensation committee to rely upon in reaching its decision. Although Crystal was not retained as a compensation consultant on the Ovitz contract, he later lamented his failure to intervene and produce a spreadsheet showing the potential costs of the employment agreement.

The compensation committee was informed that further negotiations would occur and that the stock option grant would be delayed until the final contract was worked out. The committee approved the general terms and conditions of the employment agreement, but did not condition their approval on being able to review the final agreement. Instead, the committee granted Eisner the authority to approve the final terms and conditions of the contract as long as they were within the framework of the draft agreement.

Immediately after the compensation committee met on September 26, the Old Board met. Again, no expert was present to advise the board. Nor were any documents produced to the board for it to review before the meeting regarding the Ovitz contract. The board did not ask for additional information to be collected or presented regarding Ovitz's hiring. According to the minutes, the compensation committee did not make any recommendation or report to the board concerning its resolution to hire Ovitz. Nor did Russell, who allegedly secured Ovitz's employment, make a presentation to the board. The minutes of the meeting were fifteen pages long, but only a page and a half covered Ovitz's possible employment. A portion of that page and a half was spent discussing the $250,000 fee paid to Russell for obtaining Ovitz. According to the minutes, the Old Board did not ask any questions about the details of Ovitz's salary, stock options, or possible termination. The Old Board also did not consider the consequences of a termination, or the various payout scenarios that existed. Nevertheless, at that same meeting, the Old Board decided to appoint Ovitz president of Disney. Final negotiation of the employment agreement was left to Eisner, Ovitz's close friend for over twenty-five years.

B.   *Negotiation of the Employment Agreement*

Ovitz was officially hired on October 1, 1995, and began serving as Disney's president, although he did not yet have an executed employment agreement with Disney. On October 16, 1995, the compensation committee was informed, via a brief oral report, that negotiations were ongoing with Ovitz. The committee was not given a draft of the employment agreement either before or during the meeting. A summary similar to the one given on September 26, 1995, was presented. The committee did not seek any further information about the negotiations or about the terms and conditions of Ovitz's agreement, nor was any information proffered regarding the scope of the non-fault termination provision. And, as before, no expert was available to advise the committee as to the employment agreement.

Negotiations continued among Ovitz, Eisner, and their attorneys. The lawyers circulated drafts on October 3, October 10, October 16, October 20, October 23, and December 12, 1995. The employment agreement was physically executed between Michael Ovitz and the Walt Disney Company on December 12, 1995. The employment agreement, however, was backdated to October 1, 1995, the day Ovitz began working as Disney's president. Additionally, the stock option agreement associated with the employment agreement was executed by Eisner (for Disney) on April 2, 1996. Ovitz did not countersign the stock option agreement until November 15, 1996, when he was already discussing his plans to leave Disney's employ. Neither the Old Board nor the compensation committee reviewed or approved the final employment agreement before it was executed and made binding upon Disney.

C.   *The Final Version of Ovitz's Employment Agreement*

The final version of Ovitz's employment agreement differed significantly from the drafts summarized to the compensation committee on September 26, 1995, and October 16, 1995. First, the final version caused Ovitz's stock options to be "in the money" when granted. The September 23rd draft agreement set the exercise price at the stock price on October 2, 1995, the day after Ovitz began as president. On October 16, 1995, the compensation committee agreed to change the exercise price to the price on that date (October 16, 1995), a price similar to that on October 2nd. The agreement was not signed until December 12, 1995, however, at which point the value of Disney stock had increased by eight percent-from $56.875 per share on October

16th to $61.50 per share on December 12th. The overall stock market, according to the Dow Jones Industrial Average, had also increased by about eight percent at the same time. By waiting to sign the agreement until December, but not changing the date of the exercise price, Ovitz had stock options that instantly were "in the money."[7] This allowed Ovitz to play a "win-win" game at Disney's expense—if the market price of Disney stock had fallen between October 16 and December 12, Ovitz could have demanded a downward adjustment to the option exercise price; if the price had risen (as in fact it had) Ovitz would receive "in the money" options.

Another difference in the final version of Ovitz's employment agreement concerned the circumstances surrounding a non-fault termination. The September 23rd draft agreement stated that non-fault termination benefits would only be provided if Disney wrongfully terminated Ovitz, or Ovitz died or became disabled. The October 16th draft contained a very similar definition. These were the only two drafts of which the compensation committee was made aware. The final version of the agreement, however, offered Ovitz a non-fault termination as long as Ovitz did not act with gross negligence or malfeasance. Therefore, instead of protecting Ovitz from a wrongful termination by Disney, Ovitz was able to receive the full benefits of a non-fault termination, even if he acted negligently or was unable to perform his duties, as long as his behavior did not reach the level of gross negligence or malfeasance. Additionally, a non-compete clause was not included within the agreement should Ovitz leave Disney's employ.

The employment agreement had a term of five years. Ovitz was to receive a salary of $1 million per year, a potential bonus each year from $0 to $10 million, and a series of stock options (the "A" options) that enabled Ovitz to purchase three million shares of Disney stock at the October 16, 1995 exercise price. The options were to vest at one million per year for three years beginning September 30, 1998. At the end of the contract term, if Disney entered into a new contract with Ovitz, he was entitled to the "B" options, an additional two million shares. There was no requirement, however, that Disney enter into a new contract with Ovitz.

Should a non-fault termination occur, however, the terms of the final version of the employment agreement appeared to be even more generous. Under a non-fault termination, Ovitz was to receive his salary for the remainder of the contract, discounted at a risk-free rate keyed to Disney's borrowing costs. He was also to receive a $7.5 million bonus for each year remaining on his contract, discounted at the same risk-free rate, even though no set bonus amount was guaranteed in the contract. Additionally, all of his "A" stock options

---

7. The options were apparently granted to Ovitz when the employment agreement was signed on December 12, 1995. Ovitz did not countersign the accompanying stock option agreement until November 15, 1996.

were to vest immediately, instead of waiting for the final three years of his contract for them to vest. The final benefit of the non-fault termination was a lump sum "termination payment" of $10 million. The termination payment was equal to the payment Ovitz would receive should he complete his full five-year term with Disney, but not receive an offer for a new contract. Graef Crystal opined in the January 13, 1997, edition of *California Law Business* that "the contract was most valuable to Ovitz the sooner he left Disney."

D.   *Ovitz's Performance as Disney's President*

Ovitz began serving as president of Disney on October 1, 1995, and became a Disney director in January 1996. Ovitz's tenure as Disney's president proved unsuccessful. Ovitz was not a good second-in-command, and he and Eisner were both aware of that fact. Eisner told defendant Watson, via memorandum, that he (Eisner) "had made an error in judgment in who I brought into the company." Other company executives were reported in the December 14, 1996 edition of the New York Times as saying that Ovitz had an excessively lavish office, an imperious management style, and had started a feud with NBC during his tenure. Even Ovitz admitted, during a September 30, 1996 interview on "Larry King Live," that he knew "about 1% of what I need to know."

Even though admitting that he did not know his job, Ovitz studiously avoided attempts to be educated. Eisner instructed Ovitz to meet weekly with Disney's chief financial officer, defendant Bollenbach. The meetings were scheduled to occur each Monday at 2 p.m., but every week Ovitz cancelled at the last minute. Bollenbach was quoted in a December 1996 issue of Vanity Fair as saying that Ovitz failed to meet with him at all, "didn't understand the duties of an executive at a public company[,] and he didn't want to learn."

Instead of working to learn his duties as Disney's president, Ovitz began seeking alternative employment. He consulted Eisner to ensure that no action would be taken against him by Disney if he sought employment elsewhere. Eisner agreed that the best thing for Disney, Eisner, and Ovitz was for Ovitz to gain employment elsewhere. Eisner wrote to the chairman of Sony Japan that Ovitz could negotiate with Sony without any repercussions from Disney. Ovitz and Sony began negotiations for Ovitz to become head of Sony's entertainment business, but the negotiations ultimately failed. With the possibility of having another company absorb the cost of Ovitz's departure now gone, Eisner and Ovitz began in earnest to discuss a non-fault termination.

E.   *The Non–Fault Termination*

Ovitz wanted to leave Disney, but could only terminate his employment if one of three events occurred: (1) he was not elected or retained as president and a director of Disney; (2) he was assigned duties materially inconsistent with his role as president; or (3) Disney reduced his annual salary or failed to grant his stock options, pay him discretionary bonuses, or make any required compensation payment. None of these three events occurred. If Ovitz resigned outright, he might have been liable to Disney for damages and would not have received the benefits of the non-fault termination. He also desired to protect his reputation when exiting from his position with Disney. Eisner agreed to help Ovitz depart Disney without sacrificing any of his benefits. Eisner and Ovitz worked together as close personal friends to have Ovitz receive a non-fault termination. Eisner stated in a letter to Ovitz that: "I agree with you that we must work together to assure a smooth transition and deal with the public relations brilliantly. I am committed to make this a win-win situation, to keep our friendship intact, to be positive, to say and write only glowing things. . . . Nobody ever needs to know anything other than positive things from either of us. This can all work out!"

Eisner, Litvack, and Ovitz met at Eisner's apartment on December 11, 1996, to finalize Ovitz's non-fault termination. The new complaint alleges that the New Board was aware that Eisner was negotiating with Ovitz the terms of his separation. Litvack sent a letter to Ovitz on December 12, 1996, stating that, by "mutual agreement," (1) Ovitz's term of employment would end on January 31, 1997; and (2) "this letter will for all purposes of the Employment Agreement be given the same effect as though there had been a 'Non–Fault Termination,' and the Company will pay you, on or before February 5, 1997, all amounts due you under the Employment Agreement, including those under Section 11(c) thereof. In addition, the stock options granted pursuant to Option A, will vest as of January 31, 1997 and will expire in accordance with their terms on September 30, 2002." On December 12, 1996, Ovitz's departure from Disney became public. Neither the New Board of Directors nor the compensation committee had been consulted or given their approval for a non-fault termination. In addition, no record exists of any action by the New Board once the non-fault termination became public on December 12, 1996.

On December 27, 1996, Litvack sent Ovitz a new letter superseding the December 12th letter. The December 27th letter stated that Ovitz's termination would "be treated as a 'Non–Fault Termination.'" This differed from the December 12th letter, which treated Ovitz's termination "as though there had been a 'Non–Fault Termination.'" It also made the termination of Ovitz's employment and his resignation as a Disney director effective as of the close of business on December 27th, instead of on January 31, 1997, as in the December 12th letter. Additionally, it listed the amount payable to Ovitz as $38,888,230.77, and stated that the "A" options to purchase three million shares of Disney vested on December 27th, instead of January 31, 1997, as in the December 12th letter. Both Eisner and Litvack signed the letter. Again, however, neither the New Board nor the compensation committee reviewed or approved the December 27th letter. No record exists of any New Board action after the December 27th letter became public, nor had any board member raised any questions or concerns since the original December 12th letter became public.

According to the new complaint, Disney's bylaws required board approval for Ovitz's non-fault termination. Eisner and Litvack allegedly did not have the authority to provide for a non-fault termination without board consent. No documents or board minutes currently exist showing an affirmative decision by the New Board or any of its committees to grant Ovitz a non-fault termination. The New Board was already aware that Eisner was granting the non-fault termination as of December 12, 1996, the day it became public. No record of any action by the New Board affirming or questioning that decision by Eisner either before or after that date has been produced. There are also no records showing that alternatives to a non-fault termination were ever evaluated by the New Board or by any of its committees.

II. STANDARD OF REVIEW ...

When the plaintiff alleges a derivative claim, demand must be made on the board or excused based upon futility. To determine whether demand would be futile, the Court must determine whether the particular facts, as alleged, create a reason to doubt that: "(1) the directors are disinterested and independent" or "(2) the challenged transaction was otherwise the product of a valid exercise of business judgment." ...[16]

III. ANALYSIS

The primary issue before the Court is whether plaintiffs' new complaint survives the Rule 23.1 motion to dismiss under the second prong of *Aronson v. Lewis*.[25] In order for demand to be excused under the second prong of *Aronson*, plaintiffs must allege particularized facts that raise doubt about whether the challenged transaction is entitled to the protection of the business judgment rule. Plaintiffs may rebut the presumption that the board's decision is entitled to deference by raising a reason to doubt whether the board's action was taken on an informed basis or whether the directors honestly and in good faith believed that the action was in the best interests of the corporation. Thus, plaintiffs must plead particularized facts sufficient to raise (1) a reason to doubt that the action was taken honestly and in good faith or (2) a reason to doubt that the board was adequately informed in making the decision.

---

16. *Aronson v. Lewis*, 473 A.2d 805, 814 (Del.1984).

25. 473 A.2d at 814. The Supreme Court affirmed the dismissal of plaintiffs' previous complaint under the first prong of *Aronson* and prohibited that issue from being relitigated. *Brehm*, 746 A.2d at 258 & n. 42. As discussed earlier, the new complaint must survive a Rule 23.1 motion to dismiss because it is a derivative action. The facts alleged here are the same for both the 23.1 motions and the 12(b)(6) motions. Thus, since the standard for a Rule 23.1 dismissal is more stringent than that under Rule 12(b)(6), should the new complaint survive under the second prong of *Aronson*, it will survive under Rule 12(b)(6) if its facts otherwise state a cognizable claim.

Defendants contend that the new complaint cannot be read reasonably to allege any fiduciary duty violation other than, at most, a breach of the directors' duty of due care. They further assert that even if the complaint states a breach of the directors' duty of care, Disney's charter provision, based on 8 *Del. C.* § 102(b)(7), would apply and the individual directors would be protected from personal damages liability for any breach of their duty of care. A § 102(b)(7) provision in a corporation's charter does not "eliminate or limit the liability of a director: (i)[f]or any breach of the director's duty of loyalty to the corporation or its stockholders; (ii) for acts or omissions not in good faith or which involve intentional misconduct or a knowing violation of the law; (iii) under § 174 of this title; or (iv) for any transaction from which the director derived an improper personal benefit."[28] A fair reading of the new complaint, in my opinion, gives rise to a reason to doubt whether the board's actions were taken honestly and in good faith, as required under the second prong of *Aronson*. Since acts or omissions not undertaken honestly and in good faith, or which involve intentional misconduct, do not fall within the protective ambit of § 102(b)(7), I cannot dismiss the complaint based on the exculpatory Disney charter provision.[29]

Defendants also argue that Ovitz's employment agreement was a reasonable exercise of business judgment. They argue that Ovitz's previous position as head of CAA required a large compensation package to entice him to become Disney's president. As to the non-fault termination, defendants contend that that decision was reasonable in that the board wished to avoid protracted litigation with Ovitz. The Court is appropriately hesitant to second-guess the business judgment of a disinterested and independent board of directors. As alleged in the new complaint, however, the facts belie any assertion that the New or Old Boards exercised any business judgment or made any good faith attempt to fulfill the fiduciary duties they owed to Disney and its shareholders.

A.   *The Old and New Boards*

According to the new complaint, Eisner unilaterally made the decision to hire Ovitz, even in the face of internal documents warning of potential adverse publicity and with three members of the board of directors initially objecting to the hiring when Eisner first broached the idea in August 1995. No draft employment agreements were presented to the compensation committee or to the Disney board for review before the September 26, 1995 meetings. The compensation committee met for less than an hour on September 26, 1995, and spent most of its time on two other topics, including the compensa-

---

28. 8 *Del. C.* § 102(b)(7). As to (iii), § 174 deals with a director's liability for unlawful payment of dividends or unlawful stock purchase or redemption.

29. See *Malpiede v. Townson*, 780 A.2d 1075, 1094 (Del.2001) (holding that, as a matter of law, § 102(b)(7) bars a claim only if there is an unambiguous, residual due care claim and nothing else).

tion of director Russell for helping secure Ovitz's employment. With respect to the employment agreement itself, the committee received only a summary of its terms and conditions. No questions were asked about the employment agreement. No time was taken to review the documents for approval. Instead, the committee approved the hiring of Ovitz and directed Eisner, Ovitz's close friend, to carry out the negotiations with regard to certain still unresolved and significant details.[30]

The Old Board met immediately after the committee did. Less than one and one-half pages of the fifteen pages of Old Board minutes were devoted to discussions of Ovitz's hiring as Disney's new president. Actually, most of that time appears to have been spent discussing compensation for director Russell. No presentations were made to the Old Board regarding the terms of the draft agreement. No questions were raised, at least so far as the minutes reflect. At the end of the meeting, the Old Board authorized Ovitz's hiring as Disney's president. No further review or approval of the employment agreement occurred. Throughout both meetings, no expert consultant was present to advise the compensation committee or the Old Board. Notably, the Old Board approved Ovitz's hiring even though the employment agreement was still a "work in progress." The Old Board simply passed off the details to Ovitz and his good friend, Eisner.

Negotiation over the remaining terms took place solely between Eisner, Ovitz, and attorneys representing Disney and Ovitz. The compensation committee met briefly in October to review the negotiations, but failed again to actually consider a draft of the agreement or to establish any guidelines to be used in the negotiations. The committee was apparently not otherwise involved in the negotiations. Negotiations with Eisner continued until mid-December, but Ovitz had already started serving as Disney's president as of October 1, 1995.

Eisner and Ovitz reached a final agreement on December 12, 1995. They agreed to backdate the agreement, however, to October 1, 1995. The final employment agreement also differed substantially from the original draft, but evidently no further committee or board review of it ever occurred. The final version of Ovitz's employment agreement was signed (according to the new complaint) without any board input beyond the limited discussion on September 26, 1995.

From the outset, Ovitz performed poorly as Disney's president. In short order, Ovitz wanted out, and, once again, his good friend Eisner came to the rescue, agreeing to Ovitz's request for a non-fault termination. Disney's board, however, was allegedly never consulted in this process. No board committee was ever consulted, nor were any

---

30. The allegation that Eisner and Ovitz had been close friends for over twenty-five years is not mentioned to show self-interest or domination. Instead, the allegation is mentioned because it casts doubt on the good faith and judgment behind the Old and New Boards' decisions to allow two close personal friends to control the payment of shareholders' money to Ovitz.

experts consulted. Eisner and Litvack alone granted Ovitz's non-fault termination, which became public on December 12, 1996. Again, Disney's board did not appear to question this action, although affirmative board action seemed to be required. On December 27, 1996, Eisner and Litvack, without explanation, accelerated the effective date of the non-fault termination, from January 31, 1997, to December 27, 1996. Again, the board apparently took no action; no questions were asked as to why this was done.

Disney had lost several key executives in the months before Ovitz was hired. Moreover, the position of president is obviously important in a publicly owned corporation. But the Old Board and the compensation committee (it is alleged) each spent less than an hour reviewing Ovitz's possible hiring. According to the new complaint, neither the Old Board nor the compensation committee reviewed the actual draft employment agreement. Nor did they evaluate the details of Ovitz's salary or his severance provisions. No expert presented the board with details of the agreement, outlined the pros and cons of either the salary or non-fault termination provisions, or analyzed comparable industry standards for such agreements.[31] Notwithstanding this alleged information vacuum, the Old Board and the compensation committee approved Ovitz's hiring, appointed Eisner to negotiate with Ovitz directly in drafting the unresolved terms of his employment, never asked to review the final terms, and were never voluntarily provided those terms.

During the negotiation over the unresolved terms, the compensation committee was involved only once, at the very early stages in October 1995. The final agreement varied significantly from the draft agreement in the areas of both stock options and the terms of the non-fault termination. Neither the compensation committee nor the Old Board sought to review, nor did they review, the final agreement. In addition, both the Old Board and the committee failed to meet in order to evaluate the final agreement before it became binding on Disney. To repeat, no expert was retained to advise the Old Board, the committee, or Eisner during the negotiation process.

The new complaint, fairly read, also charges the New Board with a similar ostrich-like approach regarding Ovitz's non-fault termination. Eisner and Litvack granted Ovitz a non-fault termination on December 12, 1996, and the news became public that day. Although formal board approval appeared necessary for a non-fault termination, the new complaint alleges that no New Board member even asked for a meeting to discuss Eisner's and Litvack's decision. On December 27,

---

31. In the earlier proceedings in this case, defendants represented that Graef Crystal served as the expert with regard to Ovitz's employment, arguably providing the board with the statutory safe harbor under 8 Del. C. § 141(e). The new complaint, however, alleges that Graef Crystal was hired as the expert with regard to Eisner's new employment agreement, not Ovitz's agreement. Accepting this change in facts as true for purposes of this motion, Disney's board is not entitled to invoke § 141(e)'s protection based on a board's reliance upon a qualified expert selected with reasonable care.

1996, when Eisner and Litvack accelerated Ovitz's non-fault termination by over a month, with a payout of more than $38 million in cash, together with the three million "A" stock options, the board again failed to do anything. Instead, it appears from the new complaint that the New Board played no role in Eisner's agreement to award Ovitz more than $38 million in cash and the three million "A" stock options, all for leaving a job that Ovitz had allegedly proven incapable of performing.

The New Board apparently never sought to negotiate with Ovitz regarding his departure. Nor, apparently, did it consider whether to seek a termination based on fault. During the fifteen-day period between announcement of Ovitz's termination and its effective date, the New Board allegedly chose to remain invisible in the process. The new complaint alleges that the New Board: (1) failed to ask why it had not been informed; (2) failed to inquire about the conditions and terms of the agreement; and (3) failed even to attempt to stop or delay the termination until more information could be collected. If the board had taken the time or effort to review these or other options, perhaps with the assistance of expert legal advisors, the business judgment rule might well protect its decision. In this case, however, the new complaint asserts that the New Board directors refused to explore any alternatives, and refused to even attempt to evaluate the implications of the non-fault termination—blindly allowing Eisner to hand over to his personal friend, Ovitz, more than $38 million in cash and the three million "A" stock options.[32]

These facts, if true, do more than portray directors who, in a negligent or grossly negligent manner, merely failed to inform themselves or to deliberate adequately about an issue of material importance to their corporation. Instead, the facts alleged in the new complaint suggest that the defendant directors consciously and intentionally disregarded their responsibilities, adopting a "we don't care about the risks" attitude concerning a material corporate decision. Knowing or deliberate indifference by a director to his or her duty to act faithfully and with appropriate care is conduct, in my opinion, that may not have been taken honestly and in good faith to advance the best interests of the company. Put differently, all of the alleged facts, if true, imply that the defendant directors knew that they were making material decisions without adequate information and without adequate deliberation, and that they simply did not care if the decisions caused the corporation and its stockholders to suffer injury or loss. Viewed in this light, plaintiffs' new complaint sufficiently alleges a breach of the directors' obligation to act honestly and in good faith in the corporation's best interests for a Court to conclude, if the facts are

---

32. Plaintiffs allege that the present value of the cash and the value of the stock options totaled over $140 million to Ovitz as severance. At this time I need not determine whether plaintiffs' allegations as to the value of the payout are correct or incorrect.

true, that the defendant directors' conduct fell outside the protection of the business judgment rule.[33]

Of course, the alleged facts need only give rise to a reason to doubt business judgment protection, not "a judicial finding that the directors' actions are not protected by the business judgment rule."[34] For this reason, I conclude that plaintiffs have satisfied the second prong of *Aronson*, and that demand is excused.

I also conclude that plaintiffs' pleading is sufficient to withstand a motion to dismiss under Rule 12(b)(6). Specifically, plaintiffs' claims are based on an alleged knowing and deliberate indifference to a potential risk of harm to the corporation. Where a director consciously ignores his or her duties to the corporation, thereby causing economic injury to its stockholders, the director's actions are either "not in good faith" or "involve intentional misconduct."[35] Thus, plaintiffs' allegations support claims that fall outside the liability waiver provided under Disney's certificate of incorporation.

B. Ovitz

Defendant Ovitz contends that the action against him should be dismissed because he owed no fiduciary duty not to seek the best possible employment agreement for himself. Ovitz did have the right to seek the best employment agreement possible for himself. Nevertheless, once Ovitz became a fiduciary of Disney on October 1, 1995, according to the new complaint, he also had a duty to negotiate honestly and in good faith so as not to advantage himself at the expense of the Disney shareholders. He arguably failed to fulfill that duty, according to the facts alleged in the new complaint.

Ovitz and Eisner had been close friends for over twenty-five years. Ovitz knew when he became president of Disney on October 1, 1995, that his unexecuted contract was still under negotiation. Instead of negotiating with an impartial entity, such as the compensation committee, Ovitz and his attorneys negotiated directly with Eisner, his close personal friend. Perhaps not surprisingly, the final version of the employment agreement differed significantly from the draft version summarized to the board and to the compensation committee on September 26, 1995. Had those changes been the result of arms-length bargaining, Ovitz's motion to dismiss might have merit. At this stage, however, the alleged facts (which I must accept as true) suggest that Ovitz and Eisner had almost absolute control over the terms of Ovitz's contract.

The new complaint arguably charges that Ovitz engaged in a carefully orchestrated, self-serving process controlled directly by his close friend Eisner, all designed to provide Ovitz with enormous financial benefits. The case law cited by Ovitz in support of his

---

33. *Aronson*, 473 A.2d at 812.
34. *Grobow*, 539 A.2d at 186.

35. 8 *Del. C.* § 102(b)(7)(ii).

position suggests that an officer may negotiate his or her own employment agreement as long as the process involves negotiations performed in an adversarial and arms-length manner.[36] The facts, as alleged in the new complaint, belie an adversarial, arms-length negotiation process between Ovitz and the Walt Disney Company. Instead, the alleged facts, if true, would support an inference that Ovitz may have breached his fiduciary duties by engaging in a self-interested transaction in negotiating his employment agreement directly with his personal friend Eisner.

The same is true regarding the non-fault termination. In that instance, Ovitz was also serving as a member of the Disney board of directors. The Supreme Court recently held in *Telxon Corp. v. Meyerson* that "directoral self-compensation decisions lie outside the business judgment rule's presumptive protection, so that, where properly challenged, the receipt of self-determined benefits is subject to an affirmative showing that the compensation arrangements are fair to the corporation."[37] According to the facts alleged in the new complaint, Ovitz did not advise the Disney board of his decision to seek a departure that would be fair and equitable to all parties. Instead, he went to his close friend, Eisner, and, working together, they developed a secret strategy that would enable Ovitz to extract the maximum benefit from his contract, all without board approval.

Although the strategy was economically injurious and a public relations disaster for Disney, the Ovitz/Eisner exit strategy allegedly was designed principally to protect their personal reputations, while assuring Ovitz a huge personal payoff after barely a year of mediocre to poor job performance. These allegations, if ultimately found to be true, would suggest a faithless fiduciary who obtained extraordinary personal financial benefits at the expense of the constituency for whom he was obliged to act honestly and in good faith. Because Ovitz was a fiduciary during both the negotiation of his employment agreement and the non-fault termination, he had an obligation to ensure the process of his contract negotiation and termination was both impartial and fair. The facts, as plead, give rise to a reasonable inference that, assisted by Eisner, he ignored that obligation.

IV.   CONCLUSION

It is of course true that after-the-fact litigation is a most imperfect device to evaluate corporate business decisions, as the limits of human competence necessarily impede judicial review. But our corporation law's theoretical justification for disregarding honest errors simply does not apply to intentional misconduct or to egregious process failures that implicate the foundational directoral obligation to act

36. Ovitz cites *Stifel Fin. Corp. v. Cochran*, 809 A.2d 555, 2002 WL 1316240 (Del. Supr.), as well as certain other non-precedential cases, to support his position. All cases, as pointed out directly by Ovitz in his reply brief, base the holding upon an adversarial, arms-length transaction.

37. 802 A.2d 257, 265 (Del.2002).

honestly and in good faith to advance corporate interests. Because the facts alleged here, if true, portray directors consciously indifferent to a material issue facing the corporation, the law must be strong enough to intervene against abuse of trust. Accordingly, all three of plaintiffs' claims for relief concerning fiduciary duty breaches and waste survive defendants' motions to dismiss.

The practical effect of this ruling is that defendants must answer the new complaint and plaintiffs may proceed to take appropriate discovery on the merits of their claims. To that end, a case scheduling order has been entered that will promptly bring this matter before the Court on a fully developed factual record.

IT IS SO ORDERED.

SECTION 5. DUTIES OF CONTROLLING SHAREHOLDERS

Insert the following note and case at p. 727 of the Unabridged Edition, and p. 515 of the Concise Edition, following Kahn v. Tremont Corp:

LEVCO ALTERNATIVE FUND v. THE READER'S DIGEST ASS'N, INC., 803 A.2d 428, 2002 WL 1859064 (Del. 2002). Reader's Digest Association (RDA) had two classes of common stock: Class A, which was non-voting, and Class B, which had the right to vote. RDA proposed a recapitalization under which it would, among other things, (i) create a new class of voting common stock; (ii) purchase all the shares of its Class B voting stock at a premium of 1.24 to 1 to the new voting stock; and (iii) recapitalize each share of the Class A non-voting stock into one share of the new voting common stock. The key to the recapitalization proposal was an agreement by RDA to purchase 3,636,-363 shares of Class B Voting Stock owned by two funds at $27.50 per share, for an aggregate purchase price of approximately $100 million. Prior to recapitalization, the Funds controlled 50 percent of the Class B voting stock. Following the recapitalization, the funds would hold 14 percent of the new voting common stock.

Plaintiffs, Class A shareholders, sought a preliminary injunction against the recapitalization in Delaware Chancery Court. Plaintiffs alleged that the recapitalization would result in financial detriment to the Class A shareholders. Plaintiffs also argued that a Special Committee, composed of three outside directors and established to evaluate the fairness of the transaction, breached its fiduciary duty to consider the separate interests of the Class A shareholders. RDA and its directors did not dispute that the directors owed a fiduciary duty to the Class A shareholders, but contended that they had discharged that duty through intensive negotiations between the Funds and the Special Committee. Plaintiffs asserted that the directors, including the

Special Committee, were subject to the Funds' control and therefore were required to demonstrate the entire fairness of the transaction. Plaintiffs further asserted that the directors breached their duty of care. The Court of Chancery ruled that regardless of where the burden of proof lay, the evidence did not support the view that plaintiffs would ultimately succeed in demonstrating that the activities of the Special Committee did not result in a "fair and genuinely negotiated price." Reversed.

Although the Court of Chancery did not elaborate on the burden of proof, we think it significant here that the initial burden of establishing entire fairness rests upon the party who stands on both sides of the transaction. *Kahn v. Lynch Comm. Sys., Inc.*, 638 A.2d 1110, 1117 (Del.1994). That burden may shift, of course, if an independent committee of directors has approved the transaction. *Emerald Partners v. Berlin*, 726 A.2d 1215, 1221 (Del.1999). While we agree with the Court of Chancery that the independent committee who negotiated the recapitalization believed it was operating in the interests of the corporation as an entity, we conclude that the committee's functioning, to the extent it was required to balance the conflicting interests of two distinct classes of shareholders, was flawed both from the standpoint of process and price.

With respect to the unfair dealing claim, the Special Committee never sought, nor did its financial advisor, Goldman Sachs, ever tender, an opinion as to whether the transaction was fair to the Class A shareholders. Goldman Sachs directed its fairness opinion to the interests of RDA as a corporate entity. Given the obvious conflicting interests of the shareholder classes, the conceded absence of an evaluation of the fairness of the recapitalization on the Class A shareholders is significant. While the Class A shareholders received voting rights, their equity interests decreased by at least $100 million without either their consent or an objective evaluation of the exchange. In short, while the Special Committee believed, perhaps in good faith, that the transaction was in the best interests of the corporation, arguably, it never focused on the specific impact upon the Class A shareholders of RDA's payment of $100 million to the Class B shareholders.

With respect to the premium paid to the Class B shareholders, given RDA's tenuous financial condition, having recently committed to a large acquisition, incurring additional debt in order to pay $100 million to the Class B shareholders is a matter of concern. The net result of the transaction was to significantly reduce the post-capitalization equity of the corporation. To the extent that the directors did not secure sufficient information concerning the effect of the recapitalization premium on the Class A shareholders, a serious question is raised concerning the discharge of their duty of care. *Kahn v. Tremont Corp.*, 694 A.2d 422, 430 (Del.1997) . . . .

We are not required, nor was the Court of Chancery, to determine the final merits of appellants' claims but, in our view, they stand a reasonable probability of success. It is unquestioned that the appellants will be irreparably harmed. While future monetary relief may be available, the issuance of the shares contemplated by the recapitalization may place a practical remedy beyond judicial reach.

McMullin v. Beran

Delaware Supreme Court, 2000.
765 A.2d 910.

■ HOLLAND, JUSTICE.

The plaintiff-appellant, Mary E. McMullin, a purported shareholder of ARCO Chemical Company ("Chemical"), filed this putative class action against Chemical, its directors (the "Individual Defendants" or the "Chemical Directors"), Atlantic Richfield Company ("ARCO"), Lyondell Petrochemical Company ("Lyondell"), and Lyondell's subsidiary, Lyondell Acquisition Corporation. ARCO owned 80% of Chemical's common stock. The Amended Complaint alleged that the Individual Defendants and ARCO, aided and abetted by Lyondell, breached their fiduciary duties in connection with Lyondell's acquisition of Chemical's shares at $57.75 per share (the "Transaction"). All defendants filed motions to dismiss the Amended Complaint pursuant to Court of Chancery Rule 12(b)(6). McMullin voluntarily dismissed Chemical, Lyondell and Lyondell Acquisition Corporation from this action. The Court of Chancery granted the remaining defendants' motions to dismiss. McMullin has raised three issues on appeal. Her first contention is that ARCO and the Chemical Directors were obligated to maximize value for all Chemical shareholders in the sale of the company to Lyondell. Thus, according to McMullin, the Court of Chancery erred in holding that defendants' *Revlon*[1] duty to maximize shareholder value was not "implicated" in this case. McMullin's second contention is that Chemical's Directors violated their fiduciary duties to manage the sale of Chemical by delegating control of the sale process to ARCO. According to McMullin, the Court of Chancery erred in holding that Chemical's Directors were justified in delegating their managerial responsibilities to ARCO simply because ARCO owned 80% of Chemical and no transaction could proceed without ARCO's approval. Finally, McMullin submits that the disclosure documents dis-

---

1. Revlon, Inc. v. MacAndrews & Forbes Holdings, Inc., Del.Supr., 506 A.2d 173 (1985).

seminated to Chemical's minority shareholders failed to disclose any qualitative or quantitative information about the value of the company to inform the shareholders' decision whether to tender their shares to Lyondell or seek appraisal in the ensuing merger. According to McMullin, the Court of Chancery erred in holding that the Chemical Directors had fulfilled their disclosure obligations to Chemical's minority shareholders by merely furnishing them the conclusory opinion of an investment banker that the transaction was fair to the minority shareholders from a financial point of view.

We have concluded that the Court of Chancery should not have granted the remaining defendant's motion to dismiss McMullin's Amended Complaint. Therefore, the judgment must be reversed.

Facts

McMullin is a purported former owner of Chemical common stock. Chemical was, until its purchase by Lyondell, a Delaware corporation with its principal place of business in Newtown Square, Pennsylvania. Chemical is a leading worldwide manufacturer and marketer of chemicals.

ARCO is a Delaware corporation with its principal place of business in Los Angeles, California. ARCO is an integrated oil and gas company. Before the Transaction, ARCO owned 80 million shares of Chemical's common stock, representing 80.1% of Chemical's outstanding shares. Lyondell is a Delaware corporation based in Texas.

Lyondell Acquisition Corporation is a wholly owned subsidiary of Lyondell formed to accomplish the Transaction. The Individual Defendants are former members of the board of directors of Chemical. At the time of the Transaction, one of these individuals was the chief financial officer and executive vice president of ARCO, one was a senior vice president of ARCO, four were senior vice presidents of ARCO, two were previously senior executives with various other ARCO subsidiaries, and one was the president of Chemical. The remaining three directors were not officers or employees of either ARCO or Chemical.

On February 17, 1998, ARCO received an unsolicited call from Lyondell in which Lyondell expressed an interest in acquiring Chemical. From February to June 1998, ARCO and its financial advisor, Salomon Smith Barney ("Salomon"), contacted a number of entities to gauge their interest in participating in a bidding process.

In mid-March, ARCO informed Chemical's Directors that it "had received indications of interest for an acquisition of all of the outstanding shares of the Common Stock." The Chemical Directors authorized ARCO to explore the sale of the entire company.

On May 15, Lyondell proposed to purchase all outstanding shares of Chemical in a cash tender offer at a price of $51 per share. Lyondell also proposed a second-step merger in which stockholders could elect to receive either $51 per share in cash for their stock or Lyondell common stock with a market value of $56 per share, subject to a 15.5 million cap on the number of Lyondell shares to be exchanged. Because of this cap, only a portion of the shares of Chemical would have been eligible to receive Lyondell shares rather than cash. ARCO rejected this price as inadequate and on June 4, Lyondell raised its cash offer price for all shares of Chemical to $56.60 per share. ARCO rejected the new offer.

On June 13, 1998, Lyondell made yet another revised bid, offering $57.75 in cash per share to purchase all of Chemical's outstanding stock. After negotiations, on June 17, 1998, Lyondell submitted a merger agreement and other related contracts. The Lyondell proposal contemplated a tender offer to purchase all outstanding shares of the Company for $57.75 per share, a commitment from ARCO to tender its 80 million shares of Chemical at the same $57.75 price paid to the minority, and a second-step merger whereby all untendered shares would be cashed out at the same time.

On June 18, 1998, Chemical's Board of Directors met to consider the Lyondell proposal. Representatives of ARCO and Salomon made presentations regarding the terms of the Lyondell proposal and the sale process. Merrill Lynch, Chemical's financial advisor, made a presentation and expressed its opinion that $57.75 per share was fair to Chemical's stockholders, other than ARCO, from a financial point of view. Chemical's Board of Directors unanimously approved the Transaction.

On June 24, 1998, Lyondell commenced its Tender Offer.... On July 23, 1998, the Tender Offer was completed, with 99% of Chemical's shares tendering to Lyondell. Shortly thereafter, Lyondell completed the second-step merger. None of the former Chemical shareholders sought to exercise their rights of appraisal....

Business Judgment Rule

One of the fundamental principles of the Delaware General Corporation Law statute is that the business affairs of a corporation are managed by or under the direction of its board of directors. The business judgment rule is a corollary common law precept to this statutory provision. The business judgment rule, therefore, combines a judicial acknowledgment of the managerial prerogatives that are vested in the directors of a Delaware corporation by statute with a judicial recognition that the directors are acting as fiduciaries in discharging their statutory responsibilities to the corporation and its shareholders. The business judgment rule "is a presumption that in making a business decision the directors of a corporation acted on an informed basis, in good faith and in the honest belief that the action taken was in the best interests of the company."[9]

9. Aronson v. Lewis, 473 A.2d at 812; see also Brehm v. Eisner, 746 A.2d at 264 n. 66.

The business judgment rule "operates as both a procedural guide for litigants and a substantive rule of law."[10] Procedurally, the initial burden is on the shareholder plaintiff to rebut the presumption of the business judgment rule. To meet that burden, the shareholder plaintiff must effectively provide evidence that the defendant board of directors, in reaching its challenged decision, breached any one of its "triad of fiduciary duties, loyalty, good faith or due care."[12] Substantively, "if the shareholder plaintiff fails to meet that evidentiary burden, the business judgment rule attaches" and operates to protect the individual director-defendants from personal liability for making the board decision at issue.[13]

"Burden shifting does not create per se liability on the part of the directors."[14] It is a procedure by which the Delaware judiciary determines the standard of review that is applicable to measure the board of directors' conduct. If the shareholder plaintiff succeeds in rebutting the presumption of the business judgment rule, the burden shifts to the defendant directors to prove the "entire fairness" of the transaction.

Motion to Dismiss

The fiduciary responsibilities of the Chemical Directors' with regard to the proposed Lyondell Transaction emanate from their statutory duty under 8 Del. C. § 251 "to act in an informed and deliberate manner in determining whether to approve an agreement of merger before submitting the proposal to the stockholders."[17] The Chemical Directors were obliged to make an informed, deliberate judgment, in good faith, that the merger terms, including the price, were fair. They were also obliged to disclose with entire candor all material facts concerning the merger, so that the minority stockholders would be able to make an informed decision whether to accept the tender offer price or to seek judicial remedies such as appraisal or an injunction.

In examining the Chemical Directors' motion to dismiss McMullin's Amended Complaint, the Court of Chancery was required to conduct a two-step analysis: first, to take the facts alleged as true and view all inferences from those facts in the light most favorable to the plaintiff; and, second, to determine whether with reasonable certainty,

---

10. Cinerama, Inc. v. Technicolor, Inc., Del.Supr., 663 A.2d 1156, 1162 (1995) (quoting Citron v. Fairchild Camera & Instrument Corp., Del.Supr., 569 A.2d 53, 64 (1989)).

12. Emerald Partners v. Berlin, Del. Supr., 726 A.2d 1215, 1221 (1999); Cinerama, Inc. v. Technicolor, Inc., 663 A.2d at 1162–63; In re Tri–Star Pictures, Inc., Litig., Del. Supr., 634 A.2d 319, 333 (1993).

13. Cede & Co. v. Technicolor, Inc., Del.Supr., 634 A.2d 345, 361 (1993) ("Cede II"); Citron v. Fairchild Camera & Instrument Corp., 569 A.2d at 64; Smith v. Van Gorkom, 488 A.2d at 873; Revlon, Inc. v. MacAndrews & Forbes Holdings, Inc., Del. Supr., 506 A.2d 173, 180 n. 10 (1985).

14. Cinerama, Inc. v. Technicolor, Inc., 663 A.2d at 1162; Cede II, 634 A.2d at 361.

17. Smith v. Van Gorkom, Del.Supr., 488 A.2d 858, 873 (1985); Sinclair Oil Corp. v. Levien, Del.Supr., 280 A.2d 717, 721–22 (1971).

under any set of facts that could be proven, the plaintiff would succeed in rebutting the presumption of the business judgment rule. If McMullin's Amended Complaint passed judicial muster under that two-step analysis, the motion to dismiss should have been denied. If the Amended Complaint failed to withstand that threshold level of judicial scrutiny, the motion to dismiss was properly granted because, unless effectively pled factual allegations in the shareholder plaintiff's Amended Complaint successfully rebut the procedural presumption of the business judgment rule, the Chemical Directors would be protected by the substantive operation of the business judgment rule.

Fiduciary Responsibility Is Contextually Specific

This case relates to a complete sale of Chemical. The Chemical Board owed fiduciary duties of care, loyalty and good faith to all Chemical shareholders in recommending a sale of the entire corporation. In the context of an entire sale, and in the absence of an extant majority shareholder, the directors must focus on one primary objective—to secure the transaction offering the best value reasonably available for all stockholders.[22] In pursuing that objective, the directors must be especially diligent[23] "and they must exercise their fiduciary duties to to further that end."[24]

In the absence of a majority shareholder, this Court has described some of the methods by which a board can fulfill its fiduciary obligation to seek the best value reasonably available to the stockholders when the board is engaged in the process of selling the corporation.[25] Those methods may include conducting an auction, canvassing the market, etc.[26] There is, however, "no single blueprint" that directors of Delaware corporations must follow.[27]

The statutory duties and common law fiduciary responsibilities that directors of a Delaware corporation are required to discharge depends upon the specific context that gives occasion to the board's exercise of its business judgment. Whenever the board is deciding whether to approve a proposed "all shares" tender offer that is to be

22. Paramount Communications v. QVC Network, Inc., Del.Supr., 637 A.2d 34, 44 (1994).

23. Id.; see Citron v. Fairchild Camera & Instrument Corp., Del.Supr., 569 A.2d 53, 66 (1989) (discussing "a board's active and direct role in the sale process")

24. Paramount Communications v. QVC Network, Inc., Del.Supr., 637 A.2d 34, 44 (1994); Revlon, Inc. v. MacAndrews & Forbes Holdings, Inc., Del.Supr., 506 A.2d 173, 182 (1985) ("The duty of the board ... [is] the maximization of the company's value at a sale for the stockholders' benefit."); Mills Acquisition Co. v. Macmillan, Inc., 559 A.2d at 1288 ("[I]n a sale of corporate control the responsibility of the directors is to get the highest value reasonably attainable for the shareholders."); Barkan v. Amsted Industries, Del.Supr., 567 A.2d 1279, 1286 (1989) ("[T]he board must act in a neutral manner to encourage the highest possible price for shareholders.").

25. Paramount Communications Inc. v. QVC Network, Inc., 637 A.2d at 44 (citing Barkan v. Amsted Indus., 567 A.2d at 1286–87).

26. Id.

27. Id.; Barkan v. Amsted Industries, 567 A.2d at 1286–87; Citron v. Fairchild Camera & Instrument Corp., Del.Supr., 569 A.2d 53, 68 (1989); Mills Acquisition Co. v. Macmillan, Inc., 559 A.2d at 1287.

followed by a cash-out merger, the decision constitutes a final-stage transaction for all shareholders. Consequently, the time frame for the board's analysis is immediate value maximization for all shareholders.

The questions presented in this case require an examination of the Chemical Board's statutory duty and fiduciary responsibilities to minority shareholders in the specific context of evaluating a proposal for a sale of the entire corporation to a third party at the behest of the majority shareholder. When a board is presented with the majority shareholder's proposal to sell the entire corporation to a third party, the ultimate focus on value maximization is the same as if the board itself had decided to sell the corporation to a third party. When the entire sale to a third party is proposed, negotiated and timed by a majority shareholder, however, the board cannot realistically seek any alternative because the majority shareholder has the right to vote its shares in favor of the third-party transaction it proposed for the board's consideration. Nevertheless, in such situations, the directors are obliged to make an informed and deliberate judgment, in good faith, about whether the sale to a third party that is being proposed by the majority shareholder will result in a maximization of value for the minority shareholders.

In this case, because the minority shareholders of Chemical were powerless to out-vote ARCO, they had only one decision to make: whether to accept the tender offer from Lyondell or to seek an appraisal value of their shares in the ensuing merger. Given ARCO's majority shareholder 80% voting power, under the circumstances of this case, the Chemical Directors did not have the ability to act on an informed basis to secure the best value reasonably available for all shareholders in any alternative to the third-party transaction with Lyondell that ARCO had negotiated.[34] The Chemical Directors did, however, have the duty to act on an informed basis to independently ascertain how the merger consideration being offered in the third party Transaction with Lyondell compared to Chemical's value as a going concern.

As noted, a board of directors has a duty under 8 Del. C. § 251(b) to act in an informed and deliberate manner in determining whether to approve an agreement of merger before submitting the proposal to the stockholders. In the absence of a majority shareholder, we have held that directors "may not abdicate that duty by leaving to the shareholders alone the decision to approve or disapprove the agreement."[35] A fortiori, when the proposal to merge with a third party is negotiated by the majority shareholder, the board cannot abdicate that duty by leaving it to the shareholders alone to approve or disprove the

34. See Paramount Communications v. QVC Network, Inc., Del.Supr., 637 A.2d 34 (1994).

35. See Paramount Communications, Inc. v. Time, Inc., Del.Supr., 571 A.2d 1140, 1142—43 n. 4 (1989) (quoting Smith v. Van Gorkom, Del.Supr., 488 A.2d 858, 873 (1985)). See generally Aronson v. Lewis, Del. Supr., 473 A.2d 805, 811–13 (1984). See also Pogostin v. Rice, Del.Supr., 480 A.2d 619 (1984).

merger agreement[36] because the majority shareholder's voting power makes the outcome a preordained conclusion. To paraphrase the Court of Chancery in a similar context and applying its holding to this case:

> [O]nce having assumed the position of directors of [Chemical], a corporation that had stockholders other than [ARCO], [the directors] become fiduciaries for the minority shareholders, with a concomitant affirmative duty to protect the interests of the minority, as well as the majority, stockholders. Thus, the [Chemical] Board, in carrying out its affirmative duty to protect the interests of the minority, could not abdicate its obligation to make an informed decision on the fairness of the merger by simply deferring to the judgment of the controlling shareholder . . .[37]

When a majority of a corporation's voting shares are owned by a single entity, there is a significant diminution in the voting power of the minority stockholders.[38] Consequently, minority stockholders must rely for protection on the fiduciary duties owed to them by the board of directors.[39] Under the circumstances presented in this case, although the Chemical Board could not effectively seek an alternative to the proposed Lyondell sale by auction or agreement, and had no fiduciary responsibility to engage in either futile exercise, its ultimate statutory duties under Section 251 and attendant fiduciary obligations remained inviolable.

Effective representation of the financial interests of the minority shareholders imposed upon the Chemical Board an affirmative responsibility to protect those minority shareholders' interests. This responsibility required the Chemical Board to: first, conduct a critical assessment of the third-party Transaction with Lyondell that was proposed by the majority shareholder; and second, make an independent determination whether that transaction maximized value for all shareholders. The Chemical Directors had a duty to fulfill this obligation faithfully and with due care so that the minority shareholders would be able to make an informed decision about whether to accept the Lyondell Transaction tender offer price or to seek an appraisal of their shares. McMullin's Amended Complaint alleges that these statutory duties and fiduciary responsibilities were not discharged properly by the directors of Chemical.

McMullin's Amended Complaint

McMullin does not dispute ARCO's right to sell its own 80% interest in Chemical for whatever consideration might have been acceptable to it, whether for cash or stock or a mixture of cash and

---

36. Sealy Mattress Co. of New Jersey v. Sealy, Inc., Del. Ch., 532 A.2d 1324, 1338 (1987).

37. Id.

38. Paramount Communications v. QVC Network, Inc., Del.Supr., 637 A.2d 34, 42 (1994).

39. Id. at 43.

stock. . . . The Amended Complaint does contend that the Chemical Board's recommendation to approve the Lyondell Transaction implicated the directors' ultimate fiduciary duty that was described in *Revlon* and its progeny[43]—to focus on whether shareholder value has been maximized. We agree with that contention because, rather than selling only its own 80% interest, ARCO negotiated for, with the Chemical Board's approval, the entire sale of Chemical to Lyondell.

The Amended Complaint would withstand a motion to dismiss if it successfully alleged facts that, if true, would rebut the procedural presumption of the business judgment rule. To do that, McMullin had to successfully allege that the Chemical Board had breached any one of its triad of fiduciary duties of care, loyalty or good faith. McMullin contends that the allegations in her Amended Complaint demonstrate that the Chemical Board breached both its duty of care and its duty of loyalty. If McMullin is correct with regard to either or both of her contentions, the Chemical Directors' motion to dismiss should have been denied.

Care Allegations

Under 8 Del C. § 251, a director is required "to act in an informed and deliberate manner in determining whether to approve an agreement of merger before submitting the proposal to the stockholders."[44] A director's duty to exercise an informed business judgment implicates the duty of care. Director liability for breaching the duty of care "is predicated upon concepts of gross negligence."[46]

McMullin's Amended Complaint alleges that ARCO initiated and timed the Transaction to benefit itself because ARCO needed cash to fund the $3.3 billion cash acquisition of Union Texas Petroleum Holdings that ARCO announced on May 4, 1998.[47] McMullin alleges that the Chemical Board authorized ARCO to unilaterally negotiate the merger agreement without establishing any procedural safeguards to protect the interests of the minority shareholders.[48] According to the

---

43. See, e.g., Paramount Communications, Inc. v. QVC Network, Inc., Del.Supr., 637 A.2d 34 (1994).

44. Smith v. Van Gorkom, Del.Supr., 488 A.2d 858, 873 (1985).

46. Aronson v. Lewis, Del.Supr., 473 A.2d 805, 812 (1984); Citron v. Fairchild Camera & Instrument Corp., Del.Supr., 569 A.2d 53, 66 (1989). Smith v. Van Gorkom, 488 A.2d at 873. See Brehm v. Eisner, Del. Supr., 746 A.2d 244, 259 (2000). See also Veasey & Manning, Codified Standard—Safe Harbor or Uncharted Reef? 35 Bus.Law. 919, 928 (1980).

47. Paragraph 20 of McMullin's Amended Complaint states:

On or about May 4, 1998, ARCO announced that it had agreed to acquire

Union Texas Petroleum Holdings ("UTP") for $29 per share or $3.3 billion in cash. To fund the purchase without sacrificing its single-A credit rating, according to Platt's Oilgram News, "ARCO said it will quickly move to sell $1–bil to $2–bil of non strategic assets. Analysts immediately suspected that probably meant ARCO's 82.3% stake in Chemical."

48. Paragraph 26 of McMullin's Amended Complaint states:

In January 1998, Chemical's directors established a special committee of purportedly independent directors (the "Special Committee") to negotiate with ARCO regarding the proposed Secondary Offering/Repurchase Transaction. The

Amended Complaint, ARCO not only conducted the negotiations but also placed its own cash restrictions on potential bidders.[49] McMullin alleges that ARCO gained financial advantage from the immediate all-cash Transaction with Lyondell, at the expense of the minority shareholders, by sacrificing some of the value of Chemical, which might have been realized in a differently timed or structured agreement.[50]

The Amended Complaint alleges that the Chemical Board met only once to consider the Transaction negotiated by ARCO with Lyondell. At that meeting, ARCO's financial advisor, Salomon Smith Barney, made a presentation to the Chemical Board regarding the terms of Lyondell's proposal and the sale process conducted by ARCO.[51] The Chemical Board approved the Transaction with Lyondell at that one meeting on the basis of the disclosures made to them by ARCO's financial advisor.

The business judgment rule is rebutted if the plaintiff shows that the directors failed to exercise due care in informing themselves before making their decision.[52] The imposition of time constraints on a board's decision-making process may compromise the integrity of its deliberative process.[53] History has demonstrated boards "that have

Board failed, however, to authorize the Special Committee to protect and enhance the interests of the Company and its public shareholders in connection with the subsequent sale of the Company to Lyondell. Since the Special Committee had already been authorized to act on behalf of the Company and its public shareholders in connection with the Secondary Offering/Repurchase. Transaction, the Board's failure to empower the Special Committee to actively participate in the sale of the Company is inexplicable.

49. Paragraph 29 of McMullin's Amended Complaint states:

Specifically, the Financial Times reported on June 4, 1998, that ARCO said "other companies had shown an interest in buying all or part of its chemical assets, but none had been prepared to pay what it considered a high enough price, and its 'strong preference for cash had excluded potential bidders wanting to offer only stock."

50. Paragraph 27 of McMullin's Amended Complaint states:

Additionally, the individual defendants relied upon ARCO and its financial advisor, Salomon Smith Barney ("SSB"), to conduct the solicitation of interested buyers and all negotiations for the sale of the Company, despite the fact that ARCO's need for cash and, as more fully described below, its insistence on an all-

cash bid conflicted with the interests of the public shareholders to receive maximum consideration for their shares in a sale of the Company.

51. Paragraph 27 of McMullin's Amended Complaint states:

Accordingly, it was ARCO and SSB, which made a presentation to the Board on June 18, 1998 regarding the terms of Lyondell's proposal and the sale process conducted by ARCO. Merrill Lynch, the Company's nominal financial advisor, was limited to making a presentation regarding the value of the Company and simply opined that the transaction was fair—not that it was the maximum obtainable in a sale of the Company. Indeed, given ARCO's control of the sale process, neither the individual defendants nor Merrill Lynch possessed sufficient information to make such a determination. Thus, in agreeing to the Acquisition, the individual defendants failed to properly inform themselves of Chemical's highest transactional value.

52. *Cede II*, Del.Supr., 634 A.2d 345, 366–370 (1993); Smith v. Van Gorkom, Del. Supr., 488 A.2d 858, 872–873 (1985); see also Brehm v. Eisner, Del.Supr., 746 A.2d 244, 259 (2000).

53. Citron v. Fairchild Camera & Instrument Corp., Del.Supr., 569 A.2d 53, 67 (1989).

failed to exercise due care are frequently boards that have been rushed."[54] The Amended Complaint alleges that on June 3, 1998, ARCO was asking the Chemical Board to repurchase some of its 80% holdings[55] and on June 18 was asking the Chemical board to sell the entire corporation to Lyondell.[56]

One can reasonably infer from the factual allegations in McMullin's Amended Complaint that the Chemical Board compromised its deliberative process by seeking to accommodate ARCO's immediate need for cash. The Chemical Directors were obligated to determine whether the third-party Transaction with Lyondell that was being advanced by the majority shareholder, would maximize value for the minority shareholders in the sale of Chemical. The specific allegations contained in McMullin's Amended Complaint, if true, suggest that the directors of Chemical breached their duty of care by approving the merger with Lyondell without adequately informing themselves about the transaction and without determining whether the merger consideration equaled or exceeded Chemical's appraisal value as a going concern.

Loyalty Allegations

When the Chemical Board was considering a sale of the entire corporation, it was impermissible for the directors to allow any improper influence to compromise their evaluation of whether the proposed third party transaction with Lyondell would achieve maximum value for all Chemical shareholders. The ARCO officers and designees on Chemical's board owed Chemical's minority shareholders "an uncompromising duty of loyalty."[59] There is no dilution of that obligation in a parent subsidiary context for the individuals who acted in a dual capacity as officers or designees of ARCO and as directors of Chemical.

The substantive protections of the business judgment rule can be claimed only by disinterested directors whose conduct otherwise meets the tests of the rule's procedural requirements. McMullin's

---

54. Id.

55. Paragraph 21 of McMullin's Amended Complaint states:

On June 3, 1998, Bloomberg reported that ARCO intended to reduce its stake in Chemical to 50 percent and to raise $2.15 billion by selling shares back to Chemical and to the public. At that time, the two companies anticipated ARCO would sell about 24 million of its 80 million shares to the public in a secondary offering and Chemical would spend up to $850 million to buy approximately 15 million shares from ARCO, to reduce ARCO's stake in the Company to 50 percent (the "Secondary Offering/Repurchase Transaction"). This transaction, which was expected to be completed in July 1998, would have enabled ARCO to pay off $1.4 billion in short-term debt incurred in the $3.3 billion buy-out of the UTP.

56. Paragraph 22 of McMullin's Amended Complaint states:

Instead, on June 18, 1998, Chemical and Lyondell announced that they had entered into a definitive merger agreement whereby Lyondell would acquire Chemical for $57.75 per share with an aggregate value of approximately $1.15 billion, through a cash tender offer followed by a merger for untendered shares.

59. Weinberger v. UOP, Inc., Del.Supr., 457 A.2d 701, 710 (1983).

Amended Complaint alleges that a majority of Chemical's board of directors was dominated by ARCO. In assessing director independence, Delaware courts apply a subjective "actual person" standard to determine whether a "given" director was likely to be affected in the same or similar circumstances.[62]

The Amended Complaint alleges that six of the twelve Chemical Directors were employed by ARCO, to wit: ARCO's chief financial officer and executive vice-president, another ARCO executive vice-president, and four senior vice-presidents of ARCO. Two other Chemical Directors were alleged to have prior affiliations with ARCO, as officers of other ARCO subsidiaries. McMullin alleges that none of those eight "ARCO controlled" Chemical Directors abstained from the discussions or the vote concerning the proposed transaction between Chemical and Lyondell. McMullin alleges that these ARCO connections caused the Chemical Board to enter into the third-party Transaction with Lyondell.

The allegations of loyalty to ARCO in McMullin's Amended Complaint challenge the independence of the Chemical Board. The Amended Complaint alleges that, if the Chemical Directors had analyzed the sale of Chemical to Lyondell with the goal of maximizing value for all shareholders and not just to accommodate ARCO, the Chemical board would have concluded that the minority shareholders would have fared better in an appraisal than the Lyondell Transaction that it recommended to them. The record reflects that the defendant directors should be required to file an answer to the well-pled loyalty allegations in McMullin's Amended Complaint, regarding the effects of the ARCO-related conflicts . . . [in particular,] because it is alleged that those "ARCO conflicted" directors on the Chemical Board did not abstain from participation in approving the third-party Transaction that ARCO had negotiated with Lyondell.[64]

Improper Delegation Allegations

According to McMullin, the Chemical Directors violated their fiduciary duties of care and loyalty to the minority shareholders by the initial decision to delegate the management of the sale process to a conflicted majority shareholder and by the subsequent uninformed decision to recommend approval of the third-party sale of Lyondell. The Amended Complaint charges ARCO with a conflict of interest in negotiating the sale of Chemical because ARCO insisted upon a cash only transaction. McMullin alleges that the Chemical Directors either disregarded the best interests of the minority shareholders or subordinated them to ARCO's immediate cash needs.

The defendants rely upon the decision of the Court of Chancery in *Unimation*[65] as support for their proposition that the Chemical

62. Cinerama, Inc. v. Technicolor, Inc., Del.Supr., 663 A.2d 1156, 1167 (1995).

64. Cinerama, Inc. v. Technicolor, Inc., Del.Supr., 663 A.2d 1156, 1167 (1995).

65. Van de Walle v. Unimation, Del.

Directors "breached no fiduciary duty, whether of due care or loyalty, by allowing [controlling shareholder's] representatives to speak for the minority in the negotiations." We agree that the Chemical Board could properly rely on the majority shareholder to conduct preliminary negotiations. The Chemical Board, however, had an ultimate statutory duty and fiduciary responsibility to make an informed and independent decision on whether to recommend approval of the third-party Transaction with Lyondell to the minority shareholders.[66] Fulfilling that obligation directly affected the minority shareholders' decision about whether to refrain from tendering their shares to Lyondell and pursuing an appraisal action during the second step of the Transaction.

The procedural posture in this appeal involves a motion to dismiss McMullin's Amended Complaint. In *Unimation*, the Court of Chancery reviewed a full trial record and concluded that the board satisfied its obligation to act independently and fully inform itself of the actions taken by the majority shareholder in negotiating a sale of the entire company:

> Unimation's Directors were fully informed and knowledgeable of the eight-month market search for potential buyers and of Unimation's business, prospects, and value. Those directors discussed the potential Westinghouse merger almost daily between the execution of the merger agreement and the board meeting at which the agreement was approved. Moreover, the Unimation director's meeting was preceded by an extensive meeting of the same persons, sitting as the Condec board, at which Drexel discussed the basis of its opinion that the merger was financially fair to Condec and the Unimation majority. In those circumstances, the fact that the formal Unimation directors' meeting was short is of no moment, because for months Unimation's directors had been kept fully apprised of all relevant facts on an ongoing basis, and they had already considered those facts before their formal meeting was convened.[67]

The issue of whether the directors reached an informed decision to "sell" Chemical on June 18, 1998 must be determined upon the basis of the information then reasonably available to the directors and relevant to their decision to recommend approval of the Lyondell merger proposal to the shareholders.[68] In contrast to the board of director's conduct in Unimation, the Amended Complaint filed by McMullin alleges that ARCO unilaterally initiated, structured and nego-

Ch., C.A. No. 7046, slip op. at 29, 1991 WL 29303, Jacobs, V.C. (1991).

66. See Grimes v. Donald, Del.Supr., 673 A.2d 1207, 1215 (1996) overruled in part on other grounds Brehm v. Eisner, Del.Supr., 746 A.2d 244 (2000).

67. Van de Walle v. Unimation, Del. Ch., C.A. No. 7046, slip op. at 14, 1991 WL 29303, Jacobs, V.C. (1991).

68. Smith v. Van Gorkom, Del.Supr., 488 A.2d 858, 874 (1985).

tiated the Transaction to sell all of Chemical.[69] The Amended Complaint contends that as of June 18, the Chemical Board had made no determination of Chemical's entire value as a going concern before making its expedited decision to recommend approval of ARCO's proposed third-party Transaction with Lyondell.

One can reasonably infer from the Amended Complaint that Chemical's minority shareholders might have received more than $57.75 cash in an appraisal proceeding, if the Chemical Directors had fulfilled their fiduciary duties to ascertain whether the proposed sale to Lyondell maximized value for all shareholders. When all of the facts are presented, the Court of Chancery may conclude that the Chemical Directors acted like the directors in *Unimation*—independently and on a fully informed basis. At this stage of the proceedings, however, the Chemical Directors must file an answer to the well-pled allegations to the contrary in McMullin's Amended Complaint.

Disclosure Claim

In properly discharging their fiduciary responsibilities, directors of Delaware corporations must exercise due care, good faith and loyalty whenever they communicate with shareholders about the corporation's affairs.[70] When shareholder action is requested, directors are required to provide shareholders with all information that is material to the action being requested and "to provide a balanced, truthful account of all matters disclosed in the communication with shareholders."[71] The materiality standard requires that directors disclose all facts which, "under all the circumstances, . . . would have assumed actual significance in the deliberations of the reasonable shareholder."[72] These disclosure standards are well established.

Earlier this year, we decided another case involving alleged disclosure violations when minority shareholders were presented with the choice of either tendering their shares or being "cashed out" in a third-party merger transaction that had been pre-approved by the majority shareholder.[73] In *Skeen*, it was argued that the minority shareholders should have been given all of the financial data they would need if they were making an independent determination of fair value. We declined to establish "a new disclosure standard where appraisal is an option."[74] We adhere to our holding in *Skeen*.

69. See Weinberger v. UOP, Inc., Del. Supr., 457 A.2d 701, 711(1983).

70. See Malone v. Brincat, Del.Supr., 722 A.2d 5, 10 (1998); Emerald Partners v. Berlin, Del.Supr., 726 A.2d 1215, 1223 (1999); see also Zirn v. VLI Corp., Del.Supr., 621 A.2d 773, 778 (1993).

71. Malone v. Brincat, 722 A.2d at 10. Accord Skeen v. Jo-Ann Stores, Inc., Del. Supr., 750 A.2d 1170, 1171 (2000); Arnold v. Society for Sav. Bancorp., Del.Supr., 650 A.2d 1270 (1994); Zirn v. VLI Corp., 621 A.2d at 778–79.

72. Arnold v. Society for Sav. Bancorp., 650 A.2d at 1277 (quoting TSC Indus. v. Northway, Inc., 426 U.S. 438, 449, 96 S.Ct. 2126, 48 L.Ed.2d 757 (1976)).

73. Skeen v. Jo-Ann Stores, Inc., Del. Supr., 750 A.2d 1170 (2000).

74. Id. at 1174.

McMullin's Amended Complaint alleges that the Chemical Directors breached their fiduciary duty by failing to disclose to the minority shareholders material information necessary to decide whether to accept the Lyondell tender offer or to seek appraisal under 8 Del. C. § 262.[75] The Court of Chancery summarized the plaintiff's allegations that the defendants breached their duty of disclosure by omitting from the 14D–9 the following information: indications of interest from other potential acquirers; the handling of these potential offers; the restrictions and constraints imposed by ARCO on the potential sale of Chemical; the information provided to Merrill Lynch and the valuation methodologies used by Merrill Lynch. In a similar context, the Court of Chancery has held the fact that the majority shareholder controls the outcome of the vote on the merger "makes a more compelling case for the application of the recognized disclosure standards."[76]

When a complaint alleges disclosure violations, courts are required to decide a mixed question of fact and law. In the specific context of this case, an answer to the complaint, discovery and a trial may all be necessary to develop a complete factual record before deciding whether, as a matter of law, the Chemical Directors breached their duty to disclose all material facts to the minority shareholders. The disclosure violations alleged in McMullin's Amended Complaint are, if true, sufficient to withstand a motion to dismiss.

Affirmative Defense

ARCO submits that this Court should affirm the Court of Chancery's judgment on a basis it did not reach, to wit: Article Seventh of the Chemical certificate of incorporation which was adopted pursuant to 8 Del. C. § 102(b)(7) and provides:

> To the fullest extent permitted by the General Corporation Law of Delaware as the same exists or may hereafter be amended, a director of the Company shall not be liable to the Company or its stockholders for monetary damages for breach of fiduciary duty as a director.

We have decided not to address that issue in this appeal. In *Emerald Partners*, this Court noted "for the guidance of the Court of Chancery and the parties, that the shield from liability provided by a certificate of incorporation provision adopted pursuant to 8 Del. C. § 102(b)(7) is in the nature of an affirmative defense. Defendants seeking exculpation under such a provision will normally bear the burden of establishing each of its elements."[79] We also note, however,

---

75. Paragraph 38 of McMullin's Amended Complaint states:

"Accordingly, Chemical shareholders could not determine from these materials what the intrinsic value of the shares was and why the proposed acquisition by Lyondell was preferable to other alternatives."

76. Sealy Mattress Co. of New Jersey, Inc. v. Sealy, Inc., Del.Supr., 532 A.2d 1324, 1338 (1987) (quoting Wacht v. Continental Hosts, Ltd., Del. Ch., C.A. No. 7954, slip op. at 7, 1986 WL 4492, Berger, V.C. (April 11, 1986)).

79. Emerald Partners v. Berlin, Del. Supr., 726 A.2d 1215, 1223–24 (1999) (inter-

that such provisions cannot provide protection for directors who breach their duty of loyalty.

Conclusion

The judgment of the Court of Chancery is reversed. This matter is remanded for further proceedings in accordance with this opinion.

nal citations omitted); see also Zirn v. VLI Corp., Del.Supr., 681 A.2d 1050 (1996); Arnold v. Society for Sav. Bancorp., 650 A.2d 1270.

CHAPTER X

INSIDER TRADING

SECTION 2. SECURITIES EXCHANGE ACT § 10(B) AND RULE 10B–5

Insert the following case at p. 779 of the Unabridged Edition, and page 550 of the Concise Edition, after the Note on Cady, Roberts:

The Wharf (Holdings) Limited v. United International Holdings, Inc.

Supreme Court of the United States, 2001.
532 U.S. 588.

■ JUSTICE BREYER delivered the opinion of the Court.

This securities fraud action focuses upon a company that sold an option to buy stock while secretly intending never to honor the option. The question before us is whether this conduct violates § 10(b) of the Securities Exchange Act of 1934, which prohibits using "any manipulative or deceptive device or contrivance" "in connection with the purchase or sale of any security." 48 Stat. 891, *15 U.S.C. § 78j(b)*; see also *17 C.F.R. § 240.10b–5 (2000)*. We conclude that it does.

I

Respondent United International Holdings, Inc., a Colorado-based company, sued petitioner The Wharf (Holdings) Limited, a Hong Kong firm, in Colorado's Federal District Court. United said that in October 1992 Wharf had sold it an option to buy 10% of the stock of a new Hong Kong cable system. But, United alleged, at the time of the sale Wharf secretly intended not to permit United to exercise the option. United claimed that Wharf's conduct amounted to a fraud "in connection with the . . . sale of [a] security," prohibited by § 10(b), and violated numerous state laws as well. A jury found in United's favor. The Court of Appeals for the Tenth Circuit upheld that verdict. *210 F.3d 1207 (2000)*. And we granted certiorari to consider whether the dispute fell within the scope of § 10(b).

The relevant facts, viewed in the light most favorable to the verdict winner, United, are as follows. In 1991, the Hong Kong government announced that it would accept bids for the award of an exclusive license to operate a cable television system in Hong Kong. Wharf decided to prepare a bid. Wharf's chairman, Peter Woo, instructed one of its managing directors, Stephen Ng, to find a business partner with cable system experience. Ng found United. And United sent several employees to Hong Kong to help prepare Wharf's application, negotiate contracts, design the system, and arrange financing.

United asked to be paid for its services with a right to invest in the cable system if Wharf should obtain the license. During August and September 1992, while United's employees were at work helping Wharf, Wharf and United negotiated about the details of that payment. Wharf prepared a draft letter of intent that contemplated giving United the right to become a co-investor, owning 10% of the system. But the parties did not sign the letter of intent. And in September, when Wharf submitted its bid, it told the Hong Kong authorities that Wharf would be the system's initial sole owner, Lodging to App. AY–4, although Wharf would also "consider" allowing United to become an investor, *id.*, at AY–6.

In early October 1992, Ng met with a United representative, who told Ng that United would continue to help only if Wharf gave United an enforceable right to invest. Ng then orally granted United an option with the following terms: (1) United had the right to buy 10% of the future system's stock; (2) the price of exercising the option would be 10% of the system's capital requirements minus the value of United's previous services (including expenses); (3) United could exercise the option only if it showed that it could fund its 10% share of the capital required for at least the first 18 months; and (4) the option would expire if not exercised within six months of the date that Wharf received the license. The parties continued to negotiate about how to write documents that would embody these terms, but they never reduced the agreement to writing.

In May 1993, Hong Kong awarded the cable franchise to Wharf. United raised $66 million designed to help finance its 10% share. In July or August 1993, United told Wharf that it was ready to exercise its option. But Wharf refused to permit United to buy any of the system's stock. Contemporaneous internal Wharf documents suggested that Wharf had never intended to carry out its promise. For example, a few weeks before the key October 1992 meeting, Ng had prepared a memorandum stating that United wanted a right to invest that it could exercise if it was able to raise the necessary capital. A handwritten note by Wharf's Chairman Woo replied, "No, no, no, we don't accept that." App. DT–187; Lodging to App. AI–1. In September 1993, after meeting with the Wharf board to discuss United's investment in the cable system, Ng wrote to another Wharf executive, "How do we get out?" *Id.*, at CY–1. In December 1993, after United had filed documents with the Securities Exchange Commission representing that United was negotiating the acquisition of a 10% interest in the cable system, an internal Wharf memo stated that "[o]ur next move should be to claim that our directors got quite *upset* over these representations.... Publicly, we *do not* acknowledge [United's] opportunity" to acquire the 10% interest. *Id.,* at DF–1 (emphasis in original). In the margin of a December 1993 letter from United discussing its expectation of investing in the cable system, Ng wrote, "[B]e careful, must deflect this! [H]ow?" *Id.,* at DI–1. Other Wharf documents referred to the need to "back ped[al]," *id.,* at DG–1, and "stall," *id.,* at DJ–1.

These documents, along with other evidence, convinced the jury that Wharf, through Ng, had orally sold United an option to purchase a 10% interest in the future cable system while secretly intending not to permit United to exercise the option, in violation of § 10(b) of the Securities Exchange Act and various state laws. The jury awarded United compensatory damages of $67 million and, in light of "circumstances of fraud, malice, or willful and wanton conduct," App. EM–18, punitive damages of $58.5 million on the state-law claims. As we have said, the Court of Appeals upheld the jury's award. *210 F.3d 1207 (C.A.10 2000)*. And we granted certiorari to determine whether Wharf's oral sale of an option it intended not to honor is prohibited by § 10(b).

II

Section 10(b) of the Securities Exchange Act makes it "unlawful for any person ... [t]o use or employ, in connection with the purchase or sale of any security ..., any manipulative or deceptive device or contrivance in contravention of such rules and regulations as the [SEC] may prescribe." *15 U.S.C. § 78j.*

Pursuant to this provision, the SEC has promulgated Rule 10b–5. That Rule forbids the use, "in connection with the purchase or sale of any security," of (1) "any device, scheme, or artifice to defraud"; (2) "any untrue statement of a material fact"; (3) the omission of "a material fact necessary in order to make the statements made ... not misleading"; or (4) any other "act, practice, or course of business" that "operates ... as a fraud or deceit." *17 C.F.R. § 240.10b–5 (2000)*.

To succeed in a Rule 10b–5 suit, a private plaintiff must show that the defendant used, in connection with the purchase or sale of a security, one of the four kinds of manipulative or deceptive devices to which the Rule refers, and must also satisfy certain other requirements not at issue here. See, *e.g., 15 U.S.C. § 78j* (requiring the "use of any means or instrumentality of interstate commerce or of the mails, or of any facility of any national securities exchange"); *Ernst & Ernst v. Hochfelder*, 425 U.S. 185, 193, 96 S.Ct. 1375, 47 L.Ed.2d 668 (1976) (requiring scienter, meaning "intent to deceive, manipulate, or defraud"); *Basic Inc. v. Levinson*, 485 U.S. 224, 231–232, 108 S.Ct. 978, 99 L.Ed.2d 194 (1988) (requiring that any misrepresentation be material); *id.,* at 243, 108 S.Ct. 978 (requiring that the plaintiff sustain damages through reliance on the misrepresentation).

In deciding whether the Rule covers the circumstances present here, we must assume that the "security" at issue is not the cable system stock, but the option to purchase that stock. That is because the Court of Appeals found that Wharf conceded this point. *210 F.3d, at 1221* ("Wharf does not contest on appeal the classification of the option as a security"). That concession is consistent with the language of the Securities Exchange Act, which defines "security" to include both "any . . . option . . . on any security" and "any . . . right to . . . purchase" stock. *15 U.S.C. § 78c(a)(10) (1994 ed., Supp. V)*; see also *Blue Chip Stamps v. Manor Drug Stores*, 421 U.S. 723, 751, 95 S.Ct. 1917, 44 L.Ed.2d 539 (1975) ("holders of . . . options, and other contractual rights or duties to purchase . . . securities" are " 'purchasers' . . . of securities for purposes of Rule 10b–5"). And Wharf's current effort to deny the concession, by pointing to an ambiguous statement in its Court of Appeals reply brief, comes too late and is unconvincing. See Reply Brief for Petitioners 16, n. 8 (citing Reply Brief for Appellants in Nos. 97–1421, 98–1002 (CA10), pp. 5–6). Consequently, we must decide whether Wharf's secret intent not to honor the option it sold United amounted to a misrepresentation (or other conduct forbidden by the Rule) in connection with the sale of the option.

Wharf argues that its conduct falls outside the Rule's scope for two basic reasons. First, Wharf points out that its agreement to grant United an option to purchase shares in the cable system was an oral agreement. And it says that § 10(b) does not cover oral contracts of sale. Wharf points to *Blue Chip Stamps,* in which this Court construed the Act's "purchase or sale" language to mean that only "actual purchasers and sellers of securities" have standing to bring a private action for damages. See *421 U.S., at 730–731, 95 S.Ct. 1917.* Wharf notes that the Court's interpretation of the Act flowed in part from the need to protect defendants against lawsuits that "turn largely on which oral version of a series of occurrences the jury may decide to credit." *Blue Chip Stamps, supra*, at 742, 95 S.Ct. 1917. And it claims that an oral purchase or sale would pose a similar problem of proof and thus should not satisfy the Rule's "purchase or sale" requirement.

Blue Chip Stamps, however, involved the very different question whether the Act protects a person who did not actually buy securities, but who might have done so had the seller told the truth. The Court held that the Act does not cover such a potential buyer, in part for the reason that Wharf states. But United is not a potential buyer; by providing Wharf with its services, it actually bought the option that Wharf sold. And *Blue Chip Stamps* said nothing to suggest that oral purchases or sales fall outside the scope of the Act. Rather, the Court's concern was about "the abuse potential and proof problems inherent in suits by investors who neither bought nor sold, but asserted they would have traded absent fraudulent conduct by others." *United States v. O'Hagan*, 521 U.S. 642, 664, 117 S.Ct. 2199, 138 L.Ed.2d 724 (1997). Such a "potential purchase" claim would rest on facts, including the plaintiff's state of mind, that might be "totally unknown and unknowable to the defendant," depriving the jury of "the benefit of weighing the plaintiff's version against the defendant's version." *Blue Chip Stamps, supra,* at 746, 95 S.Ct. 1917. An actual sale, even if oral, would not create this problem, because both parties would be able to testify as to whether the relevant events had occurred.

Neither is there any other convincing reason to interpret the Act to exclude oral contracts as a class. The Act itself says that it applies to "any contract" for the purchase or sale of a security. *15 U.S.C. § § 78c(a)(13), (14).* Oral contracts for the sale of securities are sufficiently common that the Uniform Commercial Code and statutes of frauds in every State now consider them enforceable. See U.C.C. § 8–113 (Supp.2000) ("A contract . . . for the sale or purchase of a security is enforceable whether or not there is a writing signed or record authenticated by a party against whom enforcement is sought"); see also 2C U.L.A. 77–81 (Supp.2000) (table of enactments of U.C.C. Revised Art. 8 (amended 1994)) (noting adoption of § 8–113, with minor variations, by all States except Rhode Island and South Carolina); *R.I. Gen. Laws § 6A–8–322 (1999)* (repealed effective July 1, 2001) (making oral contracts for the sale of securities enforceable); § 6A–8–113 (2000 Cum.Supp.) (effective July 1, 2001) (same); *S.C.Code Ann. § 36–8–113 (Supp.2000)* (same); U.C.C. § 8–113 Comment (Supp.2000) ("[T]he statute of frauds is unsuited to the realities of the securities business"). Any exception for oral sales of securities would significantly limit the Act's coverage, thereby undermining its basic purposes.

Wharf makes a related but narrower argument that the Act does not encompass oral contracts of sale that are unenforceable under state law. But we do not reach that issue. The Court of Appeals held that Wharf's sale of the option was not covered by the then-applicable Colorado statute of frauds, *Colo.Rev.Stat. § 4–8–319* (repealed 1996), and hence was enforceable under state law. Though Wharf disputes the correctness of that holding, we ordinarily will not consider such a state-law issue, and we decline to do so here.

Second, Wharf argues that a secret reservation not to permit the exercise of an option falls outside § 10(b) because it does not "relat[e] to the value of a security purchase or the consideration paid"; hence it does "not implicate [§ 10(b)'s] policy of full disclosure." Brief for Petitioners 25, 26 (emphasis deleted). But even were it the case that the Act covers only misrepresentations likely to affect the value of securities, Wharf's secret reservation was such a misrepresentation. To sell an option while secretly intending not to permit the option's exercise is misleading, because a buyer normally presumes good faith. Cf., *e.g., Restatement (Second) of Torts § 530,* Comment *c* (1976) ("Since a promise necessarily carries with it the implied assertion of an intention to perform[,] it follows that a promise made without such an intention is fraudulent"). For similar reasons, the secret reservation misled United about the option's value. Since Wharf did not intend to honor the option, the option was, unbeknownst to United, valueless.

Finally, Wharf supports its claim for an exemption from the statute by characterizing this case as a "disput[e] over the ownership of securities." Brief for Petitioners 24. Wharf expresses concern that interpreting the Act to allow recovery in a case like this one will permit numerous plaintiffs to bring federal securities claims that are in reality no more than ordinary state breach-of-contract claims—actions that lie outside the Act's basic objectives. United's claim, however, is not simply that Wharf failed to carry out a promise to sell it securities. It is a claim that Wharf sold it a security (the option) while secretly intending from the very beginning not to honor the option. And United proved that secret intent with documentary evidence that went well beyond evidence of a simple failure to perform. Moreover, Wharf has not shown us that its concern has proven serious as a practical matter in the past. Cf. *Threadgill v. Black*, 730 F.2d 810, 811–812 (C.A.D.C.) (per curiam) (suggesting in 1984 that contracting to sell securities with the secret reservation not to perform one's obligations under the contract violates § 10(b)). Nor does Wharf persuade us that it is likely to prove serious in the future. Cf. Private Securities Litigation Reform Act of *1995, Pub.L. 104–67, § 21D(b)(2), 109* Stat. 747, codified at *15 U.S.C. § 78u–4(b)(2) (1994 ed., Supp. V)* (imposing, beginning in 1995, stricter pleading requirements in private securities fraud actions that, among other things, require that a complaint "state with particularity facts giving rise to a strong inference that the defendant acted with the required [fraudulent] state of mind").

For these reasons, the judgment of the Court of Appeals is

Affirmed.

———

Insert the following case at p. 818 of the Unabridged Edition, following the Note on Causation and Reliance:

AUSA Life Ins. Co. v. Ernst and Young

United States Court of Appeals, Second Circuit.
206 F.3d 202.

■ Before: WINTER, CHIEF JUDGE, OAKES and JACOBS, CIRCUIT JUDGES.

■ JUDGE JACOBS concurs in the mandate of the opinion for the court in a separate opinion. CHIEF JUDGE WINTER dissents in a separate opinion.

■ OAKES, SENIOR CIRCUIT JUDGE:

I.   Introduction

Plaintiffs-appellants AUSA Life Insurance Company, Bankers United Life Assurance Company, Crown Life Insurance Company, General

Services Life Insurance Company, Life Investors Insurance Company of America, Modern Woodmen of America, Monumental Life Insurance Company, The Mutual Life Insurance Company of New York, and The Prudential Life Insurance Company of America (collectively, "insurance companies" or "investors") appeal from the dismissal of their Securities Act and other claims against Ernst & Young ("E & Y") after a bench trial in the United States District Court for the Southern District of New York (William C. Conner, *Judge*).

II.   Facts

The appellants are insurance companies that invested in the securities of JWP, Inc., a company which ultimately went belly-up, causing the appellants to lose most of their investments. The appellee is the accounting firm that served as the independent auditor for JWP from 1985 through 1992, the period during which the appellants invested in JWP and the period during which the allegedly fraudulent activity was occurring.

The appellants made their initial purchases of JWP's notes in November of 1988. Through March 1992, they purchased additional JWP notes, the investments totaling $149 million. The notes were purchased in accordance with agreements ("Note Agreements") which included, among other things, the financial representations made by JWP at the time of the notes' issuances, future procedures to which JWP agreed to adhere for certifying JWP's maintained financial viability, procedures to be followed in the event of a default on the notes, and the like.

In purchasing the notes, appellants relied on JWP's past financial statements, including annual reports certified by E & Y. These financial statements were required, under the Note Agreements, to be kept in accordance with generally accepted accounting principles ("GAAP"). Also, at the time of each annual audit by E & Y, E & Y was required under the Note Agreements to furnish to JWP a letter for JWP to transmit to noteholders, referred to as a "no-default certificate" or a "negative assurance letter," which stated that E & Y had audited JWP's financial statements and that JWP was in compliance with the financial covenants in the Note Agreements.

In this instance and consistently, E & Y's statements about JWP's financial health were less than accurate and were not always in accordance with GAAP or GAAS ("generally accepted auditing standards"). However, E & Y did not fail to notice that often JWP's financial representations about itself were not in accordance with GAAP; rather, E & Y consistently noticed, protested, and then acquiesced in these misrepresentations:

> E & Y's failure lay in the seeming spinelessness of John LaBarca [the partner in charge of the JWP audit] and the other E & Y accountants in their dealings with JWP, and particularly with its CEO, Ernest Grendi. . . . Grendi almost invariably succeeded in

either persuading or bullying them to agree that JWP's books required no adjustment. Part of the problem was undoubtedly the close personal relationship between Grendi and LaBarca. Grendi had been a partner of LaBarca in E & Y's predecessor firm and they continued to be good friends, regularly jogging together in preparation for the New York City Marathon.

AUSA, 991 F.Supp. at 248. "It became a well-worn inside joke to refer to the lax accounting standards at JWP as 'EGAAP,' an acronym for Ernest Grendi's Accepted Accounting Practices." *Id.* at 253.

JWP rapidly expanded between 1984 and 1992 with many aggressive acquisitions. The expansion was mainly financed by private placements of debt securities, which put JWP in an increasingly leveraged position. JWP's final, fatal acquisition was that of Businessland, Inc., in 1991. Businessland was a retailer of computers and a supplier of software. It had lost an average of ten million dollars a month over the ten months prior to the acquisition, and its auditors had issued a "going concern" qualification on its most recent audited financial statement, which indicated that the auditors doubted the company could survive.

Notwithstanding the gloomy financial picture, JWP executives saw potential. They believed that Businessland's structure could be converted into that of a "value-added" systems integrator; they thought that Businessland could be meshed into JWP's existing business which was heavily involved in installing wiring for computer networks; and they intended to capitalize on Businessland's trained sales force and existing clientele.

Unfortunately, this ambitious business venture did not evolve as envisioned. Upon JWP's acquisition of Businessland, JWP was forced to advance money to Businessland to meet the latter's operating expenditures. As well, the planned closure of most of Businessland's retail stores took longer than was initially anticipated. During the same general time period (the early 1990s), the retail computer market was the battleground for the "PC price wars," periods of intense competition, on bases including price. To nail the coffin shut, there was a downward trend in office construction which negatively impacted the electrical construction division of JWP.

In early 1992, David Sokol, JWP's new President and Chief Operating Officer, took note of what appeared to be serious accounting irregularities in JWP's records and statements. In August of 1992, JWP retained Deloitte & Touche ("D & T"), another major accounting firm, to review thoroughly JWP's books and E & Y's audits.

D & T concluded that JWP's annual reports for 1990–1992 should be restated to reduce the 1990 after-tax net income by 15% (from $59 million to $50 million), that the 1991 after-tax income should be reduced by 52% from $60 million to $29 million, and that [a] 1992 loss of $612 million with a corresponding net worth of negative $176 million should be reflected. E & Y concurred.

JWP was able to continue paying the interest due on its notes through 1992, and JWP made partial payments through April 1993. However, JWP ultimately defaulted and was placed in involuntary bankruptcy in December 1993. Some appellants sold their notes at a huge loss in 1993 and 1994, and some appellants partially exchanged some of their notes for cash and securities of a lesser total value than the original notes. At the end of the day, appellants sustained at least a loss of approximately $100 million in lost principal and unpaid interest.

Over twenty lawsuits were filed as a result of JWP's demise. A consolidated suit, comprised of plaintiffs who had purchased JWP common stock in the open market between May 1, 1991, and October 2, 1992, was settled, as was a suit comprised of those who had sold their businesses to JWP in exchange for JWP common stock ...

In the district court, plaintiffs made essentially three categories of claims against E & Y: federal securities law claims, New York common law claims for fraud, and negligent misrepresentation claims. A bench trial was conducted over eleven weeks....

The court found the following: From 1988 to 1991, E & Y was aware of serious accounting irregularities with respect to the small tool inventories which increased JWP's net income, but E & Y did not insist on the correction of the irregularities. *See AUSA*, 991 F.Supp. at 242. E & Y knew that JWP was recording anticipated future tax benefits of net operating loss (NOL) carryforwards in clear violation of GAAP (presumably for the "purpose of dressing up its year-end consolidated balance sheet"), yet E & Y saw "nothing wrong" with this practice. *Id.* After discovering more accounting abuses as to NOLs which also seemed to inflate current net operating income, E & Y again "issued unqualified audit reports for the years in question," those years including the late 1980s. *Id.* at 243. E & Y was also aware of and acquiesced in numerous other accounting abuses in claims and receivables which inflated JWP's earnings and assets at least from 1989 forward. *See id.* at 243–46. In sum, "[t]he annual no-default letters issued by E & Y were ... false in that they certified that JWP's books had been kept in accordance with GAAP, which E & Y knew was untrue." *Id.* at 246.

... The court found ... that the plaintiffs did not prove the causation element of both the federal and state law claims because the plaintiffs were not able to show loss causation—the plaintiffs could not establish that E & Y's egregious accounting idiosyncrasies caused plaintiffs' losses because JWP ultimately imploded due to Businessland's operations and the uncontrollable effects of the PC price wars.... The court found that the financial devastation of JWP was a "result of unforeseeable and independent post-audit events and not because of fiscal infirmities which were concealed by JWP's misleading financial statements." . . .

III.   Discussion

Appellants based their claims on Section 10(b) of the Securities Exchange Act of 1934, *15 U.S.C. § 78j(b)*; [and] the rules and regulations promulgated thereunder, including SEC Rule 10b–5. . . .

The appellants appeal on five bases . . . [including] the district court's refusal to find causation between E & Y's actions or inactions and the appellants' losses . . . [and] the district court's standards for assessing . . . transaction causation. . . .

We hold that transaction causation was established. We vacate and remand the loss causation determination. . . .

B.   Causation

We agree with the district court that E & Y did not perform the most efficacious accounting in this situation. . . . However, we part company with the district court on its determination that it was "unforeseeable post-audit developments [that] caused JWP's insolvency and default even if its financial condition had been fully as healthy as was represented in those reports." . . .

Causation in this context has two elements: transaction causation and loss causation. *See Schlick v. Penn–Dixie Cement Corp.*, 507 F.2d 374, 380–381 (2d Cir.1974). Loss causation is causation in the traditional "proximate cause" sense—the allegedly unlawful conduct caused the economic harm. *See id.* at 380. Transaction causation means that "the violations in question caused the appellant to engage in the transaction in question." *See id.* at 380. Transaction causation has been analogized to reliance. *See Currie v. Cayman Resources Corp.*, 835 F.2d 780, 785 (11th Cir.1988).

1.   Transaction Causation . . .

There is ample evidence in the record that the appellants relied on E & Y's certifications of the financial soundness of JWP both in making their note purchases and in continuing to hold the notes. This was not a situation where the notes were marketed en masse, and E & Y had a barely tangential role in the transaction. Rather, the purchasers of these private placement notes specifically required the audits of E & Y before purchasing the notes and as a condition of their purchase. The district court stated as much in the findings of fact: "If the plaintiffs had known the lack of quality of JWP's notes at the time of the offerings, they likely would not and in some cases could not have bought them." *See ¶ 447, Findings of Fact, Joint Appendix at 2606, AUSA*, 991 F.Supp. 234 (S.D.N.Y.1997).

Applying to these facts the legal definition of transaction causation, we find that transaction causation was established. . . .

2.   Loss Causation

Addressing loss causation is a more difficult endeavor. How far back should the line be drawn in the causal chain, before which, "because of convenience, of public policy, of a rough sense of justice," proximate cause cannot be found? *Palsgraf v. Long Island R. Co.*, 248 N.Y. 339, 352, 162 N.E. 99, 103 (1928). In the vernacular, where does the buck stop?

We agree with most of the district court's factual determinations. . . . However, given the true nature of the "loss causation" determination, as fully discussed below, the district court did not make all of the specific findings of fact required. We therefore vacate the court's determination and remand for reconsideration and more pertinent factual findings in light of this opinion.

a.   The District Court's Factual Determinations . . .

The following piecemeal factual determinations made by the district court are relevant: JWP was in default on its notes because it was in violation of the financial covenants in the Note Agreements. *See* ¶ *440, id.* at 2607. E & Y knew of these violations, but assisted in concealing them. *See* ¶ *506, id.* at 2625. This default could have allowed the plaintiffs to accelerate the due date on the notes. *See* ¶ *471, id.* at 2613. Accurate accounting, auditing, and reporting would have at least made the plaintiffs aware of the default and precarious financial position of JWP, though, at oral argument, the appellee maintained that JWP would have had thirty days to cure the default before the plaintiffs could accelerate the notes. At oral argument, the appellee also contended that, had the investors been made aware of the default, they would have waived it, and it would have become a non-issue. We need not speculate on that here. Suffice it to say that the factual findings establish that JWP was in default on its notes prior to its acquisition of Businessland, and the investors would have known of such had E & Y correctly performed their duties.

True, the district court found that "JWP would not have defaulted on its debt obligations but for its acquisition of Businessland, which turned out to be a veritable sinkhole for cash." *AUSA*, 991 F.Supp. at 250. But, as discussed above, had JWP's financial situation been accurately represented by E & Y, and had E & Y revealed the undisputed GAAP violations, JWP would have been in default on its notes prior to its acquisition of Businessland. Therefore, the acquisition of Businessland could not have taken place without a cure of the default or the investors' waivers of the default.

b.   The District Court's Application of Law to Fact

The appellee maintains—and the district court agreed—that the events leading to the demise of JWP and the loss of appellants' investments were due to external events for which appellee cannot be held accountable, and therefore loss causation was not established. The district court said specifically that

> JWP's insolvency and resulting default on its note obligations were caused not by the differences between its actual financial condition and that reflected in its audited annual reports, but by much more significant factors, including JWP's disastrous acquisition of the failing Businessland, in combination with the downturn in commercial construction and fierce competition in the PC market.

Id. at 250. We disagree, however, with this conclusion of the district court to the extent that the district court did not fully consider the legal definition of "loss causation" and the requisite factual points in determining whether loss causation was established. . . .

We have consistently said that "loss causation in effect requires that the damage complained of be one of the foreseeable consequences of the misrepresentation." *Manufacturers Hanover*, 801 F.2d at 21. . . .

In Paragraph 506(e) of the district court's Findings of Fact, the court states that the plaintiffs' reliance on JWP's annual audited reports for the years prior to their purchases "was not a proximate cause of the plaintiffs' losses." Joint Appendix at A–2625. A proximate cause determination in situations where "circumstances permit varying inferences as to the foreseeability of the intervening act" is generally a factual determination. *See Woodling v. Garrett Corp.*, 813 F.2d 543, 555 (2d Cir.1987). A foreseeability determination in and of itself is also a question of fact for resolution by the finder of fact. . . . However, we do not find in the record a discussion of facts indicating that the district court undertook to make findings of fact specifically pertinent to the foreseeability component of the proximate cause inquiry.

The foreseeability query is whether E & Y could have reasonably foreseen that their certification of false financial information could lead to the demise of JWP, by enabling JWP to make an acquisition that otherwise would have been subjected to higher scrutiny, which led to harm to the investors.[6] Given that the district court did not make factual findings as to foreseeability specifically, we remand for more factual findings. In accordance with the factual findings, the court is then instructed to reconsider proximate cause in the context of its factual determinations on foreseeability.

By way of offering a tow rope to assist the district court through this Serbonian Bog,[8] we note the following: A foreseeability finding

---

6. . . . [B]y "harm" to the investors we are referring to losses incurred for risks which the investors did not intend to take nor of which they should have (or, in this case, even could have) been aware.

8. " 'Proximate cause,' in short, has been an extraordinarily changeable concept.

'Having no integrated meaning of its own, its chameleon quality permits it to be substituted for any one of the elements of a negligence case when decision on that element becomes difficult. * * * No other formula * * * so nearly does the work of Aladdin's lamp.' " *Prosser and Keeton on Torts*, § 42,276 (*quot-*

turns on fairness, policy, and, as before, "a rough sense of justice." *Palsgraf*, 248 N.Y. at 352, 162 N.E. at 103. "A 'reasonably foreseeable act' might well be regarded as an act that a reasonable person who knew everything that the defendant knew at the time would have been able to know in advance with a fair degree of probability." *United States v. LaCroix*, 28 F.3d 223, 229 (1st Cir.1994). Where foreseeability is less than immediately obvious, it is appropriate to make a judgment based on "some social idea of justice or policy." *First Nationwide Bank*, 27 F.3d at 770; *id.* at 772 ("proximate cause determination necessarily involves a component of policy"). These considerations should be coupled with the recognition that proximate cause is a common law concept, and such concepts evolve in a manner that reflects "economic, social, and political developments." *Cullen v. BMW of North America, Inc.*, 691 F.2d 1097, 1102 (2d Cir.1982) (Oakes, J. dissenting). Therefore, it is appropriate to examine the underlying policy of the securities laws involved and the climate of securities regulation as it has evolved and as it currently exists.

"During the Great Depression, Congress enacted the 1933 and 1934 [Securities] Acts to promote investor confidence in the United States securities markets and thereby to encourage the investment necessary for capital formation, economic growth, and job creation." *Private Securities Litigation Reform Act of 1995*, P.L. 104–67, S.Rep. No. 104–98 (June 19, 1995), *reprinted in* 1995 U.S.C.C.A.N. 679, 683. The 1934 Act was intended "to impose regular reporting requirements on companies whose stock is listed on national securities exchanges." *Ernst & Ernst v. Hochfelder*, 425 U.S. 185, 195, 96 S.Ct. 1375, 47 L.Ed.2d 668 (1976). This was part of an overall broad scheme of federal regulation enacted in the early 1930s, through which Congress wanted investors to have access to comprehensive, accurate information about the companies in which they were investing. *See id.* (citing legislative reports of both the Securities Act of 1933 and the Securities Act of 1934) . . . .

We conclude that the district court failed to make sufficient factual findings relevant to the foreseeability aspects of loss causation. We therefore vacate and remand. . . .

IV.   Conclusion . . .

For the above stated reasons, we reverse the district court in part, we vacate the district court in part, and we remand for reconsideration where appropriate in light of this opinion.

■ JACOBS, CIRCUIT JUDGE, concurring: . . .

I.

In my view, the district court has made affirmable fact-findings that plaintiffs' losses were caused by the implosion of JWP's Business-

---

ing Green, *Proximate Cause in Texas Negligence Law*, 28 Tex. L.Rev. 471 (1950)). With respect to foreseeability, "[t]here is perhaps no other one issue in the law of torts over which so much controversy has raged. . . ." *Id.* at § 43, 280.

land acquisition, and therefore were not caused by E & Y's misrepresentations that JWP's books complied with GAAP. . . .

The question of loss causation has divided the panel three ways. Judge Oakes's opinion for the Court properly identifies loss causation as a fact inquiry—distinct from transaction causation—for resolution by the district court, but concludes that the categorical findings needed to decide the case have not been made, and therefore vacates the judgement and remands for further findings on whether E & Y could have reasonably foreseen that its misrepresentations could have led to JWP's demise—that is, the issue of loss causation. Chief Judge Winter's dissenting opinion argues for reversal on the ground that, in this case, further findings on the issue of loss causation are unnecessary (1) because misrepresentations of the kind in this case understate management's willingness to take risks, such as the Businessland acquisition, and (2) because such misrepresentations, if corrected, would have disclosed the material datum that management was dishonest. . . .

The three opinions on this appeal argue for three different results, a division that would cause the appeal to misfire and leave the case undecided—an unacceptable outcome in a reviewing court. . . .

In order to allow the Court to issue a mandate, I have shifted my vote on the issue of loss causation—from affirmance, to vacatur with a remand for further findings. . . .

II. . . .

In concluding that "the evidence definitely fails to establish the necessary loss causation," *id.* at 250, the district court found that there were several causes, chief among them JWP's inability to revitalize Businessland, a depressed market for commercial construction, and fierce competition in the PC market—not E & Y's misrepresentations. *See id.* at 250.

Judge Oakes believes that the district court's discussion of loss causation fails to decide whether JWP would have been able to purchase Businessland absent E & Y's misstatements. *See* Majority Opinion at 217 [hereinafter "Maj. Op."]. I think that is the wrong question. It has been found—and all opinions on appeal agree—that JWP's acquisition of Businessland was a calamity that overwhelmed all other financial circumstances and brought about JWP's bankruptcy. Therefore, I think that the loss causation inquiry should be: Was it foreseeable that E & Y's misstatement of accounts would cause the plaintiffs to suffer losses caused by the disastrous Businessland acquisition? In my view, the question is sufficiently answered by the district court's findings that the plaintiffs' chief investment concern was JWP's *actual* cash flow (which was perfectly adequate to fund plaintiffs' bonds and was unaffected by the misrepresentations) and that the disastrous nature of the Businessland investment was unforeseeable. *See AUSA Life Ins. Co.,* 991 F.Supp. at 239, 250.

Loss causation requires the plaintiffs to prove more than simply that E & Y induced them to enter into an ultimately unsuccessful investment. Such a "but-for" analysis would collapse loss causation into transaction causation. *See Citibank,* 968 F.2d at 1495 (transaction causation "requires the plaintiff to allege that the misrepresentation induced it to enter into the transaction"). Rather, loss causation requires proof that ... E & Y's "misrepresentation was the cause of the actual loss suffered." *Id.* The damages suffered by the plaintiffs must be "a foreseeable consequence of the misrepresentation." *Id.* In this sense, loss causation closely corresponds to the common law principle of proximate cause. *See Litton Indus., Inc. v. Lehman Bros. Kuhn Loeb Inc.,* 967 F.2d 742, 747 (2d Cir.1992).

I can find no flaw in the district court's application of loss causation principles to this case.

As an initial matter, the disastrous events subsequent to the Businessland acquisition were not a foreseeable consequence of E & Y's misrepresentations. JWP defaulted on the plaintiffs' notes as a result of its acquisition of Businessland in 1991. According to the testimony of JWP's former Chief Executive Officer, credited by the district court, Businessland became "a veritable sinkhole for cash" that would have bankrupted JWP even if JWP's books were as represented. *AUSA Life Ins. Co.,* 991 F.Supp. at 250. There is no credible allegation that JWP would have defaulted in 1993 in the absence of the acquisition. *See id.* Therefore, neither E & Y nor JWP could have foreseen that their misrepresentations would have resulted in JWP's insolvency and the non-payment of the bond obligations.

Judge Oakes frames the foreseeability question in terms of "whether E & Y could have reasonably foreseen that their certification of false financial information could lead to the demise of JWP, by enabling JWP to make an acquisition that otherwise would have been subjected to higher scrutiny, which led to harm to the investors." Maj. Op. at 217. I think that this "enabling" issue is a variant of but-for causation, and that the relevant inquiry (considering that JWP's failure and bankruptcy is the proximate cause of the bondholders' loss) is whether E & Y's misrepresentations could foreseeably have led to the failure of the company. As to this question, the district court's factual findings are clear enough:

> JWP's insolvency and resulting default on its note obligations were caused *not* by the differences between its actual financial condition and that reflected in its audited reports, but by much more significant factors, including JWP's disastrous acquisition of the failing Businessland, in combination with the downturn in commercial construction and fierce competition in the PC market.

AUSA Life Ins. Co., 991 F.Supp. at 250 (emphasis added).

Whether or not the acquisition was a foreseeable consequence of the misrepresentations cannot matter unless the misrepresentations are shown to have caused the resulting collapse. Even if one assumes (a stretch) that E & Y's misrepresentations allowed JWP to buy Businessland, E & Y's misrepresentations were not the reason for the resulting company's failure: JWP's ruin is easily attributable to business factors that were more potent than E & Y's misrepresentations, and were unrelated to them. *See AUSA Life Ins. Co.,* 991 F.Supp. at 238–39, 250. The dispositive question is whether the JWP/Businessland combination would have collapsed even if JWP's books were accurately stated. . . .

. . . By requiring both transaction causation *and* loss causation, section 10(b) sets a high bar for recovery, and deliberately so. There is a particular reluctance to expand liability in any direction . . . let alone merge the required elements of the cause of action.

The misrepresentations in JWP's books (concerning treatment of acquisition costs, small tool inventories, net operating losses, and software costs) were not the proximate cause—*i.e.,* the loss causation—for the plaintiffs' loss. Those misrepresentations affected JWP's *apparent* cash flow, but they had no effect on JWP's *actual* cash flow. *See AUSA Life Ins. Co.,* 991 F.Supp. at 250. This is a critical distinction. While JWP's equity investors were rightfully concerned with the discrepancies in the company's books (because such variances would have affected the company's stock price), JWP's debt holders—the plaintiffs—would not necessarily have had cause for alarm. *See id.* The primary concern of a debt holder is actual cash flow, the ability of the debt issuer to pay interest and principal as required. *See id.* Indeed, even after JWP's annual reports were restated, the company continued to meet its interest payment schedule. *See id.*

The district court's findings suggest that the plaintiffs would have remained invested in JWP notwithstanding the Businessland acquisition even if they had known of the discrepancies in JWP's books, because prior to acquisition there was no indication that Businessland would become the "sinkhole for cash" that it became. *Id.* There is also no allegation that the plaintiffs would have somehow prevented JWP from acquiring Businessland had they known of JWP's true financial condition. Therefore, JWP would still have been able to proceed with the acquisition that would have led to its insolvency and the plaintiffs' losses.

Moreover, it is hard to see how, had the auditors done a proper job, the bondholders would have been better situated or made more prescient. If, as it should have, E & Y had resisted JWP's pressure to misrepresent the company's financial condition, the bondholders would have received an accurate statement of accounts. But E & Y would not have been required to disclose management's thwarted desire to dress up the numbers. The job of the accountant is to ensure, within the parameters of the audit letter, that accounts comply with sound accounting practice. The accountant's duty is to do this regardless of pressure from managers to present the company's financial status as favorably as they can. But that obligation does not require disclosure of management's pressure to make the overly favorable representation. *See Santa Fe Indus., Inc. v. Green,* 430 U.S. 462, 477–78, 97 S.Ct. 1292, 1303, 51 L.Ed.2d 480 (1977).

Chief Judge Winter argues, however, that after the first year's misrepresentations, a restatement of accounts would have revealed that the previous financial statements had been knowingly falsified, and that such a disclosure would cause any investor, including debt holders, to jump ship. *See* Diss. Op. at 229–31. Chief Judge Winter believes that knowledge of book-cooking would have dual effects, either of which is sufficient to demonstrate loss causation: (1) it would expose management's crookedness, and (2) it would warn investors that management may have an incentive to take greater risks. *See* Diss. Op. at 230–31. Assuming (as I do not) that such a disclosure would have prevented the plaintiffs' losses, I doubt that such a disclosure would be required. No doubt, the auditors owed the plaintiffs (and others) a corrected statement of accounts over a several-year period, but there is no basis for holding that correction of the figures would require a disclosure that management corruptly insisted on making the initial (false) representations. Under *Santa Fe Industries,* 430 U.S. at 477–78, 97 S.Ct. at 1303, the duty to disclose facts (here, the numbers) does not entail a duty—on the part of the accountant—to disclose culpability or impure motives. Thus *Santa Fe Industries* holds that a section 10(b) plaintiff cannot transform a fiduciary-duty claim or a mismanagement claim into a claim of non-disclosure. . . .

In short, the proximate cause of the plaintiffs' losses was the failure of the Businessland acquisition, which was not a foreseeable result of E & Y's conduct.

■ WINTER, CHIEF JUDGE, dissenting:

I agree with the conclusions reached by Judge Oakes's opinion as to transaction causation and scienter. With regard to loss causation, I would hold that the facts found by the district court demonstrate loss causation as a matter of law. Limiting my discussion of applicable law to appellants' single federal claim, brought under Section 10(b) of the '34 Act, *15 U.S.C. § 78j(b)*, I respectfully dissent.

I

Before turning to a detailed discussion of loss causation under Section 10(b), I briefly summarize my reasoning. . . .

Both the district court and my colleagues view the loss causation issue more narrowly than I do. The district court's reasoning went more or less as follows. Because of the misleading financial statements and no-fault letters, appellants had a view of JWP's financial condition that was more rosy than the truth. However, the true financial condition of JWP was not so different from the rosy view that a fully informed reasonable investor would have apprehended a significantly greater risk of default. Rather, in the court's view, because the collapse was largely caused by the risky and mistaken business decision to acquire Businessland, it was not sufficiently connected to the misrepresentations to be deemed a foreseeable consequence of them....

III

We have stated that "loss causation" under Section 10(b) "correspond [s] ... with [the] common law notion[ ] of ... proximate causation." *Litton Indus., Inc. v. Lehman Bros. Kuhn Loeb Inc.,* 967 F.2d 742, 747 (2d Cir.1992)....

Judge Oakes correctly notes that "foreseeability" is the touchstone of loss causation.... However, the concept of foreseeability may vary according to legal context....

In the case of securities fraud, the limits of "foreseeability" must be derived from the purposes of the federal securities laws.... Those laws, as pertinent to the instant matter, impose a duty on firms to provide investors with truthful information relevant to the value of certain investments....

If the meaning of proximate cause in the present context is to be derived from the statutory purpose of making sure that firms provide the truthful information necessary to allow investors to "get what they think they are getting," then much of the requisite analysis must come from the definition of materiality under federal securities law, which governs the scope and content of the information that the firm is under a duty to provide. The test of materiality is whether a reasonable investor would consider the particular information significant or, put another way, whether the information would affect the "total mix" of information available to the investor. *See TSC Indus., Inc. v. Northway, Inc.,* 426 U.S. 438, 449, 96 S.Ct. 2126, 48 L.Ed.2d 757 (1976). The "foreseeability" of a loss in this context, therefore, turns upon the significance of the misrepresentations or omissions to the total mix of information available to the investor. Of course, in the context of common law negligence, it is generally foreseeability from the defendant's point of view that is at stake. In securities law, however, the critical issue is what a reasonable investor would have considered significant, and foreseeability is generally from the plaintiff's point of view because, once reliance and scienter are proven, the defendant is presumed to anticipate the apprehensions of a reasonable investor.

Loss causation in the context of federal securities law thus requires consideration of the significance to a reasonable investor of the truth compared to the content of the misrepresentations or omissions. If the significance of the truth is such as to cause a reasonable investor to consider seriously a zone of risk that would be perceived as remote or highly unlikely by one believing the fraud, and the loss ultimately suffered is within that zone, then a misrepresentation or omission as to that information may be deemed a foreseeable or proximate cause of the loss. This is all that is meant by our rule "that the damage complained of be one of the foreseeable consequences of the misrepresentation." *Manufacturers Hanover*, 801 F.2d at 21 (citing *Marbury Mgmt.*, 629 F.2d at 708).

A major source of confusion in this regard is the use of causation language. The issue is not whether a misstatement "caused" a loss. Rather, the issues are: (i) whether a reasonable investor would find the total mix of information so significantly altered by the truth as to apprehend a zone of risk that would seem remote to an investor still under the spell of misstatements, and (ii) whether the ultimate loss falls within that zone of risk. For example, losses due to insolvency, much less insolvency itself, are not "caused" by misrepresentations. Currently insolvent firms may (often do) survive and ultimately prosper if skillfully managed. But if a firm is not so fortunate after an investor has been misled as to solvency, the investor should not be denied recovery on the ground that it was management's lack of skill rather than the false assurances of solvency that "caused" the loss. . . .

IV

I turn now to the application of these principles to the present case. I address the situation as it existed in 1990, when appellants made their first purchase of JWP notes within the limitations period.

Finance is about risk probabilities—*i.e.,* risk allocation, diversification, and minimization. Every lender, when deciding whether and on what terms to make a loan, must evaluate the probability of default. *See* Daniel R. Fischel, *The Economics of Lender Liability*, 99 Yale L.J. 131, 134 (1989). When appellants invested in JWP, they bargained for a certain risk profile that governed the decision to lend and matters such as maturity and interest rate. They also bargained for E & Y to monitor JWP's compliance with GAAP and for contractual rights, including acceleration, that might cap their losses should JWP default. E & Y's conduct deprived them of all these bargains and subjected them to concealed risks that resulted in losses.

It appears to have been the district court's view that E & Y misrepresented only particular financial information. It found that JWP's misrepresentations as to its financial condition had a calculable effect on the solvency of the firm so marginal that the risk of a default was not significantly understated by the misrepresentations. *See AUSA*, 991 F.Supp. at 249–50. The court concluded that the risky and mistaken acquisition of Businessland was therefore not within the risks related to those misrepresentations. *See id.* at 250. If the only material information misrepresented were the treatment of certain financial matters, I would agree. E & Y's conduct, however, misrepresented far more.

In each successive JWP financial statement, E & Y incorporated by reference prior fraudulent statements. For example, the 10–K prepared for the year ending December 31, 1990 included backward-looking balance sheet and income statement data for the previous five years.

See Pl.'s Ex. 17, Part II, Item 6 at 22. The 10–K explicitly incorporated prior financial statements, including the prior year's balance sheet information and the 1988 and 1989 statements of income, cash flows, and stockholders' equity. *See id.* Part IV, Item 14(a), at 47. E & Y specifically represented:

> In our opinion, based on our audits, and for 1988 the report of other auditors, the[se] financial statements ... present fairly, in all material respects, the consolidated financial position of JWP ... at December 31, 1990 and 1989, and the consolidated results of operations and cash flows for each of the three years in the period ended December 31, 1990 in conformity with [GAAP]. *Id.* at 43.

The note purchases at issue here began in 1990. The fraud had been ongoing since 1987, and, by the time of the 1990 purchases, some of the appellants already owned millions of dollars of JWP notes. A reasonable investor receiving the financial statements (and in two cases no-default letters) would have concluded that: (i) the risk profile established by prior financial statements was accurate and stable; (ii) E & Y was monitoring JWP's compliance with GAAP in its financial statements, and no default on the outstanding notes had occurred; and (iii) the ongoing monitoring by E & Y might afford some opportunity for appellants to cap their losses should JWP encounter unexpected difficulties. None of these conclusions would have been correct.

If the true facts had become known in 1990, the inferences that a reasonable investor would have drawn would not have been limited to adjusting the estimated risk of default by discounting the dollar value involved in the misrepresentations. Obviously, the total mix of information relevant to such an investor would have been radically altered. A reasonable investor would have concluded that JWP had a management quite willing to misrepresent systematically its financial condition and an auditor willing to certify the misrepresentations.[5] The note provisions requiring the auditor to certify the lack of a default annually would have been deemed worthless. Absent an auditor willing to do its duty, such an investor would attribute no value to contractual rights to take certain action in the event of default because a fully-informed exercise would not be possible. The purchase of yet more JWP notes would have been out of the question in light of the true information. Indeed, in discussing the "investment grade" rating assigned to JWP's securities, the district court found that "[i]f the plaintiffs had known the lack of quality of JWP's Notes at the time of the offerings, they likely would not and in some cases could not have

---

5. Judge Jacobs speculates that E & Y could have issued a corrected statement of accounts for several years but would not have had to disclose that management had corruptly insisted on the earlier false statements. Even if that is so—and I am not sure that it is—such an extensive correcting of earlier years' books without any explanation would likely have had the same consequences as a full explanation for their need. Of course, any explanation that omitted a reference to management's role would have been yet another fraudulent misstatement.

bought them." Findings ¶ 447, at 2606. A reasonable noteholder would also have seriously contemplated the wisdom of retaining its present JWP notes and the need to invoke its powers under those notes, including acceleration.

The pattern of such misrepresentations itself created another risk to appellants that a reasonable investor would take into account. The management of a firm like JWP would have apprehended that, while such misstatements would reduce borrowing costs for a time, in all likelihood corrections in statements for prior years would eventually have to be made. The true financial condition of the firm would then be exposed, as would the misdeeds of JWP's management and E & Y. Investors' and analysts' evaluation of JWP would reflect both facts. Moreover, JWP's management and auditor would know that the corrections would reveal defaults on outstanding notes and perhaps trigger the exercise of the noteholders' contractual rights, including acceleration. (Indeed, the Businessland acquisition could not have proceeded if the default on the notes had been known, absent a cure by JWP—admission of years of fraud—or waiver by appellants.)

For a management facing such circumstances, the temptation to seek salvation in a risky deal is greatly heightened. Only a very profitable new venture could offset the effect of revelations of past financial misstatements and systematic fraud by existing management and the firm's auditor. To be sure, such a deal would also have a vast downside, but even the prospect of a financial collapse might not seem to management all that different from the circumstances that would prevail if profitability were not substantially increased before disclosure of the fraud.[6]

In short, when appellants began in 1990 to purchase the notes at issue, they were investing in a firm with compelling incentives that rendered it far less risk averse than the information certified by E & Y suggested. The chance that a highly risky venture would be undertaken that might lead to a default was far greater than could have been reasonably inferred from the false financial statements and no-default letters, and the contractual rights that might have minimized such a loss were in reality worthless.

Taking this view of the case, I have little difficulty in concluding that loss causation was amply shown. The essentials of appellants'

---

6. JWP's diminished risk aversion is no more than a variation on the familiar principle that highly leveraged firms are less risk averse than similar firms with less debt. "The existence of debt creates an incentive for borrowers to invest in riskier projects. This incentive arises because the lender bears the downside risk if the project turns out poorly, but he does not share in the upside potential if the project turns out well." Daniel R. Fischel, *The Economics of Lender Liability*, 99 Yale L.J. 131, 134 (1989). "This incentive to invest in risky projects is a direct function of the amount the borrower has at risk. . . . In the extreme case . . . the firm has nothing to lose and everything to gain by adopting a 'shoot the moon' investment strategy." *Id.* JWP was in effect more highly leveraged than its debt investors had been led to believe. The equity base was less than advertised. Moreover, disclosure of the fraud would have driven down equity prices and dried up access to equity capital.

bargain were a particular risk profile and contractual rights to monitor the debtor. The risk profile was false in that relevant financial information was misstated and the diminished risk averseness of the firm concealed. The contractual rights were rendered valueless because misstatements concealing existing and future defaults would forestall their exercise. In my view, therefore, the collapse of JWP as a result of the Businessland venture was well within the zone of risk concealed by the misrepresentations. . . .

I therefore respectfully dissent.

Insert the following case at p. 824 of the Unabridged Edition, following the Note on In Re Carter–Wallace Securities Litigation, and p. 592 of the Concise Edition, following the Note on Causation and Reliance:

SEC v. Zandford

Supreme Court of the United States, 2002.
2002 WL 1155996.

■ JUSTICE STEVENS delivered the opinion of the Court.

The Securities and Exchange Commission (SEC) filed a civil complaint alleging that a stockbroker violated both § 10(b) of the Securities Exchange Act of 1934, 48 Stat. 891, as amended, 15 U.S.C. § 78j(b), and the SEC's Rule 10b–5, by selling his customer's securities and using the proceeds for his own benefit without the customer's knowledge or consent. The question presented is whether the alleged fraudulent conduct was "in connection with the purchase or sale of any security" within the meaning of the statute and the rule.

I

Between 1987 and 1991, respondent was employed as a securities broker in the Maryland branch of a New York brokerage firm. In 1987, he persuaded William Wood, an elderly man in poor health, to open a joint investment account for himself and his mentally retarded daughter. According to the SEC's complaint, the "stated investment objectives for the account were 'safety of principal and income.' " App. to Pet. for Cert. 27a. The Woods granted respondent discretion to manage their account and a general power of attorney to engage in securities transactions for their benefit without prior approval. Relying on respondent's promise to "conservatively invest" their money, the Woods entrusted him with $419,255. Before Mr. Wood's death in 1991, all of that money was gone.

In 1991, the National Association of Securities Dealers (NASD) conducted a routine examination of respondent's firm and discovered that on over 25 separate occasions, money had been transferred from the Woods' account to accounts controlled by respondent. In due course, respondent was indicted in the United States District Court for the District of Maryland on 13 counts of wire fraud in violation of 18 U.S.C. § 1343. App. to Pet. for Cert. 40a. The first count alleged that respondent sold securities in the Woods' account and then made personal use of the proceeds. Id., at 42a. Each of the other counts alleged that he made wire transfers between Maryland and New York that enabled him to withdraw specified sums from the Woods' accounts. Id., at 42a–50a. Some of those transfers involved respondent writing checks to himself from a mutual fund account held by the Woods, which required liquidating securities in order to redeem the checks. Respondent was convicted on all counts, sentenced to prison for 52 months, and ordered to pay $10,800 in restitution.

After respondent was indicted, the SEC filed a civil complaint in the same District Court alleging that respondent violated § 10(b) and Rule 10b–5 by engaging in a scheme to defraud the Woods and by misappropriating approximately $343,000 of the Woods' securities without their knowledge or consent. Id., at 27a. The SEC moved for partial summary judgment after respondent's criminal conviction, arguing that the judgment in the criminal case estopped respondent from contesting facts that established a violation of § 10(b).[1] Respondent filed a motion seeking discovery on the question whether his fraud had the requisite "connection with" the purchase or sale of a security. The District Court refused to allow discovery and entered summary judgment against respondent. It enjoined him from engaging in future violations of the securities laws and ordered him to disgorge $343,000 in ill-gotten gains.

The Court of Appeals for the Fourth Circuit reversed the summary judgment and remanded with directions for the District Court to dismiss the complaint. 238 F.3d 559 (2001).... The court ... held that the civil complaint did not sufficiently allege the necessary connection because the sales of the Woods' securities were merely incidental to a fraud that "lay in absconding with the proceeds" of sales that were conducted in "a routine and customary fashion," 238 F.3d 559 at 564. Respondent's "scheme was simply to steal the Woods' assets" rather than to engage "in manipulation of a particular security." 238 F.3d 559 at 565. Ultimately, the court refused "to stretch the language of the securities fraud provisions to encompass every conversion or theft that happens to involve securities." 238 F.3d 559 at 566. Adopting what amounts to a "fraud on the market" theory of the statute's coverage, the court held that without some "relationship to market integrity or investor understanding," there is no violation of § 10(b). 238 F.3d 559 at 563.

---

1. The scope of Rule 10b–5 is coextensive with the coverage of § 10(b), see United States v. O'Hagan, 521 U.S. 642, 651 (1997); Ernst & Ernst v. Hochfelder, 425 U.S. 185, 214, 47 L. Ed. 2d 668, 96 S. Ct. 1375 (1976); therefore, we use § 10(b) to refer to both the statutory provision and the Rule....

We granted the SEC's petition for a writ of certiorari, 534 U.S. 1015, 151 L. Ed. 2d 418, 122 S. Ct. 510 (2001), to review the Court of Appeals' construction of the phrase "in connection with the purchase or sale of any security." Because the Court of Appeals ordered the complaint dismissed rather than remanding for reconsideration, we assume the allegations contained therein are true and affirm that disposition only if no set of facts would entitle petitioner to relief. See Hartford Fire Ins. Co. v. California, 509 U.S. 764, 811, 125 L. Ed. 2d 612, 113 S. Ct. 2891 (1993). We do not reach the question whether the record supports the District Court's grant of summary judgment in the SEC's favor—a question that requires all potential factual disputes to be resolved in respondent's favor. We merely hold that the allegations of the complaint, if true, entitle the SEC to relief; therefore, the Court of Appeals should not have directed that the complaint be dismissed.

II

Section 10(b) of the Securities Exchange Act makes it "unlawful for any person . . . to use or employ, in connection with the purchase or sale of any security . . ., any manipulative or deceptive device or contrivance in contravention of such rules and regulations as the [SEC] may prescribe." 15 U.S.C. § 78j. Rule 10b–5, which implements this provision, forbids the use, "in connection with the purchase or sale of any security," of "any device, scheme, or artifice to defraud" or any other "act, practice, or course of business" that "operates . . . as a fraud or deceit." 17 CFR § 240.10b–5 (2000). Among Congress' objectives in passing the Act was "to insure honest securities markets and thereby promote investor confidence" after the market crash of 1929. United States v. O'Hagan, 521 U.S. 642, 658 (1997); see also United States v. Naftalin, 441 U.S. 768, 775, 60 L. Ed. 2d 624, 99 S. Ct. 2077 (1979). More generally, Congress sought " 'to substitute a philosophy of full disclosure for the philosophy of caveat emptor and thus to achieve a high standard of business ethics in the securities industry.' " Affiliated Ute Citizens of Utah v. United States, 406 U.S. 128, 151 (1972) (quoting SEC v. Capital Gains Research Bureau, Inc., 375 U.S. 180, 186, 11 L. Ed. 2d 237, 84 S. Ct. 275 (1963)).

Consequently, we have explained that the statute should be "construed 'not technically and restrictively, but flexibly to effectuate its remedial purposes.' " 406 U.S. 128 at 151 (quoting Capital Gains Research Bureau, Inc., 375 U.S., at 195). In its role enforcing the Act, the SEC has consistently adopted a broad reading of the phrase "in connection with the purchase or sale of any security." It has maintained that a broker who accepts payment for securities that he never intends to deliver, or who sells customer securities with intent to misappropriate the proceeds, violates § 10(b) and Rule 10b–5. See, e.g., In re Bauer, 26 S. E. C. 770 (1947); In re Southeastern Securities Corp., 29 S. E. C. 609 (1949). This interpretation of the ambiguous text of § 10(b), in the context of formal adjudication, is entitled to deference if it is reasonable, see United States v. Mead Corp., 533 U.S. 218, 229–230, and n. 12 (2001). For the reasons set forth below, we think it is. While the statute must not be construed so broadly as to convert every common-law fraud that happens to involve securities into a violation of § 10(b), Marine Bank v. Weaver, 455 U.S. 551, 556, 71 L. Ed. 2d 409, 102 S. Ct. 1220 (1982) ("Congress, in enacting the securities laws, did not intend to provide a broad federal remedy for all fraud"), neither the SEC nor this Court has ever held that there must be a misrepresentation about the value of a particular security in order to run afoul of the Act.

The SEC claims respondent engaged in a fraudulent scheme in which he made sales of his customer's securities for his own benefit. Respondent submits that the sales themselves were perfectly lawful and that the subsequent misappropriation of the proceeds, though fraudulent, is not properly viewed as having the requisite connection with the sales; in his view, the alleged scheme is not materially different from a simple theft of cash or securities in an investment account. We disagree.

According to the complaint, respondent "engaged in a scheme to defraud" the Woods beginning in 1988, shortly after they opened their account, and that scheme continued throughout the 2–year period during which respondent made a series of transactions that enabled him to convert the proceeds of the sales of the Woods' securities to his own use. App. to Pet. for Cert. 27a–29a. The securities sales and respondent's fraudulent practices were not independent events. This is not a case in which, after a lawful transaction had been consummated, a broker decided to steal the proceeds and did so. Nor is it a case in which a thief simply invested the proceeds of a routine conversion in the stock market. Rather, respondent's fraud coincided with the sales themselves.

Taking the allegations in the complaint as true, each sale was made to further respondent's fraudulent scheme; each was deceptive because it was neither authorized by, nor disclosed to, the Woods. With regard to the sales of shares in the Woods' mutual fund, respondent initiated these transactions by writing a check to himself from that account, knowing that redeeming the check would require the sale of securities. Indeed, each time respondent "exercised his power of disposition for his own benefit," that conduct, "without more," was a fraud. United States v. Dunn, 268 U.S. 121, 131, 69 L. Ed. 876, 45 S. Ct. 451 (1925). In the aggregate, the sales are properly viewed as a "course of business" that operated as a fraud or deceit on a stockbroker's customer.

Insofar as the connection between respondent's deceptive practices and his sale of the Woods' securities is concerned, the case is remarkably similar to Superintendent of Ins. of N. Y. v. Bankers Life & Casualty Co., 404 U.S. 6 (1971). In that case the directors of Manhattan Casualty Company authorized the sale of the company's portfolio of treasury bonds because they had been "duped" into believing that the company would receive the proceeds of the sale. Id., at 9. We held that "Manhattan was injured as an investor through a deceptive device which deprived it of any compensation for the sale of its valuable block of securities." Id., at 10. In reaching this conclusion, we did not ask, as the Fourth Circuit did in this case, whether the directors were misled about the value of a security or whether the fraud involved "manipulation of a particular security." 238 F.3d 559 at 565. In fact, we rejected the Second Circuit's position in Superintendent of Ins. of N. Y. v. Bankers Life & Casualty Co., 430 F.2d 355, 361 (1970), that because the fraud against Manhattan did not take place within the context of a securities exchange it was not prohibited by § 10(b). 404 U.S. 6 at 10. We refused to read the statute so narrowly, noting that it "must be read flexibly, not technically and restrictively." Id., at 12. Although we recognized that the interest in " 'preserving the integrity of the securities markets,' " was one of the purposes animating the statute, we rejected the notion that § 10(b) is limited to serving that objective alone. Ibid. ("We agree that Congress by § 10(b) did not seek to regulate transactions which constitute no more than internal corporate mismanagement. But we read § 10(b) to mean that Congress meant to bar deceptive devices and contrivances in the purchase or sale of securities whether conducted in the organized markets or face to face").

Like the company directors in *Bankers Life*, the Woods were injured as investors through respondent's deceptions, which deprived them of any compensation for the sale of their valuable securities. They were duped into believing respondent would "conservatively invest" their assets in the stock market and that any transactions made on their behalf would be for their benefit for the " 'safety of principal and income.' " App. to Pet. for Cert. 27a. The fact that respondent misappropriated the proceeds of the sales provides persuasive evidence that he had violated § 10(b) when he made the sales, but misappropriation is not an essential element of the offense. Indeed, in *Bankers Life*, we flatly stated that it was "irrelevant" that "the proceeds of the sale that were due the seller were misappropriated." 404 U.S. 6 at 10. It is enough that the scheme to defraud and the sale of securities coincide.

The Court of Appeals below distinguished *Bankers Life* on the ground that it involved an affirmative misrepresentation, whereas respondent simply failed to inform the Woods of his intent to misappropriate their securities. 238 F.3d 559 at 566. We are not persuaded by this distinction. Respondent was only able to carry out his fraudulent scheme without making an affirmative misrepresentation because the Woods had trusted him to make transactions in their best interest without prior approval. Under these circumstances, respondent's fraud represents an even greater threat to investor confidence in the securities industry than the misrepresentation in *Bankers Life*. Not only does such a fraud prevent investors from trusting that their brokers are executing transactions for their benefit, but it undermines the value of a discretionary account like that held by the Woods. The benefit of a discretionary account is that it enables individuals, like the Woods, who lack the time, capacity, or know-how to supervise investment decisions, to delegate authority to a broker who will make decisions in their best interests without prior approval. If such individuals cannot rely on a broker to exercise that discretion for their benefit, then the account loses its added value. Moreover, any distinction between omissions and misrepresentations is illusory in the context of a broker who has a fiduciary duty to her clients. See Chiarella v. United States, 445 U.S. 222, 230, 63 L. Ed. 2d 348, 100 S. Ct. 1108 (1980) (noting that "silence in connection with the purchase or sale of securities may operate as a fraud actionable under § 10(b)" when there is "a duty to disclose arising from a relationship of trust and confidence between parties to a transaction"); Affiliated Ute Citizens of Utah v. United States, 406 U.S., at 153.

More recently, in Wharf (Holdings) Ltd. v. United Int'l Holdings, Inc., 532 U.S. 588 (2001), our decision that the seller of a security had violated § 10(b) focused on the secret intent of the seller when the sale occurred. The purchaser claimed "that Wharf sold it a security (the option) while secretly intending from the very beginning not to honor the option." Id., at 597. Although Wharf did not specifically argue that the breach of contract underlying the complaint lacked the requisite connection with a sale of securities, it did assert that the case was merely a dispute over ownership of the option, and that interpreting § 10(b) to include such a claim would convert every breach of contract that happened to involve a security into a violation of the federal securities laws. Id., at 596. We rejected that argument because the purchaser's claim was not that the defendant failed to carry out a promise to sell securities; rather, the claim was that the defendant sold a security while never intending to honor its agreement in the first place. Id., at 596–597. Similarly, in this case the SEC claims respondent sold the Woods' securities while secretly intending from the very beginning to keep the proceeds. In *Wharf,* the fraudulent intent deprived the purchaser of the benefit of the sale whereas here the fraudulent intent deprived the seller of that benefit, but the connection between the deception and the sale in each case is identical.

In United States v. O'Hagan, 521 U.S. 642 (1997), we held that the defendant had committed fraud "in connection with" a securities transaction when he used misappropriated confidential information for trading purposes. We reasoned that "the fiduciary's fraud is consummated, not when the fiduciary gains the confidential information, but when, without disclosure to his principal, he uses the information to purchase or sell securities. The securities transaction and the breach of duty thus coincide. This is so even though the person or entity defrauded is not the other party to the trade, but is, instead, the source of the nonpublic information." Id., at 655–656. The Court of Appeals distinguished *O'Hagan* by reading it to require that the misappropriated information or assets not have independent value to the client outside the securities market, 238 F.3d 559 at 565. We do not read *O'Hagan* as so limited. In the chief passage cited by the Court of Appeals for this proposition, we discussed the Government's position that "the misappropriation theory would not ... apply to a case in which a person defrauded a bank into giving him a loan or embezzled cash from another, and then used the proceeds of the misdeed to purchase securities," because in that situation "the proceeds would have value to the malefactor apart from their use in a securities transaction, and the fraud would be complete as soon as the money was obtained." 521 U.S. 642 at 656 (internal quotation marks omitted). Even if this passage could be read to introduce a new requirement into § 10(b), it would not affect our analysis of this case, because the Woods' securities did not have value for respondent apart from their use in a securities transaction and the fraud was not complete before the sale of securities occurred.

As in *Bankers Life*, *Wharf*, and *O'Hagan*, the SEC complaint describes a fraudulent scheme in which the securities transactions and breaches of fiduciary duty coincide. Those breaches were therefore "in connection with" securities sales within the meaning of § 10(b).[4] Accordingly, the judgment of the Court of Appeals is reversed, and the case is remanded for further proceedings consistent with this opinion.

It is so ordered.

———

Insert the following Note at p. 824 of the Unabridged Edition, following the Note on In re Carter–Wallace Securities Litigation:

IN RE CARTER–WALLACE, INC. SECURITIES LITIGATION, 220 F.3d 36 (2d Cir.2000). On remand from the decision at 150 F.3d 153, at p. 822 in the Unabridged Edition, the district court dismissed the complaint for failure to allege scienter. Essentially, scienter is a requisite degree of fault under Rule 10b–5. (See the Note on the Scienter Requirement at p. 824 of the Unabridged Edition.) The Second Circuit affirmed. The advertisements in question were all run no later than July 1999. Not until August 1999, however, did medical reports demonstrate a statistically significant link between Felbatrol and any

---

4. Contrary to the Court of Appeals' prediction, 238 F.3d 559, 566 (C.A.4 2001), our analysis does not transform every breach of fiduciary duty into a federal securities violation. If, for example, a broker embezzles cash from a client's account or takes advantage of the fiduciary relationship to induce his client into a fraudulent real estate transaction, then the fraud would not include the requisite connection to a purchase or sale of securities. Tr. of Oral Arg. 16. Likewise if the broker told his client he was stealing the client's assets, that breach of fiduciary duty might be in connection with a sale of securities, but it would not involve a deceptive device or fraud. Cf. Santa Fe Industries, Inc. v. Green, 430 U.S. 462, 474–476, 51 L. Ed. 2d 480, 97 S. Ct. 1292 (1977).

illness. Therefore, Carter–Wallace did not have the requisite degree of fault in running the advertisements.

————

Insert the following case and Note at p. 827 of the Unabridged Edition, after the Note on the Scienter Requirement:

Novak v. Kasaks

United States of Appeals, Second Circuit, 2000.
216 F.3d 300.

■ JOHN M. WALKER, JR., CIRCUIT JUDGE:

In 1996, plaintiffs-appellants filed this securities fraud class action, alleging violations of sections 10(b) and 20(a) of the Securities Exchange Act ("the 1934 Act") and Rule 10b–5 promulgated thereunder. In two opinions issued in 1998, the district court dismissed both the original complaint and the plaintiffs' amended complaint pursuant to Fed.R.Civ.P. 12(b)(6) and 15 U.S.C. § 78u–4(b)(3)(A) for failure to plead with sufficient particularity facts supporting a strong inference that the defendants had acted fraudulently. See Novak v. Kasaks, 997 F.Supp. 425 (S.D.N.Y.1998) (*"Novak I"*) (dismissing original complaint); Novak v. Kasaks, 26 F.Supp.2d 658 (S.D.N.Y.1998) (*"Novak II"*) (dismissing amended complaint). On appeal, the appellants contend that the district judge erred in granting the defendants' motions to dismiss.

In light of Second Circuit precedent and the provisions of the Private Securities Litigation Reform Act ("PSLRA"), we hold that the district court erred in: (1) concluding that the plaintiffs had failed to plead sufficient facts to support a strong inference of fraudulent intent; and (2) imposing an exceedingly onerous burden on the plaintiffs with respect to their obligation to plead facts with particularity. We see no persuasive alternative grounds for upholding the district court's dismissal of the complaint. Accordingly, we vacate the judgment of the district court and remand for further proceedings consistent with these determinations. In addition, we instruct the district court to allow the plaintiffs to replead to the extent they wish to do so in light of this opinion.

BACKGROUND

On April 25, 1996, plaintiffs Carol Novak and Robert Nieman brought this action on behalf of all purchasers of the common stock of the AnnTaylor Stores Corporation between February 3, 1994, and May 4, 1995 (the "Class Period"). In their complaint, the plaintiffs named two groups of defendants: (1) *the AnnTaylor defendants*, both the corporation itself—which, through its wholly-owned subsidiary, defendant AnnTaylor, Inc., is a specialty retailer of women's clothing, shoes, and accessories—and several officers at the highest level of management; and (2) *the Merrill Lynch defendants*, a group of entities and individuals that collectively held a dominant share of AnnTaylor stock and sold a significant fraction of their holdings during the Class Period.

The complaint—in both its original and amended forms—essentially alleges that, during the Class Period, the defendants made, or controlled others who made, materially false and misleading statements and omissions concerning the financial performance of AnnTaylor ("the Company"), primarily by failing properly to account for millions of dollars of inventory. According to the plaintiffs, the defendants knowingly and intentionally issued financial statements that overstated AnnTaylor's financial condition by accounting for inventory that they knew to be obsolete and nearly worthless at inflated values and by deliberately failing to adhere to the Company's publicly stated markdown policy. The following facts are taken largely from the plaintiffs' complaint.

The plaintiffs' specific allegations focus on AnnTaylor's so-called "Box and Hold" practice, whereby a substantial and growing quantity of out-of-date inventory was stored in several warehouses during the Class Period without being marked down. Internal Company documents ("Weekly Reports")—distributed at regular Monday morning merchandise meetings in which the AnnTaylor defendants participated—distinguished between regular inventory and "Box and Hold" inventory. According to the complaint, these reports demonstrated that: (1) much of the "Box and Hold" inventory was several years old and thus unlikely to be sold at full price, if at all; and (2) the levels of such inventory grew significantly during the Class Period, from about 10% to about 34% of total inventory. However, AnnTaylor's public financial statements did not distinguish between types of inventory, nor did AnnTaylor write off any of the "Box and Hold" inventory during the Class Period, allegedly in violation of Generally Accepted Accounting Principles ("GAAP") that required markdowns under these circumstances. Instead, the defendants made or caused to be made a series of positive statements to the public about the status of AnnTaylor's inventories, describing them at various points during the Class Period as "under control," "in good shape," and at "reasonable" or "expected" levels; stating that "no major or unusual markdowns were anticipated"; and attributing rising levels of inventory to growth, expansion, and planned future sales.

The plaintiffs contend that this course of conduct amounts to securities fraud. Had AnnTaylor taken appropriate write-downs, they argue, the Company's earnings would have been substantially lower than reported. Thus, the AnnTaylor defendants' alleged deception painted too rosy a picture of the Company's current performance and future prospects and kept the company's stock price at an artificially high level during the Class Period. According to the amended complaint, during this time,

> many AnnTaylor executives demanded that [the individual AnnTaylor] defendants . . . end the Box & Hold practice as it made no business sense and was growing out of control. Defendants' response . . . was that AnnTaylor could not "afford" to eliminate or write-down the Box & Hold inventory because doing so would "kill" the Company's reported financial results and/or profit margins and damage the Company on "Wall Street."

Ultimately, the defendants were forced to publicly acknowledge serious inventory problems—i.e., that inventories were too high and liquidation would result in much lower fiscal 1995 earnings than expected—at which point AnnTaylor stock prices fell precipitously, to the plaintiffs' detriment.

On July 1, 1996, in response to these allegations, the defendants moved to dismiss the action, and on August 16, 1996, the district judge granted a motion by the defendants to stay all discovery pending a ruling on the motions to dismiss pursuant to 15 U.S.C. § 78u–4(b)(3)(B).

On March 10, 1998, the district court issued an opinion and order granting the defendants' motions to dismiss the complaint. See *Novak I*, 997 F.Supp. at 426. The court concluded that "the fatal defect in the complaint lies in its allegations of scienter." Id. at 430. Specifically, the plaintiffs had "fail[ed] to plead facts giving rise to a strong inference of fraudulent intent" in that they did not "allege with sufficient specificity that . . . defendants . . . were aware that much of their inventory was worthless or seriously overvalued, or were reckless as to whether that was the case." Id. at 430–31. According to the district court, in order to meet the pleading requirement, the plaintiffs needed to identify the confidential sources of their information, see id. at 431–32, include written documentation of the "Box and Hold" practice in their complaint, see id. at 432, and allege facts showing that the Merrill Lynch defendants actually knew about "Box and Hold," see id. at 434.

On April 9, 1998, the plaintiffs filed an amended complaint. The defendants thereafter served motions to dismiss. On November 9, 1998, the district court dismissed the plaintiffs' amended complaint with prejudice. See *Novak II*, 26 F.Supp.2d at 660. In the district court's view, the amended complaint failed to remedy the defects of the original one, including lack of particularity in pleading, unnamed sources, and lack of specific evidence of the Merrill Lynch defendants' knowledge of the "Box and Hold" practice. See id. at 660–62. In addition, the district court found "that it would be futile to permit further amendment" of the complaint and thus dismissed it with prejudice. Id. at 663. This appeal followed.

The plaintiffs subsequently reached a settlement with the Merrill Lynch defendants and withdrew the appeal as against them. Accordingly, our discussion pertains solely to the claims against the AnnTaylor defendants....

DISCUSSION

We review *de novo* a district court's order dismissing a complaint on the pleadings and accept as true all facts alleged in the complaint. See Stevelman v. Alias Research Inc., 174 F.3d 79, 83 (2d Cir.1999) (citing Chill v. General Elec. Co., 101 F.3d 263, 267 (2d Cir.1996)). In this case, we are called upon to decide principally whether the district court, in assessing the sufficiency of the pleadings, applied appropriate standards in light of our precedents and the provisions of the PSLRA and whether it erred in concluding that the plaintiffs had failed to state a claim. We must also decide whether, even if the district court erred, there are alternative grounds for affirming the dismissal of the plaintiffs' § 10(b) claims.

I. Sufficiency of the Pleadings

The landscape of securities fraud litigation has been transformed in recent years by the passage of the PSLRA. This case requires us to determine the impact of two provisions in this legislation on the pleading standard for scienter and the required degree of particularity in pleading in this circuit.

A. The PSLRA and Anti–Fraud Provisions in Federal Securities Laws

Section 10(b) of the 1934 Act, 15 U.S.C. § 78j(b), and Rule 10b–5 promulgated thereunder, 17 C.F.R. § 240.10b–5, prohibit fraudulent activities in connection with securities transactions. Section 10(b) makes it unlawful

> [t]o use or employ, in connection with the purchase or sale of any security ..., any manipulative or deceptive device or contrivance in contravention of such rules and regulations as the Commission may prescribe as necessary or appropriate in the public interest or for the protection of investors.

15 U.S.C. § 78j(b). Rule 10b–5 specifies the following actions among the types of behavior proscribed by the statute:

> To make any untrue statement of a material fact or to omit to state a material fact necessary in order to make the statements made, in the light of the circumstances under which they were made, not misleading.... 17 C.F.R. § 240.10b–5.

In order to state a claim under these provisions, a complaint must allege that the defendants acted with scienter.... This case pertains not to the scienter requirement itself, but rather to the pleading requirement for scienter in the securities fraud context. Prior to the passage of the PSLRA, we had decided that, in order to state a claim for securities fraud, plaintiffs had to allege facts giving rise to "a strong inference of fraudulent intent." Acito v. IMCERA Group, Inc., 47 F.3d 47, 52 (2d Cir.1995).

In addition to pleading scienter, it is well-established that a securities fraud complaint must also plead certain facts with particularity in order to state a claim. Fed.R.Civ.P. 9(b) requires that, whenever a complaint contains allegations of fraud, "the circumstances constituting fraud ... shall be stated with particularity." See also *Chill*, 101 F.3d at 267 (noting that "the actual fraudulent statements or conduct and the fraud alleged must be stated with particularity") (internal citations omitted). "[A] complaint making such allegations must '(1) specify the statements that the plaintiff contends were fraudulent, (2) identify the speaker, (3) state where and when the statements were made, and (4) explain why the statements were fraudulent.' " Shields v. Citytrust Bancorp, Inc., 25 F.3d 1124, 1128 (2d Cir.1994) (quoting Mills v. Polar Molecular Corp., 12 F.3d 1170, 1175 (2d Cir.1993)).

In 1995, Congress amended the 1934 Act through passage of the PSLRA. See Private Securities Litigation Reform Act of 1995, Pub.L. No. 104–67, 109 Stat. 737 (codified at 15 U.S.C. §§ 77k, 77l, 77z–1, 77z–2, 78a, 78j–1, 78t, 78u, 78u–4, 78u–5). Legislators were apparently motivated in large part by a perceived need to deter strike suits wherein opportunistic private plaintiffs file securities fraud claims of dubious merit in order to exact large settlement recoveries. See H.R. Conf. Rep. No. 104–369, at 31 (1995) (noting "significant evidence of abuse in private securities lawsuits," including "the routine filing of lawsuits against issuers of securities and others whenever there is a significant change in an issuer's stock price, without regard to any underlying culpability of the issuer," and "the abuse of the discovery process to impose costs so burdensome that it is often economical for the victimized party to settle"), *reprinted in* 1995 U.S.C.C.A.N. 730, 730.

In order "to curtail the filing of meritless lawsuits," the PSLRA imposed stringent procedural requirements on plaintiffs pursuing private securities fraud actions. See id. at 41. This case concerns two of these provisions in particular. First, the statute requires that,

> [i]n any private action arising under this chapter in which the plaintiff may recover money damages only on proof that the defendant acted with a particular state of mind, the complaint shall, with respect to each act or omission alleged to violate this chapter, state with particularity facts giving rise to a strong inference that the defendant acted with the *required state of mind*.

15 U.S.C. § 78u–4(b)(2) (emphasis added) [hereinafter "paragraph (b)(2)"].

Second, the statute requires that,

[i]n any private action arising under this chapter in which the plaintiff alleges that the defendant—

(A) made an untrue statement of a material fact; or

(B) omitted to state a material fact necessary in order to make the statements made, in the light of the circumstances in which they were made, not misleading; the complaint shall specify each statement alleged to have been misleading, the reason or reasons why the statement is misleading, and, *if an allegation regarding the statement or omission is made on information and belief, the complaint shall state with particularity all facts on which that belief is formed*.

15 U.S.C. § 78u–4(b)(1) (emphasis added) [hereinafter "paragraph (b)(1)"]. In addition, § 21D(b)(3)(A) of the PSLRA requires courts to dismiss complaints that fail to meet the pleading requirements of paragraphs (b)(1) and (b)(2). See 15 U.S.C. § 78u–4(b)(3)(A). We must determine the impact of these new requirements in order to decide whether the plaintiffs in this case have pleaded sufficient facts with enough particularity to state a claim under the 1934 Act.

B.   The Pleading Standard for Scienter

1.   The Second Circuit's Pre–PSLRA Pleading Standard

We can easily summarize the pleading standard for scienter that prevailed in this circuit prior to the PSLRA:

[P]laintiffs must allege facts that give rise to a strong inference of fraudulent intent. "The requisite 'strong inference' of fraud may be established either (a) by alleging facts to show that defendants had both motive and opportunity to commit fraud, or (b) by alleging facts that constitute strong circumstantial evidence of conscious misbehavior or recklessness."

Acito, 47 F.3d at 52 (quoting *Shields*, 25 F.3d at 1128) (internal citations omitted). However, this statement of the standard conceals the complexity and uncertainty that often surround its application. This difficulty in application stems, at least in part, from the "inevitable tension" between the interests in deterring securities fraud and deterring strike suits. See In re Time Warner Inc. Sec. Litig., 9 F.3d 259, 263 (2d Cir.1993). As a result, different courts applying the pleading standard to differing factual circumstances may reach seemingly disparate results. See id. at 264. Nevertheless, we discern some basic patterns in our case law under § 10(b) and Rule 10b–5 that help to provide substance to the general language of the standard itself.

We described the type of motive and opportunity required to plead scienter under our pre-reform standard as follows:

Motive would entail concrete benefits that could be realized by one or more of the false statements and wrongful nondisclosures alleged. Opportunity would entail the means and likely prospect of achieving concrete benefits by the means alleged.

Shields, 25 F.3d at 1130. Plaintiffs could not proceed based on motives possessed by virtually all corporate insiders, including: (1) the desire to maintain a high corporate credit rating, see San Leandro Emergency Med. Group Profit Sharing Plan v. Philip Morris Cos., Inc., 75 F.3d 801, 814 (2d Cir.1996), or otherwise sustain "the appearance of corporate profitability, or of the success of an investment," *Chill*, 101 F.3d at 268; and (2) the desire to maintain a high stock price in order to increase executive compensation, see *Acito*, 47 F.3d at 54, or prolong the benefits of holding corporate office, see *Shields*, 25 F.3d at 1130. Rather, plaintiffs had to allege that defendants benefitted in some concrete and personal way from the purported fraud. This requirement was generally met when corporate insiders were alleged to have misrepresented to the public material facts about the corporation's performance or prospects in order to keep the stock price artificially high while they sold their own shares at a profit. See, e.g., *Stevelman*, 174 F.3d at 85; Goldman v. Belden, 754 F.2d 1059, 1070 (2d Cir. 1985). Accordingly, in the ordinary case, adequate motive arose from the desire to profit from extensive insider sales.

Plaintiffs could also meet the pre-PSLRA pleading standard by alleging facts that constituted strong circumstantial evidence of conscious misbehavior or recklessness on the part of defendants. Intentional misconduct is easily identified since it encompasses deliberate illegal behavior, such as securities trading by insiders privy to undisclosed and material information, see Simon DeBartolo Group, L.P. v. Richard E. Jacobs Group, Inc., 186 F.3d 157, 168–69 (2d Cir.1999), or knowing sale of a company's stock at an unwarranted discount, see Schoenbaum v. Firstbrook, 405 F.2d 215, 219 (2d Cir.1968) (in banc).

Recklessness is harder to identify with such precision and consistency. In 1978, when we first held that recklessness suffices to plead scienter under § 10(b) and Rule 10b–5, we defined reckless conduct as:

> at the least, conduct which is "highly unreasonable" and which represents
>
> > "an extreme departure from the standards of ordinary care . . . to the extent that the danger was either known to the defendant or so obvious that the defendant must have been aware of it."

Rolf v. Blyth, Eastman Dillon & Co., Inc., 570 F.2d 38, 47 (2d Cir.1978) (quoting Sanders v. John Nuveen & Co., 554 F.2d 790, 793 (7th Cir.1977)) (ellipsis in original). Similarly, we later noted that " '[a]n egregious refusal to see the obvious, or to investigate the doubtful, may in some cases give rise to an inference of . . . recklessness.' " *Chill*, 101 F.3d at 269 (quoting Goldman v. McMahan, Brafman, Morgan & Co., 706 F.Supp. 256, 259 (S.D.N.Y.1989)) (ellipsis in original).

However, these general standards offer little insight into precisely what actions and behaviors constitute recklessness sufficient for § 10(b) liability. It is the actual facts of our securities fraud cases that provide the most concrete guidance as to the types of allegations required to meet the pre-PSLRA pleading standard in this circuit.

According to these cases, securities fraud claims typically have sufficed to state a claim based on recklessness when they have specifically alleged defendants' knowledge of facts or access to information contradicting their public statements. Under such circumstances, defendants knew or, more importantly, should have known that they were misrepresenting material facts related to the corporation. Thus, for example, the pleading standard was met where the plaintiffs alleged that the defendants made or authorized statements that sales to China would be "an important new source of revenue" when they knew or should have known that Chinese import restrictions in place at the time would severely limit such sales. See Cosmas v. Hassett, 886 F.2d 8, 12 (2d Cir.1989). Similarly, the pleading standard was met where the plaintiffs alleged that the defendants released to the investing public several highly positive predictions about the marketing prospects of a computer system to record hotel guests' long-distance telephone calls when they knew or should have known several facts about the system and its consumers that revealed "grave uncertainties and problems concerning future sales of" the system. *Goldman*, 754 F.2d at 1063, 1070.

Under certain circumstances, we have found allegations of recklessness to be sufficient where plaintiffs alleged facts demonstrating that defendants failed to review or check information that they had a duty to monitor, or ignored obvious signs of fraud. Thus, the pleading standard was met where the plaintiff alleged that the defendant, his broker, consistently reassured the plaintiff that the investment advisor responsible for the plaintiff's portfolio "knew what he was doing" but never actually investigated the advisor's decisions to determine "whether there was a basis for the [defendant's] assertions." *Rolf*, 570 F.2d at 47–48. Similarly, the pleading standard was met where the defendant allegedly included false statements in SEC filings despite "the obviously evasive and suspicious statements made to him" by the corporate officials upon whom he was relying for this information and despite outside counsel's recommendation that these statements not be included. SEC v. McNulty, 137 F.3d 732, 741 (2d Cir.1998).

At the same time, however, we have identified several important limitations on the scope of liability for securities fraud based on reckless conduct. First, we have refused to allow plaintiffs to proceed with allegations of "fraud by hindsight." See Stevelman, 174 F.3d at 85. Corporate officials need not be clairvoyant; they are only responsible for revealing those material facts reasonably available to them. See

Denny v. Barber, 576 F.2d 465, 470 (2d Cir.1978). Thus, allegations that defendants should have anticipated future events and made certain disclosures earlier than they actually did do not suffice to make out a claim of securities fraud. See *Acito*, 47 F.3d at 53.

Second, as long as the public statements are consistent with reasonably available data, corporate officials need not present an overly gloomy or cautious picture of current performance and future prospects. See *Stevelman*, 174 F.3d at 85; *Shields*, 25 F.3d at 1129–30. Where plaintiffs contend defendants had access to contrary facts, they must specifically identify the reports or statements containing this information. See San Leandro, 75 F.3d at 812 ("Plaintiffs' unsupported general claim of the existence of confidential company sales reports that revealed the larger decline in sales is insufficient to survive a motion to dismiss.").

Third, there are limits to the scope of liability for failure adequately to monitor the allegedly fraudulent behavior of others. Thus, the failure of a non-fiduciary accounting firm to identify problems with the defendant-company's internal controls and accounting practices does not constitute reckless conduct sufficient for § 10(b) liability. See Decker v. Massey–Ferguson, Ltd., 681 F.2d 111, 120 (2d Cir.1982). Similarly, the failure of a parent company to interpret extraordinarily positive performance by its subsidiary—specifically, the "unprecedented and dramatically increasing profitability" of a particular form of trading—as a sign of problems and thus to investigate further does not amount to recklessness under the securities laws. See *Chill*, 101 F.3d at 269–70.

Finally, allegations of GAAP violations or accounting irregularities, standing alone, are insufficient to state a securities fraud claim. See *Stevelman*, 174 F.3d at 84; *Chill*, 101 F.3d at 270. Only where such allegations are coupled with evidence of "corresponding fraudulent intent," Chill, 101 F.3d at 270, might they be sufficient.

We now examine to what extent these lessons from our prior case law have survived the recent reform of the securities laws.

2.   Implications of the PSLRA for the Pleading Standard for Scienter in This Circuit

Courts have disagreed on the proper interpretation of the new pleading requirement imposed by paragraph (b)(2) in light of the text of the PSLRA and its legislative history. They have generally come to one of two conclusions:

(1) The statute effectively adopts the Second Circuit's pleading standard for scienter wholesale, and thus plaintiffs may continue to state a claim by pleading either motive and opportunity or strong circumstantial evidence of recklessness or conscious misbehavior. See In re Advanta Corp. Sec. Litig., 180 F.3d 525 (3d Cir.1999); Press v. Chemical Invest. Servs. Corp., 166 F.3d 529,

538 (2d Cir.1999) (dicta); Rubinstein v. Skyteller, Inc., 48 F.Supp.2d 315, 320 (S.D.N.Y.1999) (following *Press*).

(2) The statute strengthens the Second Circuit's standard by rejecting the simple pleading of motive and opportunity. See Bryant v. Avado Brands, Inc., 187 F.3d 1271, 1283 (11th Cir. 1999); In re Silicon Graphics Inc. Sec. Litig., 183 F.3d 970, 979 (9th Cir.1999); In re Comshare, Inc. Sec. Litig., 183 F.3d 542, 550–51 (6th Cir.1999); *Novak I*, 997 F.Supp. at 430; In re Glenayre Tech., Inc. Sec. Litig., 982 F.Supp. 294, 298 (S.D.N.Y.1997); In re Baesa Sec. Litig., 969 F.Supp. 238, 241–42 (S.D.N.Y.1997).

Our own review of the text and legislative history leads us to a middle ground. We conclude that the PSLRA effectively raised the nationwide pleading standard to that previously existing in this circuit and no higher (with the exception of the "with particularity" requirement). At the same time, however, we believe that Congress's failure to include language about motive and opportunity suggests that we need not be wedded to these concepts in articulating the prevailing standard. We are led to these conclusions by the considerations that follow.

In order to gauge the implications of paragraph (b)(2), we apply familiar canons of statutory construction. We look first to the text of the statute. If that language is plain and its meaning sufficiently clear, we need look no further. See Connecticut Nat'l Bank v. Germain, 503 U.S. 249, 254, 112 S.Ct. 1146, 117 L.Ed.2d 391 (1992). Only if the text of the statute is not unambiguous do we turn for guidance to legislative history and the purposes of the statute. See Dowling v. United States, 473 U.S. 207, 218, 105 S.Ct. 3127, 87 L.Ed.2d 152 (1985). Applying these principles, we conclude that the enactment of paragraph (b)(2) did not change the basic pleading standard for scienter in this circuit.

In this case, our interpretive task begins and ends with the text of the statute. In drafting paragraph (b)(2), Congress specifically incorporated this circuit's "strong inference" language to define the pleading standard for securities fraud cases. Compare 15 U.S.C. § 78u–4(b)(2) (requiring plaintiffs to "state with particularity facts giving rise to a strong inference that the defendant acted with the required state of mind"), with *Acito*, 47 F.3d at 52 ("[P]laintiffs must allege facts that give rise to a strong inference of fraudulent intent."). We agree with the Third Circuit that this "use of the Second Circuit's language compels the conclusion that the Reform Act establishes a pleading standard approximately equal in stringency to that of the Second Circuit." In re Advanta Corp., 180 F.3d at 534. Cf. United States v. Johnson, 14 F.3d 766, 770 (2d Cir.1994) (finding that Congress's use of "substantially identical language" to that of an earlier statute "bespeaks an intention to import" judicial interpretations of that language into the new statute).

Given the absence of ambiguity in the statutory text, no resort to legislative history or the purposes of the PSLRA is required. In any event, there is nothing in these sources that would alter our conclusion. As far as the general purposes of the PSLRA are concerned, Congress plainly sought to impose a stricter nationwide pleading standard and did so. But this purpose does not require raising the standard above that of this circuit, particularly in light of the explicit Congressional recognition that our pre-PSLRA standard was the most stringent in the nation. See H.R. Conf. Rep. No. 104–369, at 41. "In many jurisdictions, adoption of a 'strong inference' standard will substantially heighten the barriers to pleading scienter, a result Congress expressly intended. Moreover, even in jurisdictions already employing the Second Circuit standard, the additional requirement that plaintiffs state facts 'with particularity' represents a heightening of the standard." In re Advanta Corp., 180 F.3d at 534.

Meanwhile, in our view, as is so often the case with legislative history generally, the legislative history of the PSLRA contains "conflicting expressions of legislative intent" with respect to the pleading requirement. Id. at 533. For example, while the Conference Committee rejected language from the Senate bill that would have adopted the Second Circuit rule wholesale, including language about motive and opportunity and recklessness, see H.R. Conf. Rep. No. 104–369, at 41 & 48 n. 23, the Senate Committee reporting the bill stated that it was proposing not "a new and untested pleading standard that would generate additional litigation," but rather "a uniform standard modeled upon the pleading standard of the Second Circuit." S.Rep. No. 104–98, at 15 (1995), reprinted in 1995 U.S.C.C.A.N. 679, 694 (noting that courts interpreting the proposed "strong inference" pleading standard might find Second Circuit case law "instructive").

When all is said and done, we believe that the enactment of paragraph (b)(2) did not change the basic pleading standard for scienter in this circuit (except by the addition of the words "with particularity"). Accordingly, we hold that the PSLRA adopted our "strong inference" standard:

In order to plead scienter, plaintiffs must "state with particularity facts giving rise to a strong inference that the defendant acted with the required state of mind," as required by the language of the Act itself. Although litigants and lower courts need and should not employ or rely on magic words such as "motive and opportunity," we believe that our prior case law may be helpful in providing guidance as to how the "strong inference" standard may be met. Therefore, in applying this standard, district courts should look to the cases and factors discussed in Section I.B.1 above to determine whether plaintiffs have pleaded facts giving rise to the requisite "strong inference." These cases suggest, in brief, that the inference may arise where the complaint sufficiently alleges that the defendants: (1) benefitted in a concrete and personal way from the purported fraud . . . ; (2) engaged in deliberately illegal behavior ...; (3) knew facts or had access to information suggesting that their public statements were not accurate ...; or (4) failed to check information they had a duty to monitor.... We now turn to the complaint in this case to determine whether the plaintiffs have met their burden to plead scienter.

3. Strong Inference of Fraudulent Intent on the Part of the AnnTaylor Defendants

The district court concluded that the plaintiffs had failed to plead facts giving rise to a strong inference of the defendants' fraudulent intent, as required to state a claim under § 10(b). We disagree.

According to the complaint, the AnnTaylor defendants knew at all relevant times that the Company had serious inventory problems that they sought to disguise by adopting the "Box and Hold" scheme. By refusing to mark down inventory they knew to be "worthless," "obsolete," and "unsalable," the defendants acted "intentionally and deliberately" to artificially inflate AnnTaylor's reported financial results. They discussed the need to mark down inventory but refused to do so because that would damage the Company's financial prospects. Further, in approving the inventory management practices of "Box and Hold," the defendants knowingly sanctioned procedures that violated the Company's own markdown policy, as stated in the Company's public filings. In doing so, they caused those filings to be materially misleading in that the disclosed policy no longer reflected actual practice. Lastly, despite knowledge of the true reasons for rising inventory levels, the defendants made repeated statements to the investment community either offering false reassurances that inventory was under control or giving false explanations for its growth. In short, the Complaint alleges that the defendants engaged in conscious misstatements with the intent to deceive. There is no doubt that this pleading satisfies the standard for scienter under *Hochfelder*, and the requirement of the PSLRA that plaintiffs state facts with particularity that give rise to a strong inference of the required state of mind.

In the end, we believe that the district court applied the correct standard but erroneously found that this standard was not met on these pleadings. According to the district court, the scienter requirement can be satisfied by pleading either "conscious recklessness"— i.e., a state of mind "approximating actual intent, and not merely a heightened form of negligence"—or "actual intent." *Novak I*, 997 F.Supp. at 430. This was an accurate statement of the law. However, the district court believed that the facts pleaded by the plaintiffs supported nothing more than an inference that the managers of AnnTaylor disagreed over matters of business judgment, such as the valuation of inventory and the timing of markdowns. See *Novak II*, 26 F.Supp.2d at 660. This was incorrect as a matter of law. When managers deliberately make materially false statements concerning inventory with the intent to deceive the investment community, they have engaged in conduct actionable under the securities laws.

C.   Particularity of the Facts Pleaded

The district court also found the facts pleaded by the plaintiffs insufficiently particularized, in large part because they did not reveal the identity of the personal sources of their critical factual allegations. We disagree with the district court's reasoning and accordingly vacate and remand for further proceedings consistent with the discussion that follows.

As discussed above, Rule 9(b) has long required plaintiffs in securities fraud cases to state "the circumstances constituting fraud . . . with particularity." The PSLRA imposed an additional requirement: whenever plaintiffs allege, on information and belief, that defendants made material misstatements or omissions, the complaint must "state with particularity all facts on which that belief is formed." 15 U.S.C. § 78u–4(b)(1). This requirement plainly applies in this case. In numerous places in their complaint, the plaintiffs allege, based on information and belief, that the AnnTaylor defendants made materially misleading statements or omissions. Most importantly, they allege that the defendants made false statements concerning the value of inventory because "Box and Hold" merchandise was "unsalable," "obsolete," and "nearly worthless," and its "actual value was nearly zero." In order to survive at this stage, the complaint must state with particularity sufficient facts to support the belief that the "Box and Hold" inventory was of limited value, and accordingly that the defendants' positive public statements concerning inventory growth were false and misleading.

The district court concluded that the plaintiffs had failed to meet these particularity requirements, in substantial part because they failed to reveal their confidential sources for some of the facts on which their belief in the essential worthlessness of the "Box and Hold" inventory was based. See *Novak I*, 997 F.Supp. at 431–32; *Novak II*, 26 F.Supp.2d at 660–61. The lower court found the plaintiffs' allegations in this respect at worst "conclusory, unsupported and inflammatory," and at best "based upon reports by . . . anonymous 'former employees' who should have been identified by name." *Novak II*, 26 F.Supp.2d at 661. The district court's reasoning and conclusions were flawed in several respects.

For one thing, the complaint provides specific facts concerning the Company's significant write-off of inventory directly following the Class Period, which tends to support the plaintiffs' contention that inventory was seriously overvalued at the time the purportedly misleading statements were made. Specifically, the plaintiffs allege that: (1) in AnnTaylor's May 1995 reporting of its first quarter fiscal 1995 results, the Company "admitted to analysts that its inventories were too high" and that "inventory liquidation" would follow; (2) in

AnnTaylor's July 29, 1995 10–Q filed with the SEC, it "admitted that the decrease in the Company's gross profit percentage was attributable to 'increased cost of goods sold as a percentage of net sales, *primarily resulting from markdowns*' "; and (3) a January 22, 1996 Weekly Report showed that even six months after the Class Period, substantial amounts of "Box and Hold" inventory still dated from 1993 and 1994, which supports the inference that inventory during the Class Period was similarly dated. Thus, the complaint identifies with particularity several documentary sources that support the plaintiffs' belief that serious inventory problems existed during the Class Period itself.

We recognize that the complaint does not state with particularity every fact upon which this belief was based, since it is apparent that there were also personal sources who were not specifically identified. However, plaintiffs who rely on confidential sources are not always required to name those sources, even when they make allegations on information and belief concerning false or misleading statements, as here.

First, there is nothing in the caselaw of this circuit that requires plaintiffs to reveal confidential sources at the pleading stage. The defendants rely heavily on Segan v. Dreyfus Corp., 513 F.2d 695 (2d Cir.1975), in which we held that a plaintiff's complaint was insufficiently specific and rejected the argument that further disclosure would, among other things, identify a confidential informant. See id. at 696. But in Dreyfus, we held only that the plaintiff had to plead additional facts, not that the plaintiff was required to reveal the name of the informant. See id. ("A suit charging fraud may not be based on facts so secret that the defendants cannot be told what they are.") (emphasis added). Some district courts in this circuit have on occasion stated that Rule 9(b) requires plaintiffs in securities fraud cases to allege the "sources that support the alleged specific facts," e.g., Blanchard v. Katz, 705 F.Supp. 1011, 1012 (S.D.N.Y.1989); Crystal v. Foy, 562 F.Supp. 422, 425 (S.D.N.Y.1983), but in no case have they dismissed a complaint for failure to identify confidential sources.

Second, while paragraph (b)(1) may compel revelation of confidential sources under certain circumstances, such circumstances are not necessarily present in this case. The defendants point to district court decisions outside this circuit that hold or imply that the PSLRA generally requires plaintiffs to include the names of their confidential sources. See In re Silicon Graphics Inc. Sec. Litig., 970 F.Supp. 746, 763 (N.D.Cal.1997); In re Aetna Inc. Sec. Litig., No. CIV. A. MDL 1219, 1999 WL 354527, at *4 (E.D.Pa. May 26, 1999). However, this rule is based on a misreading of the legislative history of the PSLRA. Specifically, the court in *Silicon Graphics* relied primarily on the hyperbolic statements of legislators attempting (unsuccessfully) to amend the proposed Act to lighten plaintiffs' pleading burden. See *Silicon Graphics*, 970 F.Supp. at 763–64. In fact, the applicable provision of the law as ultimately enacted requires plaintiffs to plead only facts and makes no mention of the sources of these facts. See 15 U.S.C. § 78u–4(b)(1).

More fundamentally, our reading of the PSLRA rejects any notion that confidential sources must be named as a general matter. In our view, notwithstanding the use of the word "all," paragraph (b)(1) does not require that plaintiffs plead with particularity every single fact upon which their beliefs concerning false or misleading statements are based. Rather, plaintiffs need only plead with particularity *sufficient* facts to support those beliefs.[1] Accordingly, where plaintiffs rely on confidential personal sources but also on other facts, they need not name their sources as long as the latter facts provide an adequate basis for believing that the defendants' statements were false. Moreover, even if personal sources must be identified, there is no requirement that they be named, provided they are described in the complaint with sufficient particularity to support the probability that a person in the position occupied by the source would possess the information alleged. In both of these situations, the plaintiffs will have pleaded enough facts to support their belief, even though some arguably relevant facts have been left out. Accordingly, a complaint can meet the new pleading requirement imposed by paragraph (b)(1) by providing documentary evidence and/or a sufficient general description of the personal sources of the plaintiffs' beliefs.

Thus, we find no requirement in existing law that, in the ordinary course, complaints in securities fraud cases must name confidential sources, and we see no reason to impose such a requirement under the circumstances of this case. "The primary purpose of Rule 9(b) is to afford defendant fair notice of the plaintiff's claim and the factual ground upon which it is based." Ross v. Bolton, 904 F.2d 819, 823 (2d Cir.1990). This purpose, which also underlies paragraph (b)(1), can be served without requiring plaintiffs to name their confidential sources as long as they supply sufficient specific facts to support their allegations. Imposing a general requirement of disclosure of confidential sources serves no legitimate pleading purpose while it could deter informants from providing critical information to investigators in meritorious cases or invite retaliation against them.

We express no view as to whether the plaintiffs' allegations in this case were sufficiently particularized. Instead, we remand to the district court with instructions to: (1) allow the plaintiffs to replead in light of

---

1. Paragraph (b)(1) is strangely drafted. Reading "all" literally would produce illogical results that Congress cannot have intended. Contrary to the clearly expressed purpose of the PSLRA, it would allow complaints to survive dismissal where "all" the facts supporting the plaintiff's information and belief were pled, but those facts were patently insufficient to support that belief. Equally peculiarly, it would require dismissal where the complaint pled facts fully sufficient to support a convincing inference if any known facts were omitted. Our reading of the provision focuses on whether the facts alleged are sufficient to support a reasonable belief as to the misleading nature of the statement or omission.

our discussion above; and (2) reconsider the particularity of the plaintiffs' pleadings in light of the proper standards.

II. Alternative Grounds for Dismissal

The appellees argue that we still may affirm the district court's dismissal because: (1) the appellants have not adequately alleged that statements made by securities analysts can be attributed to the Ann-Taylor defendants; and (2) the alleged false and misleading statements made during the Class Period are not actionable in any event. We reject both arguments.

Under the law of this circuit, plaintiffs may state a claim against corporate officials for false and misleading information disseminated through analysts' reports by alleging that the officials either: (1) "intentionally foster[ed] a mistaken belief concerning a material fact" that was incorporated into reports; or (2) adopted or placed their "imprimatur" on the reports. See Elkind v. Liggett & Myers, Inc., 635 F.2d 156, 163–64 (2d Cir.1980). This was plainly the case here. The plaintiffs alleged that the AnnTaylor defendants both made misstatements that were later incorporated into analysts' reports and subsequently (at least implicitly) adopted the contents of those reports. These allegations were sufficiently detailed to meet the pleading threshold because generally the circumstances of the statements—including dates and participants—were particularized. See *Acito*, 47 F.3d at 51.

Moreover, the types of statements the defendants are alleged to have made or adopted are actionable. While statements containing simple economic projections, expressions of optimism, and other puffery are insufficient, see, e.g., Friedman v. Mohasco Corp., 929 F.2d 77, 79 (2d Cir.1991), defendants may be liable for misrepresentations of existing facts, see In re Prudential Sec. Inc. Ltd. Partnerships Litig., 930 F.Supp. 68, 74–75 (S.D.N.Y.1996). Here, the complaint alleges that the defendants did more than just offer rosy predictions; the defendants stated that the inventory situation was "in good shape" or "under control" while they allegedly knew that the contrary was true. Assuming, as we must at this stage, the accuracy of the plaintiffs' allegations about AnnTaylor's "Box and Hold" practices, these statements were plainly false and misleading.

CONCLUSION

For the foregoing reasons, we hold, first, that: (a) in order to plead scienter in securities fraud cases, plaintiffs must "state with particularity facts giving rise to a strong inference that the defendant acted with the required state of mind"; and (b) the plaintiffs here pleaded sufficient facts to establish a strong inference of fraudulent intent on the part of the AnnTaylor defendants. Second, we hold that the district court erred, under the circumstances of this case, by requiring the plaintiffs to reveal the names of their confidential sources in order to meet the particularity requirements of the PSLRA. On remand, we instruct the district court to: (a) permit the plaintiffs to replead; and (b) evaluate their pleadings anew in light of our interpretation of these requirements. Finally, we see no alternative grounds for affirming the district court's dismissal of the plaintiffs' complaint. Accordingly, the judgment of the district court is vacated and the case remanded for further proceedings consistent with these rulings.

———

PHILADELPHIA v. FLEMING COMPANIES, 264 F.3d 1245 (10th Cir.2001). "The circuit courts of appeals are currently split on the question of whether plaintiffs may still use motive and opportunity pleadings to demonstrate scienter under the heightened pleading requirements set forth in the PSLRA. Two circuits have held that evidence of motive and opportunity to commit securities fraud may still satisfy the requirements for pleading scienter under the PSLRA. See *Press*, 166 F.3d at 537–38 [2d Cir.] (upholding previous Second Circuit standard without analysis of the PSLRA); *Advanta*, 180 F.3d at 534–35 [3d Cir.] (analyzing the PSLRA and upholding Second Circuit standard). At least one circuit has held that motive and opportunity pleadings alone can never satisfy the scienter pleading requirements of the PSLRA. See *In re Silicon Graphics*, 183 F.3d at 979 [9th Cir.]. And at least two, and arguably three, more circuits have adopted a middle ground between these two approaches, holding that motive and opportunity pleadings are relevant to a finding of scienter, but that they do not constitute a separate, alternative method of pleading scienter. See [*Greebel v. FTP Software, Inc.*, 194 F.3d 185 (1st Cir. 1999); *Helwig v. Vencor, Inc.*, 251 F.3d 540 (6th Cir.2001); *Bryant v. Avado Brands, Inc.*, 187 F.3d 1271 (11th Cir.1999)].

"We agree with the middle ground chosen by the First and Sixth Circuits, and arguably by the Eleventh Circuit. These circuits have determined that courts must look to the totality of the pleadings to determine whether the plaintiffs' allegations permit a strong inference of fraudulent intent. Allegations of motive and opportunity may be important to that totality, but are typically not sufficient in themselves to establish a 'strong inference' of scienter."

———

Insert the following material at p.829 of the Unabridged Edition, and p. 594 of the Concise Edition, after the Note on the Use Test Under Rule 10b–5:

SECURITIES AND EXCHANGE COMMISSION RELEASE NO. 33–7881 (2000)

SELECTIVE DISCLOSURE AND INSIDER TRADING

... [I]nsider trading law has developed on a case-by-case basis under the antifraud provisions of the federal securities laws, primarily

Section 10(b) of the Exchange Act and Rule 10b–5. As a result, from time to time there have been issues on which various courts disagreed. [Rule 10b5–1 resolves one such issue.]

A. Rule 10b5–1: Trading "On the Basis of" Material Nonpublic Information

1. Background

... [O]ne unsettled issue in insider trading law has been what, if any, causal connection must be shown between the trader's possession of inside information and his or her trading. In enforcement cases, we have argued that a trader may be liable for trading while in "knowing possession" of the information. The contrary view is that a trader is not liable unless it is shown that he or she "used" the information for trading. Until recent years, there has been little case law discussing this issue. Although the Supreme Court has variously described an insider's violations as trading "on"[95] or "on the basis of"[96] material nonpublic information, it has not addressed the use/possession issue. Three recent courts of appeals cases addressed the issue but reached different results.[97]

... [I]n our view, the goals of insider trading prohibitions—protecting investors and the integrity of securities markets—are best accomplished by a standard closer to the "knowing possession" standard than to the "use" standard. At the same time, we recognize that an absolute standard based on knowing possession, or awareness, could be overbroad in some respects. The new rule attempts to balance these considerations by means of a general rule based on "awareness" of the material nonpublic information, with several carefully enumerated affirmative defenses. This approach will better enable insiders and issuers to conduct themselves in accordance with the law....

... Scienter remains a necessary element for liability under Section 10(b) of the Exchange Act and Rule 10b–5 thereunder, and Rule 10b5–1 does not change this.

2. Provisions of Rule 10b5–1

We are adopting ... the general rule set forth in Rule 10b5–1(a), and the definition of "on the basis of" material nonpublic information in Rule 10b5–1(b). A trade is on the basis of material nonpublic information if the trader was aware of the material, nonpublic information when the person made the purchase or sale.

---

95. *See Dirks v. SEC*, 463 U.S. 646, 654 (1983).

96. *See O'Hagan*, 521 U.S. at 651–52.

97. *Compare United States v. Teicher*, 987 F.2d 112, 120–21 (2d Cir.), cert. denied, 510 U.S. 976 (1993) (suggesting that "knowing possession" is sufficient) with *SEC v. Adler*, 137 F.3d 1325, 1337 (11th Cir.1998) ("use" required, but proof of possession provides strong inference of use) and *United States v. Smith*, 155 F.3d 1051, 1069 & n. 27 (9th Cir.1998), cert. denied, 525 U.S. 1071 (1999) (requiring that "use" be proven in a criminal case).

... The awareness standard reflects the common sense notion that a trader who is aware of inside information when making a trading decision inevitably makes use of the information. Additionally, a clear awareness standard will provide greater clarity and certainty than a presumption or "strong inference" approach.[105] Accordingly, we have determined to adopt the awareness standard as proposed....

... [T]he affirmative defense [in Rule 10b5–1] allows purchases and sales pursuant to contracts, instructions, and plans. [The defense provides] appropriate flexibility to persons who wish to structure securities trading plans and strategies when they are not aware of material nonpublic information, and do not exercise any influence over the transaction once they do become aware of such information.

As adopted, paragraph (c)(1)(i) sets forth an affirmative defense from the general rule, which applies both to individuals and entities that trade. To satisfy this provision, a person must establish several factors.

- First, the person must demonstrate that before becoming aware of the information, he or she had entered into a binding contract to purchase or sell the security, provided instructions to another person to execute the trade for the instructing person's account, or adopted a written plan for trading securities.

- Second, the person must demonstrate that, with respect to the purchase or sale, the contract, instructions, or plan either: (1) expressly specified the amount, price, and date; (2) provided a written formula or algorithm, or computer program, for determining amounts, prices, and dates; or (3) did not permit the person to exercise any subsequent influence over how, when, or whether to effect purchases or sales; provided, in addition, that any other person who did exercise such influence was not aware of the material nonpublic information when doing so.

- Third, the person must demonstrate that the purchase or sale that occurred was pursuant to the prior contract, instruction, or plan. A purchase or sale is not pursuant to a contract, instruction, or plan if, among other things, the person who entered into the contract, instruction, or plan altered or deviated from the contract, instruction, or plan or entered into or altered a corresponding or hedging transaction or position with respect to those securities.[111]

---

105. Some commenters stated that "aware" was an unclear term that may be interpreted to mean something less than "knowing possession." We disagree. "Aware" is a commonly used and well-defined English word, meaning "having knowledge; conscious; cognizant." We believe that "awareness" has a much clearer meaning that "knowing possession," which has not been defined by case law.

111. Rule 10b5–1(c)(1)(i)(C). However, a person acting in good faith may modify a prior contract, instruction, or plan before becoming aware of material nonpublic information. In that case, a purchase or sale that complies with the modified contract, instruction, or plan will be considered pursuant to a new contract, instruction, or plan.

Under paragraph (c)(1)(ii), ... the exclusion provided in paragraph (c)(1)(i) will be available only if the contract, instruction, or plan was entered into in good faith and not as part of a scheme to evade the prohibitions of this section.

Paragraph (c)(1)(iii) defines several key terms in the exclusion.... ["Amount"] means either a specified number of shares or a specified dollar value of securities.... [Price] means market price on a particular date or a limit price or a particular dollar price. "Date" means either the specific day of the year on which a market order is to be executed, or a day or days of the year on which a limit order is in force.

Taken as a whole, the revised defense is designed to cover situations in which a person can demonstrate that the material nonpublic information was not a factor in the trading decision. We believe this provision will provide appropriate flexibility to those who would like to plan securities transactions in advance at a time when they are not aware of material nonpublic information, and then carry out those pre-planned transactions at a later time, even if they later become aware of material nonpublic information.

For example, an issuer operating a repurchase program will not need to specify with precision the amounts, prices, and dates on which it will repurchase its securities. Rather, an issuer could adopt a written plan, when it is not aware of material nonpublic information, that uses a written formula to derive amounts, prices, and dates. Or the plan could simply delegate all the discretion to determine amounts, prices, and dates to another person who is not aware of the information—provided that the plan did not permit the issuer to (and in fact the issuer did not) exercise any subsequent influence over the purchases or sales.

Similarly, an employee wishing to adopt a plan for exercising stock options and selling the underlying shares could, while not aware of material nonpublic information, adopt a written plan that contained a formula for determining the specified percentage of the employee's vested options to be exercised and/or sold at or above a specific price. The formula could provide, for example, that the employee will exercise options and sell the shares one month before each date on which her son's college tuition is due, and link the amount of the trade to the cost of the tuition.

An employee also could acquire company stock through payroll deductions under an employee stock purchase plan or a Section 401(k) plan. The employee could provide oral instructions as to his or her plan participation, or proceed by means of a written plan. The transaction price could be computed as a percentage of market price, and the transaction amount could be based on a percentage of salary to be deducted under the plan. The date of a plan transaction could be determined pursuant to a formula set forth in the plan. Alternatively, the date of a plan transaction could be controlled by the plan's administrator or investment manager, assuming that he or she is not aware of the material, nonpublic information at the time of executing the transaction, and the employee does not exercise influence over the timing of the transaction.

The proposal included an additional affirmative defense available only to trading parties that are entities.... [T]his defense is available to entities as an alternative to the other enumerated defenses described above.

Under this provision, an entity will not be liable if it demonstrates that the individual making the investment decision on behalf of the entity was not aware of the information, and that the entity had implemented reasonable policies and procedures to prevent insider trading....

Insert the following material at p.866 of the Unabridged Edition, and p. 618 of the Concise Edition, after United States v. O'Hagan:

SECURITIES AND EXCHANGE COMMISSION
RELEASE NO. 33–7881 (2000)
SELECTIVE DISCLOSURE AND INSIDER TRADING

... [I]nsider trading law has developed on a case-by-case basis under the antifraud provisions of the federal securities laws, primarily Section 10(b) of the Exchange Act and Rule 10b–5. As a result, from time to time there have been issues on which various courts disagreed. [Rule 10b5–2 resolves one such issue.] ...

... *Rule 10b5–2: Duties of Trust or Confidence in Misappropriation Insider Trading Cases* ...

1. Background

... [A]n unsettled issue in insider trading law has been under what circumstances certain non-business relationships, such as family and personal relationships, may provide the duty of trust or confidence required under the misappropriation theory. Case law has produced the following anomalous result. A family member who receives a "tip" (within the meaning of *Dirks*) and then trades violates Rule 10b–5. A family member who trades in breach of an express promise of confidentiality also violates Rule 10b–5. A family member who trades in breach of a reasonable expectation of confidentiality, however, does not necessarily violate Rule 10b–5.

... [W]e think that this anomalous result harms investor confidence in the integrity and fairness of the nation's securities markets. The family member's trading has the same impact on the market and investor confidence in the third example as it does in the first two examples. In all three examples, the trader's informational advantage stems from "contrivance, not luck," and the informational disadvantage to other investors "cannot be overcome with research or skill." Additionally, the need to distinguish among the three types of cases may require an unduly intrusive examination of the details of particular family relationships. Accordingly, we believe there is good reason for the broader approach we adopt today for determining when family or personal relationships create "duties of trust or confidence" under the misappropriation theory.

... [Rule 10b5–2] is not designed to interfere with particular family or personal relationships; rather, its goal is to protect investors and the fairness and integrity of the nation's securities markets against improper trading on the basis of inside information. Moreover, we do not believe that the rule will require a more intrusive examination of family relationships than would be required under existing case law without the rule. Current case law ... already establishes a regime under which questions of liability turn on the nature of the details of the relationships between family members, such as their prior history and patterns of sharing confidences. By providing more of a bright-line test for certain enumerated close family relationships, we believe the rule will mitigate, to some degree, the need to examine the details of particular relationships in the course of investigating suspected insider trading.

2. Provisions of Rule 10b5–2

[Rule 10b5–2] sets forth a non-exclusive list of three situations in which a person has a duty of trust or confidence for purposes of the "misappropriation" theory of the Exchange Act and Rule 10b–5 thereunder.

First ... we provide that a duty of trust or confidence exists whenever a person agrees to maintain information in confidence.

Second, we provide that a duty of trust or confidence exists when two people have a history, pattern, or practice of sharing confidences such that the recipient of the information knows or reasonably should know that the person communicating the material nonpublic information expects that the recipient will maintain its confidentiality. This is a "facts and circumstances" test based on the expectation of the parties in light of the overall relationship. Some commenters were concerned that, as proposed, this provision examined the reasonable expectation of confidentiality of the person communicating the material nonpublic information rather than examining the expectations of the recipient of the information and/or both parties to the communication. We believe that mutuality was implicit in the proposed rule because an inquiry into the reasonableness of the recipient's expectation necessarily involves considering the relationship as a whole, including the other party's expectations. Nevertheless, we have revised the provision to make this mutuality explicit. . . .

Third, we are adopting as proposed a bright-line rule that states that a duty of trust or confidence exists when a person receives or obtains material nonpublic information from certain enumerated close family members: spouses, parents, children, and siblings. An affirmative defense permits the person receiving or obtaining the information to demonstrate that under the facts and circumstances of that family relationship, no duty of trust or confidence existed. Some commenters noted that the enumerated relationships do not include domestic partners, step-parents, or step-children. We have determined not to include these relationships in this paragraph, although paragraphs (b)(1) and (b)(2) could reach them. Our experience in this area indicates that most instances of insider trading between or among family members involve spouses, parents and children, or siblings; therefore, we have enumerated these relationships and not others. . . .

Insert the following case at p. 866 of the Unabridged Edition, after United States v. O'Hagan:

United States v. Falcone

United States Court of Appeals, Second Circuit, 2001.
257 F.3d 226.

■ Before: FEINBERG, VAN GRAAFEILAND, and SOTOMAYOR, CIRCUIT JUDGES.

■ SOTOMAYOR, CIRCUIT JUDGE:

Defendant Joseph Falcone appeals from a judgment of the United States District Court for the Eastern District of New York (Platt, J.) convicting him after a jury trial of thirteen counts of securities fraud, in violation of section 10(b) of the Securities Exchange Act of 1934, *15 U.S.C. § 78j(b)* ("section 10(b)"), and one count of conspiracy to commit securities fraud, in violation of *18 U.S.C. § 371*, based on the "misappropriation theory" of insider trading. The charges arose from a scheme involving the misappropriation of pre-release confidential copies of a magazine column that discussed securities for the purpose of trading in the securities of the featured companies. In challenging the district court's finding that this case is governed by this Court's decision in *United States v. Libera*, 989 F.2d 596 (2d Cir.1993), which upheld a conviction based on a similar scheme, defendant argues on appeal that *Libera* should not govern the result in this case because: 1) under the Supreme Court's more recent decision in *United States v. O'Hagan*, 521 U.S. 642, 117 S.Ct. 2199, 138 L.Ed.2d 724 (1997), the misappropriations at issue in both *Libera* and the instant case would not satisfy section 10(b)'s requirement that the misappropriation be "in connection with" the purchase or sale of a security; and 2) this case is materially distinguishable from *Libera*. We disagree and affirm the judgment of conviction.

BACKGROUND

Defendant's conviction arose from his participation in a scheme in which an employee of Hudson News, a magazine wholesaler, faxed a stockbroker acquaintance of defendant's, Larry Smath, pre-release confidential copies of a column in *Business Week* magazine—"Inside Wall Street"—that discussed companies and their stocks. *Business Week* is a weekly financial publication owned by McGraw–Hill, Inc. Smath himself used the information to trade securities and also passed the information along to defendant, who likewise traded in the securities discussed in the column.

Evidence was introduced at trial indicating that the value of stocks discussed favorably in the column tended to increase after the magazine was released to the public and that, because of this impact, *Business Week* imposed a strict confidentiality policy prior to that release on all those involved in the magazine's production and distribution. This policy applied to Hudson News and was implemented through a broader company policy, applicable to all the magazines Hudson News distributed, prohibiting employees from taking copies of the magazines or portions thereof out of the company's delivery department.

After the jury returned a guilty verdict, the district court denied defendant's motion to set the verdict aside. Although expressing concern about the "boundless expansion of the misappropriation theory," the district court reluctantly declared that it was bound by this court's imposition of liability on virtually identical facts in *United States v. Libera*, 989 F.2d 596 (2d Cir.1993). *Libera* dealt with the criminal liability of individuals who, like defendant here, received pre-release copies of the same "Inside Wall Street" column in *Business Week* magazine in violation of *Business Week*'s confidentiality policy and traded on the information. *See id.* at 598–99. In *Libera*, the information was passed to the defendants after it had been misappropriated by an employee of *Business Week*'s printer. *Id.*

Here, employees of entities further down the chain of distribution were the misappropriators. According to the evidence at trial, after being printed, *Business Week* magazine is sent to a national distributor of magazines, Curtis Circulation Company ("Curtis"). *See United States v. Falcone*, 97 F.Supp.2d 297, 299 (E.D.N.Y.2000). Curtis sells the magazine to various wholesalers, including Hudson News. Gregory Salvage, a 22–year employee of Hudson News, arranged for a subordinate to fax copies of the "Inside Wall Street" column—prior to the close of the stock market on Thursdays and prior to the public release of the magazine later that evening—to Smath, a stockbroker at Renaissance Securities and Salvage's neighbor. Smath himself traded based on this information and also passed it on to defendant, who likewise traded in reliance thereon.

On appeal, defendant argues that under the misappropriation theory as defined in *O'Hagan*, it is not sufficient for the purposes of section 10(b) liability that a misappropriation ultimately results in securities trading. Instead, he argues, the misappropriation in breach of a duty must itself have a certain nexus with securities trading that is lacking in the scenario at issue in *Libera* and the instant case....

DISCUSSION

I.   *The Law of Insider Trading*

A.   *Relevant Statutory Authority*

Section 10(b) of the Securities Exchange Act of 1934 is violated when: (1) "any manipulative or deceptive device" is used, (2) "in connection with the purchase or sale of any security." *15 U.S.C. § 78j(b)*. Pursuant to this section, the Securities and Exchange Commission has adopted Rule 10b–5, which provides in relevant part that:

> It shall be unlawful for any person, directly or indirectly, by the use of any means or instrumentality of interstate commerce, or of the mails or of any facility of any national securities exchange,
>
> (b) To employ any device, scheme, or artifice to defraud, [or] . . .
>
> (c) To engage in any act, practice, or course of business which operates or would operate as a fraud or deceit upon any person, in connection with the purchase or sale of any security.

17 C.F.R. § 240.10b–5.

B.   *The Traditional Theory*

Under traditional insider trading theory, section 10(b) is violated when a corporate insider, such as an officer of the corporation, "trades in the securities of his corporation on the basis of material, non-public information." *O'Hagan,* 521 U.S. at 651–52, 117 S.Ct. 2199. Such trading constitutes deception under section 10(b) because "a relationship of trust and confidence [exists] between the shareholders of a corporation and those insiders who have obtained confidential information by reason of their position with that corporation," and this relationship gives rise to "a duty to disclose [or to abstain from trading] because of the necessity of preventing a corporate insider from . . . tak[ing] unfair advantage of . . . uninformed . . . stockholders." *Id.* at 652, 117 S.Ct. 2199 (internal quotation marks omitted; alterations in original). Although the requirement that the deception be "in connection with" the purchase or sale of a security is not often discussed in traditional insider trading case law, the connection is almost self-evident: the duty of disclosure being breached is to persons with whom the insider is engaging in securities transactions, and the insider breaches that duty when he or she engages in the securities transaction without disclosure.

In *Dirks v. SEC,* 463 U.S. 646, 103 S.Ct. 3255, 77 L.Ed.2d 911 (1983), the Supreme Court held that under the traditional theory, it is equally a section 10(b) violation if, under certain circumstances, the corporate officer does not actually trade but instead "tips" a corporate outsider (*e.g.,* a friend or a family member) with the information for the purpose of having the outsider trade. *See id.* at 660, 103 S.Ct. 3255. In deciding *Dirks,* the first issue for the Supreme Court was what duty of disclosure, if any, a corporate outsider was subject to, such that his or her trading in violation of that duty would constitute deception under section 10(b). The Court emphasized that there was no general duty of disclosure between all those who invest in the stock market, *id.* at 657–58, 103 S.Ct. 3255, and that, unlike corporate officers, corporate outsiders have no relationship with the corporation's shareholders from which any duty to disclose could arise, *id.* at 654–55, 103 S.Ct. 3255. While the Court ultimately determined that tippees could nevertheless still be in violation of section 10(b), it held that the circumstances under which that could occur were limited:

> [A] tippee assumes a fiduciary duty to the shareholders of a corporation not to trade on material nonpublic information only when the insider has breached his fiduciary duty to the shareholders by disclosing the information to the tippee and the tippee knows or should know that there has been a breach. *Id.* at 660, 103 S.Ct. 3255.

The second issue for the Court in *Dirks* was to determine when an insider's duty was breached where the insider had not himself or herself traded based on material non-public information but had simply given outsiders such information. In *Dirks,* the corporate insider had given the defendant, an officer of a securities broker-dealer, information that a massive fraud was occurring at the corporation, in an attempt to expose that fraud. *Id.* at 667, 103 S.Ct. 3255. The defendant informed others of what he had been told and certain investors sold their securities in the corporation. *Id.* at 649 103 S.Ct. 3255. The question was whether the insider's actions constituted a breach of the insider's fiduciary duty to shareholders because, notwithstanding the insider's benign motives, trading in the corporation's securities without disclosure had still resulted from his provision of information to the defendant. The Court held that no such breach had occurred. *Id.* at 666–67, 103 S.Ct. 3255.

To constitute a violation of section 10(b), according to *Dirks,* "the test is whether the insider personally will benefit, directly or indirectly, from his disclosure. Absent some personal gain, there has been no breach of duty to stockholders. And absent a breach by the insider, there is no derivative breach." *Id.* at 662, 103 S.Ct. 3255. Thus, the tippee could not be held liable for a federal securities fraud violation simply because he or she in fact traded in securities or helped others to trade in securities based on the material nonpublic information. Rather, the key factor was the tipper's intent in providing the information.

C. *The Misappropriation Theory*

1. *The Theory in the Second Circuit*

The Second Circuit was the first to recognize a different theory of insider trading: the misappropriation theory. *See generally United States v. Chestman*, 947 F.2d 551, 566–67 (2d Cir.1991) (*en banc*) (setting forth history of application of misappropriation theory in this Circuit). Under the misappropriation theory,

> a person violates Rule 10b–5 when he misappropriates material nonpublic information in breach of a fiduciary duty or similar relationship of trust and confidence and uses that information in a securities transaction. In contrast to [the traditional theory], the misappropriation theory does not require that the buyer or seller of securities be defrauded. Focusing on the language "fraud or deceit upon *any* person" (emphasis added), we have held that the predicate act of fraud may be perpetrated on the source of the nonpublic information, even though the source may be unaffiliated with the buyer or seller of securities. *Chestman*, 947 F.2d at 566.

Under this theory, this Court (prior to *Chestman*) upheld the securities fraud convictions of a newspaper reporter, a former newspaper clerk, and a stockbroker who traded securities based on misappropriated information similar to the type of information at issue in this case: "the timing and content of the *Wall Street Journal's* confidential schedule of columns of acknowledged influence in the securities market." *United States v. Carpenter,* 791 F.2d 1024, 1027 (2d Cir. 1986). While under the misappropriation theory, the duty that had been breached no longer was a duty owed to a party to a securities transaction, we found in *Carpenter* that such deception still satisfied the "in connection with" standard because

> the use of the misappropriated information for the financial benefit of the defendants and to the financial detriment of those investors with whom appellants traded supports the conclusion that appellants' fraud was "in connection with" the purchase or sale of securities under section 10(b) and Rule 10b–5. We can deduce reasonably that those who purchased or sold securities without the misappropriated information would not have purchased or sold, at least at the transaction prices, had they had the benefit of that information. Certainly the protection of investors is the major purpose of section 10(b) and Rule 10b 5. Further, investors are endangered equally by fraud by non-inside misappropriators as by fraud by insiders.

Id. at 1032 (internal citations omitted). Rejecting the argument made by the *Carpenter* dissent that the "in connection with" requirement was not met because no "securities-related" information had been misappropriated, we added that the deception was "in connection with" securities transactions because "the misappropriated information regarding the timing and content of certain *Journal* columns had 'no value whatsoever [to appellants] except "in connection with" their subsequent purchase[s] [and sales] of securities.' " *Id.* at 1033 (quoting *SEC v. Materia*, 745 F.2d 197, 203 (2d Cir.1984)). Furthermore, we pointed out that "[t]he 'sole purpose' of the scheme was to purchase and sell securities," *id.* (quoting *United States v. Newman*, 664 F.2d 12, 18 (2d Cir.1981)), "and thereby virtually to 'reap instant no-risk profits in the stock market,' " *id.* (quoting *Materia*, 745 F.2d at 203).[2]

We found ourselves applying the theory in the context of information obtained from a publication again in 1993 in *United States v. Libera*, 989 F.2d 596 (2d Cir.1993). *Libera* involved the same magazine at issue in this case—*Business Week*—and a similar scheme involving the pre-release misappropriation of the "Inside Wall Street" column. *Id.* at 598–99. However, unlike in *Carpenter*, in *Libera*, the misappropriators of the information did not trade—or have others trade on their behalf—based on the misappropriated information. *Id.* The initial misappropriator in *Libera*, in fact, did not receive any financial payment at all for advance copies of the column; eventually, when that individual was unable to continue, his replacement was paid $20 and later $30 per column. *Id.*

The main issue in *Libera* was whether, in order to find the tippees liable under Section 10(b) pursuant to the misappropriation theory, "the tipper must have known that his breach of a fiduciary obligation would lead to the tippee's trading on the misappropriated information." *Id.* at 597. Under the traditional theory of insider trading, tippee liability was in fact premised on the intent of the tipper to provide the tippee with information that the tippee could use to make money in securities trading. *See Dirks*, 463 U.S. at 664, 103 S.Ct. 3255 (holding that tippees and tippers would be liable where there existed a "relationship between the insider and the recipient that suggests a *quid pro quo* from the latter, or an intention to benefit the particular recipient. The elements of fiduciary duty and exploitation of nonpublic information also exist when an insider makes a gift of confidential information to a trading relative or friend.") *Libera* held, however, that tippee liability under the misappropriation theory did not require this type of knowledge by the tipper, and that

> [t]he tipper's knowledge that he or she was breaching a duty to the owner of confidential information suffices to establish the tipper's expectation that the breach will lead to some kind of a misuse of the information. This is so because it may be presumed

---

2. On appeal, the Supreme Court—missing one justice—split 4–4 on the question of the validity of the securities fraud convictions, thus affirming the judgment of the court below. *See Carpenter v. United States*, 484 U.S. 19, 24, 108 S.Ct. 316, 98 L.Ed.2d 275 (1987) (observing in its recitation of the facts that "[a]lthough the victim of the fraud, the *Journal*, was not a buyer or seller of the stocks traded in or otherwise a market participant, the fraud was nevertheless considered [by the lower courts] to be 'in connection with' a purchase or sale of securities within the meaning of the statute and the rule," but ultimately holding that the court was "evenly divided with respect to the convictions under the securities laws and for that reason affirms the judgment below").

that the tippee's interest in the information is, in contemporary jargon, not for nothing. To allow a tippee to escape liability solely because the government cannot prove to a jury's satisfaction that the tipper knew exactly what misuse would result from the tipper's wrongdoing would not fulfill the purpose of the misappropriation theory, which is to protect property rights in information. *Libera,* 989 F.2d at 600.

Thus, *Libera* held that the only required elements for tippee liability were: "(i) a breach by the tipper of a duty owed to the owner of the nonpublic information; and (ii) the tippee's knowledge that the tipper had breached the duty." *Id.* at 600. Other than in its recitation of the standard set forth in Rule 10b–5, *Libera* made no mention of the "in connection with" requirement.

2.   *The Supreme Court's Decision in O'Hagan*

In *O'Hagan,* the Supreme Court resolved an inter-circuit conflict regarding the validity of the misappropriation theory and held that a lawyer who traded in the shares of the target company of a proposed acquisition based on information misappropriated from his law firm and its client, the company seeking to acquire the target, violated section 10(b). *O'Hagan,* 521 U.S. at 653, 117 S.Ct. 2199. The Court agreed that section 10(b)'s deception requirement could be predicated on a fraud on the source of confidential information instead of a buyer or seller of securities, but it did not fully endorse the broad rationale this Circuit provided in *Carpenter* for why the deception of a source of confidential information was "in connection with" the purchase or sale of a security.

As defined by the Supreme Court in *O'Hagan,* the misappropriation theory holds that a section 10(b) violation occurs when an individual "misappropriates confidential information for securities trading purposes, in breach of a duty owed to the source of the information." *Id.* at 652, 117 S.Ct. 2199. Under *O'Hagan,* the "deception" requirement of section 10(b) is satisfied by the misappropriator's "feigning fidelity to the source of [the confidential] information." *Id.* at 655, 117 S.Ct. 2199. According to the Court, "[a] company's confidential information . . . qualifies as property to which the company has a right of exclusive use" and "[t]he undisclosed misappropriation of such information, in violation of a fiduciary duty . . . constitutes fraud akin to embezzlement—the fraudulent appropriation to one's own use of the money or goods entrusted to one's care by another." *Id.* at 654, 117 S.Ct. 2199 (internal quotation marks and citations omitted). Because the lawyer O'Hagan had breached the fiduciary duty he owed both to his law firm and to the firm's client to keep their information confidential and not appropriate such information to his own use, he had engaged in deception within the meaning of section 10(b).

The Court held that section 10(b)'s requirement that the deception be "in connection with the purchase or sale of any security" was satisfied because "the fiduciary's fraud is consummated, not when the fiduciary gains the confidential information, but when, without disclosure to his principal, he uses the information to purchase or sell securities. The securities transaction and the breach of duty thus coincide." *Id.* at 656, 117 S.Ct. 2199. That is, O'Hagan legitimately possessed the information given his fiduciary relationship with the source of the information, and the "misappropriation" occurred only when he used that information to trade securities.

The Court distinguished, as not satisfying the "in connection with" requirement, a scenario in which an employee embezzles money from his or her employer for the purpose of buying securities. The Court did so on the ground that "money can buy, if not anything, then at least many things; its misappropriation may thus be viewed as sufficiently detached from a subsequent securities transaction that § 10(b)'s 'in connection with' requirement would not be met." *Id.* at 656–57, 117 S.Ct. 2199. In contrast, the Court stated, the information targeted by the misappropriation theory is information of the sort that "misappropriators ordinarily capitalize upon to gain no-risk profits through the purchase or sale of securities," *id.* at 656, 117 S.Ct. 2199 *i.e.,* information that "ordinarily" "derives its value . . . from its utility in securities trading." *Id.* at 657, 117 S.Ct. 2199. The misappropriation of such information thus possesses a sufficient connection to securities trading to satisfy section 10(b) and Rule 10b–5.

II. *Application in This Case*

A. *Do Libera and Carpenter Still Provide the Governing Rule After O'Hagan?*

While, as the district court in the instant case pointed out, the coincidence of a securities transaction and breach of duty—identified in *O'Hagan* as contributing to the satisfaction of the "in connection with" requirement—is not present where, as here, the misappropriator tips the information to an outsider but does not trade or have others trade on his or her behalf, the Supreme Court in *O'Hagan* did not purport to set forth the sole combination of factors necessary to establish the requisite connection in all contexts. Accordingly, this Circuit after *O'Hagan* has applied the misappropriation theory to schemes involving nontrading tippers, albeit without discussion of the "in connection with" requirement. *See United States v. McDermott,* 245 F.3d 133 (2d Cir.2001) (applying theory to hold that sufficient evidence supported insider trading conviction of non-trading tipper— the president, CEO and chairman of an investment bank specializing in mergers and acquisitions—who gave material, non-public information for trading purposes to a woman with whom he was having an affair). Application of *Libera* to the instant case is therefore not undermined by the lack of a trading tipper here, notwithstanding the intervening decision in *O'Hagan.*

O'Hagan's requirement that the misappropriated information "ordinarily" be valuable due to "its utility in securities trading," *O'Hagan,* 521 U.S. at 657, 117 S.Ct. 2199, appears to be a more generally applicable factor in determining whether section 10(b)'s "in connection with" requirement is satisfied. That requirement is met in a case where, as here, the misappropriated information is a magazine column that has a known effect on the prices of the securities of the companies it discusses. *See Carpenter,* 791 F.2d at 1033 (holding that "the misappropriated information regarding the timing and content of certain *Journal* columns had no value whatsoever to appellants except in connection with their subsequent purchases and sales of securities") (internal quotation marks and brackets omitted).

Libera, therefore, continues to provide the relevant criteria by which to evaluate defendant's conviction.

B.   *Breach of Duty and Tippee's Knowledge Under Libera*

To support a conviction of the tippee defendant, the government was simply required to prove a breach by Salvage, the tipper, of a duty owed to the owner of the misappropriated information, and defendant's knowledge that the tipper had breached the duty. *See Libera,* 989 F.2d at 600. Defendant argues that this case differs factually from *Libera* because no fiduciary duty existed here and, even if it did, he did not know that the information he was receiving from Salvage had been obtained in violation of that duty. We disagree.

Defendant claims that while the confidentiality of the "Inside Wall Street" column may have been clearly communicated to *Business Week*'s printer under the facts of *Libera,* with corresponding acceptance by the printer of the responsibility to maintain the confidentiality of that information to protect *Business Week*'s interests, such confidentiality was not made sufficiently clear here to those further down the distribution chain—such as Hudson News. Thus, he claims, there was no fiduciary duty to be breached. It is true that this Circuit has held that "a fiduciary duty cannot be imposed unilaterally by entrusting a person with confidential information," *Chestman,* 947 F.2d at 567, and that a fiduciary relationship, or its functional equivalent, exists only where there is explicit acceptance of a duty of confidentiality or where such acceptance may be implied from a similar relationship of trust and confidence between the parties. *Id.* at 567–68. Qualifying relationships are marked by the fact that the party in whom confidence is reposed has entered into a relationship in which he or she acts to serve the interests of the party entrusting him or her with such information. *Id.* at 568–69.

Sufficient evidence was introduced at trial, however, from which a reasonable jury could find that these elements were present here. The evidence indicated that periodically *Business Week* would ask Curtis, the distributor, to issue "a policy statement to the wholesalers requesting that *Business Week* not be distributed before 5:00 p.m. on Thursday afternoon." Curtis understood and communicated to Hudson News that this policy was needed because there was highly confidential information in the "Inside Wall Street" column that "*Business Week* had agreed not to make known to the general public before 5 p.m. on Thursday." A representative from Hudson News testified that Hudson News employees understood that *Business Week* "like[d] to make sure that the information in that magazine is held very closely," that Hudson had a "unique deal" to carry out that purpose, and that the magazines were "a product entrusted to Hudson News that didn't belong to us. It belonged to the publisher. They entrusted it to us." Hudson had a policy prohibiting the theft of copies of the magazine or the removal of the magazine or articles therein from the premises, and Curtis at one point actually sent representatives to check that this policy was being enforced. *Falcone,* 97 F.Supp.2d at 299–300. Finally, a representative from Hudson News testified that the misappropriator Salvage, in fact, was the "top person in the delivery room area" and therefore was not only informed of such policies and rules but was responsible for enforcing them.

Defendant also claims that he did not know the source of the information he received from Smath. However, as the district court noted, Smath testified that in fact he told defendant the details of the scheme. In addition, Smath testified that defendant paid him $200 for each column, substantially in excess of the magazine's sale price. *See Falcone,* 97 F.Supp.2d at 300. The jury could therefore believe Smath rather than defendant in finding that defendant knew he was obtaining stolen information.

CONCLUSION

For the reasons set forth above, we affirm defendant's convictions.

————

Insert the following material at p.876 of the Unabridged Edition, at the end of Section 2:

SECURITIES AND EXCHANGE COMMISSION RELEASE NO. 33–7881 (2000)

SELECTIVE DISCLOSURE AND INSIDER TRADING

Selective Disclosure: Regulation FD

A. *Background*

. . . [W]e we have become increasingly concerned about the selective disclosure of material information by issuers. As reflected in recent publicized reports, many issuers are disclosing important non-public information, such as advance warnings of earnings results, to securities analysts or selected institutional investors or both, before making full disclosure of the same information to the general public. Where this has happened, those who were privy to the information beforehand were able to make a profit or avoid a loss at the expense of those kept in the dark.

We believe that the practice of selective disclosure leads to a loss of investor confidence in the integrity of our capital markets. Investors who see a security's price change dramatically and only later are given access to the information responsible for that move rightly question whether they are on a level playing field with market insiders.

Issuer selective disclosure bears a close resemblance in this regard to ordinary "tipping" and insider trading. In both cases, a privileged few gain an informational edge—and the ability to use that edge to profit—from their superior access to corporate insiders, rather than from their skill, acumen, or diligence. Likewise, selective disclosure has an adverse impact on market integrity that is similar to the adverse impact from illegal insider trading: Investors lose confidence in the fairness of the markets when they know that other participants may exploit "unerodable informational advantages" derived not from hard work or insights, but from their access to corporate insiders. The economic effects of the two practices are essentially the same. Yet, as a result of judicial interpretations, tipping and insider trading can be severely punished under the antifraud provisions of the federal securities laws, whereas the status of issuer selective disclosure has been considerably less clear.

Regulation FD is also designed to address another threat to the integrity of our markets: the potential for corporate management to treat material information as a commodity to be used to gain or maintain favor with particular analysts or investors.... [I]n the absence of a prohibition on selective disclosure, analysts may feel pressured to report favorably about a company or otherwise slant their analysis in order to have continued access to selectively disclosed information. We are concerned, in this regard, with reports that analysts who publish negative views of an issuer are sometimes excluded by that issuer from calls and meetings to which other analysts are invited.

Finally, ... technological developments have made it much easier for issuers to disseminate information broadly. Whereas issuers once may have had to rely on analysts to serve as information intermediaries, issuers now can use a variety of methods to communicate directly with the market. In addition to press releases, these methods include, among others, Internet webcasting and teleconferencing. Accordingly, technological limitations no longer provide an excuse for abiding the threats to market integrity that selective disclosure represents.

To address the problem of selective disclosure, we proposed Regulation FD. It targets the practice by establishing new requirements for full and fair disclosure by public companies....

B. *Discussion of Regulation FD*

Rule 100 of Regulation FD sets forth the basic rule regarding selective disclosure. Under this rule, whenever:

(1) an issuer, or person acting on its behalf,

(2) discloses material nonpublic information,

(3) to certain enumerated persons (in general, securities market professionals or holders of the issuer's securities who may well trade on the basis of the information),

(4) the issuer must make public disclosure of that same information:

(a) simultaneously (for intentional disclosures), or

(b) promptly (for non-intentional disclosures).

As a whole, the regulation requires that when an issuer makes an intentional disclosure of material nonpublic information to a person covered by the regulation, it must do so in a manner that provides general public disclosure, rather than through a selective disclosure. For a selective disclosure that is non-intentional, the issuer must publicly disclose the information promptly after it knows (or is reckless in not knowing) that the information selectively disclosed was both material and nonpublic. . . .

1. *Scope of Communications and Issuer Personnel Covered by the Regulation*

[Regulation FD] is designed to address the core problem of selective disclosure made to those who would reasonably be expected to trade securities on the basis of the information or provide others with advice about securities trading. Accordingly, Rule 100(a) of Regulation FD . . . makes clear that the general rule against selective disclosure applies only to disclosures made to the categories of persons enumerated in Rule 100(b)(1).

Rule 100(b)(1) enumerates four categories of persons to whom selective disclosure may not be made absent a specified exclusion. The first three are securities market professionals—(1) broker-dealers and their associated persons, (2) investment advisers, certain institutional investment managers and their associated persons, and (3) investment companies, hedge funds, and affiliated persons. These categories will include sell-side analysts, many buy-side analysts, large institutional investment managers, and other market professionals who may be likely to trade on the basis of selectively disclosed information. The fourth category of person included in Rule 100(b)(1) is any holder of the issuer's securities, under circumstances in which it is reasonably foreseeable that such person would purchase or sell securities on the basis of the information. Thus, as a whole, Rule 100(b)(1) will cover the types of persons most likely to be the recipients of improper selective disclosure, but should not cover persons who are engaged in ordinary-course business communications with the issuer, or interfere with disclosures to the media or communications to government agencies.

Rule 100(b)(2) sets out four exclusions from coverage. The first, as proposed, is for communications made to a person who owes the issuer a duty of trust or confidence—*i.e.*, a "temporary insider"—such as an attorney, investment banker, or accountant. The second exclusion is for communications made to any person who expressly agrees to maintain the information in confidence. Any misuse of the information for trading by the persons in these two exclusions would thus be covered under either the "temporary insider" or the misappropriation theory of insider trading. This approach recognizes that issuers and their officials may properly share material nonpublic information with outsiders, for legitimate business purposes, when the outsiders are subject to duties of confidentiality.

The third exclusion from coverage in Rule 100(b)(2) is for disclosures to an entity whose primary business is the issuance of credit ratings, provided the information is disclosed solely for the purpose of developing a credit rating and the entity's ratings are publicly available.... [R]atings organizations often obtain nonpublic information in the course of their ratings work. We are not aware, however, of any incidents of selective disclosure involving ratings organizations. Ratings organizations, like the media, have a mission of public disclosure; the objective and result of the ratings process is a widely available publication of the rating when it is completed. And under this provision, for the exclusion to apply, the ratings organization must make its credit ratings publicly available. For these reasons, we believe it is appropriate to provide this exclusion from the coverage of Regulation FD.

The fourth exclusion from coverage is for communications made in connection with most offerings of securities registered under the Securities Act....

b. *Disclosures by a Person Acting on an Issuer's Behalf.* ... We define the term ["person acting on behalf of an issuer"] to mean: (1) Any senior official of the issuer[34] or (2) any other officer, employee, or agent of an issuer who regularly communicates with any of the persons described in Rule 100(b)(1)(i), (ii), or (iii), or with the issuer's security holders. By revising the definition in this manner, we provide that the regulation will cover senior management, investor relations professionals, and others who regularly interact with securities market professionals or security holders. Of course, neither an issuer nor such a covered person could avoid the reach of the regulation merely by having a non-covered person make a selective disclosure. Thus, to the extent that another employee had been *directed* to make a selective disclosure by a member of senior management, that member of senior

34. "Senior official" is defined in Rule 101(f) as any director, executive officer, investor relations or public relations officer, or other person with similar functions....

management would be responsible for having made the selective disclosure. *See* Section 20(b) of the Exchange Act. In addition, as was proposed, the definition expressly states that a person who communicates material nonpublic information in breach of a duty to the issuer would not be considered to be acting on behalf of the issuer. Thus, an issuer is not responsible under Regulation FD when one of its employees improperly trades or tips.

2. *Disclosures of Material Nonpublic Information*

[Regulation FD] applies to disclosures of "material nonpublic" information about the issuer or its securities. The regulation does not define the terms "material" and "nonpublic," but relies on existing definitions of these terms established in the case law. Information is material if "there is a substantial likelihood that a reasonable shareholder would consider it important" in making an investment decision. To fulfill the materiality requirement, there must be a substantial likelihood that a fact "would have been viewed by the reasonable investor as having significantly altered the total mix of information made available." Information is nonpublic if it has not been disseminated in a manner making it available to investors generally.

. . . While it is not possible to create an exhaustive list, the following items are some types of information or events that should be reviewed carefully to determine whether they are material: (1) Earnings information; (2) mergers, acquisitions, tender offers, joint ventures, or changes in assets; (3) new products or discoveries, or developments regarding customers or suppliers (*e.g.,* the acquisition or loss of a contract); (4) changes in control or in management; (5) change in auditors or auditor notification that the issuer may no longer rely on an auditor's audit report; (6) events regarding the issuer's securities—*e.g.,* defaults on senior securities, calls of securities for redemption, repurchase plans, stock splits or changes in dividends, changes to the rights of security holders, public or private sales of additional securities; and (7) bankruptcies or receiverships.

By including this list, we do not mean to imply that each of these items is *per se* material. The information and events on this list still require determinations as to their materiality (although some determinations will be reached more easily than others). For example, some new products or contracts may clearly be material to an issuer; yet that does not mean that *all* product developments or contracts will be material. This demonstrates, in our view, why no "bright-line" standard or list of items can adequately address the range of situations that may arise. Furthermore, we do not and cannot create an exclusive list of events and information that have a higher probability of being considered material.

One common situation that raises special concerns about selective disclosure has been the practice of securities analysts seeking "guidance" from issuers regarding earnings forecasts. When an issuer official engages in a private discussion with an analyst who is seeking guidance about earnings estimates, he or she takes on a high degree of risk under Regulation FD. If the issuer official communicates selectively to the analyst nonpublic information that the company's anticipated earnings will be higher than, lower than, or even the same as what analysts have been forecasting, the issuer likely will have violated Regulation FD. This is true whether the information about earnings is communicated expressly or through indirect "guidance," the meaning of which is apparent though implied. Similarly, an issuer cannot render material information immaterial simply by breaking it into ostensibly non-material pieces.

At the same time, an issuer is not prohibited from disclosing a non-material piece of information to an analyst, even if, unbeknownst to the issuer, that piece helps the analyst complete a "mosaic" of information that, taken together, is material. Similarly, since materiality is an objective test keyed to the reasonable investor, Regulation FD will not be implicated where an issuer discloses immaterial information whose significance is discerned by the analyst. Analysts can provide a valuable service in sifting through and extracting information that would not be significant to the ordinary investor to reach material conclusions. We do not intend, by Regulation FD, to discourage this sort of activity. The focus of Regulation FD is on whether the issuer discloses material nonpublic information, not on whether an analyst, through some combination of persistence, knowledge, and insight, regards as material information whose significance is not apparent to the reasonable investor.

. . . Rule 101(a) states that a person acts "intentionally" only if the person knows, or is reckless in not knowing, that the information he or she is communicating is both material and nonpublic. . . . [T]his aspect of the regulation provides additional protection that issuers need not fear being second-guessed by the Commission in enforcement actions for mistaken judgments about materiality in close cases.

3. Intentional and Non-intentional Selective Disclosures: Timing of Required Public Disclosures

A key provision of Regulation FD is that the timing of required public disclosure differs depending on whether the issuer has made an "intentional" selective disclosure or a selective disclosure that was not intentional. For an "intentional" selective disclosure, the issuer is required to publicly disclose the same information simultaneously.

a. *Standard of "Intentional" Selective Disclosure.* Under the regulation, a selective disclosure is "intentional" when the issuer or person acting on behalf of the issuer making the disclosure either knows, or is reckless in not knowing, prior to making the disclosure, that the information he or she is communicating is both material and nonpublic. . . .

b. *"Prompt" Public Disclosure After Non-intentional Selective Disclosures.* Under Rule 100(a)(2), when an issuer makes a covered non-intentional disclosure of material nonpublic information, it is required to make public disclosure promptly. . . .

Commenters expressed varying views on the definition of "promptly" provided in the rule. Some said that the time period provided for disclosure was appropriate; others said it was too short; and still others said that it was too specific, and should require disclosure only as soon as reasonably possible or practicable. We believe that it is preferable for issuers and the investing public that there be a clear delineation of when "prompt" disclosure is required. We also believe that the 24–hour requirement strikes the appropriate balance between achieving broad, non-exclusionary disclosure and permitting issuers time to determine how to respond after learning of the non-intentional selective disclosure. However, recognizing that sometimes non-intentional selective disclosures will arise close to or over a weekend or holiday, we have slightly modified the final rule to state that the outer boundary for prompt disclosure is the later of 24 hours or the commencement of the next day's trading on the New York Stock Exchange, after a senior official learns of the disclosure and knows (or is reckless in not knowing) that the information disclosed was material and nonpublic. . . .

4. *"Public Disclosure" Required by Regulation FD*

Rule 101(e) defines the type of "public disclosure" that will satisfy the requirements of Regulation FD. As proposed, Rule 101(e) gave issuers considerable flexibility in determining how to make required public disclosure. The proposal stated that issuers could meet Regulation FD's "public disclosure" requirement by filing a Form 8–K, by distributing a press release through a widely disseminated news or wire service, or by any other non-exclusionary method of disclosure that is reasonably designed to provide broad public access—such as announcement at a conference of which the public had notice and to which the public was granted access, either by personal attendance, or telephonic or electronic access. This definition was designed to permit issuers to make use of current technologies, such as webcasting of conference calls, that provide broad public access to issuer disclosure events. . . .

We believe that issuers could use the following model, which employs a combination of methods of disclosure, for making a planned disclosure of material information, such as a scheduled earnings release:

● First, issue a press release, distributed through regular channels, containing the information;

● Second, provide adequate notice, by a press release and/or website posting, of a scheduled conference call to discuss the announced results, giving investors both the time and date of the conference call, and instructions on how to access the call; and

• Third, hold the conference call in an open manner, permitting investors to listen in either by telephonic means or through Internet webcasting.[71]

By following these steps, an issuer can use the press release to provide the initial broad distribution of the information, and then discuss its release with analysts in the subsequent conference call, without fear that if it should disclose additional material details related to the original disclosure it will be engaging in a selective disclosure of material information. . . .

5.   Issuers Subject to Regulation FD

Regulation FD will apply to all issuers with securities registered under Section 12 of the Exchange Act, and all issuers required to file reports under Section 15(d) of the Exchange Act, including closed-end investment companies, but not including other investment companies, foreign governments, or foreign private issuers. . . .

7.   Liability Issues

We recognize that the prospect of private liability for violations of Regulation FD could contribute to a "chilling effect" on issuer communications. Issuers might refrain from some informal communications with outsiders if they feared that engaging in such communications, even when appropriate, would lead to their being charged in private lawsuits with violations of Regulation FD. . . .

. . . Rule 102 . . . expressly provides that no failure to make a public disclosure required solely by Regulation FD shall be deemed to be a violation of Rule 10b–5. This provision makes clear that Regulation FD does not create a new duty for purposes of Rule 10b–5 liability. Accordingly, private plaintiffs cannot rely on an issuer's violation of Regulation FD as a basis for a private action alleging Rule 10b–5 violations.

Rule 102 is designed to exclude Rule 10b–5 liability for cases that would be based "solely" on a failure to make a public disclosure required by Regulation FD. As such, it does not affect any existing grounds for liability under Rule 10b–5. Thus, for example, liability for "tipping" and insider trading under Rule 10b–5 may still exist if a selective disclosure is made in circumstances that meet the *Dirks* "personal benefit" test. In addition, an issuer's failure to make a public disclosure still may give rise to liability under a "duty to correct" or "duty to update" theory in certain circumstances. And an issuer's contacts with analysts may lead to liability under the "entanglement" or "adoption" theories. In addition, if an issuer's report or

---

71. Giving the public the opportunity to listen to the call does not also require that the issuer give all members of the public the opportunity to ask questions.

public disclosure made under Regulation FD contained false or misleading information, or omitted material information, Rule 102 would not provide protection from Rule 10b–5 liability.

Finally, if an issuer failed to comply with Regulation FD, it would be subject to an SEC enforcement action alleging violations of Section 13(a) or 15(d) of the Exchange Act . . . and Regulation FD. We could bring an administrative action seeking a cease-and-desist order, or a civil action seeking an injunction and/or civil money penalties.[90] In appropriate cases, we could also bring an enforcement action against an individual at the issuer responsible for the violation, either as "a cause of" the violation in a cease-and-desist proceeding,[91] or as an aider and abetter of the violation in an injunctive action.[92]

---

90. Regulation FD does not expressly require issuers to adopt policies and procedures to avoid violations, but we expect that most issuers will use appropriate disclosure policies as a safeguard against selective disclosure. We are aware that many, if not most, issuers already have policies and regarding disclosure practices, the dissemination of material information, and the question of which issuer personnel are authorized to speak to analysts, the media, or investors. The existence of an appropriate policy, and the issuer's general adherence to it, may often be relevant to determining the issuer's intent with regard to a selective disclosure.

91. Section 21C of the Exchange Act, *15 U.S.C. 78u–3*. A failure to file or otherwise make required public disclosure under Regulation FD will be considered a violation for as long as the failure continues; in our enforcement actions, we likely will seek more severe sanctions for violations that continue for a longer period of time.

92. Section 20(e) of the Exchange Act, *15 U.S.C. 78t*(e).

CHAPTER XI

SHAREHOLDER SUITS

SECTION 6. DEMAND ON THE BOARD AND TERMINATION OF DERIVATIVE ACTIONS OF THE RECOMMENDATION OF THE BOARD OR A COMMITTEE

Insert the following case at p. 993 of the Unabridged Edition, and p. 705 of the Concise Edition, at the end of Section 6:

Einhorn v. Culea

Supreme Court of Wisconsin, 2000.
235 Wis.2d 646, 612 N.W.2d 78.

■ SHIRLEY S. ABRAHAMSON, CHIEF JUSTICE.

This is a review of a published decision of the court of appeals affirming a judgment and order of the circuit court for Ozaukee County, Joseph D. McCormack, Circuit Judge. The circuit court dismissed the derivative shareholder action of Stephen Einhorn, a minority shareholder and member of the board of directors of Northern Labs. The circuit court concluded that the threshold for determining whether a member of the special litigation committee is independent within the meaning of Wis. Stat. § 180.0744 (1997–98) is "extremely low" and found that the special litigation committee was independent. Accordingly, the circuit court dismissed Einhorn's derivative action pursuant to § 180.0744(1).[3]

The court of appeals affirmed the judgment of the circuit court, concluding that the circuit court's assessment of whether each member of the special litigation committee was independent was based on facts supported by the record and was not clearly erroneous.

The issue raised in the present case is the proper interpretation and application of the standard set forth in Wis. Stat. § 180.0744 of whether a member of a special litigation committee is independent.

---

3. Wisconsin Stat. § 180.0744(1) reads as follows:

180.0744. Dismissal

The court shall dismiss a derivative proceeding on motion by the corporation if the court finds that [a special litigation committee] ... has determined, acting in good faith after conducting a reasonable inquiry upon which its conclusions are based, that maintenance of the derivative proceeding is not in the best interests of the corporation....

The issue is not whether the derivative action will succeed, but whether the derivative action should be dismissed on the basis of the decision of the special litigation committee. For the reasons set forth, we conclude that the circuit court and the court of appeals erred in declaring that the threshold established by the legislature in § 180.0744 in determining whether a member of a special litigation committee is independent is "extremely low." We further conclude that in deciding whether members of the special litigation committee are independent, the circuit court should determine whether, considering the totality of the circumstances, a reasonable person in the position of the member of the special litigation committee can base his or her decision on the merits of the issue rather than on extraneous considerations or influences. In other words, the test is whether a member of the committee has a relationship with an individual defendant or the corporation that would reasonably be expected to affect the member's judgment with respect to the litigation at issue. Because the circuit court did not make sufficient findings of fact and did not apply the correct legal standard to determine whether the members of the special litigation committee were independent, we reverse the decision of the court of appeals and remand the cause to the circuit court for further proceedings not inconsistent with this decision.

I

We set forth the background of the dispute here. Additional facts relevant to the issue of whether the members of the special litigation committee were independent are set forth later in the opinion.

In December 1985, James D. Culea (the defendant), Stephen Einhorn (the plaintiff), and Einhorn's business partner, Orville Mertz, acquired Northern Labs. The Northern Labs stock was distributed as follows: Culea 56.09%, Einhorn 20.60% and Mertz 20.06%. The remaining stock was owned by other managers and directors. Culea has served as president, manager, director and majority shareholder of Northern Labs since 1986. Einhorn has been a director and minority shareholder.

At the time of its acquisition in 1985, Northern Labs had annual sales of $16 million and generated little profit. During the period between 1986 and 1992, Northern Labs' sales and profits increased. In the 1993 fiscal year, Northern Labs generated $33 million in sales and $1.9 million in profits.

In 1992, Culea sought a retroactive performance bonus, asserting that he had been undercompensated in the years following the acquisition. In May 1992, he sent a notice to the directors scheduling a compensation committee meeting and a board of directors meeting for July 29, 1992. At that time the board of directors consisted of Culea, his wife Shelly Culea, Einhorn, Mertz, and the company's vice president of finance, Robert Bonk. Culea, Mertz and Bonk comprised the compensation committee.

On July 29, 1992, the compensation committee unanimously approved a retroactive bonus to Culea of approximately $300,000, a portion of which was to be paid with Northern Labs stock. A board of directors meeting was held immediately after the compensation committee meeting. The four directors in attendance—Culea, Mertz, Bonk and Shelly Culea—voted unanimously to ratify the compensation committee's decisions. Einhorn did not attend the July 29, 1992, board of directors meeting. Following Culea's stock compensation, the stock was allocated as follows: Culea 76%, Einhorn 22%, and Bonk 2%.[6]

On December 9, 1993, Einhorn filed a direct action against Culea, alleging that Culea had willfully breached his fiduciary duty to Einhorn by participating in and causing the corporation to award a self-dealing retroactive bonus to Culea of $300,000 and to issue stock for no consideration or at a grossly inadequate price. Einhorn alleged that he had been "damaged by the dilution of his percentage of ownership in the companies and by a reduction in the value of his interest in the companies...." Einhorn sought a judgment ordering Culea to surrender stock to Northern Labs and to reimburse Northern Labs for all cash payments received by him for the retroactive bonus.

On May 3, 1994, Culea filed a motion for summary judgment arguing, among other things, that Einhorn improperly filed his suit as a direct action instead of a derivative action. The circuit court agreed with Culea and gave Einhorn 30 days to amend his complaint.

Einhorn amended his complaint in November 1994 to state a derivative action with allegations similar to those in his original complaint. The members of the board of directors in November 1994 were, pursuant to a stock agreement, appointees of Culea and Einhorn. In addition to himself and his wife, Culea appointed his neighbor Dwight Chewning, Northern Labs CFO Robert Bonk, and Lolita Chua, a friend of Shelly Culea. Einhorn appointed himself and his business partner, John Beagle.

Following Einhorn's amended complaint, on December 9, 1994, Culea issued a notice of a special meeting of the board of directors for December 16, 1994. Culea's notice indicated that Chewning and Chua were new members of the board and that the board would be voting on whether the maintenance of Einhorn's derivative action was in the best interests of the corporation. Einhorn requested to bring an attorney to the meeting but his request was denied by the corporate counsel for Northern Labs. Corporate counsel's firm represented Culea in the action filed by Einhorn.

---

6. Prior to the board meeting, Mertz and two other stockholders had sold their   holdings.

The board of directors met as scheduled on December 16, 1994. Northern Labs' corporate counsel advised that because Einhorn, Culea and Shelly Culea had an interest in the dispute, they should not participate in any vote, whether as directors or as potential members of any special litigation committee. The board then created a special litigation committee composed of Chewning, Bonk, Chua and Beagle.

After five months of meetings and approximately 500 hours of inquiry, the special litigation committee voted three to one that continuation of Einhorn's derivative action was not in the best interests of the corporation.[8] Based on this vote and pursuant to Wis. Stat. § 180.0744(1), Culea moved the circuit court to dismiss Einhorn's derivative action.

In a decision and order dated October 30, 1995, the circuit court denied Culea's motion to dismiss the action, stating that it was not prepared to find that the special litigation committee met the criteria of being independent set forth in Wis. Stat. § 180.0744. After a seven-day trial to the circuit court on the issue of whether the members of the special litigation committee were independent under § 180.0744, the circuit court concluded that the threshold established by the legislature in determining whether members of the special litigation committee were independent is "extremely low." The circuit court found that the members of the committee were independent within the meaning of § 180.0744, that they acted in good faith and that they made their determination from conclusions based upon a reasonable inquiry.[9] The circuit court dismissed the derivative action. The court of appeals affirmed the judgment of the circuit court.

II

The present case is a derivative action. A derivative action differs from ordinary commercial litigation and from a representative action such as a class action. In a derivative action, the claims belong to the corporation, not to the complaining shareholder. The complaining shareholder is challenging, on behalf of the corporation that has been unwilling to bring the suit, specific corporate conduct.

A derivative action reflects competing interests: On the one hand, the action allows shareholders to assert the corporation's rights when corporate management refuses to do so. On the other hand, the board of directors or majority shareholders of a corporation, not the courts or minority shareholders, should resolve internal conflicts. A derivative action raises the specter of undue judicial interference with the business judgment of corporate management. In other words, a derivative action is a means to curb managerial misconduct, yet it also undermines the basic principle of corporate governance that the

---

8. The lone dissenting vote was John Beagle, Einhorn's business partner.

9. The issues of whether the members acted in good faith and conducted a reasonable inquiry are not before us. Einhorn does not challenge these conclusions.

decisions of a corporation, including the decision to initiate litigation, should be made by the board of directors.

Courts and legislatures have allowed corporations to use special litigation committees to dismiss derivative actions in an attempt to balance the competing interests at issue: the shareholders' need to protect the corporation and the corporation's need to prevent meritless or harmful litigation. If the special litigation committee is independent from the alleged wrongdoers, acts in good faith and conducts a reasonable inquiry upon which its conclusion is based, the committee's recommendation not to proceed with a derivative action is viewed as a proper exercise of the directors' business judgment and the court will dismiss the action.

The concept of the special litigation oversight committee flows from the business judgment rule, a judicially created doctrine that limits judicial review of corporate decision-making when corporate directors make business decisions on an informed basis, in good faith and in the honest belief that the action taken is in the best interests of the company. The business judgment rule shields, to a large extent, the substantive bases for a corporate decision from judicial inquiry. The business judgment rule also ensures that management remains in the hands of the board of directors and protects courts from becoming too deeply implicated in internal corporate matters.

Under Wis. Stat. § 180.0744, the corporation may create a special litigation committee consisting of two or more independent directors appointed by a majority vote of independent directors present at a meeting of the board of directors. The independent special litigation committee determines whether the derivative action is in the best interests of the corporation. If the independent special litigation committee acts in good faith, conducts a reasonable inquiry upon which it bases its conclusions and concludes that the maintenance of the derivative action is not in the best interests of the corporation, the circuit court shall dismiss the derivative action. The statute thus requires the circuit court to defer to the business judgment of a properly composed and properly operating special litigation committee.[15]

The provisions of the Wisconsin statute relevant to the present case read as follows:

180.0744. Dismissal

(1) The court shall dismiss a derivative proceeding on motion by the corporation if the court finds, subject to the burden of proof assigned under sub. (5) or (6), that one of the groups specified in sub. (2) or (6) has determined, acting in good faith after conducting a reasonable inquiry upon which its conclusions

---

15. 2 Model Business Corporation Act Annotated, Introductory Comment to Sub-   chapter D, Derivative Proceedings, § 7.40 at 7–253 (3d ed. 1997 Supp.).

are based, that maintenance of the derivative proceeding is not in the best interests of the corporation.

(2) Unless a panel is appointed under sub. (6), the determination in sub.(1) shall be made by any of the following: ...

(b) A majority vote of a committee consisting of 2 or more independent directors appointed by majority vote of independent directors present at a meeting of the board of directors, whether or not the voting, independent directors constitute a quorum.

The most common challenge to the decision of a special litigation committee, and the one made in the present case, is that the members are not independent. Given the finality of the ultimate decision of the committee to dismiss the action, judicial oversight is necessary to ensure that the special litigation committee is independent so that it acts in the corporation's best interest.[16] At issue is whether the special litigation committee created in the present case under Wis. Stat. § 180.0744 was composed of independent directors as required by statute.

Although the plain language of Wis. Stat. § 180.0744 requires the directors who are members of the special litigation committee to be independent, the statute does not define the word "independent." Rather, § 180.0744(3) merely instructs that whether a director on the committee is independent should not be determined solely on the basis of any of the following three factors set forth in the statute: (1) whether the director is nominated to the special litigation committee or elected by persons who are defendants in the derivative action, (2) whether the director is a defendant in the action, or (3) whether the act being challenged in the derivative action was approved by the director if the act resulted in no personal benefit to the director.

Wisconsin Stat. § 180.0744(3) provides as follows:

(3) Whether a director is independent for purposes of this section may not be determined solely on the basis of any one or more of the following factors:

(a) The nomination or election of the director by persons who are defendants in the derivative proceeding or against whom action is demanded.

(b) The naming of the director as a defendant in the derivative proceeding or as a person against whom action is demanded.

(c) The approval by the director of the act being challenged in the derivative proceeding or demand if the act resulted in no personal benefit to the director.

To determine the meaning of the word "independent" in Wis. Stat. § 180.0744, we examine the language of the statute, and its

---

16. 2 Model Business Corporation Act Annotated, Introductory Comment to Sub- chapter D, Derivative Proceedings, § 7.40 at 7–253 (3d ed. 1997 Supp.).

history, context, subject matter and purpose. See UFE, Inc. v. LIRC, 201 Wis.2d 274, 282, 548 N.W.2d 57 (1996).

The factors identified in Wis. Stat. § 180.0744(3) that cannot be solely determinative of whether a director is independent would appear at first blush to render a director not independent. For example, by instructing a court that whether a director is independent may not be determined solely on the basis that the director is a named defendant in the derivative action, Wis. Stat. § 180.0744(3)(b) appears to direct a court to adopt a relaxed, lenient standard for the word "independent." Relying on this subsection and reviewing the legislative history, the circuit court concluded that "the threshold established by the legislature is extremely low. This conclusion is inescapable under a statute where a director who is a defendant in a derivative suit cannot be excluded from an independent committee by that fact alone."

A more nuanced examination of the statute shows, however, that the circuit court's reliance on Wis. Stat. § 180.0744(3) for an "extremely low threshold" standard is incorrect. The legislature understood the significance of the factors it listed. It allows the circuit court to give weight to these factors; the statute simply states that the presence of one or more of these factors is not solely determinative of the issue of whether a director is independent.

The legislature recognized, for example, that a shareholder could prevent the entire board of directors from serving on the special litigation committee merely by naming all the directors as defendants in the derivative action. Section 180.0744(3)(b) instructs a court to examine whether a director who is a member of the special litigation committee is a nominal defendant or a defendant with a personal interest in the dispute. The statute thus instructs the court that this factor is not solely determinative.

The Official Comment to § 7.44 of the Model Business Corporation Act upon which Wis. Stat. § 180.0744 is based explains that "the mere fact that a director has been named as a defendant ... does not cause the director to be considered not independent.... It is believed that a court will be able to assess any actual bias in deciding whether the director is independent without any presumption arising out of ... the mere naming of the director as a defendant...."

We conclude that the circuit court's interpretation that the statute sets forth an "extremely low" threshold for determining whether a director is independent does not comport with the statute. The legislature directs in Wis. Stat. § 180.0744(3) that a court is not to adopt a per se exclusion of directors from the special litigation committee when these directors have certain relations with the corporation. Instead the legislature directs a court to examine the characteristics of each member's relationship to a defendant director and the corporation carefully to determine whether the member is independent.

The statute requires judicial adherence to the decision of a special litigation committee that is independent and is operating in accordance with the statute. Judicial review to determine whether the members of the committee are independent and whether the committee's procedure complies with the statute is of utmost importance, because the court is bound by the substantive decision of a properly constituted and acting committee. The power of a corporate defendant to obtain a dismissal of an action by the ruling of a committee of independent directors selected by the board of directors is unique in the law. The threshold established by the legislature in Wis. Stat. § 180.0744 to determine whether members of a committee are independent is decidedly not "extremely low," as the circuit court stated. We conclude the legislature intended a circuit court to examine carefully whether members of a special litigation committee are independent.

The legislative history of Wis. Stat. § 180.0744 supports our interpretation of the word "independent" and the role of the circuit court.

Wisconsin Stat. § 180.0744 is based on § 7.44 of the Model Business Corporation Act, which was adopted in 1989. The Wisconsin version of the Model Business Corporation Act, Wis. Stat. § 180.0744, was created by 1991 Act 16, § 27, effective May 13, 1991. Thus our inquiry into the meaning of the word "independent" under the Wisconsin statute considers the history of the enactment of both the Wisconsin statute and the Model Business Corporation Act.

The language of Wis. Stat. § 180.0744(1), as originally adopted, differed from § 7.44 of the Model Business Corporation Act in its final phrase. The final phrase of § 180.0744(1) as originally adopted, in contrast to the Model Business Corporation Act, provided that a court shall adhere to the decision of the special litigation committee to dismiss the derivative action **"unless the court finds that the members of the group so voting were not independent or were not acting in good faith"**[24] (emphasis added).

24. The original enactment of Wis. Stat. § 180.0744(1) provided:

(1) The court shall dismiss a derivative proceeding on motion by the corporation if one or more of the groups specified in sub. (2) or (6) has determined in good faith after conducting a reasonable inquiry upon which its conclusions are based that maintenance of the derivative proceeding is not in the best interests of the corporation, unless the court finds that the members of the group so voting were not independent or were not acting in good faith (emphasis of the final phrase added).

See 1991 Wis. Act 16, § 27.

Section 7.44(a) of the Model Business Corporation Act reads as follows:

(a) A derivative proceeding shall be dismissed by the court on motion by the corporation if one of the groups specified in subsections (b) or (f) has determined in good faith after conducting a reasonable inquiry upon which its conclusions are based that the maintenance of the derivative proceeding is not in the best interests of the corporation.

According to the bill-drafting file for Wis. Stat. § 180.0744, the purpose of the final clause, which could be considered merely redundant, was to make explicit that under the statute a court is to examine the rationality of the decision-making process and whether the members of the group were independent and acted in good faith.[25] The final clause "strikes a proper balance between shareholders' rights and the business judgment principle of corporate governance."[26]

According to the legislative history, the statute does not dictate judicial adherence to the decision of a special litigation committee unless the committee members are independent under the statute. A court is required to adhere to the decision of the special litigation committee regarding dismissal of a derivative action on the ground that the committee's decision constitutes a matter of business judgment delegated by the board of directors to the committee. Thus, under the Wisconsin statute, judicial oversight is necessary to determine whether the members of the special litigation committee are independent.

In October 1991, the Committee on Business Corporation Law of the State Bar of Wisconsin sought amendment of Wis. Stat. § 180.744(1), as the attorneys explained, to retain the purpose of the final phrase but to clarify that the final phrase of the Wisconsin statute did not change the burden of proof set forth in the statute.[28] The amendment proposed by the lawyers, described as "nonsubstantive and 'housekeeping' in nature," and adopted by the legislature, thus expressly retains the concept of judicial review of whether members of the special litigation committee are independent.[29]

The legislative history contradicts the conclusion of the circuit court and court of appeals in the present case that the legislature intended an "extremely low" threshold for determining whether members of a special litigation committee are independent. The legislative history of Wis. Stat. § 180.0744 demonstrates the legislature's intent that the courts scrutinize whether the members of a special litigation committee are independent in order to protect the shareholders' and the corporation's interests.

III

We now discuss the appropriate test to be applied to determine whether directors who are members of a special litigation committee

25. Letter from Attorney Jeffrey Bartell to Senator Charles Chvala dated January 23, 1991, Bill–Drafting File, 1991 Wis. Act 16, Legislative Reference Bureau, Madison, Wisconsin.

26. Letter from Attorney Jeffrey Bartell to Senator Charles Chvala dated January 23, 1991, Bill–Drafting File, 1991 Wis. Act 16, Legislative Reference Bureau, Madison, Wisconsin.

28. Memorandum to the Committee on Business Corporation Law from Jeffrey Bartell and Molly Martin dated October 31, 1991, Bill–Drafting File, 1991 Wis. Act 16, Legislative Reference Bureau, Madison, Wisconsin.

29. See 1991 Wis. Act 173, § 2 (effective April 28, 1992). See also Christopher S. Berry, Kenneth B. Davis, Jr., Frank C. DeGuire and Clay R. Williams, Wisconsin Business Corporation Law at 7–116 (State Bar of Wisconsin CLE Books 1992).

are independent under Wis. Stat. § 180.0744. This question is one of first impression in Wisconsin. Nothing in the statute expressly states the factors to be examined to determine whether directors who are members of a committee are independent.

The Model Business Corporation Act (upon which Wis. Stat. § 180.0744 is based) builds on the law relating to special litigation committees developed by a number of states. We are therefore informed by the case law of other states, and we derive from this case law the following test to determine whether a member of a special litigation committee is independent.

Whether members are independent is tested on an objective basis as of the time they are appointed to the special litigation committee.[33] Considering the totality of the circumstances, a court shall determine whether a reasonable person in the position of a member of a special litigation committee can base his or her decision on the merits of the issue rather than on extraneous considerations or influences.[34] In other words, the test is whether a member of a committee has a relationship with an individual defendant or the corporation that would reasonably be expected to affect the member's judgment with respect to the litigation in issue. The factors a court should examine to determine whether a committee member is independent include, but are not limited to, the following:

(1) *A committee member's status as a defendant and potential liability*. Optimally members of a special litigation committee should not be defendants in the derivative action and should not be exposed to personal liability as a result of the action.

(2) *A committee member's participation in or approval of the alleged wrongdoing or financial benefits from the challenged transaction*. Optimally members of a special litigation committee should not have been members of the board of directors when the transaction in question occurred or was approved. Nor should they have participated in the transaction or events underlying the derivative action. Innocent or pro forma involvement does not necessarily render a member not independent, but substantial participation or approval or personal financial benefit should.

(3) *A committee member's past or present business or economic dealings with an individual defendant*. Evidence of a committee member's employment and financial relations with an individual defendant should be considered in determining whether the member is independent.

33. An independent member might stop being independent while serving on a special litigation committee.

34. This standard for determining whether a person is independent fits the dictionary definitions of independent. Black's Law Dictionary at 774 (7th ed.1999) defines "independent" as "not subject to the control or influence of another." The American Heritage Dictionary of the English Language at 917 (3d ed.1992) defines "independent" as, among other things, "free from the influence, guidance, or control of another or others."

(4) *A committee member's past or present personal, family, or social relations with individual defendants.* Evidence of a committee member's non-financial relations with an individual defendant should be considered in determining whether the member is independent. A determination of whether a member is independent is affected by the extent to which a member is directly or indirectly dominated by, controlled by or beholden to an individual defendant.

(5) *A committee member's past or present business or economic relations with the corporation.* For example, if a member of the special litigation committee was outside counsel or a consultant to the corporation, this factor should be considered in determining whether the member is independent.

(6) *The number of members on a special litigation committee.* The more members on a special litigation committee, the less weight a circuit court may assign to a particular disabling interest affecting a single member of the committee.

(7) *The roles of corporate counsel and independent counsel.* Courts should be more likely to find a special litigation committee independent if the committee retains counsel who has not represented individual defendants or the corporation in the past.

Some courts and commentators have suggested that a "structural bias" exists in special litigation committees that taints their decisions. They argue that members of a committee, appointed by the directors of the corporation, are instinctively sympathetic and empathetic towards their colleagues on the board of directors and can be expected to vote for dismissal of any but the most egregious charges. They assert that the committees are inherently biased and untrustworthy. Wisconsin Stat. § 180.0744 and the Model Business Corporation Act are designed to combat this possibility.

Wisconsin Stat. § 180.0744 requires that only independent directors vote to create a special litigation committee and only independent directors serve on the committee. The statute recognizes that independent directors serving as members of a special litigation committee are capable of rendering an independent decision even though they are members of the board of directors which includes defendants in the derivative action.

A court should not presuppose that a special litigation committee is inherently biased. Although members of a special litigation committee may have experiences similar to those of the defendant directors and serve with them on the board of directors, the legislature has declared that independent members of a special litigation committee are capable of rendering an independent decision. The test we set forth today is designed, as is the statute, to overcome the effects of any "structural bias."

A circuit court is to look at the totality of the circumstances. A finding that a member of the special litigation committee is independent does not require the complete absence of any facts that might point to non-objectivity. A director may be independent even if he or she has had some personal or business relation with an individual director accused of wrongdoing. Although the totality of the circumstances test does not necessitate the complete absence of any facts that might point to a member not being independent, a circuit court is required to apply the test for determining whether a member is independent with care and rigor. If the members are not independent, the court will, in effect, be allowing the defendant directors to render a judgment on their own alleged misconduct. The value of a special litigation committee depends on the extent to which the members of the committee are independent.

It is vital for a circuit court to review whether each member of a special litigation committee is independent. The special litigation committee is, after all, the "only instance in American Jurisprudence where a defendant can free itself from a suit by merely appointing a committee to review the allegations of the complaint. . . ."[40] We agree with the Delaware Court of Chancery that the trial court must be "certain that the SLC [special litigation committee] is truly independent."[41] While ill suited to assessing business judgments, courts are well suited by experience to evaluate whether members of a special litigation committee are independent.

The test we set forth attains the balance the legislature intended by empowering corporations to dismiss meritless derivative litigation through special litigation committees, while checking this power with appropriate judicial oversight over the composition and conduct of the special litigation committee.

IV

The circuit court declined to grant summary judgment for the defendant because there was a dispute of material facts. After seven days of testimony on the issue of whether the members of the special litigation committee were independent, the circuit court made findings of fact and concluded that the threshold the legislature established for determining whether the members of the committee were independent is "extremely low." Applying this "extremely low" standard, the circuit court determined that the members of the special litigation committee in the present case were independent.[42]

40. Lewis v. Fuqua, 502 A.2d 962, 967 (Del.Ch.1985).

41. Lewis v. Fuqua, 502 A.2d 962, 967 (Del.Ch.1985).

42. The question of which party has the burden of proving, Wis. Stat. § 180.0744(5), whether members of the special litigation committee in the present case were independent has been raised in this case. At the trial before the circuit court, plaintiff Einhorn presented his case first. We do not address the issue of burden of proof because it was not fully analyzed or fully briefed by the parties.

We briefly explore the relations of the members of the special litigation committee to the corporation and the defendant Culea. In this case no member of the special litigation committee is a named defendant in the derivative action.

One member of the committee, Robert Bonk, received a $25,000 bonus at the same meeting of the compensation committee at which Culea's challenged bonus was approved. The circuit court found that "while [Bonk] did receive a bonus at the same meeting of the board where Mr. Culea received his bonus, it does not appear that there was a quid pro quo or any other type of linkage between the two bonuses. In fact, it should be noted that the plaintiff [Einhorn] has not made Bonk's $25,000 bonus a subject of this lawsuit." Einhorn has made the bonus an issue in this court.

Bonk is an employee of the corporation, is a subordinate of Culea and considers Culea a friend. Bonk acknowledged that it would be "very difficult for [him] to even consider the possibility that Mr. Culea would do something improper...." Bonk's ability to independently evaluate the litigation may have been compromised by his own admission. The circuit court merely stated that "with the exception of him being an employee of Northern Labs, this Court fails to find any inherent basis upon which his independence could be challenged."

Outside counsel retained by the special litigation committee questioned whether Robert Bonk was independent: "[Bonk's] independence is questionable.... Because his interests in the financial outcome ~~would~~ [strikethrough in original] was affected but it is such a small amount.... The input of [Bonk] throughout the process may taint the vote because his independence may be questioned." Whether Bonk was independent should be determined on the basis of his employment status, his financial interest in the outcome and his personal relation with Culea.

Another member of the committee, John Beagle, was characterized by the circuit court as Einhorn's "right-hand man." Beagle admitted that he and Einhorn "have a very good business relationship" and are "also very good friends." Beagle wrote, in explaining his lone vote to maintain the derivative action, that "the special litigation committee is not, and never was, unbiased or independent ... each of us is too close to one party or the other to have a chance at being independent...." John Beagle, plaintiff Einhorn's good friend and close business partner, openly admits that he was not independent.

The other two members of the special litigation committee had personal and social relationships with Culea and Culea's wife. Einhorn argues strenuously that Culea's neighbor and friend, Dwight Chewning, and Culea's wife's friend, Lolita Chua, were not independent. The exact extent of these friendships is vigorously contested by the parties, but the existence of some relationship is evidenced in the record.

The circuit court did not make findings of fact specifying the relationships of Chewning and Chua to Culea other than describing Chewning as a "neighbor" and Chua as a "social friend" of Mrs.

Culea. In its discussion of Chewning and Chua, the circuit court examined their performance as witnesses and as members of the special litigation committee. While the care, attention and sense of individual responsibility of a member may touch on the issue of whether the member was independent, the test is primarily concerned with whether factors exist at the time the committee was formed that would prevent a reasonable person from basing his or her decisions on the merits of the issue. Whether members of the special litigation committee are independent is critical. "Good faith, reasonable inquiry, and the best interests of the corporation are not enough."[47]

As we stated previously, mere acquaintanceship and social interaction are not per se bars to finding a member independent. Relationships with an individual defendant and the corporation are, however, factors the circuit court must consider in the totality of circumstances.

Einhorn also argues strenuously that the role of the corporation's counsel tainted the formation of the special litigation committee, in that the corporation's counsel was acting both as Culea's personal counsel and as the corporation's counsel. Relatively late in its investigation the special litigation committee retained a separate law firm from Washington, D.C., to act as its counsel. But the exact extent of the corporation's counsel's role in advising the special litigation committee is contested. The circuit court did not make findings about the roles of the corporation's counsel and outside counsel. The role of the corporation's counsel should be considered as one of the circumstances in determining whether the committee is independent. Several courts have stated that retention of objectively independent counsel is highly recommended, although failure to do so does not necessarily prevent a special litigation committee from being independent.[48]

The circuit court did not apply the totality of the circumstances standard to determine whether a reasonable person in the position of the member of the special litigation committee could base his or her decision on the merits of the issue rather than on extraneous conditions or influences. Considered together, the relationships in the

---

47. See Christopher S. Berry, Kenneth B. Davis, Jr., Frank C. DeGuire and Clay R. Williams, Wisconsin Business Corporation Law at 7–116 (State Bar of Wisconsin CLE Books 1992).

48. See, e.g., In re Par Pharm. Inc., 750 F.Supp. 641, 647 (S.D.N.Y.1990) ("Both New York and Delaware law contemplate that a special litigation committee be represented by independent counsel."); Kaplan v. Wyatt, 499 A.2d 1184, 1190 (Del.1985)(although use of in-house counsel is not recommended, it is not fatal to the special litigation committee's investigation).

A comment to Wis. SCR 20:1.13 of the Code of Professional Conduct states the following about derivative actions:

The question can arise whether counsel for the organization may defend such an action. The proposition that the organization is the lawyer's client does not alone resolve the issue. Most derivative actions are a normal incident of an organization's affairs, to be defended by the organization's lawyer like any other suit. However, if the claim involves serious charges of wrongdoing by those in control of the organization, a conflict may arise between the lawyer's duty to the organization and the lawyer's relationship with the board. In those circumstances, Rule 1.7 [relating to conflict of interest] governs who should represent the directors and the organization.

present case raise significant questions concerning whether the members of the special litigation committee were independent.[49] The decision of this court is not intended to cast doubt on any committee member's integrity, honesty or hard work on the special litigation committee. Rather, we are concerned that, at the time of the formation of the special litigation committee, the members of the committee had relationships with the individual defendant and the corporation that call into question whether a reasonable person could base his or her decision on the merits of the issue rather than on extraneous considerations or influences.

The application of a statute to undisputed facts is ordinarily a question of law that this court determines independently of the circuit court and the court of appeals, benefiting from the analyses of these courts. But in this case the facts are in dispute, and the circuit court has not made sufficient findings of fact upon which this court can apply the legal test set forth. Accordingly, we remand the cause to the circuit court to make findings of fact and to apply the proper legal standard to the facts of this case.

The decision of the court of appeals is reversed and the cause is remanded.

SECTION 10. INDEMNIFICATION AND INSURANCE

(a) INDEMNIFICATION

Add the following Note at p. 1041 of the Unabridged Edition, after the Note on Plate v. Sun–Diamond Growers:

STIFEL FINANCIAL CORP. v. COCHRAN, 809 A.2d 555 (Del. Supr. 2002). Cochran, an investment banker, had been discharged as an officer and director of Stifel Nicolaus corporation, a wholly owned subsidiary of Stifel Financial Corporation ("Stifel"). Cochran then refused to repay to Stifel Nicolaus excess compensation and the balance of a promissory note, as required by his employment agree-

---

49. Wisconsin Stat. § 180.0744 draws no distinction between publicly held corporations and closely held corporations. See §§ 180.1801–180.1837 relating to close corporations. We acknowledge that it may be difficult for closely held corporations to assemble special litigation committees. If it is difficult for the corporation to create an independent special litigation committee, the remedy has been provided by the legislature. The corporation may move the court, pursuant to Wis. Stat. § 180.0744(6), to "appoint a panel of one or more independent persons to determine whether maintenance of the derivative proceedings is in the best interests of the corporation."

ment. To recover these amounts, Stifel Nicolaus instituted an arbitration proceeding against Cochran. The arbitrators ruled in favor of Stifel Nicolaus on the excess-compensation and promissory-note claims, and ordered Cochran to repay Stifel Nicolaus approximately $1.2 million. The arbitration award was confirmed by the United States District Court for the Eastern District of Missouri.

Stifel's bylaws contained the following indemnification provision:

> The Corporation [Stifel] shall indemnify to the full extent authorized by law any person made or threatened to be made a party to any action, suit, or proceeding, whether criminal, civil, administrative or investigative, by reason of the fact that he . . . is or was a director, officer or employee of the Corporation or any predecessor of the Corporation or serves or served any other enterprise as a director, officer or employee at the request of the Corporation or any predecessor of the Corporation.

Cochran filed an action seeking indemnification from Stifel pursuant to this bylaw. The Delaware Supreme Court held that Cochran was not entitled to indemnification for the amounts he was required to pay to Stifel on the basis of the compensation and promissory note claims because the liability did not result from actions by Stifel in his official capacity:

> The arbitration action was brought against Cochran to enforce certain provisions of an employment contract and promissory note, which Cochran had entered into with Stifel Nicolaus. The Court of Chancery's explanation bears repeating:
>
> > When a corporate officer signs an employment contract committing to fill an office, he is acting in a personal capacity in an adversarial, arms-length transaction. To the extent that he binds himself to certain obligations under that contract, he owes a personal obligation to the corporation. When the corporation brings a claim and proves its entitlement to relief because the officer has breached his individual obligations, it is problematic to conclude that the suit has been rendered an "official capacity" suit subject to indemnification under § 145 and implementing bylaws. Such a conclusion would render the officer's duty to perform his side of the contract in many respects illusory.
>
> We agree that the claims litigated in the arbitration action were properly characterized as personal, not directed at Cochran in his "official capacity" as an officer and director of Stifel Nicolaus. . . . Stifel Nicolaus based the Compensation Claim [and] the Promissory Note Claim . . . on the employment contract Cochran entered into with the company. Although Cochran's termination is the event that triggered the relevant provisions of the employment contract, Cochran's decision to breach the contract was entirely a personal one, pursued for his sole benefit. . . .

———

CHAPTER XII

STRUCTURAL CHANGES: CORPORATE COMBINATIONS AND TENDER OFFERS

SECTION 1: CORPORATE COMBINATIONS

Insert the following case at p. 1128 of the Unabridged Edition, and page 797 of the Concise Edition, after the Note on Alpert v. 28 Williams St. Corp.:

Glassman v. Unocal Exploration Corp.

Supreme Court of Delaware, 2001.
777 A.2d 242.

■ Before VEASEY, CHIEF JUSTICE, WALSH, HOLLAND, BERGER and STEELE, JUSTICES, constituting the Court en Banc.

■ BERGER, JUSTICE.

In this appeal, we consider the fiduciary duties owed by a parent corporation to the subsidiary's minority stockholders in the context of a "short-form" merger. Specifically, we take this opportunity to reconcile a fiduciary's seemingly absolute duty to establish the entire fairness of any self-dealing transaction with the less demanding requirements of the short-form merger statute. The statute authorizes the elimination of minority stockholders by a summary process that does not involve the "fair dealing" component of entire fairness. Indeed, the statute does not contemplate any "dealing" at all. Thus, a parent corporation cannot satisfy the entire fairness standard if it follows the terms of the short-form merger statute without more.

Unocal Corporation addressed this dilemma by establishing a special negotiating committee and engaging in a process that it believed would pass muster under traditional entire fairness review. We find that such steps were unnecessary. By enacting a statute that authorizes the elimination of the minority without notice, vote, or other traditional indicia of procedural fairness, the General Assembly effectively circumscribed the parent corporation's obligations to the minority in a short-form merger. The parent corporation does not have to establish entire fairness, and, absent fraud or illegality, the only recourse for a minority stockholder who is dissatisfied with the merger consideration is appraisal.

I. Factual and Procedural Background

Unocal Corporation is an earth resources company primarily engaged in the exploration for and production of crude oil and natural gas. At the time of the merger at issue, Unocal owned approximately 96% of the stock of Unocal Exploration Corporation ("UXC"), an oil and gas company operating in and around the Gulf of Mexico. In 1991, low natural gas prices caused a drop in both companies' revenues and earnings. Unocal investigated areas of possible cost savings and decided that, by eliminating the UXC minority, it would reduce taxes and overhead expenses.

In December 1991 the boards of Unocal and UXC appointed special committees to consider a possible merger. The UXC committee consisted of three directors who, although also directors of Unocal, were not officers or employees of the parent company. The UXC committee retained financial and legal advisors and met four times before agreeing to a merger exchange ratio of .54 shares of Unocal stock for each share of UXC. Unocal and UXC announced the merger on February 24, 1992, and it was effected, pursuant to *8 Del. C. § 253*, on May 2, 1992. The Notice of Merger and Prospectus stated the terms of the merger and advised the former UXC stockholders of their appraisal rights.

Plaintiffs filed this class action, on behalf of UXC's minority stockholders, on the day the merger was announced. They asserted, among other claims, that Unocal and its directors breached their fiduciary duties of entire fairness and full disclosure. The Court of Chancery conducted a two day trial and held that: (i) the Prospectus did not contain any material misstatements or omissions; (ii) the entire fairness standard does not control in a short-form merger; and (iii) plaintiffs' exclusive remedy in this case was appraisal. The decision of the Court of Chancery is affirmed.

II. Discussion

The short-form merger statute, as enacted in 1937, authorized a parent corporation to merge with its wholly-owned subsidiary by filing and recording a certificate evidencing the parent's ownership and its merger resolution. In 1957, the statute was expanded to include parent/subsidiary mergers where the parent company owns at least 90% of the stock of the subsidiary. The 1957 amendment also made it possible, for the first time and only in a short-form merger, to pay the minority cash for their shares, thereby eliminating their ownership interest in the company. In its current form, which has not changed significantly since 1957, *8 Del. C. § 253* provides in relevant part:

> (a) In any case in which at least 90 percent of the outstanding shares of each class of the stock of a corporation . . . is owned

by another corporation ..., the corporation having such stock ownership may ... merge the other corporation ... into itself ... by executing, acknowledging and filing, in accordance with § 103 of this title, a certificate of such ownership and merger setting forth a copy of the resolution of its board of directors to so merge and the date of the adoption; provided, however, that in case the parent corporation shall not own all the outstanding stock of ... the subsidiary corporation[ ], ... the resolution ... shall state the terms and conditions of the merger, including the securities, cash, property or rights to be issued, paid delivered or granted by the surviving corporation upon surrender of each share of the subsidiary corporation....

* * *

(d) In the event that all of the stock of a subsidiary Delaware corporation ... is not owned by the parent corporation immediately prior to the merger, the stockholders of the subsidiary Delaware corporation party to the merger shall have appraisal rights as set forth in Section 262 of this Title....

The ... question [was then] presented to this Court ... whether any equitable relief is available to minority stockholders who object to a short-form merger. In *Stauffer v. Standard Brands Incorporated*,[3] minority stockholders sued to set aside the contested merger or, in the alternative, for damages. They alleged that the merger consideration was so grossly inadequate as to constitute constructive fraud and that Standard Brands breached its fiduciary duty to the minority by failing to set a fair price for their stock. The Court of Chancery held that appraisal was the stockholders' exclusive remedy, and dismissed the complaint. This Court affirmed, but explained that appraisal would not be the exclusive remedy in a short-form merger tainted by fraud or illegality:

[T]he exception [to appraisal's exclusivity] ... refers generally to all mergers, and is nothing but a reaffirmation of the ever-present power of equity to deal with illegality or fraud. But it has no bearing here. No illegality or overreaching is shown. The dispute reduces to nothing but a difference of opinion as to value. Indeed it is difficult to imagine a case under the short merger statute in which there could be such actual fraud as would entitle a minority to set aside the merger. This is so because the very purpose of the statute is to provide the parent corporation with a means of eliminating the minority shareholder's interest in the enterprise. Thereafter the former stockholder has only a monetary claim.[4]

The *Stauffer* doctrine's viability rose and fell over the next four decades ...

3. Del.Supr., 187 A.2d 78 (1962).   **4.** 187 A.2d at 80.

In 1977, this Court [held in] . . . *Singer v. Magnavox Co.*[7] . . . that a controlling stockholder breaches its fiduciary duty if it effects a cash-out merger under § 251 for the sole purpose of eliminating the minority stockholders. . . .

Singer's business purpose test was extended to short-form mergers two years later in *Roland International Corporation v. Najjar* . . . .[9]

After *Roland*, there was not much of *Stauffer* that safely could be considered good law. . . . But that changed in 1983, in *Weinberger v. UOP, Inc.*,[11] when the Court dropped the business purpose test, made appraisal a more adequate remedy, and said that it was "return[ing] to the well established principles of *Stauffer* . . . mandating a stockholder's recourse to the basic remedy of an appraisal." *Weinberger* focused on two subjects—the "unflinching" duty of entire fairness owed by self-dealing fiduciaries, and the "more liberalized appraisal" it established.

With respect to entire fairness, the Court explained that the concept includes fair dealing (how the transaction was timed, initiated, structured, negotiated, disclosed and approved) and fair price (all elements of value); and that the test for fairness is not bifurcated. On the subject of appraisal, the Court made several important statements: (i) courts may consider "proof of value by any techniques or methods which are generally considered acceptable in the financial community and otherwise admissible in court. . . .;" (ii) fair value must be based on "all relevant factors," which include not only "elements of future value . . . which are known or susceptible of proof as of the date of the merger" but also, when the court finds it appropriate, "damages, resulting from the taking, which the stockholders sustain as a class;" and (iii) "a plaintiff's monetary remedy ordinarily should be confined to the more liberalized appraisal proceeding herein established. . . ."

By referencing . . . *Stauffer* . . ., one might have thought that the *Weinberger* court intended appraisal to be the exclusive remedy "ordinarily" in non-fraudulent mergers where "price . . . [is] the preponderant consideration outweighing other features of the merger." In *Rabkin v. Philip A. Hunt Chemical Corp.*,[18] however, the Court dispelled that view. The *Rabkin* plaintiffs claimed that the majority stockholder breached its fiduciary duty of fair dealing by waiting until a one year commitment to pay $25 per share had expired before effecting a cash-out merger at $20 per share. The Court of Chancery dismissed the complaint, reasoning that, under *Weinberger*, plaintiffs could obtain full relief for the alleged unfair dealing in an appraisal proceeding. This Court reversed, holding that the trial court read *Weinberger* too narrowly and that appraisal is the exclusive remedy only if stockholders' complaints are limited to "judgmental factors of valuation."

---

7. Del. Supr., 380 A.2d 969 (1977).

9. Del. Supr., 407 A.2d 1032 (1979).

11. Del.Supr., 457 A.2d 701 (1983).

18. *Del.Supr.*, 498 A.2d 1099 (1985).

Rabkin, through its interpretation of *Weinberger*, effectively eliminated appraisal as the exclusive remedy for any claim alleging breach of the duty of entire fairness. But *Rabkin* involved a long-form merger, and the Court did not discuss, in that case or any others, how its refinement of *Weinberger* impacted short-form mergers. . . .

Mindful of this history, we must decide whether a minority stockholder may challenge a short-form merger by seeking equitable relief through an entire fairness claim. Under settled principles, a parent corporation and its directors undertaking a short-form merger are self-dealing fiduciaries who should be required to establish entire fairness, including fair dealing and fair price. The problem is that § 253 authorizes a summary procedure that is inconsistent with any reasonable notion of fair dealing. In a short-form merger, there is no agreement of merger negotiated by two companies; there is only a unilateral act—a decision by the parent company that its 90% owned subsidiary shall no longer exist as a separate entity. The minority stockholders receive no advance notice of the merger; their directors do not consider or approve it; and there is no vote. Those who object are given the right to obtain fair value for their shares through appraisal.

The equitable claim plainly conflicts with the statute. If a corporate fiduciary follows the truncated process authorized by § 253, it will not be able to establish the fair dealing prong of entire fairness. If, instead, the corporate fiduciary sets up negotiating committees, hires independent financial and legal experts, etc., then it will have lost the very benefit provided by the statute—a simple, fast and inexpensive process for accomplishing a merger. We resolve this conflict by giving effect the intent of the General Assembly.[24] In order to serve its purpose, § 253 must be construed to obviate the requirement to establish entire fairness.

Thus, we again return to *Stauffer*, and hold that, absent fraud or illegality, appraisal is the exclusive remedy available to a minority stockholder who objects to a short-form merger. In doing so, we also reaffirm *Weinberger's* statements about the scope of appraisal. The determination of fair value must be based on *all* relevant factors, including damages and elements of future value, where appropriate. So, for example, if the merger was timed to take advantage of a depressed market, or a low point in the company's cyclical earnings, or to precede an anticipated positive development, the appraised value may be adjusted to account for those factors. We recognize that these are the types of issues frequently raised in entire fairness claims, and we have held that claims for unfair dealing cannot be litigated in an appraisal.[26] But our prior holdings simply explained that equitable claims may not be engrafted onto a statutory appraisal proceeding; stockholders may not receive rescissionary relief in an appraisal. Those

24. *Klotz v. Warner Communications, Inc.*, Del.Supr., 674 A.2d 878, 879 (1995).

26. *Alabama By–Products Corporation v. Neal*, Del.Supr., 588 A.2d 255, 257 (1991).

decisions should not be read to restrict the elements of value that properly may be considered in an appraisal.

Although fiduciaries are not required to establish entire fairness in a short-form merger, the duty of full disclosure remains, in the context of this request for stockholder action. Where the only choice for the minority stockholders is whether to accept the merger consideration or seek appraisal, they must be given all the factual information that is material to that decision. The Court of Chancery carefully considered plaintiffs' disclosure claims and applied settled law in rejecting them. We affirm this aspect of the appeal on the basis of the trial court's decision.

III.   Conclusion

Based on the foregoing, we affirm the Court of Chancery and hold that plaintiffs' only remedy in connection with the short-form merger of UXC into Unocal was appraisal.

SECTION 2.   TENDER OFFERS

Add the following case at p. 1230 of the Unabridged Edition and p. 874 of the Concise Edition, after Quickturn Design Systems, Inc. v. Shapiro:

Omnicare, Inc., v. NCS Healthcare, Inc.
Supreme Court of Delaware 2003.
818 A.2d 914.

■ Before: VEASEY, CHIEF JUSTICE, WALSH, HOLLAND, BERGER and STEELE, JUSTICES, constituting the Court en Banc.

■ HOLLAND, JUSTICE, for the majority: . . .

NCS Healthcare, Inc. ("NCS"), a Delaware corporation, was the object of competing acquisition bids, one by Genesis Health Ventures, Inc., ("Genesis"), a Pennsylvania Corporation, and the other by Omnicare, Inc. ("Omnicare"), a Delaware corporation. . . .

NCS, is a Delaware corporation headquartered in Beachwood, Ohio. NCS is a leading independent provider of pharmacy services to long-term care institutions including skilled nursing facilities, assisted living facilities and other institutional healthcare facilities. NCS common stock consists of Class A shares and Class B shares. The Class B shares are entitled to ten votes per share and the Class A shares are entitled to one vote per share. The shares are virtually identical in every other respect.

The defendant Jon H. Outcalt is Chairman of the NCS board of directors. Outcalt owns 202,063 shares of NCS Class A common stock and 3,476,086 shares of Class B common stock. The defendant Kevin B. Shaw is President, CEO and a director of NCS. At the time the merger agreement at issue in this dispute was executed with Genesis, Shaw owned 28,905 shares of NCS Class A common stock and 1,141,134 shares of Class B common stock.

The NCS board has two other members, defendants Boake A. Sells and Richard L. Osborne. Sells is a graduate of the Harvard Business School. He was Chairman and CEO at Revco Drugstores in Cleveland, Ohio from 1987 to 1992, when he was replaced by new owners. Sells currently sits on the boards of both public and private companies. Osborne is a full-time professor at the Weatherhead School of Management at Case Western Reserve University. He has been at the university for over thirty years. Osborne currently sits on at least seven corporate boards other than NCS.

The defendant Genesis is a Pennsylvania corporation with its principal place of business in Kennett Square, Pennsylvania. It is a leading provider of healthcare and support services to the elderly....

The plaintiffs in the class action own an unspecified number of shares of NCS Class A common stock. They represent a class consisting of all holders of Class A common stock. As of July 28, 2002, NCS had 18,461,599 Class A shares and 5,255,210 Class B shares outstanding.

Omnicare is a Delaware corporation with its principal place of business in Covington, Kentucky. Omnicare is in the institutional pharmacy business, with annual sales in excess of $2.1 billion during its last fiscal year....

FACTUAL BACKGROUND ...

NCS Seeks Restructuring Alternatives

Beginning in late 1999, changes in the timing and level of reimbursements by government and third-party providers adversely affected market conditions in the health care industry. As a result, NCS began to experience greater difficulty in collecting accounts receivables, which led to a precipitous decline in the market value of its stock. NCS common shares that traded above $20 in January 1999 were worth as little as $5 at the end of that year. By early 2001, NCS was in default on approximately $350 million in debt, including $206 million in senior bank debt and $102 million of its 5 3/4 %Convertible Subordinated Debentures (the "Notes"). After these defaults, NCS common stock traded in a range of $0.09 to $0.50 per share until days before the announcement of the transaction at issue in this case.

NCS began to explore strategic alternatives that might address the problems it was confronting....

Omnicare's Initial Negotiations

In the summer of 2001, NCS invited Omnicare, Inc. to begin discussions with Brown Gibbons [NCS's investment banker] regarding a possible transaction. On July 20, Joel Gemunder, Omnicare's President and CEO, sent Shaw [NCS's CEO] a written proposal to acquire

NCS in a bankruptcy sale under Section 363 of the Bankruptcy Code. This proposal was for $225 million subject to satisfactory completion of due diligence....

NCS Financial Improvement

... In March 2002, NCS decided to form an independent committee of board members who were neither NCS employees nor major NCS stockholders (the "Independent Committee") [to consider transactions that would provide some value for NCS's stockholders]. The NCS board thought this was necessary because, due to NCS's precarious financial condition, it felt that fiduciary duties were owed to the enterprise as a whole rather than solely to NCS stockholders.

Sells and Osborne were selected as the members of the committee, and given authority to consider and negotiate possible transactions for NCS. The entire four member NCS board, however, retained authority to approve any transaction. The Independent Committee retained the same legal and financial counsel as the NCS board.

The Independent Committee met for the first time on May 14, 2002. At that meeting Pollack suggested that NCS seek a "stalking-horse merger partner" to obtain the highest possible value in any transaction. The Independent Committee agreed with the suggestion.

Genesis Initial Proposal

Two days later, on May 16, 2002, Scott Berlin of Brown Gibbons, Glen Pollack [also of Brown Gibbons] and Boake Sells [a member of NCS's independent committee] met with George Hager, CFO of Genesis, and Michael Walker, who was Genesis's CEO. At that meeting, Genesis made it clear that if it were going to engage in any negotiations with NCS, it would not do so as a "stalking horse." As one of its advisors testified, "We didn't want to be someone who set forth a valuation for NCS which would only result in that valuation ... being publicly disclosed, and thereby creating an environment where Omnicare felt to maintain its competitive monopolistic positions, that they had to match and exceed that level." Thus, Genesis "wanted a degree of certainty that to the extent [it] w[as] willing to pursue a negotiated merger agreement ..., [it] would be able to consummate the transaction [it] negotiated and executed."

In June 2002, Genesis proposed a transaction for the acquisition of NCS.... As discussions continued, the terms proposed by Genesis continued to improve....

Genesis Exclusivity Agreement

NCS's financial advisors and legal counsel met again with Genesis and its legal counsel on June 26, 2002, to discuss a number of transaction-related issues....

At the June 26 meeting, Genesis's representatives demanded that, before any further negotiations take place, NCS agree to enter into an exclusivity agreement with it. As Hager from Genesis explained it: "[I]f they wished us to continue to try to move this process to a definitive agreement, that they would need to do it on an exclusive basis with us. We were going to, and already had incurred significant expense, but we would incur additional expenses ... , both internal and external, to bring this transaction to a definitive signing. We wanted them to work with us on an exclusive basis for a short period of time to see if we could reach agreement." On June 27, 2002, Genesis's legal counsel delivered a draft form of exclusivity agreement for review and consideration by NCS's legal counsel.

The Independent Committee met on July 3, 2002, to consider the proposed exclusivity agreement. Pollack presented a summary of the terms of a possible Genesis merger, which had continued to improve. The then-current Genesis proposal included (1) repayment of the NCS senior debt in full, (2) payment of par value for the Notes (without accrued interest) in the form of a combination of cash and Genesis stock, (3) payment to NCS stockholders in the form of $24 million in Genesis stock, plus (4) the assumption, because the transaction was to be structured as a merger, of additional liabilities to trade and other unsecured creditors.

NCS director Sells testified [that] Pollack told the Independent Committee at a July 3, 2002 meeting that Genesis wanted the Exclusivity Agreement to be the first step towards a completely locked up transaction that would preclude a higher bid from Omnicare:

A. [Pollack] explained that Genesis felt that they had suffered at the hands of Omnicare and others. I guess maybe just Omnicare. I don't know much about Genesis [sic] acquisition history. But they had suffered before at the 11:59:59 and that they wanted to have a pretty much bulletproof deal or they were not going to go forward.

Q. When you say they suffered at the hands of Omnicare, what do you mean?

A. Well, my expression is that that was related to—a deal that was related to me or explained to me that they, Genesis, had tried to acquire, I suppose, an institutional pharmacy, I don't remember the name of it. Thought they had a deal and then at the last minute, Omnicare outbid them for the company in a like 11:59 kind of thing, and that they were unhappy about that. And once burned, twice shy.

After NCS executed the exclusivity agreement, Genesis provided NCS with a draft merger agreement, a draft Noteholders' support agreement, and draft voting agreements for Outcalt and Shaw, who together held a majority of the voting power of the NCS common stock. Genesis and NCS negotiated the terms of the merger agreement over the next three weeks. During those negotiations, the Independent Committee and [an Ad Hoc Committee that had been formed to represent the Noteholders] persuaded Genesis to improve the terms of its merger. . . .

Omnicare Proposes Negotiations . . .

On the afternoon of July 26, 2002, Omnicare faxed to NCS a letter outlining a proposed acquisition. . . . Omnicare's proposal, however, was expressly conditioned on negotiating a merger agreement, obtaining certain third party consents, and completing its due diligence. . . .

Late in the afternoon of July 26, 2002, NCS representatives received voicemail messages from Omnicare asking to discuss the letter. The exclusivity agreement prevented NCS from returning those calls. In relevant part, that agreement precluded NCS from "engag[ing] or particpat[ing] in any discussions or negotiations with respect to a Competing Transaction or a proposal for one." The July 26 letter from Omnicare met the definition of a "Competing Transaction."

. . . Nevertheless, the Independent Committee [decided] to use Omnicare's letter to negotiate for improved terms with Genesis.

Genesis Merger Agreement and Voting Agreements

Genesis responded to the NCS request to improve its offer as a result of the Omnicare fax the next day. On July 27, Genesis proposed substantially improved terms. . . . In return for [its] concessions, Genesis stipulated that the transaction had to be approved by midnight the next day, July 28, or else Genesis would terminate discussions and withdraw its offer. . . .

. . . [The NCS board met on July 28.] After receiving similar reports and advice from its legal and financial advisors, the board concluded that "balancing the potential loss of the Genesis deal against the uncertainty of Omnicare's letter, results in the conclusion that the only reasonable alternative for the Board of Directors is to approve the Genesis transaction." The board first voted to authorize the voting agreements [described below] with Outcalt and Shaw, for purposes of Section 203 of the Delaware General Corporation Law ("DGCL"). The board was advised by its legal counsel that "under the terms of the merger agreement and because NCS shareholders representing in excess of 50% of the outstanding voting power would be required by Genesis to enter into stockholder voting agreements contemporaneously with the signing of the merger agreement, and would agree to vote their shares in favor of the merger agreement, shareholder approval of the merger would be assured even if the NCS Board were to withdraw or change its recommendation. *These facts would prevent NCS from engaging in any alternative or superior transaction in the future.*" (emphasis added).

After listening to a summary of the merger terms, the board then resolved that the merger agreement and the transactions contemplated thereby were advisable and fair and in the best interests of all the NCS stakeholders. The NCS board further resolved to recommend the transactions to the stockholders for their approval and adoption. A definitive merger agreement between NCS and Genesis and the stockholder voting agreements were executed later that day. . . .

NCS/Genesis Merger Agreement

Among other things, the NCS/Genesis merger agreement provided the following:

- NCS stockholders would receive 1 share of Genesis common stock in exchange for every 10 shares of NCS common stock held;
- NCS stockholders could exercise appraisal rights under 8 Del. C. § 262;
- NCS would redeem NCS's Notes in accordance with their terms;
- NCS would submit the merger agreement to NCS stockholders regardless of whether the NCS board continued to recommend the merger;
- NCS would not enter into discussions with third parties concerning an alternative acquisition of NCS, or provide non-public information to such parties, unless (1) the third party provided an unsolicited, bona fide written proposal documenting the terms of the acquisition; (2) the NCS board believed in good faith that the proposal was or was likely to result in an acquisition on terms superior to those contemplated by the NCS/Genesis merger agreement; and (3) before providing non-public information to that third party, the third party would execute a confidentiality agreement at least as restrictive as the one in place between NCS and Genesis; and
- If the merger agreement were to be terminated, under certain circumstances NCS would be required to pay Genesis a $6 million termination fee and/or Genesis's documented expenses, up to $5 million.

[The merger agreement did not include a fiduciary out. A fiduciary out is a term in a merger agreement that provides that *another* term (or terms) in the agreement, which restricts in a certain way the discretion of the board of the corporation that is to be acquired, does not apply if the restriction would result in a breach of the board's fiduciary duties to the corporation and its shareholders. Among the kinds of terms to which a fiduciary out may apply are no-talk clauses, which prohibit the Board from discussing a merger of the Corporation into a third party, and provisions, like the one in *Omnicare*, that require the Board to submit the merger to the shareholders for their approval.]

Voting Agreements

[Contemporaneously with, and as required by, the merger agreement,] Outcalt and Shaw, in their capacity as NCS stockholders, entered into voting agreements with Genesis. NCS was also required to be a party to the voting agreements by Genesis. Those agreements provided, among other things, that:

- Outcalt and Shaw were acting in their capacity as NCS stockholders in executing the agreements, not in their capacity as NCS directors or officers;

- Neither Outcalt nor Shaw would transfer their shares prior to the stockholder vote on the merger agreement;

- Outcalt and Shaw agreed to vote all of their shares in favor of the merger agreement; and

- Outcalt and Shaw granted to Genesis an irrevocable proxy to vote their shares in favor of the merger agreement.

- The voting agreement was specifically enforceable by Genesis.

The merger agreement further provided that if either Outcalt or Shaw breached the terms of the voting agreements, Genesis would be entitled to terminate the merger agreement and potentially receive a $6 million termination fee from NCS. Such a breach was impossible since Section 6 provided that the voting agreements were specifically enforceable by Genesis.

Omnicare's Superior Proposal . . .

On October 6, 2002, Omnicare irrevocably committed itself to a transaction with NCS. Pursuant to the terms of its proposal, Omnicare agreed to acquire all the outstanding NCS Class A and Class B shares [through a tender offer] at a price of $3.50 per share in cash. [The Omnicare bid offered the NCS stockholders cash equal to more than twice the then-current market value of the shares to be received in the Genesis merger. The transaction offered by Omnicare also treated NCS's other stakeholders on equal terms with the Genesis agreement.]

The merger agreement between Genesis and NCS contained a provision authorized by Section 251(c) of Delaware's corporation law. It required that the Genesis agreement be placed before the corporation's stockholders for a vote, even if the NCS board of directors no longer recommended it. At the insistence of Genesis, the NCS board also agreed to omit any effective fiduciary clause from the merger agreement. In connection with the Genesis merger agreement, two stockholders of NCS, who held a majority of the voting power, agreed unconditionally to vote all of their shares in favor of the Genesis merger. Thus, the combined terms of the voting agreements and merger agreement guaranteed, ab initio, that the transaction proposed by Genesis would obtain NCS stockholder's approval. As a result of this irrevocable offer, on October 21, 2002, the NCS board withdrew its recommendation that the stockholders vote in favor of the NCS/Genesis merger agreement. NCS's financial advisor withdrew its fairness opinion of the NCS/Genesis merger agreement as well....

LEGAL ANALYSIS ...

Deal Protection Devices Require Enhanced Scrutiny

The dispositive issues in this appeal involve the defensive devices that protected the Genesis merger agreement. The Delaware corporation statute provides that the board's management decision to enter into and recommend a merger transaction can become final only when ownership action is taken by a vote of the stockholders. Thus, the Delaware corporation law expressly provides for a balance of power between boards and stockholders which makes merger transactions a shared enterprise and ownership decision. Consequently, a board of directors' decision to adopt defensive devices to protect a merger agreement may implicate the stockholders' right to effectively vote contrary to the initial recommendation of the board in favor of the transaction.

It is well established that conflicts of interest arise when a board of directors acts to prevent stockholders from effectively exercising their right to vote contrary to the will of the board. The "omnipresent specter" of such conflict may be present whenever a board adopts defensive devices to protect a merger agreement. The stockholders' ability to effectively reject a merger agreement is likely to bear an inversely proportionate relationship to the structural and economic devices that the board has approved to protect the transaction....

There are inherent conflicts between a board's interest in protecting a merger transaction it has approved, the stockholders' statutory right to make the final decision to either approve or not approve a merger, and the board's continuing responsibility to effectively exercise its fiduciary duties at all times after the merger agreement is executed. These competing considerations require a threshold determination that board-approved defensive devices protecting a merger transaction are within the limitations of its statutory authority and consistent with the directors' fiduciary duties. Accordingly, in *Paramount v. Time*, we held that the business judgment rule applied to the Time board's original decision to merge with Warner.[33] We further held, however, that defensive devices adopted by the board to protect the original merger transaction must withstand enhanced judicial scrutiny under the *Unocal* standard of review, even when that merger transaction does not result in a change of control.[34]

33. *Paramount Communications, Inc. v. Time Inc.*, 571 A.2d at 1152.

34. Id. at 1151–55; *Unocal Corp. v. Mesa Petroleum Co.*, 493 A.2d 946 (Del.1985); see *In re Santa Fe Pacific Corp. Shareholder Litigation*, 669 A.2d 59 (Del.1995).

Enhanced Scrutiny Generally . . .

A board's decision to protect its decision to enter a merger agreement with defensive devices against uninvited competing transactions that may emerge is analogous to a board's decision to protect against dangers to corporate policy and effectiveness when it adopts defensive measures in a hostile takeover contest. In applying *Unocal's* enhanced judicial scrutiny in assessing a challenge to defensive actions taken by a target corporation's board of directors in a takeover context, this Court held that the board "does not have unbridled discretion to defeat perceived threats by any draconian means available."[46] Similarly, just as a board's statutory power with regard to a merger decision is not absolute, a board does not have unbridled discretion to defeat any perceived threat to a merger by protecting it with any draconian means available.

Since *Unocal*, "this Court has consistently recognized that defensive measures which are either preclusive or coercive are included within the common law definition of draconian." . . . .

Therefore, in applying enhanced judicial scrutiny to defensive devices designed to protect a merger agreement, a court must first determine that those measures are not preclusive or coercive *before* its focus shifts to the "range of reasonableness" in making a proportionality determination. . . .

Deal Protection Devices

Defensive devices, as that term is used in this opinion, is a synonym for what are frequently referred to as "deal protection devices." Both terms are used interchangeably to describe any measure or combination of measures that are intended to protect the consummation of a merger transaction. Defensive devices can be economic, structural, or both.

Deal protection devices need not all be in the merger agreement itself. In this case, for example, the Section 251(c) provision in the merger agreement was combined with the separate voting agreements to provide a structural defense for the Genesis merger agreement against any subsequent superior transaction. Genesis made the NCS board's defense of its transaction absolute by insisting on the omission of any effective fiduciary out clause in the NCS merger agreement. . . .

In this case, the stockholder voting agreements were inextricably intertwined with the defensive aspects of the Genesis merger agreement. In fact, the voting agreements with Shaw and Outcalt were the linchpin of Genesis' proposed tripartite defense. Therefore, Genesis made the execution of those voting agreements a non-negotiable condition precedent to its execution of the merger agreement. In the case before us, the Court of Chancery held that the acts which locked-

46. *Unocal Corp. v. Mesa Petroleum Co.,* 493 A.2d at 955.

up the Genesis transaction were the Section 251(c) provision and "the execution of the voting agreement by Outcalt and Shaw."

With the assurance that Outcalt and Shaw would irrevocably agree to exercise their majority voting power in favor of its transaction, Genesis insisted that the merger agreement reflect the other two aspects of its concerted defense, i.e., the inclusion of a Section 251(c) provision and the omission of any effective fiduciary out clause. Those dual aspects of the merger agreement would not have provided Genesis with a complete defense in the absence of the voting agreements with Shaw and Outcalt.

These Deal Protection Devices Unenforceable

In this case, the Court of Chancery correctly held that the NCS directors' decision to adopt defensive devices to completely "lock up" the Genesis merger mandated "special scrutiny" under the two-part test set forth in *Unocal*.[59] That conclusion is consistent with our holding in *Paramount v. Time* that "safety devices" adopted to protect a transaction that did not result in a change of control are subject to enhanced judicial scrutiny under a *Unocal* analysis.[60] . . . .

Pursuant to the judicial scrutiny required under *Unocal*'s two-stage analysis, the NCS directors must first demonstrate "that they had reasonable grounds for believing that a danger to corporate policy and effectiveness existed. . . ." To satisfy that burden, the NCS directors are required to show they acted in good faith after conducting a reasonable investigation. The threat identified by the NCS board was the possibility of losing the Genesis offer and being left with no comparable alternative transaction.

The second stage of the *Unocal* test requires the NCS directors to demonstrate that their defensive response was "reasonable in relation to the threat posed." This inquiry involves a two-step analysis. The NCS directors must first establish that the merger deal protection devices adopted in response to the threat were not "coercive" or "preclusive," and then demonstrate that their response was within a "range of reasonable responses" to the threat perceived. In *Unitrin*, we stated:

- A response is "coercive" if it is aimed at forcing upon stockholders a management-sponsored alternative to a hostile offer.

- A response is "preclusive" if it deprives stockholders of the right to receive all tender offers or precludes a bidder from seeking control by fundamentally restricting proxy contests or otherwise.

59. *In re NCS Healthcare, Inc.*, 2002 WL 31720732, at *16 (Del.Ch. Nov.22, 2002). See *Unocal Corp. v. Mesa Petroleum Co.*, 493 A.2d 946, 955 (Del.1985).

60. See *Paramount Communications, Inc. v. Time Inc.*, 571 A.2d 1140, 1151 (Del. 1989) (holding that "structural safety devices" in a merger agreement are properly subject to a *Unocal* analysis).

This aspect of the *Unocal* standard provides for a disjunctive analysis. If defensive measures are either preclusive or coercive they are draconian and impermissible. In this case, the deal protection devices of the NCS board were both preclusive and coercive.

This Court enunciated the standard for determining stockholder coercion in the case of *Williams v. Geier*.[67] A stockholder vote may be nullified by wrongful coercion "where the board or some other party takes actions which have the effect of causing the stockholders to vote in favor of the proposed transaction for some reason other than the merits of that transaction.". . . .

. . . [A]ny stockholder vote [in this case] would have been robbed of its effectiveness by the impermissible coercion that predetermined the outcome of the merger without regard to the merits of the Genesis transaction at the time the vote was scheduled to be taken. Deal protection devices that result in such coercion cannot withstand *Unocal*'s enhanced judicial scrutiny standard of review because they are not within the range of reasonableness.

Although the minority stockholders were not forced to vote for the Genesis merger, they were required to accept it because it was a fait accompli. The record reflects that the defensive devices employed by the NCS board are preclusive and coercive in the sense that they accomplished a fait accompli. In this case, despite the fact that the NCS board has withdrawn its recommendation for the Genesis transaction and recommended its rejection by the stockholders, the deal protection devices approved by the NCS board operated in concert to have a preclusive and coercive effect. Those tripartite defensive measures—the Section 251(c) provision, the voting agreements, and the absence of an effective fiduciary out clause—made it "mathematically impossible" and "realistically unattainable" for the Omnicare transaction or any other proposal to succeed, no matter how superior the proposal.[72]

The deal protection devices adopted by the NCS board were designed to coerce the consummation of the Genesis merger and preclude the consideration of any superior transaction. The NCS directors' defensive devices are not within a reasonable range of responses to the perceived threat of losing the Genesis offer because they are preclusive and coercive. Accordingly, we hold that those deal protection devices are unenforceable.

Effective Fiduciary Out Required

The defensive measures that protected the merger transaction are unenforceable not only because they are preclusive and coercive but, alternatively, they are unenforceable because they are invalid as they

67. *Williams v. Geier*, 671 A.2d 1368 (Del.1996).

72. See *Unitrin, Inc. v. Am. Gen. Corp.*, 651 A.2d at 1388–89; see also *Carmody v.* *Toll Bros., Inc.*, 723 A.2d 1180, 1195 (Del.Ch. 1998) (citations omitted).

operate in this case. Given the specifically enforceable irrevocable voting agreements, the provision in the merger agreement requiring the board to submit the transaction for a stockholder vote and the omission of a fiduciary out clause in the merger agreement completely prevented the board from discharging its fiduciary responsibilities to the minority stockholders when Omnicare presented its superior transaction. "To the extent that a [merger] contract, or a provision thereof, purports to require a board to act or not act in such a fashion as to limit the exercise of fiduciary duties, it is invalid and unenforceable."[74] . . .

Under the circumstances presented in this case, where a cohesive group of stockholders with majority voting power was irrevocably committed to the merger transaction, "[e]ffective representation of the financial interests of the minority shareholders imposed upon the [NCS board] an affirmative responsibility to protect those minority shareholders' interests."[79] The NCS board could not abdicate its fiduciary duties to the minority by leaving it to the stockholders alone to approve or disapprove the merger agreement because two stockholders had already combined to establish a majority of the voting power that made the outcome of the stockholder vote a foregone conclusion. . . .

Taking action that is otherwise legally possible . . . does not ipso facto comport with the fiduciary responsibilities of directors in all circumstances.[81] The synopsis to the amendments that resulted in the enactment of Section 251(c) in the Delaware corporation law statute specifically provides: "the amendments are not intended to address the question of whether such a submission requirement is appropriate in any particular set of factual circumstances." Section 251 provisions, like the no-shop provision examined in *QVC*, are "presumptively valid in the abstract."[82] Such provisions in a merger agreement may not, however, "validly define or limit the directors' fiduciary duties under Delaware law or prevent the [NCS] directors from carrying out their fiduciary duties under Delaware law."[83]

Genesis admits that when the NCS board agreed to its merger conditions, the NCS board was seeking to assure that the NCS creditors were paid in full and that the NCS stockholders received the highest value available for their stock. In fact, Genesis defends its

---

74. *Paramount Communications Inc. v. QVC Network Inc.*, 637 A.2d 34, 51 (Del.1993) (citation omitted). Restatement (Second) of Contracts § 193 explicitly provides that a "promise by a fiduciary to violate his fiduciary duty or a promise that tends to induce such a violation is unenforceable on grounds of public policy." The comments to that section indicate that "[d]irectors and other officials of a corporation act in a fiduciary capacity and are subject to the rule stated in this Section." Restatement (Second) of Contracts § 193 (1981) (emphasis added).

79. *McMullin v. Beran*, 765 A.2d 910, 920 (Del.2000).

81. *MM Companies v. Liquid Audio, Inc.*, 813 A.2d 1118, 1132 (Del.2003) (citation omitted).

82. *Paramount Communications Inc. v. QVC Network Inc.*, 637 A.2d at 48.

83. Id.

"bulletproof" merger agreement on that basis. We hold that the NCS board did not have authority to accede to the Genesis demand for an absolute "lock-up."

The directors of a Delaware corporation have a continuing obligation to discharge their fiduciary responsibilities, as future circumstances develop, after a merger agreement is announced. Genesis anticipated the likelihood of a superior offer after its merger agreement was announced and demanded defensive measures from the NCS board that completely protected its transaction.[84] Instead of agreeing to the absolute defense of the Genesis merger from a superior offer, however, the NCS board was required to negotiate a fiduciary out clause to protect the NCS stockholders if the Genesis transaction became an inferior offer. By acceding to Genesis' ultimatum for complete protection in futuro, the NCS board disabled itself from exercising its own fiduciary obligations at a time when the board's own judgment is most important,[85] i.e. receipt of a subsequent superior offer.

Any board has authority to give the proponent of a recommended merger agreement reasonable structural and economic defenses, incentives, and fair compensation if the transaction is not completed. To the extent that defensive measures are economic and reasonable, they may become an increased cost to the proponent of any subsequent transaction. Just as defensive measures cannot be draconian, however, they cannot limit or circumscribe the directors' fiduciary duties. Notwithstanding the corporation's insolvent condition, the NCS board had no authority to execute a merger agreement that subsequently prevented it from effectively discharging its ongoing fiduciary responsibilities.

The stockholders of a Delaware corporation are entitled to rely upon the board to discharge its fiduciary duties at all times.[86] The fiduciary duties of a director are unremitting and must be effectively discharged in the specific context of the actions that are required with regard to the corporation or its stockholders as circumstances change.[87] The stockholders with majority voting power, Shaw and Outcalt, had an absolute right to sell or exchange their shares with a third party at any price. This right was not only known to the other directors of NCS, it became an integral part of the Genesis agreement. In its answering brief, Genesis candidly states that its offer "came with a condition—Genesis would not be a stalking horse and would not

84. The marked improvements in NCS's financial situation during the negotiations with Genesis strongly suggests that the NCS board should have been alert to the prospect of competing offers or, as eventually occurred, a bidding contest.

85. See *Malone v. Brincat*, 722 A.2d 5, 10 (Del.1998) (directors' fiduciary duties do

not operate intermittently). See also *Moran v. Household Int'l, Inc.*, 500 A.2d 1346 (Del. 1985).

86.   *Malone v. Brincat*, 722 A.2d at 10.

87.   Id.; *Moran v. Household Int'l, Inc.*, 500 A.2d at 1357 (use of defense evaluated if and when the issue arises).

agree to a transaction to which NCS's controlling shareholders were not committed."

The NCS board was required to contract for an effective fiduciary out clause to exercise its continuing fiduciary responsibilities to the minority stockholders.[88] The issues in this appeal do not involve the general validity of either stockholder voting agreements or the authority of directors to insert a Section 251(c) provision in a merger agreement. In this case, the NCS board combined those two otherwise valid actions and caused them to operate in concert as an absolute lock up, in the absence of an effective fiduciary out clause in the Genesis merger agreement.

In the context of this preclusive and coercive lock up case, the protection of Genesis' contractual expectations must yield to the supervening responsibility of the directors to discharge their fiduciary duties on a continuing basis. The merger agreement and voting agreements, as they were combined to operate in concert in this case, are inconsistent with the NCS directors' fiduciary duties. To that extent, we hold that they are invalid and unenforceable.[89] . . .

■ Veasey, Chief Justice, with whom Steele, Justice, joins dissenting. . . .

. . . [T]he Majority has removed from their proper context the contractual merger protection provisions. The lock-ups here cannot be reviewed in a vacuum. A court should review the entire bidding process to determine whether the independent board's actions permitted the directors to inform themselves of their available options and whether they acted in good faith.

Going into negotiations with Genesis, the NCS directors knew that, up until that time, NCS had found only one potential bidder, Omnicare. Omnicare had refused to buy NCS except at a fire sale price through an asset sale in bankruptcy. Omnicare's best proposal at that stage would not have paid off all creditors and would have provided nothing for stockholders. The Noteholders, represented by the Ad Hoc Committee, were willing to oblige Omnicare and force NCS into bankruptcy if Omnicare would pay in full the NCS debt. Through the NCS board's efforts, Genesis expressed interest that became increasingly attractive. Negotiations with Genesis led to an offer paying creditors off and conferring on NCS stockholders $24 million—an amount infinitely superior to the prior Omnicare proposals.

But there was, understandably, a sine qua non. In exchange for offering the NCS stockholders a return on their equity and creditor payment, Genesis demanded certainty that the merger would close. If

---

88. See *Paramount Communications Inc. v. QVC Network Inc.*, 637 A.2d at 42–43. Merger agreements involve an ownership decision and, therefore, cannot become final without stockholder approval. Other contracts do not require a fiduciary out clause because they involve business judgments that are within the exclusive province of the board of directors' power to manage the affairs of the corporation. See *Grimes v. Donald*, 673 A.2d 1207, 1214–15 (Del.1996).

89. *Paramount Communications, Inc. v. QVC Network, Inc.*, 637 A.2d at 51.

the NCS board would not have acceded to the Section 251(c) provision, if Outcalt and Shaw had not agreed to the voting agreements and if NCS had insisted on a fiduciary out, there would have been no Genesis deal! Thus, the only value-enhancing transaction available would have disappeared. NCS knew that Omnicare had spoiled a Genesis acquisition in the past, and it is not disputed by the Majority that the NCS directors made a reasoned decision to accept as real the Genesis threat to walk away.

When Omnicare submitted its conditional eleventh-hour bid, the NCS board had to weigh the economic terms of the proposal against the uncertainty of completing a deal with Omnicare. Importantly, because Omnicare's bid was conditioned on its satisfactorily completing its due diligence review of NCS, the NCS board saw this as a crippling condition, as did the Ad Hoc Committee. As a matter of business judgment, the risk of negotiating with Omnicare and losing Genesis at that point outweighed the possible benefits. The lock-up was indisputably a sine qua non to any deal with Genesis.

A lock-up permits a target board and a bidder to "exchange certainties."[97] Certainty itself has value. The acquirer may pay a higher price for the target if the acquirer is assured consummation of the transaction. The target company also benefits from the certainty of completing a transaction with a bidder because losing an acquirer creates the perception that a target is damaged goods, thus reducing its value. . . .

The Majority invalidates the NCS board's action by announcing a new rule that represents an extension of our jurisprudence. That new rule can be narrowly stated as follows: A merger agreement entered into after a market search, before any prospect of a topping bid has emerged, which locks up stockholder approval and does not contain a "fiduciary out" provision, is per se invalid when a later significant topping bid emerges. As we have noted, this bright-line, per se rule would apply regardless of (1) the circumstances leading up to the agreement and (2) the fact that stockholders who control voting power had irrevocably committed themselves, as stockholders, to vote for the merger. Narrowly stated, this new rule is a judicially-created "third rail" that now becomes one of the given "rules of the game," to be taken into account by the negotiators and drafters of merger agreements. In our view, this new rule is an unwise extension of existing precedent. . . .

The very measures the Majority cites as "coercive" were approved by Shaw and Outcalt through the lens of their independent assessment of the merits of the transaction. The proper inquiry in this case is whether the NCS board had taken actions that "have the effect of causing the stockholders to vote in favor of the proposed transaction

97. See *Rand v. Western Air Lines*, 1994 WL 89006 at *6 (Del.Ch.).

for some reason other than the merits of that transaction."[109] Like the termination fee upheld as a valid liquidated damages clause against a claim of coercion in *Brazen v. Bell Atlantic Corp.*, the deal protection measures at issue here were "an integral part of the merits of the transaction" as the NCS board struggled to secure—and did secure—the only deal available.[110]

Outcalt and Shaw were fully informed stockholders. As the NCS controlling stockholders, they made an informed choice to commit their voting power to the merger. The minority stockholders were deemed to know that when controlling stockholders have 65% of the vote they can approve a merger without the need for the minority votes. Moreover, to the extent a minority stockholder may have felt "coerced" to vote for the merger, which was already a fait accompli, it was a meaningless coercion—or no coercion at all—because the controlling votes, those of Outcalt and Shaw, were already "cast." Although the fact that the controlling votes were committed to the merger "precluded" an overriding vote against the merger by the Class A stockholders, the pejorative "preclusive" label applicable in a *Unitrin* fact situation has no application here. Therefore, there was no meaningful minority stockholder voting decision to coerce.

In applying *Unocal* scrutiny, we believe the Majority incorrectly preempted the proportionality inquiry. In our view, the proportionality inquiry must account for the reality that the contractual measures protecting this merger agreement were necessary to obtain the Genesis deal. The Majority has not demonstrated that the director action was a disproportionate response to the threat posed. Indeed, it is clear to us that the board action to negotiate the best deal reasonably available with the only viable merger partner (Genesis) who could satisfy the creditors and benefit the stockholders, was reasonable in relation to the threat, by any practical yardstick.

An Absolute Lock-up is Not a Per Se Violation of Fiduciary Duty

We respectfully disagree with the Majority's conclusion that the NCS board breached its fiduciary duties to the Class A stockholders by failing to negotiate a "fiduciary out" in the Genesis merger agreement. What is the practical import of a "fiduciary out?" It is a contractual provision, articulated in a manner to be negotiated, that would permit the board of the corporation being acquired to exit without breaching the merger agreement in the event of a superior offer.

In this case, Genesis made it abundantly clear early on that it was willing to negotiate a deal with NCS but only on the condition that it would not be a "stalking horse." Thus, it wanted to be certain that a third party could not use its deal with NCS as a floor against which to

109. *Geier*, 671 A.2d at 1382–83 (citations omitted).

110. 695 A.2d 43, 50 (Del.1997).

begin a bidding war. As a result of this negotiating position, a "fiduciary out" was not acceptable to Genesis. The Majority Opinion holds that such a negotiating position, if implemented in the agreement, is invalid per se where there is an absolute lock-up. We know of no authority in our jurisprudence supporting this new rule, and we believe it is unwise and unwarranted. . . .

Conclusion

It is regrettable that the Court is split in this important case. One hopes that the Majority rule announced here—though clearly erroneous in our view—will be interpreted narrowly and will be seen as sui generis. By deterring bidders from engaging in negotiations like those present here and requiring that there must always be a fiduciary out, the universe of potential bidders who could reasonably be expected to benefit stockholders could shrink or disappear. Nevertheless, if the holding is confined to these unique facts, negotiators may be able to navigate around this new hazard.

Accordingly, we respectfully dissent.

[The separate dissenting opinion of Justice Steele is omitted.]

Insert the following two cases at p. 1233 of the Unabridged Edition, at the end of Chapter 12:

Solomon v. Pathe

Supreme Court of Delaware, 1996
672 A.2d 35

■ Before HOLLAND, HARTNETT, and BERGER, JJ.

■ HARTNETT, JUSTICE.

In this appeal, we affirm the dismissal of this action by the Court of Chancery which held that the complaint fails to state a claim upon which relief can be granted. . . .

The suit dismissed is a putative shareholder class action that challenges the fairness of a tender offer made by Credit Lyonnais Banque Nederland N.V. ("CLBN") to purchase 5.9 million shares of the publicly-traded common stock of Pathe Communications Corporation ("Pathe"). . . . The Plaintiff–Appellant, Robert Solomon ("Solomon"), is a shareholder who purportedly represents a class holding ten percent of Pathe's common stock.

CLBN is a Netherlands corporation. Giancarlo Parretti ("Parretti") was the Chief Executive Officer of Pathe when it purchased MGM/UA Communications Corporation ("MGM"). The purchase price was funded principally by loans from CLBN totalling approximately one billion dollars. As part of this loan transaction, CLBN took a perfected security interest in eighty-nine percent of Pathe's stock and ninety-eight percent of MGM's stock. Additionally, in exchange for the granting of credit, CLBN acquired the right, under two voting trust agreements, to vote 89.5 percent of Pathe's shares and substantially all of MGM's shares....

... [Prior to May 1992,] CLBN offered to make a tender offer for an unspecified number of Pathe's publicly held shares of common stock. In response, Pathe appointed a special committee to review the proposal with the assistance of its own legal and financial advisers.

On May 1, 1992 ... CLBN agreed to make a public tender offer of $1.50 per share for up to 5.8 million of Pathe's publicly held shares.... On May 7th, CLBN ... made the promised tender offer for the Pathe shares.

... The amended complaint asserted that the tender offer was unfair to all shareholders (except the Defendants) who tendered their shares in response to the tender offer. Additionally, it asserted that the tender offer price was "coercive" and amounted to a breach of loyalty by CLBN as controlling shareholder of Pathe and MGM. Solomon also asserted in his amended complaint that the Pathe Board was under the control of CLBN; that the Defendants exhibited impropriety by failing to retain independent advisers; and that the Defendants failed "to assure that no conflict of interest existed."

CLBN moved, pursuant to Chancery Rule 12(b), to dismiss the suit, arguing that ... the complaint failed to state a claim upon which relief could be granted.... [The Court of Chancery dismissed the complaint with prejudice.]

After a careful review of the amended complaint, we agree with the Chancellor that it fails to state a claim upon which relief can be granted....

... [The complaint] attempts to assert a breach of the duty of fair dealing by the directors because they did not oppose the tender offer. The asserted unfairness of the tender offer is based on its allegedly inadequate price. The Chancellor's holding that none of the facts cited by Solomon "can be said to arouse as much as a fleeting doubt of the fairness of the [disclosure] or the $1.50 tender offer" price is correct as a matter of law.

In the case of totally voluntary tender offers, as here, courts do not impose any right of the shareholders to receive a particular price.... Delaware law recognizes that, as to allegedly voluntary tender offers (in contrast to cash-out mergers), the determinative factor as to voluntariness is whether coercion is present, or whether there is "materially false or misleading disclosures made to shareholders in connection with the offer." *Eisenberg v. Chicago Milwaukee Corp.*, Del.Ch., 537 A.2d 1051, 1056 (1987) (citations omitted). A transaction may be considered involuntary, despite being voluntary in appearance and form, if one of these factors is present. *Id.* There is no well-plead allegation of any coercion or false or misleading disclosures in the present case, however.

Moreover, in the absence of coercion or disclosure violations, the adequacy of the price in a voluntary tender offer cannot be an issue. *Weinberger*, 457 A.2d at 703.... Solomon has plead no facts from which there could be drawn a reasonable inference that there was coercion or lack of complete disclosure. The amended complaint focuses mainly on a conclusory allegation that coercion was present. The complaint, therefore, falls well short of the minimum notice requirements. "Conclusions ... will not be accepted as true without specific allegations of fact to support them." ...

For the foregoing reasons, the Court of Chancery's dismissal of Solomon's claim under Rule 12(b)(6) for failure to state a claim upon which relief can be granted is AFFIRMED.

————

In re Pure Resources, Inc. Shareholders Litigation

Court of Chancery of Delaware, 2002
808 A.2d 421

■ STRINE, VICE CHANCELLOR.

This is the court's decision on a motion for preliminary injunction. The lead plaintiff in the case holds a large block of stock in Pure Resources, Inc., 65% of the shares of which are owned by Unocal Corporation. The lead plaintiff and its fellow plaintiffs seek to enjoin a now-pending exchange offer (the "Offer") by which Unocal hopes to acquire the rest of the shares of Pure in exchange for shares of its own stock.

The plaintiffs believe that the Offer is inadequate and is subject to entire fairness review, consistent with the rationale of *Kahn v. Lynch Communication Systems, Inc.*[1] and its progeny. Moreover, they claim that the defendants, who include Unocal and Pure's board of directors, have not made adequate and non-misleading disclosure of the material facts necessary for Pure stockholders to make an informed decision whether to tender into the Offer.

By contrast, the defendants argue that the Offer is a non-coercive one that is accompanied by complete disclosure of all material facts. As such, they argue that the Offer is not subject to the entire fairness standard, but to the standards set forth in cases like *Solomon v. Pathe Communications Corp.*,[2] standards which they argue have been fully met.

In this opinion, I conclude that the Offer is subject, as a general matter, to the *Solomon* standards, rather than the *Lynch* entire fairness

1. 638 A.2d 1110 (Del.1994).   2. 672 A.2d 35 (Del.1996).

standard. I conclude, however, that many of the concerns that justify the *Lynch* standard are implicated by tender offers initiated by controlling stockholders, which have as their goal the acquisition of the rest of the subsidiary's shares. These concerns should be accommodated within the *Solomon* form of review, by requiring that tender offers by controlling shareholders be structured in a manner that reduces the distorting effect of the tendering process on free stockholder choice and by ensuring minority stockholders a candid and unfettered tendering recommendation from the independent directors of the target board. In this case, the Offer for the most part meets this standard, with one exception that Unocal may cure.

But I also find that the Offer must be preliminarily enjoined because material information relevant to the Pure stockholders' decision-making process has not been fairly disclosed. Therefore, I issue an injunction against the Offer pending an alteration of its terms to eliminate its coercive structure and to correct the inadequate disclosures.

I

These are the key facts as I find them for purposes of deciding this preliminary injunction motion.

A.

Unocal Corporation is a large independent natural gas and crude oil exploration and production company with far-flung operations. In the United States, its most important operations are currently in the Gulf of Mexico. Before May 2000, Unocal also had operations in the Permian Basin of western Texas and southeastern New Mexico. During that month, Unocal spun off its Permian Basin unit and combined it with Titan Exploration, Inc. Titan was an oil and gas company operating in the Permian Basin, south central Texas, and the central Gulf Coast region of Texas. It also owned mineral interests in the southern Gulf Coast.

The entity that resulted from that combination was Pure Resources, Inc. Following the creation of Pure, Unocal owned 65.4% of Pure's issued and outstanding common stock. The remaining 34.6% of Pure was held by Titan's former stockholders, including its managers who stayed on to run Pure. The largest of these stockholders was Jack D. Hightower, Pure's Chairman and Chief Executive Officer, who now owns 6.1% of Pure's outstanding stock before the exercise of options. As a group, Pure's management controls between a quarter and a third of the Pure stock not owned by Unocal, when options are considered.

B.

Several important agreements were entered into when Pure was formed. The first is a Stockholders Voting Agreement. That Agreement requires Unocal and Hightower to vote their shares to elect to the Pure board five persons designated by Unocal (so long as Unocal owns greater than 50% of Pure's common stock), two persons designated by

Hightower, and one person to be jointly agreed upon by Unocal and Hightower. Currently, the board resulting from the implementation of the Voting Agreement is comprised as follows:

Unocal Designees:

- Darry D. Chessum—Chessum is Unocal's Treasurer and is the owner of one share of Pure stock.
- Timothy H. Ling—Ling is President, Chief Operating Officer, and director of Unocal. He owns one share of Pure stock.
- Graydon H. Laughbaum, Jr.—Laughbaum was an executive for 34 years at Unocal before retiring at the beginning of 1999. For most of the next three years, he provided consulting services to Unocal. Laughbaum owns 1,301 shares of Pure stock.
- HD Maxwell—Maxwell was an executive for many years at Unocal before 1992. Maxwell owns one share of Pure stock.
- Herbert C. Williamson, III—Williamson has no material ties to Unocal. He owns 3,364 shares of Pure stock.

Hightower Designees:

- Jack D. Hightower—As mentioned, he is Pure's CEO and its largest stockholder, aside from Unocal.
- George G. Staley—Staley is Pure's Chief Operating Officer and also a large stockholder, controlling 625,261 shares.

Joint Designee of Unocal and Hightower:

- Keith A. Covington—Covington's only tie to Unocal is that he is a close personal friend of Ling, having gone to business school with him. He owns 2,401 Pure shares. . . .

II. . . .

B.

[In part because of Unocal's concerns about Hightower's aggressive business plans for Pure, and in part to integrate Unocal's North American production base, Unocal decided to acquire the minority interest in Pure. On August 20, 2002, Unocal informed Pure's board that it intended to acquire the Pure shares it did not already own through a tender offer pursuant to which the Pure stockholders other than Unocal would be offered 0.6527 shares of common stock of Unocal for each outstanding share of Pure common stock they owned. Based on the closing price of Unocal's shares on August 20, 2002, the offer would provide a 27% premium to the closing price of Pure common stock on that date.]

Unocal management asked Ling and Chessum to make calls to the Pure board about the Offer. In their talking points, Ling and Chessum were instructed to suggest that any Special Committee formed by Pure should have powers "limited to hiring independent advisors (bank and lawyers) and to coming up with a recommendation to the Pure shareholders as to whether or not to accept UCL's offer; any greater delegation is not warranted".

The next day the Pure board met to consider this event.... [T]he Pure board voted to establish a Special Committee comprised of Williamson and Covington to respond to the Unocal bid....

The precise authority of the Special Committee to act on behalf of Pure was left hazy at first, but seemed to consist solely of the power to retain independent advisors, to take a position on the offer's advisability on behalf of Pure, and to negotiate with Unocal to see if it would increase its bid. Aside from this last point, this constrained degree of authority comported with the limited power that Unocal had desired.

During the early days of its operation, the Special Committee was aided by company counsel, Thompson & Knight, and management in retaining its own advisors and getting started. Soon, though, the Special Committee had retained two financial advisors and legal advisors to help it....

After the formation of the Special Committee, Unocal formally commenced its Offer, which had these key features:

- An exchange ratio of 0.6527 of a Unocal share for each Pure share.

- A non-waivable majority of the minority tender provision, which required a majority of shares not owned by Unocal to tender. Management of Pure, including Hightower and Staley, are considered part of the minority for purposes of this condition, not to mention Maxwell, Laughbaum, Chessum, and Ling.

- A waivable condition that a sufficient number of tenders be received to enable Unocal to own 90% of Pure and to effect a short-form merger under 8 Del.C. § 253.

- A statement by Unocal that it intends, if it obtains 90%, to consummate a short-form merger as soon as practicable at the same exchange ratio....

Thereafter, the Special Committee sought to, in its words, "clarify" its authority. The clarity it sought was clear: the Special Committee wanted to be delegated the full authority of the board under Delaware law to respond to the Offer. With such authority, the Special Committee could have searched for alternative transactions, speeded up consummation of the Royalty Trust [a device, which had been under consideration by Pure, under which Pure would monetize the value of certain mineral rights and sell portions of the interests in those rights to third parties], evaluated the feasibility of a self-tender, and put in place a shareholder rights plan (a.k.a., poison pill) to block the Offer.

What exactly happened at this point is shrouded by invocations of privilege. But this much is clear. [Chessum and Ling, who had earlier] recused themselves from the Pure board process ..., reentered it in full glory when the Special Committee asked for more authority. Chessum took the lead in raising concerns and engaged Unocal's in-house and outside counsel to pare down the resolution proposed by the Special Committee. After discussions between Counsel for Unocal and the Special Committee, the bold resolution drafted by Special Committee counsel was whittled down to take out any ability on the part of the Special Committee to do anything other than study the Offer, negotiate it, and make a recommendation on behalf of Pure in the required 14D–9.

The record does not illuminate exactly why the Special Committee did not make this their Alamo.... [and failed] to insist on the power to deploy a poison pill—the by-now de rigeur tool of a board responding to a third-party tender offer....

The most reasonable inference that can be drawn from the record is that the Special Committee was unwilling to confront Unocal as aggressively as it would have confronted a third-party bidder....

Contemporaneous with these events, the Special Committee met on a more or less continuous basis. On a few occasions, the Special Committee met with Unocal and tried to persuade it to increase its offer. On September 10, for example, the Special Committee asked Unocal to increase the exchange ratio from 0.6527 to 0.787. Substantive presentations were made by the Special Committee's financial advisors in support of this overture.

After these meetings, Unocal remained unmoved and made no counteroffer. Therefore, on September 17, 2002, the Special Committee voted not to recommend the Offer, based on its analysis and the advice of its financial advisors. The Special Committee prepared the 14D–9 on behalf of Pure, which contained the board's recommendation not to tender into the Offer. Hightower and Staley also announced their personal present intentions not to tender, intentions that if adhered to would make it nearly impossible for Unocal to obtain 90% of Pure's shares in the Offer.

During the discovery process, a representative of the lead plaintiff, which is an investment fund, testified that he did not feel coerced by the Offer. The discovery record also reveals that a great deal of the Pure stock held by the public is in the hands of institutional investors.

III.   The Plaintiffs' Demand For A Preliminary Injunction

A.   The Merits ...

Distilled to the bare minimum, the plaintiffs argue that the Offer should be enjoined because: (i) the Offer is subject to the entire fairness standard and the record supports the inference that the transaction cannot survive a fairness review; (ii) in any event, the Offer is actionably coercive and should be enjoined on that ground; and (iii) the disclosures provided to the Pure stockholders in connection with the Offer are materially incomplete and misleading.

In order to prevail on this motion, the plaintiffs must convince me that one or more of its merits arguments have a reasonable probability of success, that the Pure stockholders face irreparable injury in the absence of an injunction, and that the balance of hardships weighs in favor of an injunction.

B. *The Plaintiffs' Substantive Attack on the Offer*

1.

The primary argument of the plaintiffs is that the Offer should be governed by the entire fairness standard of review. In their view, the structural power of Unocal over Pure and its board, as well as Unocal's involvement in determining the scope of the Special Committee's authority, make the Offer other than a voluntary, non-coercive transaction. In the plaintiffs' mind, the Offer poses the same threat of (what I will call) "inherent coercion" that motivated the Supreme Court in *Kahn v. Lynch Communication Systems, Inc.* to impose the entire fairness standard of review on any interested merger involving a controlling stockholder, even when the merger was approved by an independent board majority, negotiated by an independent special committee, and subject to a majority of the minority vote condition.

In support of their argument, the plaintiffs contend that the tender offer method of acquisition poses, if anything, a greater threat of unfairness to minority stockholders and should be subject to the same equitable constraints. More case-specifically, they claim that Unocal has used inside information from Pure to foist an inadequate bid on Pure stockholders at a time advantageous to Unocal. Then, Unocal acted self-interestedly to keep the Pure Special Committee from obtaining all the authority necessary to respond to the Offer. As a result, the plaintiffs argue, Unocal has breached its fiduciary duties as majority stockholder, and the Pure board has breached its duties by either acting on behalf of Unocal (in the case of Chessum and Ling) or by acting supinely in response to Unocal's inadequate offer (the Special Committee and the rest of the board). Instead of wielding the power to stop Unocal in its tracks and make it really negotiate, the Pure board has taken only the insufficient course of telling the Pure minority to say no.

In response to these arguments, Unocal asserts that the plaintiffs misunderstand the relevant legal principles. Because Unocal has proceeded by way of an exchange offer and not a negotiated merger, the rule of *Lynch* is inapplicable. Instead, Unocal is free to make a tender offer at whatever price it chooses so long as it does not: i) "structurally coerce" the Pure minority by suggesting explicitly or implicitly that injurious events will occur to those stockholders who fail to tender; or ii) mislead the Pure minority into tendering by concealing or misstating the material facts. This is the rule of law articulated by, among other cases, *Solomon v. Pathe Communications Corp.* Because Unocal has conditioned its Offer on a majority of the minority provision and intends to consummate a short-form merger at the same price, it argues that the Offer poses no threat of structural coercion and that the Pure minority can make a voluntary decision. Because the Pure minority has a negative recommendation from the Pure Special Committee and because there has been full disclosure (including of any material information Unocal received from Pure in formulating its bid), Unocal submits that the Pure minority will be able to make an informed decision whether to tender. For these reasons, Unocal asserts that no meritorious claim of breach of fiduciary duty exists against it or the Pure directors.

2.

This case therefore involves an aspect of Delaware law fraught with doctrinal tension: what equitable standard of fiduciary conduct applies when a controlling shareholder seeks to acquire the rest of the company's shares? ...

In building the common law, judges ... cannot escape making normative choices, based on imperfect information about the world. This reality clearly pervades the area of corporate law implicated by this case. When a transaction to buy out the minority is proposed, is it more important to the development of strong capital markets to hold controlling stockholders and target boards to very strict (and litigation-intensive) standards of fiduciary conduct? Or is more stockholder wealth generated if less rigorous protections are adopted, which permit acquisitions to proceed so long as the majority has not misled or strong-armed the minority? Is such flexibility in fact beneficial to minority stockholders because it encourages liquidity-generating tender offers to them and provides incentives for acquirers to pay hefty premiums to buy control, knowing that control will be accompanied by legal rules that permit a later "going private" transaction to occur in a relatively non-litigious manner?

At present, the Delaware case law has two strands of authority that answer these questions differently. In one strand, which deals with situations in which controlling stockholders negotiate a merger agreement with the target board to buy out the minority, our decisional law emphasizes the protection of minority stockholders against unfairness. In the other strand, which deals with situations when a controlling stockholder seeks to acquire the rest of the company's shares through a tender offer followed by a short-form merger under 8 Del.C. § 253, Delaware case precedent facilitates the free flow of capital between willing buyers and willing sellers of shares, so long as the consent of the sellers is not procured by inadequate or misleading information or by wrongful compulsion.

These strands appear to treat economically similar transactions as categorically different simply because the method by which the controlling stockholder proceeds varies. This disparity in treatment persists even though the two basic methods (negotiated merger versus tender offer/short-form merger) pose similar threats to minority stockholders. Indeed, it can be argued that the distinction in approach

subjects the transaction that is more protective of minority stockholders when implemented with appropriate protective devices—a merger
negotiated by an independent committee with the power to say no
and conditioned on a majority of the minority vote—to more stringent
review than the more dangerous form of a going private deal—an
unnegotiated tender offer made by a majority stockholder. The latter
transaction is arguably less protective than a merger of the kind
described, because the majority stockholder-offeror has access to
inside information, and the offer requires disaggregated stockholders
to decide whether to tender quickly, pressured by the risk of being
squeezed out in a short-form merger at a different price later or being
left as part of a much smaller public minority. This disparity creates a
possible incoherence in our law.

3.

To illustrate this possible incoherence in our law, it is useful to
sketch out these two strands. I begin with negotiated mergers. In
Kahn v. Lynch Communication Systems, Inc., the Delaware Supreme
Court addressed the standard of review that applies when a controlling stockholder attempts to acquire the rest of the corporation's
shares in a negotiated merger pursuant to 8 Del.C. § 251. The Court
held that the stringent entire fairness form of review governed regardless of whether: i) the target board was comprised of a majority of
independent directors; ii) a special committee of the target's independent directors was empowered to negotiate and veto the merger; and
iii) the merger was made subject to approval by a majority of the
disinterested target stockholders.

The Supreme Court concluded that even a gauntlet of protective
barriers like those would be insufficient protection because of (what I
will term) the "inherent coercion" that exists when a controlling
stockholder announces its desire to buy the minority's shares. In
colloquial terms, the Supreme Court saw the controlling stockholder
as the 800–pound gorilla whose urgent hunger for the rest of the
bananas is likely to frighten less powerful primates like putatively
independent directors who might well have been hand-picked by the
gorilla (and who at the very least owed their seats on the board to his
support).

The Court also expressed concern that minority stockholders
would fear retribution from the gorilla if they defeated the merger and
he did not get his way. This inherent coercion was felt to exist even
when the controlling stockholder had not threatened to take any
action adverse to the minority in the event that the merger was voted
down and thus was viewed as undermining genuinely free choice by
the minority stockholders.

All in all, the Court was convinced that the powers and influence
possessed by controlling stockholders were so formidable and daunting to independent directors and minority stockholders that protective

devices like special committees and majority of the minority conditions (even when used in combination with the statutory appraisal remedy) were not trustworthy enough to obviate the need for an entire fairness review.[20] The Court did, however, recognize that these safety measures had utility and should be encouraged. Therefore, it held that their deployment could shift the burden of persuasion on the issue of fairness from the controlling stockholders and the target board as proponents of the transaction to shareholder-plaintiffs seeking to invalidate it.

The policy balance struck in *Lynch* continues to govern negotiated mergers between controlling stockholders and subsidiaries. If anything, later cases have extended the rule in *Lynch* to a broader array of transactions involving controlling shareholders.[22]

4.

The second strand of cases involves tender offers made by controlling stockholders—i.e., the kind of transaction Unocal has proposed. The prototypical transaction addressed by this strand involves a tender offer by the controlling stockholder addressed to the minority stockholders. In that offer, the controlling stockholder promises to buy as many shares as the minority will sell but may subject its offer to certain conditions. For example, the controlling stockholder might condition the offer on receiving enough tenders for it to obtain 90% of the subsidiary's shares, thereby enabling the controlling stockholder to consummate a short-form merger under 8 Del.C. § 253 at either the same or a different price.

As a matter of statutory law, this way of proceeding is different from the negotiated merger approach in an important way: neither the tender offer nor the short-form merger requires any action by the subsidiary's board of directors. The tender offer takes place between the controlling shareholder and the minority shareholders so long as the offering conditions are met. And, by the explicit terms of § 253, the short-form merger can be effected by the controlling stockholder itself, an option that was of uncertain utility for many years because it was unclear whether § 253 mergers were subject to an equitable requirement of fair process at the subsidiary board level. That uncertainty was recently resolved in *Glassman v. Unocal Exploration Corp.*,[23] an important recent decision, which held that a short-form

20. Another underpinning of the *Lynch* line of cases is an implicit perception that the statutory remedy of appraisal is a less than fully adequate protection for stockholders facing Inherent Coercion from a proposed squeeze-out merger. These imperfections have been commented on elsewhere. See, e.g., *Clements v. Rogers*, 790 A.2d 1222, 1238 n. 46 (Del.Ch.2001); *Andra v. Blount*, 772 A.2d 183, 184 (Del.Ch.2000); Randall S. Thomas, *Revising the Delaware Appraisal Statute*, 3 DEL.L.REV. 1, 1–2 (2000); Bradley R. Aronstam et al., *Delaware's Going Private Dilemma: Fostering Protections for Minority Shareholders in the Wake of Siliconix and Unocal Exploration* 33–35 (Aug. 28, 2002) [hereinafter "Aronstam"] (unpublished manuscript).

22. See, e.g., *Emerald Partners v. Berlin*, 787 A.2d 85, 93 n. 52 (Del.2001); *Kahn v. Tremont Corp.*, 694 A.2d 422, 428 (Del.1997).

23. 777 A.2d 242 (Del.2001).

merger was not reviewable in an action claiming unfair dealing, and that, absent fraud or misleading or inadequate disclosures, could be contested only in an appraisal proceeding that focused solely on the adequacy of the price paid.

Before *Glassman*, transactional planners had wondered whether the back-end of the tender offer/short-form merger transaction would subject the controlling stockholder to entire fairness review. *Glassman* seemed to answer that question favorably from the standpoint of controlling stockholders, and to therefore encourage the tender offer/short-form merger form of acquisition as presenting a materially less troublesome method of proceeding than a negotiated merger.

Why? Because the legal rules that governed the front end of the tender offer/short-form merger method of acquisition had already provided a more flexible, less litigious path to acquisition for controlling stockholders than the negotiated merger route. Tender offers are not addressed by the Delaware General Corporation Law ("DGCL"), a factor that has been of great importance in shaping the line of decisional law addressing tender offers by controlling stockholders— but not, as I will discuss, tender offers made by third parties.

Because no consent or involvement of the target board is statutorily mandated for tender offers, our courts have recognized that "[i]n the case of totally voluntary tender offers . . . courts do not impose any right of the shareholders to receive a particular price. Delaware law recognizes that, as to allegedly voluntary tender offers (in contrast to cash-out mergers), the determinative factors as to voluntariness are whether coercion is present, or whether there are materially false or misleading disclosures made to stockholders in connection with the offer."[24] . . .

The differences between this approach, which I will identify with the *Solomon* line of cases, and that of *Lynch* are stark. To begin with, the controlling stockholder is said to have no duty to pay a fair price, irrespective of its power over the subsidiary. Even more striking is the different manner in which the coercion concept is deployed. In the tender offer context addressed by *Solomon* and its progeny, coercion is defined in the more traditional sense as a wrongful threat that has the effect of forcing stockholders to tender at the wrong price to avoid an even worse fate later on, a type of coercion I will call structural coercion.[26] The inherent coercion that *Lynch* found to exist when

24. *Solomon v. Pathe Communications Corp.*, 672 A.2d 35, 39 (Del.1996) (citations and quotations omitted).

26. See *In re Marriott Hotel Props. II Ltd. P'ship*, 2000 WL 128875, (Del.Ch. Jan.24, 2000). I include within the concept of structural coercion an offer that is coercive because the controlling stockholder threatens to take action after the tender offer that is harmful to the remaining minority (e.g., to seek affirmatively to delist the company's shares) or because the offer's back-end is so unattractive as to induce tendering at an inadequate price to avoid a worse fate (e.g., a pledge to do a § 253 merger involving consideration in the form of high risk payment-in-kind bonds).

controlling stockholders seek to acquire the minority's stake is not even a cognizable concern for the common law of corporations if the tender offer method is employed.

This latter point is illustrated by those cases that squarely hold that a tender is not actionably coercive if the majority stockholder decides to: (i) condition the closing of the tender offer on support of a majority of the minority and (ii) promise that it would consummate a short-form merger on the same terms as the tender offer.[27] In those circumstances, at least, these cases can be read to bar a claim against the majority stockholder even if the price offered is below what would be considered fair in an entire fairness hearing ("fair price") or an appraisal action ("fair value"). That is, in the tender offer context, our courts consider it sufficient protection against coercion to give effective veto power over the offer to a majority of the minority.[28] Yet that very same protection is considered insufficient to displace fairness review in the negotiated merger context.

5.

The parties here cross swords over the arguable doctrinal inconsistency between the *Solomon* and *Lynch* lines of cases, with the plaintiffs arguing that it makes no sense and Unocal contending that the distinction is non-foolish. . . . I turn more directly to that dispute now.

I begin by discussing whether the mere fact that one type of transaction is a tender offer and the other is a negotiated merger is a sustainable basis for the divergent policy choices made in *Lynch* and *Solomon*? . . .

[It is clear] that Delaware law has not regarded tender offers as involving a special transactional space, from which directors are altogether excluded from exercising substantial authority. To the contrary, much Delaware jurisprudence during the last twenty years has dealt with whether directors acting within that space comported themselves consistently with their duties of loyalty and care. It therefore is by no means obvious that simply because a controlling stockholder proceeds by way of a tender offer that either it or the target's directors fall outside the constraints of fiduciary duty law.

In this same vein, the basic model of directors and stockholders adopted by our M & A case law is relevant. Delaware law has seen directors as well-positioned to understand the value of the target company, to compensate for the disaggregated nature of stockholders by acting as a negotiating and auctioning proxy for them, and as a bulwark against structural coercion. Relatedly, dispersed stockholders

---

27. See, e.g., *In re Aquila Inc.*, 2002 Del.Ch. Lexis 5, (Del.Ch. Jan. 3, 2002).

28. See, e.g., [*Siliconix Inc. S'holders Litig.*, 2001 WL 716787, (Del.Ch. June 21, 2001)].

have been viewed as poorly positioned to protect and, yes, sometimes, even to think for themselves.

6.

Because tender offers are not treated exceptionally in the third-party context, it is important to ask why the tender offer method should be consequential in formulating the equitable standards of fiduciary conduct by which courts review acquisition proposals made by controlling stockholders. Is there reason to believe that the tender offer method of acquisition is more protective of the minority, with the result that less scrutiny is required than of negotiated mergers with controlling stockholders?

Unocal's answer to that question is yes and primarily rests on an inarguable proposition: in a negotiated merger involving a controlling stockholder, the controlling stockholder is on both sides of the transaction. That is, the negotiated merger is a self-dealing transaction, whereas in a tender offer, the controlling stockholder is only on the offering side and the minority remain free not to sell.

As a formal matter, this distinction is difficult to contest. When examined more deeply, however, it is not a wall that can bear the full weight of the *Lynch/Solomon* distinction. In this regard, it is important to remember that the overriding concern of *Lynch* is [that] the controlling shareholders have the ability to take retributive action in the wake of rejection by an independent board, a special committee, or the minority shareholders. That ability is so influential that the usual cleansing devices that obviate fairness review of interested transactions cannot be trusted.

The problem is that nothing about the tender offer method of corporate acquisition makes the 800–pound gorilla's retributive capabilities less daunting to minority stockholders. Indeed, many commentators would argue that the tender offer form is more coercive than a merger vote. In a merger vote, stockholders can vote no and still receive the transactional consideration if the merger prevails.[39] In a tender offer, however, a non-tendering shareholder individually faces an uncertain fate. That stockholder could be one of the few who holds out, leaving herself in an even more thinly traded stock with little hope of liquidity and subject to a § 253 merger at a lower price or at the same price but at a later (and, given the time value of money, a less valuable) time. The 14D–9 warned Pure's minority stockholders of just this possibility. For these reasons, some view tender offers as creating a prisoner's dilemma—distorting choice and creating incentives for stockholders to tender into offers that they believe are

---

39. They may or may not receive appraisal rights. In this case, for example, *Unocal* notes that appraisal rights would not be available to dissenters if it had negotiated a merger agreement with Pure. Because it has proceeded by the tender offer route with a hoped-for § 253 merger, such rights will be available even though Unocal is offering widely traded stock, rather than cash, consideration.

inadequate in order to avoid a worse fate.[40] But whether or not one views tender offers as more coercive of shareholder choice than negotiated mergers with controlling stockholders, it is difficult to argue that tender offers are materially freer and more reliable measures of stockholder sentiment.

Furthermore, the common law of corporations has long had a structural answer to the formal self-dealing point Unocal makes: a non-waivable majority of the minority vote condition to a merger. By this technique, the ability of the controlling stockholder to both offer and accept is taken away, and the sell-side decision-making authority is given to the minority stockholders. That method of proceeding replicates the tender offer made by Unocal here, with the advantage of not distorting the stockholders' vote on price adequacy in the way that a tendering decision arguably does.

Lynch, of course, held that a majority of the minority vote provision will not displace entire fairness review with business judgment rule review. Critically, the *Lynch* Court's distrust of the majority of the minority provision is grounded in a concern that also exists in the tender offer context. The basis for the distrust is the concern that before the fact ("ex ante") minority stockholders will fear retribution after the fact ("ex post") if they vote no—i.e., they will face inherent coercion—thus rendering the majority of the minority condition an inadequate guarantee of fairness. But if this concern is valid, then that same inherent coercion would seem to apply with equal force to the tender offer decision-making process, and be enhanced by the unique features of that process. A controlling stockholder's power to force a squeeze-out or cut dividends is no different after the failure of a tender offer than after defeat on a merger vote.[41]

Finally, some of the other factors that are said to support fairness review of negotiated mergers involving controlling stockholders also apply with full force to tender offers made by controlling stockholders. The informational advantage that the controlling stockholder possesses is not any different; in this case, for example, Unocal was able to proceed having had full access to non-public information about Pure. The tender offer form provides no additional protection against this concern.

Furthermore, the tender offer method allows the controlling stockholder to time its offer and to put a bull rush on the target stockholders. Here, Unocal studied an acquisition of Pure for nearly a

---

40. See Lucian Arye Bebchuk, *Toward Undistorted Choice and Equal Treatment in Corporate Takeovers*, 98 Harv.L.Rev. 1695, 1696 (1985); Lucian Arye Bebchuk, *The Case for Facilitating Competing Tender Offers*, 95 Harv.L.Rev. 1028, 1039–40 (1982); Louis Lowenstein, *Pruning Deadwood in Hostile Takeovers: A Proposal for Legislation*, 83 Colum.L.Rev. 249, 307–09 (1983)....

41. A different view might be taken, of course, which recognizes that the constraints of equity and the appraisal statute, when combined, act as a sufficient check on retribution to allow (increasingly sophisticated and active) stockholders to vote on mergers freely. But *Lynch* does not embrace this view.

year and then made a "surprise" offer that forced a rapid response from Pure's Special Committee and the minority stockholders.

Likewise, one struggles to imagine why subsidiary directors would feel less constrained in reacting to a tender offer by a controlling stockholder than a negotiated merger proposal. Indeed, an arguably more obvious concern is that subsidiary directors might use the absence of a statutory role for them in the tender offer process to be less than aggressive in protecting minority interests, to wit, the edifying examples of subsidiary directors courageously taking no position on the merits of offers by a controlling stockholder. Or, as here, the Special Committee's failure to demand the power to use the normal range of techniques available to a non-controlled board responding to a third-party tender offer.

For these and other reasons that time constraints preclude me from explicating, I remain less than satisfied that there is a justifiable basis for the distinction between the *Lynch* and *Solomon* lines of cases. Instead, their disparate teachings reflect a difference in policy emphasis that is far greater than can be explained by the technical differences between tender offers and negotiated mergers, especially given Delaware's director-centered approach to tender offers made by third-parties, which emphasizes the vulnerability of disaggregated stockholders absent important help and protection from their directors.

7.

The absence of convincing reasons for this disparity in treatment inspires the plaintiffs to urge me to apply the entire fairness standard of review to Unocal's offer. Otherwise, they say, the important protections set forth in the *Lynch* line of cases will be rendered useless, as all controlling stockholders will simply choose to proceed to make subsidiary acquisitions by way of a tender offer and later short-form merger.

I admit being troubled by the imbalance in Delaware law exposed by the *Solomon/Lynch* lines of cases. Under *Solomon*, the policy emphasis is on the right of willing buyers and sellers of stock to deal with each other freely, with only such judicial intervention as is necessary to ensure fair disclosure and to prevent structural coercion. The advantage of this emphasis is that it provides a relatively non-litigious way to effect going private transactions and relies upon minority stockholders to protect themselves. The cost of this approach is that it arguably exposes minority stockholders to the more subtle form of coercion that *Lynch* addresses and leaves them without adequate redress for unfairly timed and priced offers. The approach also minimizes the potential for the minority to get the best price, by arguably giving them only enough protection to keep them from being structurally coerced into accepting grossly insufficient bids but not necessarily merely inadequate ones.

Admittedly, the *Solomon* policy choice would be less disquieting if Delaware also took the same approach to third-party offers and thereby allowed diversified investors the same degree of unrestrained access to premium bids by third-parties. In its brief, Unocal makes a brave effort to explain why it is understandable that Delaware law emphasizes the rights of minority stockholders to freely receive structurally, non-coercive tender offers from controlling stockholders but not their right to accept identically structured offers from third parties. Although there may be subtle ways to explain this variance, a forest-eye summary by a stockholder advocate might run as follows: As a general matter, Delaware law permits directors substantial leeway to block the access of stockholders to receive substantial premium tender offers made by third-parties by use of the poison pill but provides relatively free access to minority stockholders to accept buy-out offers from controlling stockholders.

In the case of third-party offers, these advocates would note, there is arguably less need to protect stockholders indefinitely from structurally non-coercive bids because alternative buyers can emerge and because the target board can use the poison pill to buy time and to tell its story. By contrast, when a controlling stockholder makes a tender offer, the subsidiary board is unlikely—as this case demonstrates—to be permitted by the controlling stockholder to employ a poison pill to fend off the bid and exert pressure for a price increase and usually lacks any real clout to develop an alternative transaction. In the end, however, I do not believe that these discrepancies should lead to an expansion of the *Lynch* standard to controlling stockholder tender offers.

Instead, the preferable policy choice is to continue to adhere to the more flexible and less constraining *Solomon* approach, while giving some greater recognition to the inherent coercion and structural bias concerns that motivate the *Lynch* line of cases. Adherence to the *Solomon* rubric as a general matter, moreover, is advisable in view of the increased activism of institutional investors and the greater information flows available to them. Investors have demonstrated themselves capable of resisting tender offers made by controlling stockholders on occasion, and even the lead plaintiff here expresses no fear of retribution. This does not mean that controlling stockholder tender offers do not pose risks to minority stockholders; it is only to acknowledge that the corporate law should not be designed on the assumption that diversified investors are infirm but instead should give great deference to transactions approved by them voluntarily and knowledgeably.

To the extent that my decision to adhere to *Solomon* causes some discordance between the treatment of similar transactions to persist, that lack of harmony is better addressed in the *Lynch* line, by affording greater liability-immunizing effect to protective devices such as majority of minority approval conditions and special committee negotiation and approval.

8.

To be more specific about the application of *Solomon* in these circumstances, it is important to note that the *Solomon* line of cases does not eliminate the fiduciary duties of controlling stockholders or target boards in connection with tender offers made by controlling stockholders. Rather, the question is the contextual extent and nature of those duties, a question I will now tentatively,[44] and incompletely, answer.

The potential for coercion and unfairness posed by controlling stockholders who seek to acquire the balance of the company's shares by acquisition requires some equitable reinforcement, in order to give proper effect to the concerns undergirding *Lynch*. In order to address the prisoner's dilemma problem, our law should consider an acquisition tender offer by a controlling stockholder non-coercive only when: 1) it is subject to a non-waivable majority of the minority tender condition; 2) the controlling stockholder promises to consummate a prompt § 253 merger at the same price if it obtains more than 90% of the shares; and 3) the controlling stockholder has made no retributive threats. Those protections ... minimize the distorting influence of the tendering process on voluntary choice. They also recognize the adverse conditions that confront stockholders who find themselves owning what have become very thinly traded shares. These conditions also provide a partial cure to the disaggregation problem, by providing a realistic non-tendering goal the minority can achieve to prevent the offer from proceeding altogether.[46]

The informational and timing advantages possessed by controlling stockholders also require some countervailing protection if the minority is to truly be afforded the opportunity to make an informed, voluntary tender decision. In this regard, the majority stockholder owes a duty to permit the independent directors on the target board both free rein and adequate time to react to the tender offer, by (at the very least) hiring their own advisors, providing the minority with a recommendation as to the advisability of the offer, and disclosing adequate information for the minority to make an informed judgment.[47] For their part, the independent directors have a duty to undertake these tasks in good faith and diligently, and to pursue the best interests of the minority.

44. As befits the development of the common law in expedited decisions.

46. They achieve this at some detriment to individual rights, a detriment that seems justifiable as helping the minority increase its leverage to hold out for a truly attractive offer. This protection still may not render the disaggregated minority capable of extracting the offeror's full reserve price, in contrast to a board with the actual power to stop an offer for at least a commercially significant period of time and to force meaningful give-and-take at the bargaining table, which is not available as an option in the take it-or-leave it tender process.

47. This is not to slight the controlling stockholder's fiduciary duty of fair disclosure and its duty to avoid misleading the independent directors and the minority.

When a tender offer is non-coercive in the sense I have identified and the independent directors of the target are permitted to make an informed recommendation and provide fair disclosure, the law should be chary about superimposing the full fiduciary requirement of entire fairness upon the statutory tender offer process. Here, the plaintiffs argue that the Pure board breached its fiduciary duties by not giving the Special Committee the power to block the Offer by, among other means, deploying a poison pill. Indeed, the plaintiffs argue that the full board's decision not to grant that authority is subject to the entire fairness standard of review because a majority of the full board was not independent of Unocal.

That argument has some analytical and normative appeal, embodying as it does the rough fairness of the goose and gander rule. I am reluctant, however, to burden the common law of corporations with a new rule that would tend to compel the use of a device that our statutory law only obliquely sanctions and that in other contexts is subject to misuse, especially when used to block a high value bid that is not structurally coercive. When a controlling stockholder makes a tender offer that is not coercive in the sense I have articulated, therefore, the better rule is that there is no duty on its part to permit the target board to block the bid through use of the pill. Nor is there any duty on the part of the independent directors to seek blocking power.[50] But it is important to be mindful of one of the reasons that make a contrary rule problematic—the awkwardness of a legal rule requiring a board to take aggressive action against a structurally non-coercive offer by the controlling stockholder that elects it. This recognition of the sociology of controlled subsidiaries puts a point on the increased vulnerability that stockholders face from controlling stockholder tenders, because the minority stockholders are denied the full range of protection offered by boards in response to third party offers. This factor illustrates the utility of the protective conditions that I have identified as necessary to prevent abuse of the minority.

9.

Turning specifically to Unocal's Offer, I conclude that the application of these principles yields the following result. The Offer, in its present form, is coercive because it includes within the definition of the "minority" those stockholders who are affiliated with Unocal as directors and officers. It also includes the management of Pure, whose incentives are skewed by their employment, their severance agreements [which gave the managers the right to severance payments, up to three times their annual salaries and bonuses, upon successful completion of the tender offer], and their Put Agreements [which give the managers the right to sell their Pure shares to Unocal upon the

---

50. If our law trusts stockholders to protect themselves in the case of a controlling stockholder tender offer that has the characteristics I have described, this will obviously be remembered by advocates in cases involving defenses against similarly non-coercive third-party tender offers.

occurrence of certain events, arguably including the successful completion of Unocal's tender offer, at an amount that could exceed the tender-offer price]. This is, of course, a problem that can be cured if Unocal amends the Offer to condition it on approval of a majority of Pure's unaffiliated stockholders. Requiring the minority to be defined exclusive of stockholders whose independence from the controlling stockholder is compromised is the better legal rule (and result). Too often, it will be the case that officers and directors of controlled subsidiaries have voting incentives that are not perfectly aligned with their economic interest in their stock and who are more than acceptably susceptible to influence from controlling stockholders. Aside, however, from this glitch in the majority of the minority condition, I conclude that Unocal's Offer satisfies the other requirements of "non-coerciveness." Its promise to consummate a prompt § 253 merger is sufficiently specific,[51] and Unocal has made no retributive threats.

Although Unocal's Offer does not altogether comport with the above-described definition of non-coercive, it does not follow that I believe that the plaintiffs have established a probability of success on the merits as to their claim that the Pure board should have blocked that Offer with a pill or other measures. Putting aside the shroud of silence that cloaked the board's (mostly, it seems, behind the scenes) deliberations, there appears to have been at least a rational basis to believe that a pill was not necessary to protect the Pure minority against coercion, largely, because Pure's management had expressed adamant opposition to the Offer. Moreover, the board allowed the Special Committee a free hand: to recommend against the Offer—as it did; to negotiate for a higher price—as it attempted to do; and to prepare the company's 14D–9—as it did.

For all these reasons, therefore, I find that the plaintiffs do not have a probability of success on the merits of their attack on the Offer, with the exception that the majority of the minority condition is flawed.

C. *The Plaintiffs' Disclosure Claims*

[In contrast to the claims based on the merits of the Offer, the court concluded that plaintiffs had a reasonable probability of success on their claims that Unocal had omitted material information and made misleading statements.]

V. *Conclusion*

For all these reasons, the plaintiffs' motion for a preliminary injunction is hereby granted, and the consummation of the Offer is hereby enjoined. . . .

---

51. A note is in order here. I believe Unocal's statement of intent to be sufficiently clear as to expose it to potential liability in the event that it were to obtain 90% and not consummate the short-form merger at the same price (e.g., if it made the exchange ratio in the short-form merger less favorable). The promise of equal treatment in short-form merger is what renders the tender decision less distorting.

*

APPENDIX

THE COLLAPSE OF ENRON

The events surrounding the collapse of Enron have spurred a wide-ranging reexamination of corporate-governance issues in the United States. Some of the key elements of the Enron story are set out in this Appendix, for possible use as a teaching tool.

Appendix I consists of three Parts.

Part A is an excerpt from an article by Professor William Bratton, in which he describes Enron's business model.

Part B is a Note entitled "Three Weddings and a Funeral." This Note is based largely on the Powers Report, which was issued by an internal investigative committee that was created by Enron's board of directors after the debacle. The first part of the Note describes several key actions by Enron involving issues of board and management accountability, conflicts of interest, and accounting practices. The second part of the Note sets out the Powers Report's evaluations of the conduct of Enron's board and management in connection with these actions.

Finally, Part C of the Appendix consists of a second excerpt from Professor Bratton's article, in which he sets out four different stories to explain Enron's collapse.

Appendix I focuses on Enron's internal corporate-governance mechanisms. Accordingly, there is no direct discussion of the roles of either Enron's accountant, Arthur Andersen, or its outside law firm, Vinson & Elkins.

PART A

WILLIAM BRATTON, ENRON AND THE DARK SIDE OF SHAREHOLDER VALUE, 76 TULANE L. REV. 1275 (2002)*

[In the following excerpt, Professor Bratton discusses Enron's business model.]

In early 2001 Enron was in a process of transformation, determined to leave behind its original business, an asset-laden producer and transporter of natural gas, to become a pure financial intermediary. Its intermediary business had two aspects. First, there was a proprietary marketplace in which Enron matched up energy producers, carriers, and users. Enron was expanding this business to cover anything which could be traded—pulp and paper, metals, even broadband services. There was reason for optimism—Enron had just started up an exemplary online operation which made access to its marketplace cheap and user-friendly. Enron acknowledged few limits to its marketplace. Only "unique" products—"knickknacks"—could not be brought within its trading model. Second, Enron sold risk management products. These over-the-counter derivative contracts covered its customers' exposure to price risks, making participation in Enron's market more attractive.

To get a better look at Enron's intermediary operation, let us hypothesize Enron's entry as a trader into a new market, say pulp and paper. To effect entry as a seller, Enron first had to assure itself of sources of supply, whether through contracting or through direct ownership of the sources of the product, here timber tracts. Once it established itself as a seller, Enron would start bringing other sellers together with timber buyers. As Enron saw it, such a new market could grow spectacularly if many timber users had captive sources of supply. In this scenario, the vertically-integrated forest products companies notice the Enron market and see that it has sufficient volume to supply their needs. They begin to draw on it for marginal supplies. It becomes clear that Enron's market offers timber at lower prices than do their captive timber sources. Ultimately, these companies unbundle themselves, selling off their forest tracts, pocketing the gain, and relying on Enron's market for future supplies.

Enron claimed to provide a level of intelligence higher than that of a marketplace, traditionally conceived:

> [We] provide high-value products and services other wholesale service providers cannot. We can take physical components and repackage them to suit the specific needs of customers. We treat term, price and delivery as variables that are blended into a single, comprehensive solution.

One key to this addition of value was diversification. Enron's network of contacts respecting supply of a given product caused a reduction of risk for buyers of the product, a risk reduction effect unachievable by isolated producer-sellers in the an industry. Skilling explained:

> [T]he fundamental advantage of a virtually integrated system vs. a physically integrated system is you need less capital to provide the same reliability. . . . Delivery is a nonsystematic risk. If a pipeline blows up or a compressor goes down or a wire breaks, the bigger your portfolio, the greater your ability to wire around that. So, if for example, I'm just starting in the gas merchant business and I'm selling gas from central Kansas to Kansas City, if the pipeline blows up, I'm out of business. For Enron, if that pipeline blows up, I'll back haul out of New York, or I'll bring Canadian gas in and spin it through some storage facilities. If you can diversify your infrastructure, you can reduce nonsystematic risk, which says there's a . . . very strong tangible network effect. . . . But you've

got to be big, you've got to get that initial market share, or you're toast. . . .

One obstacle to this market creation scenario concerned price risk to buyers. Product users who procure captive sources of supply seek insulation from price fluctuations, particularly upward price fluctuations in times of high demand. To divest one's source of supply and rely on a trading market, particularly another firm's proprietary trading market, is to expose oneself to this risk. The solution to the problem, for both Enron and the product user, lay in derivative contracts entered into with a market intermediary. These can provide protection against price increases at reasonable cost, at least for the short and intermediate durations. Thus did Enron supplement its activities as a market maker by entering into these contracts with its customers. As Enron stated in its 2000 Annual Report:

> In Volatile Markets, Everything Changes But Us. When customers do business with Enron, they get our commitment to reliably deliver their product at a predictable price, regardless of market condition. This commitment is possible because of Enron's unrivaled access to markets and liquidity. . . . We offer a multitude of predictable pricing options. Market access and information allow Enron to deliver comprehensive logistical solutions that work in volatile markets or markets undergoing fundamental changes, such as energy or broadband.

Enron, in short, aspired to be *better* than a market. It was reducing the costs of finding, contracting with, and communicating with outside suppliers and customers—costs that formerly meant bringing disparate operations under a single corporate roof. From this there followed a staggering claim: Enron would apply enough raw intelligence and superior information the [to] provision of products and risk services to cause a change in the prevailing mode of industrial organization. Said Skilling:

> There's only been a couple of times in history when these costs of interaction have radically changed. One was the railroads, and then the telephone and the telegraph. . . . [W]e're going through another right now. The costs of interaction are collapsing because of the Internet, and as those costs collapse, I think the economics of temporarily assembled organizations will beat the economics of the old vertically integrated organization.
>
> The old way they reduced the risk is they'd vertically integrate. If you were Exxon in the old days, you integrated across the whole chain. . . . If you were afraid crude-oil prices would go down, you'd own the refinery, too, because [then] you liked it if crude prices went down. . . . That made a lot of sense . . . because it was very expensive to make sure you could get reliable supplies of crude oil to go into a refinery if you didn't own the crude oil. Well, now you can go on your computer and get it instantaneously. If you have somebody [like Enron] who comes along and says

hey, look, I'm going to virtually vertically integrate because it's a whole lot cheaper, you're not going to be cost-competitive.

In Skilling's projection, virtual integration force would force Big Oil, Big Coal, or Big Anything to split up into multitudinous micro-firms, each working a niche. Enron would put the whole back together through its trading operation, all the while securing lower prices for all.

The "nexus of contracts" firm hypothesized by Jensen and Meckling in 1976 would be realized in fact. Jensen and Meckling took the large firm and explained it as by product of equilibrium contracting by rational economic actors. Given the complexity of relations among actors in the complex, agency cost reduction emerged as the problem for solution in the economics of firm organization. Enron was going to use real world market contracting to unwind Jensen and Meckling's contractual complexes into simpler, more transparent units. With each unit directly disciplined by the market for its own product, agency costs inevitably would be less of a problem.

Skilling saw one further implication: Assets were a bad thing to have. This followed from the shareholder value maximization norm. Skilling liked the numbers on return on equity capital yielded by financial institutions, insurance companies, and pension funds better than the returns capital yielded in the energy industry: "[I]t's very hard to earn a compensatory rate of return on a traditional asset investment. . . . In today's world, you have to bring intellectual content to the product, or you will not earn a fair rate of return." Under this line of thinking, Enron could justify owning a bricks-and-mortar operation or other hard asset only to the extent necessary to support a trading operation—as with the timber tracts in the foregoing example or Enron's building of a national broadband network as the start point for a broadband trading market. Meanwhile, Enron would divest its extensive collection of pipelines and other properties. Wall Street applauded—here was a firm that "doesn't linger over troubled assets," dumping them in order to "help fund its vast ambitions."

It should be noted that Enron's plan to become the real world embodiment of the contractarian ideal has profound implications for industrial organization. Of course, there is nothing new about restructuring, downsizing, and unbundling. These became everyday events in corporate America as the shareholder value maximization norm came to drive management decisions in the 1990s. But even as many corporations regrouped around "core competencies" they remained big, asset-rich entities, vertically integrating the production, supply, and distribution functions feeding in and out of their cores. Enron's vision held out a much more radical degree of divestiture, leading to smaller entities under tighter market constraints and deprived of institutional stability.

For a glimpse of the world Skilling envisioned for everybody else, we need only look within Enron's glass box in Houston to see the way he treated his own employees. Questions about executive decisions were not tolerated. Nor were fairness complaints. Employees labored under tremendous pressure to take significant risks and bring in favorable results in the short term. And the end justified the means. In 2000 Skilling publicly praised the employee who started Enron's online trading operation even though she had been explicitly forbidden so to do. Said an officer present at that meeting: "The moral of the story is, 'You can break the rules, you can cheat, you can lie, but as long as you make money, it's all right.' "

Enron's whiz kid recruits entered a perpetual tournament. They termed it the "rank or yank" system. Each got to pick 10 other employees to rank his or her performance. But the system also allowed coworkers to make unsolicited evaluations into an online database. At year's end, Skilling threw everybody's results onto a bell curve. Those on the wrong end of the curve were terminated. Those who remained scratched and clawed to get or stay in the winners' circle. Winners got million dollar bonuses and were privileged to accompany Skilling for glacier hiking in Patagonia or Land Cruiser racing in Australia.

Differences between winners and losers within Enron became starker as 2001 unfolded. All of the employees became losers as their 401(k)s gave up a billion [dollars] in value. Management froze the plan accounts on October 17, 2001, the day Enron revealed a third quarter loss of $638 million. Meanwhile, top executives holding Enron stock purchased through the stock option plan were not similarly restricted and continued the heavy selling in which they had been engaged for some months. Market sales of personal Enron stock yielded Kenneth Lay proceeds of $23 million in 2001; redemptions of Lay's stock by Enron itself during the year netted him an additional $70.1 million. Skilling sold $15.6 million worth before he resigned and $15 million thereafter. Amalgamated Bank, the plaintiff in a lawsuit against Enron's officers and directors, alleged gross sales of $1 billion of Enron stock by its officer and director defendants over a three-year period.

———

PART B

NOTE–THREE WEDDINGS AND A FUNERAL

This Note sets out some of the critical transactions that Enron engaged in prior to its collapse. The account in this Note is for the most part based on findings and conclusions in the Report of the Special Investigative Committee of the Board of Directors of Enron Corporation (the Powers Report). Although the Note employs the names of real people, real entities, and real transactions, the account in this Note cannot be taken as conclusively accurate. There are several reasons for this.

First, some important Enron officers and employees either refused to talk to the Powers Committee or talked to the Committee on only a very limited basis. If these actors had talked to the Committee, they might have provided information that would have led the Committee to make different findings and come to different conclusions.

Second, to simplify the transactions for purposes of discussion, where the Powers Report found there was conflicting evidence, this Note takes as hypothetically true the conclusions the Report reached or, where the Report did not reach an explicit conclusion, the conclusion that seemed most likely, without rehearsing the conflicting evidence. In some or all such cases it may be that the conclusion that the Report reached, or the conclusion here deemed most likely, is not in fact true.

Third, this Note sometimes stylizes the facts by omitting details that do not seem significant. For example, the Note disregards various intermediate entities, so that actions that are attributed to a given entity may actually have been performed to or on behalf of one or more intermediate entities.

Finally, the Powers Report rested in large part on unsworn testimony, and in some part on hearsay.

1. *Some of the Players*

Some of the key players in the transactions described in this Note are as follows:

Kenneth Lay—Enron's CEO for much of the relevant period. Also a director.

Jeffrey Skilling—Enron's COO for part of the relevant period; later CEO. Also a director.

Andrew Fastow—Enron's Executive Vice President and CFO.

Michael Kopper—An Enron manager who reported to Fastow; not a senior officer of Enron

Jeffrey McMahon—Enron's Treasurer. Reported to Fastow.

Richard Causey—Enron's Chief Accounting Officer.

Richard Buy—Enron's Senior Risk Officer

2. *Accounting Principles and SPEs*

Most of the problems concerning Enron that have come to public attention directly or indirectly concern Special Purpose Entities (SPEs). SPEs are sometimes employed by corporations that want to accomplish certain financial objectives indirectly that accounting principles do not allow them to accomplish directly. A central issue here is the accounting principle of consolidation. There is a presumption that when one of the companies in a group has a controlling financial interest in the other companies, consolidated financial statements are more meaningful than unconsolidated statements, and are usually necessary for a fair presentation. Ordinarily, therefore, a corporate majority holder of the equity in an entity should consolidate that entity in its financials. This presumption can be overcome, however, in the case of an SPE, if but only if two conditions are met:

1. The SPE must have one or more independent owners, who must make a substantive equity capital investment in the SPE, and the investment must carry substantive risks and rewards of ownership during the entire term of the transaction. The SEC staff has taken the position that 3% of an SPE's total equity capital held by independent owners is the minimum acceptable at-risk investment.

2. The independent owners must exercise control over the SPE.

Enron's SPEs—or, at least, the SPEs that figure in this Note—had several purposes, including the following:

1. To allow Enron to treat the transfer of appreciated assets, such as stock, as a "sale," and thereby to treat the difference between Enron's cost for the asset and the value of the asset at the time it was transferred as "profit," even though the asset was not really disposed of, but instead remained in an entity affiliated with Enron.

2. To allow Enron to include in income appreciation in the value of Enron stock held by an SPE, even though normally a corporation cannot treat appreciation in the value of its own stock as income.

3. To allow Enron to raise billions of dollars in debt financing through the SPEs without showing the debt on Enron's own financial statements, thereby making Enron's financial statements look better, so that Enron could maintain a good credit rating and borrow at lower interest rates.

4. To allow Enron to claim that it had "hedged" its risk on an investment, and thereby keep losses in the investment off its books, by getting an agreement in the form of a hedge from an SPE, even though the SPE's assets consisted mainly of Enron stock, so that there was only a paper hedge, not a true economic hedge.

Parts 3 and 4 of this Note will develop scenarios involving three of SPEs created by Enron: Chewco, LJM1, and LJM2.

3. *Chewco*

Chewco was formed as a Delaware limited liability company in early November 1997. It took over the business of an entity named JEDI. JEDI was an investment vehicle that prior to the formation of Chewco had been owned 50–50 by Enron and the California Public Employees' Retirement System (CalPERS). It is not entirely clear why Enron wanted to retain JEDI in the form of an SPE after Enron bought out CalPERS. However, an article on Enron in the Wall Street Journal on April 30, 2002, states that Enron used Chewco to keep more than $700 million in debt off Enron's books. Also, it seems likely that Enron wanted to be able to recognize investment gains made by JEDI that Enron could not have recognized if it had either liquidated JEDI or had treated JEDI on a consolidated basis. In particular, JEDI had major income from appreciation in the rise of stock in Enron itself, which Enron could not have recognized if it either owned the JEDI assets directly or had to consolidate JEDI.

To maintain JEDI as an unconsolidated entity, Enron needed a new at-risk investor. Fastow initially proposed that he act as the manager of, and an investor in, Chewco. Fastow told Enron employees that Skilling (then Enron's COO) had approved Fastow's participation, as long as the participation would not have to be disclosed in Enron's proxy statement. Enron's Code of Conduct provided that no full-time officer or employee could "[o]wn an interest in or participate, directly or indirectly, in the profits of any other entity which does business with or is a competitor of the Company, unless such ownership or participation has been previously disclosed in writing to the Chairman of the Board and Chief Executive Officer of Enron [at this point, Lay] and such officer has determined that such interest or participation does not adversely affect the best interests of the Company." Both Enron's in-house counsel and its longstanding outside counsel, Vinson & Elkins, advised Fastow that his participation in Chewco would require disclosure in Enron's proxy statement and approval from Lay under the Code of Conduct. As a result, Kopper, an Enron employee who reported to Fastow, was substituted as the manager of Chewco. Because Kopper, unlike Fastow, was not a senior officer of Enron, Kopper's role in Chewco would not require disclosure in the proxy statement (but would require Lay's approval under Enron's Code of Conduct). As initially formed, therefore, Kopper, through intermediary entities, was the sole manager of Chewco.

While Chewco was being formed, an Enron employee, on behalf of Enron, and Kopper, on behalf of Chewco, were negotiating the economic terms. During the negotiations, Fastow contacted Enron's negotiator, who reported to him, and suggested that he was pushing too hard for Enron, and that the deal needed to be closed. Enron's negotiator explained to Fastow the status of the discussions with Kopper; said that he believed it was his job to obtain the best economic terms for Enron; and added that accepting Kopper's current position would result in greater benefits to Chewco than would be required if the negotiations continued. Fastow indicated that he was comfortable closing the transaction on the terms then proposed by Kopper. Enron's negotiator was uncomfortable with this discussion and Fastow's intervention, and believed that Enron could have improved its position if he had been permitted to continue the negotiations, but he acquiesced.

The Board of Directors, other than Skilling, was unaware that an Enron employee (Kopper) was an investor in or manager of Chewco. Because substantial loan guarantees from Enron were required to permit Chewco to acquire the CalPERS interest in JEDI, the Chewco transaction was brought before the Board's Executive Committee, at a meeting held by telephone conference call, in November 1997. Fastow made the presentation describing Chewco as an SPE not affiliated with either Enron or CalPERS. There was no disclosure to the Executive Committee of Kopper's role. Neither the Executive Committee nor Lay made the finding necessary under Enron's Code of Conduct to permit Kopper to have a financial interest in Chewco.

Enron could not secure a true outside equity investor for Chewco. Eventually Barclay's Bank agreed to put up funds. Barclay's recorded these funds as a loan, but Enron treated part of the funds as at-risk capital. Although much smoke and mirrors was involved, various Enron employees, including Kopper, were aware of the relevant facts, and no one who knew those facts could have reasonably concluded that at least 3% of Chewco's equity had been supplied by an outside investor on an at-risk basis.

From December 1997 through December 2000, Kopper was paid approximately $2 million in fees relating to Chewco. Chewco required little management, and Kopper did little or nothing to justify those fees or indeed almost any fees.

JEDI was an investment fund that carried its assets at fair value. Changes in the fair value of its investments were recorded in JEDI's income statement. From the inception of JEDI in 1993 through the first quarter of 2000, Enron picked up its contractual share of income or losses from JEDI, using the equity method of accounting. Under generally accepted accounting principles, a company is normally precluded from recognizing an increase in the value of its own stock as income. However JEDI held 12 million shares of Enron stock, which it marked to market. Enron stock appreciated significantly during this period. As a result, Enron recorded significant income resulting from appreciation in the value of shares of its own stock held by JEDI. But in the first quarter of 2001, when the Enron stock held by JEDI declined in value by $94 million. Enron's internal accountants decided not to record the loss.

During the first quarter of 2000, senior personnel in Enron's Finance area came to the conclusion that JEDI was essentially in a liquidation mode, and had become an expensive off-balance sheet financing vehicle. They approached Fastow, who agreed with their conclusion. The next step was to determine an appropriate buyout price for Chewco's interest in JEDI.

The discussions concerning the buyout terms involved, among others, Fastow, Kopper, and Jeffrey McMahon (then Enron's Treasurer and Senior Vice President of Finance). Because JEDI's assets had increased in value since 1997, on paper Chewco's interest in JEDI had become valuable. In March 2001, Enron repurchased Chewco's interest in JEDI. Fastow was personally involved in the negotiations and decision-making concerning this repurchase.

The repurchase resulted in an enormous financial gain to Kopper. Kopper had invested only $125,000 in Chewco. McMahon proposed to Fastow that the buyout be structured to provide a $1 million return to the Chewco investors (essentially, Kopper). This would give the investors a 152% internal rate of return on their investment, and a return-on-capital multiple of 7.99. Fastow received the proposal, said he would discuss it with Kopper, and later reported back to McMahon that he had negotiated a payment of $10 million. Subsequently, Kopper was paid an additional $2.6 million on a tax-indemnification claim. The Powers Committee concluded that "Much of this [$12.6 million] payout ... is difficult to justify or understand from Enron's perspective, and at least $2.6 million of the payout appears inappropriate on its face," because it was based on a claim that Enron's in-house counsel unequivocally advised Fastow had no legal basis.

Shortly after Kopper was paid the $12.5 million, he purchased Fastow's remaining interests in LJM2, another SPE. (LJM2 is discussed in Part IV.) The Wall Street Journal April 30 article on Enron reports suspicions by the Powers Committee and by government prosecutors that Fastow caused Enron to pay the $12.5 million to Kopper so that Kopper could use part or all of the money to buy Fastow's stake in LJM2.

Kopper's $10,000,000 return on his $125,000 investment in Chewco represented an internal rate of return of more than 360%, even without taking into account the $2.6 million on the indemification claim and $1.6 million in management fees that Kopper received.

4. *The LJMs*

(a) LJM1

Following the creation of Chewco, Enron created two SPEs called LJM1 and LJM2. The first transaction with the LJMs involved LJM1. It centered on stock that Enron held in Rhythms NetConnections, Inc., a privately-held internet service provider for businesses using digital subscriber-line technology. In March 1998, Enron had invested $10 million in Rhythms by purchasing 5.4 million shares of stock at $1.85 per share. In April 1999, Rhythms went public at $21 per share. By the close of the trading day, the stock price reached $69. By May 1999, Enron's investment in Rhythms was worth approximately $300 million, but Enron was prohibited by a lock-up agreement from selling its shares before the end of 1999.

Because Enron accounted for the Rhythms investment as part of its trading portfolio, it marked the Rhythms stock to market, so that increases and decreases in the value of Rhythms stock were reflected on Enron's income statement. However, Skilling was concerned about the volatility of Rhythms stock, and wanted to hedge Enron's position to capture the value already achieved and protect against future volatility. Given the size of Enron's position, the relative illiquidity of Rhythms stock, and the lack of comparable securities in the market, it would have been virtually impossible or prohibitively expensive to hedge the Rhythms investment commercially.

Enron was also looking for a way to take advantage of an increase in the value of Enron stock that was reflected in forward contracts, under which Enron had the right to purchase a specified number of Enron shares, at a fixed price that was lower than the current market price of the stock, from an investment bank. As already noted, under generally accepted accounting principles a company is normally precluded from recognizing an increase in value of its own stock (including forward contracts) as income. Enron sought to make use of what it viewed as this "trapped" value.

Fastow developed a plan to create LJM1, which would be capitalized primarily with the appreciated value of the forward contracts. LJM1 would engage in a hedging transaction with Enron involving the Rhythms stock, which would allow Enron to offset losses on Rhythms if the price of Rhythms declined. Fastow would form the partnership and serve as the general partner.

At a Board meeting in June 1999, Fastow presented the proposal. He described the structure of LJM1 and the hedging transaction. He disclosed that he would serve as the general partner of LJM1, and represented that he would invest $1 million. He described the distribution formula for earnings of LJM1 and said he would receive certain management fees from the partnership. He told the Board that all proceeds from appreciation in the value of Enron stock would go to the limited partners in LJM1, not to him; that 100% of the proceeds from all other assets would go to him until he had received a rate of return of 25% on his invested capital; and that of any remaining income, half would go to him and half would be divided among the partners (including Fastow) in proportion to their capital commitments. Fastow also told the Board that the proposal required action pursuant to Enron's Code of Conduct–action within Lay's authority– based on a determination that Fastow's participation as the managing partner of LJM1 "will not adversely affect the interests" of Enron. After discussion, the Board adopted a resolution approving the proposed transaction with LJM1 and ratifying a determination by Lay that Fastow's participation in LJM1 would not adversely affect Enron's interests.

LJM1 was formed in June 1999. Fastow became the sole and managing member. He raised $15 million from two limited partners. Enron then transferred the forward contracts on 3.4 million Enron shares to LJM1, along with 1.6 million Enron shares and $3.75 million in cash. LJM1, in turn, gave Enron a put (that is, a right to require a counterparty to buy shares at a designated price) on 5.4 million shares of Rhythms stock. Under the put, Enron could require LJM1 to purchase the Rhythms shares at $56 per share in June 2004. Enron obtained a fairness opinion from PricewaterhouseCoopers on the exchange.

To satisfy the requirement for non-consolidation, LJM1 needed to have a minimum of outside 3% at-risk equity. At its formation, however, LJM1 had negative equity, because its liability (the Rhythms put) greatly exceeded its assets.

The "hedge" that Enron obtained on its Rhythms position affected the gains and losses Enron reported on its income statement. However, there was not a true economic hedge. LJM1's ability to make good on the Rhythms put rested largely on the value of Enron stock. If Enron stock performed well, LJM1 could perform under the put even if Rhythms stock declined. But if Enron stock and Rhythms stock both declined, LJM1 would be unable to perform under the put, and Enron's hedge on Rhythms would fail. This structure is in sharp contrast to a typical economic hedge, which is obtained by paying a market price to a creditworthy counterparty who will take on the economic risk of a loss. In early 2000, Enron's analysts determined there was a 68% probability that LJM1 would default and would be unable to meet its obligations to Enron on the put.

Around this time, Enron decided to liquidate its Rhythms position. Once Enron decided to liquidate the Rhythms position, it had to unwind the transaction with LJM1. On March 8, 2000, as the unwinding negotiations were underway, Enron gave LJM1 a put on 3.1 million shares of Enron stock at $71.31 per share. LJM1 did not pay any consideration for the put. On March 8, the closing price of Enron stock was $67.19 per share. The put was therefore "in the money" to LJM1 by $4.12 per share (or approximately $12.8 million) on the day it was executed. The put was given to LJM1 to stabilize LJM1's structure and freeze the economics so that the unwinding negotiations could be completed.

Fastow proposed that LJM1 receive $30 million from Enron in connection with the unwind. Enron agreed to the proposal.

The unwind transaction resulted in a huge windfall to LJM1. Enron did not seek or obtain a fairness opinion on the unwind. Neither the Board nor any Board Committee was informed of the transaction. Lay was unaware of the transaction. Skilling was aware that Enron had sold its Rhythms position, but was not aware of the terms on which the hedge was unwound. There was no Enron Deal Approval Sheet, summarizing the transaction and showing required approvals, concerning the unwind.

Because of a decline in price of Rhythms stock, Enron's right to put the Rhythms stock to LJM1 was substantially in the money to Enron when the LJM1 structure was unwound. Enron calculated the put as having a value of $207 million. In exchange for Enron's termination of the put, plus $27 million cash, LJM1 returned to Enron shares of Enron stock that had a market value of $234 million if unrestricted. Enron's accounting personnel determined that the exchange was fair, using the unrestricted value of the shares. However, Enron shares were not unrestricted. They carried a (partly amortized) four-year contractual restriction. Because of the restriction, at the closing a valuation discount of 38% was applied to those shares.

Unbeknown to virtually everyone at Enron, in March 2000 several Enron employees, including Fastow, Kopper, Ben Glisan (Enron's Treasurer and a Fastow protégé) and Kristan Mordaunt (an Enron lawyer), had obtained financial interests in the unwind of LJM1 through limited partnerships in Southampton Place, L.P. (named after the neighborhood in which Fastow lived), which was formed on March 20, 2000. The Fastow Family Foundation was also a limited partner in Southampton. Around this time, Glisan was representing Enron in negotiations with other Fastow-led partnerships, and Mordaunt represented Enron in a transaction with one such partnership.

Shortly thereafter, Enron paid Southampton $17 million to buy back some of its own stock, which the Wall Street Journal, based on the Powers Report, suggest was a overpayment, creating a huge windfall for Southampton and the limited partners. Just two months after their initial investment, the limited partners in Southhampton reaped huge returns. In return for a $25,000 two-month investment, the Fastow Family Foundation received $4.5 million. The Enron employees, Glisan and Mordaunt, each received approximately $1 million in return for two-month investments of $5,800 each.

(b)   LJM2

LJM2 was much more active than LJM1. The two LJMs together engaged in around twenty and perhaps more transactions, almost all on the part of LJM2. (These included the by-now semi-famous "Raptor" transactions.) It would be tedious to rehearse all these transactions, although many of them have some interest. For present purposes, the important points about the transactions are as follows:

1.   The high number of transactions seems to be somewhat inconsistent, although perhaps not absolutely inconsistent, with the concept of a Special Purpose Entity, which is often conceived as an enterprise that is created for one well-defined special purpose and then goes on autopilot, so that it is not under the immediate control of the corporation that created it.

2.   Fastow put pressure on the employees who were negotiating with LJM2 on Enron's behalf—some of whom reported to Fastow—to give LJM2 better terms than the employees had been negotiating before Fastow's intervention. Usually these interventions were successful.

C. *Fastow's Gains on the LJMs*

Fastow's partnership capital in LJM1 and LJM2 apparently increased by $31 million in 1999 and 2000. Fastow also received partnership distributions of $18.7 million in 2000, perhaps on top of the increase in his capital. Recall too that the Fastow Family Foundation received a return of $4.5 million on an investment of $25,000 in LJM1. Approximate total: $54 million, on an investment of just over $1 million.

5. *The Funeral*

On October 16, 2001, Enron announced that it was taking a $544 million after-tax charge against earnings related to transactions with LJM2. It also announced a reduction of shareholders' equity of $1.2 billion related to transactions with LJM2.

Less than one month later, Enron announced that it was restating its financial statements for the period from 1997 through 2001 because of accounting errors relating to transactions with LJM1 and Chewco. The LJM1 and Chewco restatements, like the earlier $544 million charge against earnings and reduction of shareholders' equity, were very large. They reduced Enron's reported net income by $28 million in 1997 (of $105 million total), by $133 million in 1998 (of $703 million total), by $248 million in 1999 (of $893 million total), and by $99 million in 2000 (of $979 million total). The restatement reduced reported shareholders' equity by $258 million in 1997, by $391 million in 1998, by $710 million in 1999, and by $754 million in 2000. It increased reported debt by $711 million in 1997, by $561 million in 1998, by $685 million in 1999, and by $628 million in 2000.

Enron's use of LJM1 and LJM2 allowed Enron to avoid reflecting almost $1 billion in losses on its investments over a period spanning just a little more than one year. Without LJM1 and LJM2, Enron's pre-tax earnings from the third quarter of 2000 through the third quarter of 2001 would have been $429 million, rather than the $1.5 billion that Enron reported.

Shortly thereafter, Enron collapsed.

6. *The Powers Committee Conclusions*

This Part sets out the Powers Committee's conclusions concerning board and management responsibility for Enron's conduct. Although quotation marks are not employed, all the material in this Part consists of excerpts from the Powers Report, except as otherwise indicated. However, some of the excerpts have been transposed.

The Board of Directors

With respect to the issues that are the subject of this investigation, the Board of Directors failed, in our judgment, in its oversight duties.

This had serious consequences for Enron, its employees, and its shareholders.

The Board of Directors approved the arrangements that allowed the Company's CFO to serve as general partner in partnerships that participated in significant financial transactions with Enron.... This decision was fundamentally flawed. The Board substantially underestimated the severity of the conflict and overestimated the degree to which management controls and procedures could contain the problem.

After having authorized a conflict of interest creating as much risk as this one, the Board had an obligation to give careful attention to the transactions that followed. It failed to do this. It cannot be faulted for the various instances in which it was apparently denied important information concerning certain of the transactions in question. However, it can and should be faulted for failing to demand more information, and for failing to probe and understand the information that did come to it....

The Board had agreed to permit Enron to take on the risks of doing business with its CFO, but had done so on the condition that the Audit and Compliance Committee (and later also the Finance Committee) review Enron's transactions with the LJM partnerships. These reviews were a significant part of the control structure, and should have been more than just another brief item on the agenda.

In fact, the reviews were brief, reportedly lasting ten to fifteen minutes. More to the point, the specific economic terms, and the benefits, to LJM1 or LJM2 (or to Fastow), were not discussed. There does not appear to have been much, if any, probing with respect to the underlying basis for Causey's [the Chief Accounting Officer's] representation that the transactions were at arm's-length and that "the process was working effectively." The reviews did provide the Committees with what they believed was an assurance that Causey had in fact looked at the transactions–an entirely appropriate objective for a Board Committee-level review of ordinary transactions with outside parties. But these were not normal transactions.

There was little point in relying on Audit and Compliance Committee review as a control over these transactions if that review did not have more depth or substance.*

* According to a story in the New York Times, a document prepared by David Duncan, Arthur Andersen's lead accountant for Enron, told the audit committee on February 7, 1999 that there were high risks in the way that Enron was accounting for many aspect of its business.

" 'Obviously, we [Arthur Andersen] are on board with all of these,' the Andersen partner, David Duncan, wrote in the document, his talking points for a presentation to the [audit] committee. 'But many push limits and have a high "others could have a different view" risk profile.' Mr. Duncan pleaded guilty last month to obstruction of justice for destroying documents related to the Enron debacle.

"In a letter to Mr. Levin's committee, another Andersen partner, Tom Bauer, said that at that same 1999 audit committee meeting, Andersen officials told the Enron directors that some aspects of the company's

Review of Fastow's Compensation

Committee-mandated procedures required reviewing Fastow's compensation from LJM I and LJM2. This should have been an important control. As much as any other procedure, it might have provided a warning if the transactions were on terms too generous to LJM1 or LJM2. It might have indicated whether the representation that Fastow would not profit from increases in the price of Enron stock was accurate. It might have revealed whether Fastow's gains were inconsistent with the understanding reported by a number of Board members that he would be receiving only modest compensation from LJM, commensurate with the approximately three hours per week he told the Finance Committee in May 2000 he was spending on LJM matters. . . .

The Board's review apparently never occurred until October 2001, after newspaper reports focused attention on Fastow's involvement in LJM1 and LJM2. . . . [At] the October 6, 2000, meeting of the Finance Committee. . . . Fastow told the Committee (in Skilling's presence) that Skilling received "a review of [Fastow's] economic interest in [Enron] and the LJM funds," and the Committee then unanimously agreed that the Compensation Committee should review Fastow's compensation from LJM1 and LJM2. Although a number of members of the Compensation Committee were present at this Finance Committee meeting, it does not appear that the Compensation Committee thereafter performed a review. . . . The Board, and in particular the Audit and Compliance Committee, has the duty of ultimate oversight over the Company's financial reporting. While the primary responsibility for the financial reporting abuses discussed in the Report lies with Management, [this Committee believes] those abuses could and should have been prevented or detected at an earlier time had the Board been more aggressive and vigilant. . . .

The Audit and Compliance Committee, and later the Finance Committee, took on a specific role in the control structure by carrying out periodic reviews of the LJM transactions. This was an opportunity to probe the transactions thoroughly, and to seek outside advice as to any issues outside the Board members' expertise. Instead, these reviews appear to have been too brief, too limited in scope, and too superficial to serve their intended function. The Compensation Committee was given the role of reviewing Fastow's compensation from

accounting were 'pushing the limits' and 'at the edge.' . . .

"Robert K. Jaedicke, the longtime chairman of the audit committee, told the panel that he did not recall Andersen auditors using that language to describe the accounting. 'I don't remember the word "push limits," ' said Mr. Jaedicke, a retired accounting professor who left the Enron board earlier this year.

" 'We knew that the company was engaged in high risk, in innovative transactions,' he continued, adding, 'if David Duncan had given this to the audit committee, my guess is the discussion would have been a lot different than it was.' . . ."

Richard A. Oppel Jr., The Directors—Harsh Words from Senators to the Board, New York Times, May 8, 2002, C7, at col. 1. (Footnote by ed.)

the LJM entities, and did not carry out this review. This remained the case even after the Committees were on notice that the LJM transactions were contributing very large percentages of Enron's earnings. In sum, the Board did not effectively meet its obligation with respect to the LJM transactions.

Enron's Management

Individually, and collectively, Enron's Management failed to carry out its substantive responsibility for ensuring that the transactions were fair to Enron—which in many cases they were not—and its responsibility for implementing a system of oversight and controls over the transactions with the LJM partnerships. There were several direct consequences of this failure: transactions were executed on terms that were not fair to Enron and that enriched Fastow and others; Enron engaged in transactions that had little economic substance and misstated Enron's financial results; and the disclosures Enron made to its shareholders and the public did not fully or accurately communicate relevant information. . . .

Management had the primary responsibility for implementing the Board's resolutions and controls. Management failed to do this in several respects. No one accepted primary responsibility for oversight, the controls were not executed properly, and there were apparent structural defects in the controls that no one undertook to remedy or to bring to the Board's attention. In short, no one was minding the store.

The most fundamental management control flaw was the lack of separation between LJM and Enron personnel, and the failure to recognize that the inherent conflict was persistent and unmanageable. Fastow, as CFO, knew what assets Enron's business units wanted to sell, how badly and how soon they wanted to sell them, and whether they had alternative buyers. He was in a position to exert great pressure and influence, directly or indirectly, on Enron personnel who were negotiating with LJM. We have been told of instances in which he used that pressure to try to obtain better terms for LJM, and where people reporting to him instructed business units that LJM would be the buyer of the asset they wished to sell. . . . Enron employees worked for LJM while still sitting in their Enron offices, side by side with people who were acting on behalf of Enron. Simply put, there was little of the separation and independence required to enable Enron employees to negotiate effectively against LJM2.

In many cases, the safeguard requiring that a transaction could be negotiated on behalf of Enron only by employees who did not report to Fastow was ignored. We have identified at least 13 transactions between Enron and LJM2 in which the individuals negotiating on behalf of Enron reported directly or indirectly to Fastow.

This situation led one Fastow subordinate, then-Treasurer Jeff McMahon, to complain to Skilling in March 2000. While McMahon's and Skilling's recollections of their conversation differ, McMahon's contemporaneous handwritten discussion points, which he says he followed in the meeting, include these notations:

- "LJM situation where AF [Andy Fastow] wears 2 hats and upside comp is so great creates a conflict I am right in the middle of"
- "I find myself negotiating with Andy [to whom he then reported] on Enron matters and am pressured to do a deal that I do not believe is in the best interests of the shareholders."
- "Bonuses do get affected—MK [Michael Kopper], JM [Jeff McMahon]" . . .

Skilling has said he recalls the conversation focusing only on McMahon's compensation. Even if that is true, it still may have suggested that Fastow's conflict was placing pressure on an Enron employee. The conversation presented an issue that required remedial action: a solution by Management, a report to the Board that its controls were not working properly, or both. Skilling took no action of which we are aware, and shortly thereafter McMahon accepted a transfer within Enron that removed him from contact with LJM. Neither Skilling nor McMahon raised the issue with Lay or the Board . . .

The Board's first and most-relied-on control was review of transactions by the Chief Accounting Officer, Causey, and the Chief Risk Officer, Buy. Neither ignored his responsibility completely, but neither appears to have given the transactions anywhere near the level of scrutiny the Board understood they were giving. Neither imposed a procedure for identifying all LJM1 or LJM2 transactions and for assuring that they went through the required procedures. It appears that some of the transactions . . . did not even come to Causey or Buy for review. . . .

Even with respect to the transactions that he did review, Causey said he viewed his role as being primarily determining that the appropriate business unit personnel had signed off. Buy said he viewed his role as being primarily to evaluate Enron's risk. It does not appear that Causey or Buy had the necessary time, or spent the necessary time, to provide an effective check, even though the Board was led to believe they had done so.

Skilling appears to have been almost entirely uninvolved in overseeing the LJM transactions, even though in October 2000 the Finance Committee was told by Fastow apparently in Skilling's presence that Skilling had undertaken substantial duties. Fastow told the Committee that there could be no transactions with the LJM entities without Skilling's approval, and that Skilling was reviewing Fastow's compensation. Skilling described himself to us as having little or no role with respect to the individual LJM transactions. . . . His signature is absent from many LJM Deal Approval Sheets, even though the Finance Committee was told that his approval was required. Skilling said he would sign off on transactions if Causey and Buy had signed off, suggesting he made no independent assessment of the transactions' fairness. This was not sufficient in light of the representations to the Board.

It does not appear that Lay had, or was intended to have, any managerial role in connection with LJM once the entities became operational. His involvement was principally on the same basis as other Directors. By the accounts of both Lay and Skilling, the division of labor between them was that Skilling, as President and COO (later CEO) had full responsibility for domestic operational activities such as these. Skilling said he would keep Lay apprised of major issues, but does not recall discussing LJM matters with him. . . . Still, during the period while Lay was CEO, he bore ultimate management responsibility.

Still other controls were not properly implemented. The LJM Deal Approval Sheet process was not well-designed, and it was not consistently followed. We have been unable to locate Approval Sheets for some transactions. Other Approval Sheets do not have all the required signatures. The Approval Sheet form contained pre-printed check marks in boxes signifying compliance with a number of, controls and disclosure concerns, with the intention that a signature would be added to certify the accuracy of the preprinted check-marks. Some transactions closed before the Approval Sheets were completed. The Approval Sheets did not require any documentation of efforts to find third party, unrelated buyers for Enron assets other than LJM I or LJM2, and it does not appear that such efforts were systematically pursued. Some of the questions on the Approval Sheets were framed with boilerplate conclusions ("Was this transaction done strictly on an arm's-length basis?"), and others were worded in a fashion that set unreasonably low standards or were worded in the negative ("Was Enron advised by any third party that this transaction was not fair, from a financial perspective, to Enron?"). In practice, it appears the LJM Deal Approval Sheets were a formality that provided little control.

Apart from these failures of execution, perhaps the most basic reason the controls failed was structural. Most of the controls were based on a model in which Enron's business units were in full command of transactions and had the time and motivation to find the highest price for assets they were selling. In some cases, transactions were consistent with this model, but in many of the transactions the assumptions underlying this model did not apply. The [LJM] transactions had little economic substance. In effect, they were transfers of economic risk from one Enron pocket to another, apparently to create income that would offset mark-to-market losses on merchant investments on Enron's income statement. The Chief Accounting Officer was not the most effective guardian against transactions of this sort, because the Accounting Department was at or near the root of the transactions. Other transactions were temporary transfers of assets

Enron wanted off its balance sheet. It is unclear in some of the cases whether economic risk ever passed from Enron to LJM1 or LJM2. The fundamental flaw in these transactions was not that the price was too low. Instead, as a matter of economic substance, it is not clear that anything was really being bought or sold. Controls that were directed at assuring a fair price to Enron were ineffective to address this problem.

In sum, the controls that were in place were not ... effectively implemented by Management, and the conflict was so fundamental and pervasive that it overwhelmed the controls as the relationship progressed. The failure of any of Enron's Senior Management to oversee the process, and the failure of Skilling to address the problem of Fastow's influence over the Enron side of transactions on the one occasion when, by McMahon's account, it did come to his attention, permitted the problem to continue unabated until late 2001.

———

PART C

WILLIAM BRATTON, ENRON AND THE DARK SIDE OF SHAREHOLDER VALUE, 76 TULANE L. REV. 1275 (2002)*

[In the following excerpt, Professor Bratton sets out "four distinct stories" that may account for Enron's collapse.]

A. Enron as Conventional Market Reversal

Enron's results for 1998, 1999, and 2000 suggest some interesting comparisons. The firm's revenues increased by $10 billion from 1998 to 1999, and by $60 billion (to $100 billion) from 1999 to 2000. During the period, revenues contributed by Enron's old economy asset businesses—its pipelines and water companies—stayed stable. The revenue growth came from Enron's new economy trading business. Meanwhile, net after tax income rose much more slowly, as the chart below shows. Pre-tax profits (not depicted on the chart) increased by $1 billion in 1998, and then by only $500 million in each of 1999 and 2000. These simple horizontal analyses suggest declining returns in the trading business. More particularly, even as Enron had opened more and more new trading territory, entrance barriers were low. As time went on, Enron had to deal with dozens of competitors who hired away its employees to compete in what had become its bread and butter business, undercutting its profit margins. According to one analyst, Enron's trading margins collapsed from 5.3 percent in early 1998 to 1.7 percent in the third quarter of 2001. Investor attention to the problem was deferred for a time because the California energy crisis and the attendant period of sky high electricity prices led to extraordinary returns to all traders in that market. As California's prices dropped back to normal, Enron's shrinking trading returns became more apparent.

	1996	1997	1998	1999	2000
Revenue (billions)	13.2	20.2	31.2	40.1	100.7
Net Income (millions)	493	515	698	957	1,266

Enron's managers saw that rapid maturation of its new markets presented a problem for its growth numbers. Their strategy for dealing with it was to step up of the process of market creation, moving into new commodities like pulp and paper, steel, and, most daringly, bandwidth. In addition, in 1999 they successfully launched EnronOn-Line, a Net-based commodity trading platform. But these initiatives did not make up for the shrinking returns in Enron's bigger volume energy trading business. And there was another problem. Good as they were at opening markets, Enron's managers were less adept at the old economy discipline of cost control. Indeed, extravagant spending was an everyday incident of life at the firm.

Bandwidth emerged as a special problem. Enron had invested $1.2 billion to build and operate a fiber optic network. In 2001 it found itself with an operation with 1,700 employees which devoured $700 million a year with no sign of profitability. These numbers emerged just as severe overcapacity and financial distress hit the broadband business as a whole. The negative implications for Enron's stock price far outstripped the drain on cash flow. According to some outside analysts, when Enron's stock peaked in August 2000, priced at 90 with a price/earnings ratio of 60, a third of the price stemmed from expected growth in the broadband trading operation.

Old economy-related factors also contributed to Enron's problems. A number of big-ticket investments abroad—most prominently, the $3 billion power plant in Dahbol, India, a $1.3 billion purchase of the main power distributor to Sao Paulo, Brazil, and the $2.4 billion purchase of the Wessex Water Works in Britain—all were performing badly. These global mistakes were adding up in public view.

Finally, Enron's managers, laser focused on earnings as they were, had to keep an eye on its portfolio of "merchant investments." This contained many large block holdings of stock in technology and energy companies. Many of these positions were illiquid; hedges were either expensive or unavailable. Enron accounted for these investments as trading securities. Under this treatment, unrealized increases in the stocks' prices had flowed through to its income statement as gains. Thus had the rising stock market benefited Enron's numbers. A falling market would have the opposite effect, however.

The combination of the foregoing conditions and the stock market's general decline caused Enron's stock to fall precipitously even before resignations and scandals beset the company. The stock lost 39 percent of its value in the first six months of 2001. Had Enron gone into Chapter 11 at this point in the story due to these factors (taken together with a recession), the story would be unremarkable. The distress would stem from garden-variety risks and problems faced by all firms. Such failures bespeak erroneous business judgment and bad luck on the part of managers, but present no policy problem for business regulation. Enron captures our interest because these causes were necessary but not sufficient for its collapse, at least on the present state of the record.

B.   Enron as Derivative Speculation Gone Wrong

As we have seen, risk management through derivative contracting was a central component of Enron's trading business. These risk management services imply risks to the service provider. Enron nicely described these in its 2000 Annual Report:

> Wholesale Services manages its portfolio of contracts and assets in order to maximize value, minimize the associated risks and provide overall liquidity. In doing so, Wholesale Services uses portfolio and risk management disciplines, including offsetting or hedging transactions, to manage exposures to market price movements (commodities, interest rates, foreign currencies and equities). Additionally, Wholesale Services manages its liquidity and exposure to third party credit risk through monetization of its contract portfolio or third-party insurance contracts. Wholesale Services also sells interests in certain investments and other assets to improve liquidity and overall return, the timing of which is dependent on market conditions and management's expectations of the investments' value. . . .

> The use of financial instruments by Enron's businesses may expose Enron to market and credit risks resulting from adverse changes in commodity and equity prices, interest and foreign exchange rates.

The last sentence just quoted makes a critical point respecting the risk profile of firms that deal in derivatives. The degree of risk exposure depends on whether the "rocket scientists" in the firm's derivatives department fully or partially hedge their positions. Anything other than full hedging can mean a loss (or windfall gain) in the event of price volatility. Management's Discussion and Analysis (MD&A) in Enron's 2000 Annual Report makes a state-of-the-art governance assurance:

> Enron manages market risk on a portfolio basis, subject to parameters established by its Board of Directors. Market risks are monitored by an independent risk control group operating separately from the units that create or actively manage these risk

exposures to ensure compliance with Enron's stated risk management policies.

What Enron's "stated risk management policies" actually said was not disclosed. Some observers of Enron's fall suspect that, whatever the "stated policy," the practice might have been imprudent. More particularly, they hypothesize that Enron's derivatives traders had been pumping up its earnings with bets that energy prices would rise. Such bets would have meant significant profits in 1999 and 2000. In 2001, however, such betting would have meant significant losses as energy prices fell. On this scenario, Enron's fall mimics the 1998 case of Long Term Capital Management, with two differences. Here the high-tech bets were on energy prices rather than on interest rates, as there, and here there was no bailout engineered by the Federal Reserve, as there.

Others press a different, but concomitant derivative story. They allege that Enron's trading floor was a nest of corruption. The traders, it is said, routinely, overstated their own trading profits, impelled no doubt by the tournament system's demand for good numbers. The traders also abused the fair value accounting which now applies to their operation. Under this, some derivative positions are "marked to market" (MTM) each reporting period. Under MTM accounting, even though the position remains open and gain or loss has not yet been realized, the firm's income statement reflects the gain or loss implied by the contract's current value. For over-the-counter derivatives, no trading market sets this figure. The contract's value must be derived from an economic model. Unfortunately, generally accepted approaches to valuation did not yet exist for many items in Enron's vast stock of innovative derivative products, particularly those with longer terms. An opportunity for income statement legerdemain resulted, and it is alleged that Enron's traders took liberal advantage.

Similar accounting treatment, along with similar problems of speculative valuation, applied to Enron's long-term energy trading contracts. Here Enron aggressively exploited a special rule obtained for the energy industry, booking estimated gains for the lives of long-term supply contracts on a present basis, rather than spreading the recognition of revenues over the lives such contracts as would be done under conventional accounting. Indeed, it now appears that Enron marketed these and similar transactions to potential counterparties, selling accounting and tax treatments along with energy and financial products, with the treatments importing more substance than the transactions themselves.

If some or all of the foregoing allegations turn out to be true—and many have turned out to be true already—then derivatives trading very well may have brought Enron down in 2002 or thereafter. But in 2001, when Enron filed for bankruptcy, none of the foregoing was known to the financiers and related actors who determined Enron's fate. Strictly speaking, then, a malfunctioning derivatives operation did not bring Enron down. Whether the lion's share of these allegations prove out remains to be seen. It bears noting that in January 2002, UBS Warburg purchased the Enron's energy trading operation from the Chapter 11 debtor in possession, implying a judgment of soundness.

A cautionary, counterfactual note enters the story nonetheless: Even if Enron's derivative positions were appropriately managed, many observers were ready to believe the company to be a candidate for derivative distress in light of the direction of energy prices in 2001. Given that distress stemming from other quarters would make it difficult for Enron to maintain its credit rating and liquidity, and thus its relationships with contract and derivative counterparties, suspicions respecting derivatives exposure could not have helped matters. Enron's famously opaque financials only fueled suspicions . . . .

If Enron's derivative operation turns out to have been corrupt, there arise two powerful regulatory implications. First, the Commodity Futures Modernization Act should not have exempted Enron and similarly-situated firms from oversight. Second, the achievement of transparency respecting derivative positions for all financial intermediaries should take first place on the federal regulatory agenda.

C.   Enron as a Den of Thieves

[Professor Bratton begins by discussing the transactions set out in Part B of this Appendix (Note—Three Weddings and a Funeral). This portion of Professor Bratton's article is omitted.]

The Powers Committee report on LJM1 and 2, released in February 2002 . . . would establish beyond peradventure that the transactions between Enron, the SPEs and LJM1 and LJM2 involved breaches of fiduciary duties owed by Fastow and others to Enron. Terms of many sales contracts were skewed to favor LJM (and thus Fastow's equity interest). As a result of this, returns to LJM's outside equity investors were quite fantastic.

But no one knew any of this on October 17, 2001, when the only news was the fact that returns to Fastow amounted to $30 million. Given that previous disclosures held out the possibility of a significant upside possibility for Fastow, why all the brouhaha? As a matter of corporate law, deals like this do not breach fiduciary duties on a *per se* basis. If we follow the Delaware cases, the disinterested directors' approval means that a plaintiff seeking to make out a breach of the duty of loyalty has to bear the burden of showing that the transactions were unfair. Unfairness obtains only if Fastow's $30 million was out of line with the returns of managers of comparable limited partnerships, or if plaintiff could show that the terms of the transactions between Enron and LJM unduly favored LJM. In October 2001, neither situation obtained on the face of the public record. Given the large numbers involved in the Enron–LJM SPE transactions and a practice of large rewards for promoters of private equity schemes, a finding of fiduciary breach respecting the $30 million taken by Fastow would have seemed unlikely, absent Enron's other problems.

We can draw several lessons from the fact that, despite all of this, disclosure of the $30 million taken alone caused a scandal. First, contrary to the efficient market hypothesis, actors in the financial markets are selective so far as concerns assimilation of facts rendered in fine print sections of financials and other SEC documents. Second, the strength of the norm against self dealing brought to bear in the financial community varies with corporate results. On the upside, no one pays much attention. The operative norm is that of the corporate law duty—self-dealing transactions are acceptable so long as the consideration stays in the same ballpark as that of comparable transactions. Since everyone is making money, magnanimity makes sense. Disturbing the side deal could destabilize a productive employment arrangement. On the downside, everything is different. The same officer touted as an entrepreneurial genius on the upside starts to look like a thief and his or her self-dealing transaction causes a scandal even though it already was disclosed.

This could be called scapegoating. It is defensible nonetheless. The officer who succumbs to temptation on the upside assumes the downside risk of reputational ruin. The financial community and the law only tolerate self dealing transactions as a matter of expediency. Beneath that tolerance runs a strong a norm of aversion which can rear its head viciously in bad times. Neither Andy Fastow nor any other self dealing corporate actor plausibly can express surprise when a spate of red ink triggers his or her denunciation as a miscreant. Legal liability easily could follow: The transaction that did not breach the duty of loyalty when entered into in good times can breach the duty by virtue of the fact that unrelated subsequent events make it look unfair to an *ex post* decision maker.

To sum up on Fastow and his $30 million, this previously disclosed self-dealing transaction, taken alone, makes an implausible candidate for a leading role in an account of Enron's collapse. For that we must look to the broader terrain of Enron's dealings with its SPEs and affiliated companies. . . .

The confidence-based account of Enron's collapse becomes more compelling with a closer look at transactions between Enron and the SPEs related to LJM 1 and 2.

(a) *The Watered Stock.*

Recall that Enron funded the LJM-related SPEs with $1.2 billion of its own common stock, along with other assets, exchanged for debt instruments of the SPEs. A century ago, corporate law barred such transactions, prohibiting the use of debt or other promissory consideration in connection with the issue of new common stock. The risk that insiders would take the stock and enjoy an upside play without ever delivering on their promises was deemed great enough to support a *per se* prohibition. Today corporate law has a more relaxed attitude, remitting the decision as to the adequacy of the consideration to the discretion of the board of directors. Accountants retain a healthy suspicion: Notes received in exchange for a company's own common stock must be booked as deductions from shareholders' equity. The newly-issued stock is credited to the capital stock account at the purchase price, but the capital stock accounts elsewhere are debited (reduced) in the amount of the note. The result is a wash at the time the note is issued. As the note is paid, the reduction gradually is reduced, with a corresponding net increase to the shareholders' equity account.

Such niceties, however, did not fall within the purview of Enron's aggressive accounting practices. When it capitalized the LJM-related. . . . SPEs, Enron booked the notes issued by the SPEs as assets on its balance sheet and increased its shareholders' equity in a like amount, as one would do when selling newly issued common for cash in a public offering. Enron and Andersen later thought better of the treatment. Unwinding it meant the sudden and highly embarrassing disappearance of $1.2 billion from Enron's net shareholders' equity.

Significantly, the matter at least had been mentioned in the footnotes to Enron's 2000 financials. We see the stock going into the SPEs, and then some sentences later we read of "a special distribution from the Entities in the form of $1.2 billion in notes receivable. . . ."

(b) *The Equity Swaps That Weren't.*

Enron used the LJM-related SPEs . . . as counterparties in equity swaps. The swaps hedged Enron's exposure to downside risk on large block positions of publicly-traded equity it held in its "merchant" portfolio. Enron needed hedges of theses exposures to protect its income statement. Since the stocks were accounted for as trading securities, any unrealized decreases in their market values were deducted from Enron's net earnings. So far so good: It is normal for holders of a large, undiversified equity stakes, such as executives holding sizable positions in their own companies' stock, to enter into such contracts. Ordinarily this is done with a financial institution for a short or intermediate term. To describe a very simple transaction, if the stock subject to the swap goes up during the period of the swap, the executive pays the bank the amount of the price increase. Since the executive's own block of stock has gone up as well, the transaction is a wash so far as the executive is concerned. If the stock goes down, the bank pays the amount of the decrease to the executive. The bank in turn hedges its downside risk on the stock by selling the stock short or purchasing a put option on the stock.

The LJM-related SPEs acted in the position of the financial institution. But they did not make hedging contracts to cover their exposure in the event the stock subject to the swap lost value. Such contracts would have been expensive if available at all. Instead, the Enron common stock (issued in exchange for the SPE notes) used to fund the SPEs was to cover any SPE loss on the swap.

The Enron portfolio stocks under the swap did lose value. Enron set up the swaps just as the subject stock prices hit peaks. According to the Powers Report the value of the portfolio under the swaps fell by $1.1 billion across five fiscal quarters, so that the SPEs owed Enron $1.1 billion under the contracts. Enron, using the new "fair value" accounting, marked the value of its rights under the swap contracts to market for income statement purposes. Enron's reported numbers are lower than the later Powers figures: Enron's Annual Report for 2000 showed a $500 million gain on the swap contracts which exactly offset its loss on the stock portfolio. This $500 million made up about one third of Enron's earnings for 2000 (prior to restatement in 2001).

Problems arose. The Enron common used to fund the SPEs with capital to support the swaps also started falling. Where its value fell below the SPE's exposure on the swap, the SPE was technically insolvent. There resulted a series of improvised restructurings of the transactions, carried out by Enron's middle managers and concealed from its board of directors.

Worse, the whole transaction structure followed from a very faulty premise. The stock protected by the swaps was not going to go back up. The SPEs had not hedged, so under the deal, their losses on the stock would have to be covered by the stock issued by Enron. Collapsing everything into one transaction, Enron was issuing its own common to itself to cover its own income statement loss, thereby increasing its own net earnings by a total over the life of the swaps by a figure in excess of $500 million; $1.1 billion according to the Powers Report.

This one may not do under the most basic rules of accounting, indeed, under the most basic rules of capitalism. One issues stock to raise capital. One then uses the capital to do business and generate income. One cannot skip the step, and enter the capital stock directly into income. The value of a firm stems from its ability to take the capital and earn money over time; its stock market capitalization reflects projections of its ability so to do. Here Enron perverts the system, using its market capitalization—the value of its common—to support the value of its common.

At Ken Lay's direction, Enron folded the SPEs and the swaps in the third quarter of 2001, restating past earnings downward by almost $600 million. It had at least noted the arrangement in the footnotes to its 2000 Annual Report. The Report tells us of the hedges, and we see that Enron owes the SPEs "premiums" totaling $36 million. Further: "Enron recognized revenues of approximately $500 million related to the subsequent change in the market value of these derivatives, which offset market value changes in certain . . . investments. . . . " However, we are not told how the SPE will be covering its $500 million loss exposure.

Nor are we told why "premiums" were due and owing. It took the Powers Report to clear that up. Fastow negotiated a deal for LJM that guaranteed a windfall profit out of each SPE even before a single swap was put in place. The SPE would write a put on its Enron common and sell the put to Enron. Enron would pay a premium on the put at the market rate for such a contract. The SPE transferred the premium to LJM [as] an immediate return on capital. For example, with LJM1 and the Talon SPE, this was a $41 million payment, making for a 193 percent annualized return on the LJM investment. . . .

(c) *Summary*.

At around the same time Enron revealed the aforementioned downward restatements of its previously reported results, Enron announced a 2001 third quarter loss of $618 million (compared with around $300 million profits a year earlier). Just looking at the numbers for the year 2000—the downward adjustment stemming due to LJM-related entries was $519.9 million, a significant number in view of the fact that Enron's restated net earnings for 2000 amounted to only $847 million. The problem went beyond the numbers, which were not large enough to bring down Enron, taken alone. The terms of the transactions showed that Enron had been pumping up its earnings by abusing the SPE device. Whenever economics had gotten in the way of a result it wanted, it had used its own high-flying common stock to surmount the sticking point. On the upside this might pass; with the stock falling through the floor this meant trouble. Even worse, Enron no longer had any credibility—no one can believe anything asserted by a firm that covers up losses by entering into sham derivative contracts with itself.

It is possible that the credibility deficit in time could have brought down the firm. As to that we can only speculate, for independent reasons brought about Enron's collapse before the implications of its SPE accounting could be assimilated fully.

D.   Enron as a Bank Run

As a part of Skilling's "asset light" strategy, Enron had moved hard assets worth billions into affiliated entities. Many were majority owned by Enron and consolidated into its financials, some of these even having their own credit ratings. Many more were unconsolidated affiliates accounted for under the equity method. We have seen that with its SPEs Enron could divest itself of financial assets, even as it needed to sell only a relatively small stake to outside equity investors. With Enron's unconsolidated affiliates, bigger outside equity stakes were required.

But why would smart money from the financial community commit significant money as Enron divested junk assets? Leverage appears to provide a good working explanation. Enron wanted to realize as much cash as possible from its asset divestments. So in many cases

Enron and its outside equity turned to outside lenders to provide debt capital for the equity affiliate. Had the affiliates borrowed nonrecourse to Enron, these deals would not have threatened Enron's stability.

But it seems that in many cases outside lenders were unwilling to lend on the credit of the junk assets Enron was dumping into its equity affiliates. They insisted that Enron itself be liable on a contingent basis. As an example, the debt of Marlin Water Trust, an affiliate through which another affiliate, Atlantic Water Trust (in which Enron had a one-third equity interest) invested in a company called Azurix Corp., . . . which owned a waterworks in Britain. Marlin was capitalized with $125 million in equity and $915 million in debt. "Trigger events" in its debt contracts provided that Enron would become liable on its debt if either Enron lost its investment grade credit rating or its common stock price fell below $59.78. If either trigger went off, Enron had 90 days to register and sell sufficient common stock to pay down the debt. To the extent Enron did not raise the cash to pay the debt with a stock offering, Enron was obligated to make up the difference in cash. Similarly, Enron had backed $2.4 billion of debt of another equity affiliate, Osprey, with a contingent promise to issue Enron equity, and ultimately to assume the debt should the value of the stock prove inadequate.

The Marlin and Osprey debt obligations show us why Enron's house of cards finally collapsed. As Enron transferred hard assets from its balance sheet into the affiliates, it sought cash consideration for the assets rather than dodgy debt paper issued by the affiliate. Some cash would come in from outside equity participants, but not much. The affiliates had to be levered in order to attract private equity, which would accordingly be putting up only a small fraction of the value of the assets purchased. Significant cash consideration for the assets therefore meant outside lenders. To swing deals in the private placement debt market, Enron gambled on the price of its own high-flying stock. If the stock remained buoyant, the obligation to pay the debt came due only on the debt's maturity. At that time, the still-buoyant stock would provide a painless vehicle for paying off the debt should the value of the affiliate's assets fall short. If Enron's stock fell gradually and caused the trigger to go off, Enron could get out from under the debt by minting more stock. It would have a problem on only one scenario. If the triggering stock decline was a free fall, Enron would be unable to bail itself out with a new stock offering and the debt would be accelerated directly against it. It was the last scenario which actually occurred.

Here was high-leverage financing in a mode that the promoters of the leveraged buyouts of the 1980s never would have dared to imagine. The 1980s deals were old economy deals, in which lenders looked to the earning power of hard assets and took mortgages and security interests in the assets. New economy company that it was, Enron borrowed on a virtual basis: It took on contingent obligations secured in the first instance by its own market capitalization and incurred for the purpose of divesting itself of its own assets. In the 1980s, a highly-leveraged deal presupposed a projection that the company would generate earnings before interest and taxes sufficient to cover the debt. At Enron in the virtual 1990s, the value to back the deal came not from such an inside projection of what the firm could earn, but from the market stock price. Stock prices also result from future earnings projections—projections made by outside traders with limited information about the company. Sometimes, in runaway stock markets, the projections are dispensed with entirely as the traders chase trends.

Unfortunately, Enron took this gamble on its own stock price in such a bubble stock market. And so the gamble failed. As we have seen, Enron's stock declined for independent reasons as 2001 unfolded. This, together with the crisis in confidence triggered by the SPE disclosures, caused further price declines. Contract contingencies began to trigger obligations on billions of off-balance sheet debt. And, in a conjuring trick unimaginable to the principals of Drexel Burnham Lambert in their most creative moments, Enron had incurred these contingent liabilities without bothering fully to disclose them in its financial statements, whether on the balance sheet or in the footnotes. Indeed, it delayed public disclosure until the last possible point—mid-November 2001.

The sudden appearance of $4 billion of additional obligations struck Enron with more devastating effect than would have been the case with an old-fashioned, hard assets company. Enron already was frantically trying to prop itself up with new borrowing, including a $1.5 billion infusion from its partner in a bailout merger, Dynegy. Dynegy, on hearing of the $4 billion immediately insisted that the $9 billion merger price be reduced to $4.17 billion. At the same time, analysts reckoned that Enron needed $4 billion of immediate cash from somewhere to sustain its trading operation. But no cash was forthcoming. Enron's trading business melted away; in the last weeks almost all of its volume stemmed from unwind orders from parties going elsewhere. Dynegy waited a week after learning of the $4 billion, and then called off the deal. This happened just after Standard & Poors, having concluded that there would be no rescue, downgraded Enron to junk status. Enron had nowhere to go but [bankruptcy proceedings], where it ended up in a few days' time.

It was, as erstwhile CEO Jeff Skilling later observed, a "classic run on the bank." No wonder he had bailed out in August.

Skilling's description is apt. Enron had come to look more and more like a financial intermediary, whether a bank or a broker dealer. Such businesses depend on customer confidence. As we have seen, Enron already was looking less than confidence-inspiring by October 2001. But a financial intermediary's customers do not necessarily care about earnings management and executive self-dealing transactions so long as their own contracts are performed to the letter. Here "confidence" in the first instance means creditworthiness signified by an investment grade rating, particularly when the intermediary does business in derivative transactions. (That is why banks do this business through special-purpose subsidiaries with independent credit rating.) To lose the rating is to lose the derivatives business, as counterparties take their business risks to a shop able to enter into derivative contracts entailing no significant default risk.

As with the watered stock and the equity swaps that weren't, a good part of the story of the hidden liabilities was there to be gleaned in Enron's 2000 Annual Report. Although many affiliates and SPEs were unconsolidated, the magnitude of Enron's asset transfer program was apparent. Of $23.4 billion of assets reported on its balance sheet, $5.3 billion (22.6 percent) represented investments in "unconsolidated equity affiliates." Footnote 9 shows that these entities' liabilities exceeded that of Enron—they had a total of $4.7 billion current liabilities, $9.7 billion long term debt, and $6.148 billion of "other noncurrent liabilities." We also see clearly on Enron's income statement that its percentage share of affiliate earnings (accounted for under the equity method) could impact its bottom line significantly. In 1999, this figure was $309 million, 34.6 percent of Enron's net earnings of $893 million. The figure fell to $87 million in 2000, 8.8 percent of that year's reported $979 million of operating net income.

Two paragraphs above all in Enron's 2000 MD&A stand out in light of hindsight. They disclosure the contingent affiliate liabilities and triggers:

> Enron is a party to certain financial contracts which contain provisions for early settlement in the event of a significant market price decline in Enron's common stock falls below certain levels (prices ranging from $28.20 to $55.00 per share) or if the credit ratings on Enron's unsecured, senior long-term debt obligations fall below investment grade. The impact of this early settlement could include the issuance of additional shares of Enron common stock.

> ... Enron's continued investment grade status is critical to the success of its wholesale businesses as well as its ability to maintain liquidity. Enron's management believes it will be able to maintain its credit rating.

The paragraphs omit at least two material facts—that the "financial contracts" are affiliate debt contracts and derivative contracts unconsolidated on Enron's balance sheet and that Enron's contingent liabilities under the "provisions" amount to $4 billion, a figure which looms large in comparison to the $1.7 billion of short-term debt and $8.55 billion of long-term debt booked on Enron's 2000 balance sheet. Belated disclosure of the $4 billion total in November 2001 was by itself sufficient to bring down the firm.

E.   Summary and Analysis

All four of the preceding stories figure into a final account of
Enron's collapse. Had Enron suffered no reverses in its basic business
and no crisis of confidence, the contingencies respecting the $4 billion
of obligations that pushed Enron into Chapter 11 might never have
occurred. At the same time, had $4 billion of additional obligations
not come out of the woodwork after Enron entered into a merger
agreement with Dynegy, the merger might have been consummated.
We can pare down the account by coupling the crisis of confidence
and the hidden $4 billion of obligations as primary causes. The
coupling works well—both stories involve equity affiliate and SPE
transactions incident to Skilling's "asset light" strategy and aggressive
earnings management. Both stories also involve heavy use of Enron's
common stock as a back up currency importing stability to an otherwise shaky deal structure.

Viewed with the benefit of hindsight, the equity affiliate and SPE
transactions appear foolish, reckless, or fraudulent. There arises a
question as to just what the top officers of Enron thought they were
doing. Clearly, they pursued much more than the realization of
Skilling's promise of higher return on invested capital through divest-
ment of hard assets. Short term stakes loomed larger. Viewed in the
short term, Enron's asset sales to SPEs generated revenues and gains
which helped Enron's net earnings meet market expectations during
the interval prior to the realization of earning from Enron's new
investments. Had the financial assets sold to the SPEs been sold for
cash to third parties at arm's length, they still would have been a
source of funds. But one suspects that the net earnings impact of
arm's length sales would have been much less favorable. It accordingly
made perfect sense to put Fastow on both sides of the SPE transfers.
His divided loyalty assured a purchase price pitched to Enron's bottom
line, even as his limited partnership solved the Chewco problem and
stood ready to serve as three percent outside investor. At the same
time, Enron used its equity affiliates as a source of debt capital. This
borrowing helped the affiliates yield attractive returns for their outside
equity investors (and presumably to provide a source of funds for new
investments in the push to expand trading markets). Deflecting high-
leverage equity investment to the affiliates made perfect sense for
Enron since it had to limit direct borrowing in order to maintain the
investment-grade credit rating on which its trading business depend-
ed.

The equity affiliate strategy hit a snag only with the terms imposed
by the outside lenders. They wanted security beyond that afforded by
the affiliates' assets. Enron's managers responded with a gamble and
borrowed against their own stock price. This reflects a belief in their
own business plan. They must have figured that the stock price
eventually would become bulletproof, once the firm was awash in
earnings from broadband and other new initiatives. The same projec-

tion figured centrally in the LJM-related SPE derivative strategy. In the interim period before the new investments paid off, the sham equity swaps supported earnings per share. Had its stock price stayed buoyant, Enron might have covered the SPE's losses on the derivative contracts with all eyes remaining averted from the economic substance of the transactions. The decision to stay silent about the magnitude of contingent obligations similarly figured into the gamble. Had the stock price stayed up, the only downside on the borrowing was an incidental dilution of the common stock interest. And had the stock stayed up, the strategy might have worked. Unfortunately, with the stock price falling and Skilling pulling out of the company with no explanation, investors and reporters started to ask questions.

So, what now seems foolish, reckless or fraudulent, does so only because the gamble failed. Of course, gambling is what high risk-high return businesses are all about. Rarely, however, do we see managers of large firms stake so much (the whole company and their own liberty) on so little (concealment of off-balance sheet obligations and earnings manipulation).

Thus did Enron's managers cross the line from risk-averse to risk-prone behavior. Did they so rationally? We have seen that they had their reasons. We should add compensation to the list. Like most managers today, Enron's received significant compensation in the form of stock options. Option holding dulls the actor's sensitivity to degrees of distress on the downside, and at the same time gives the actor an incentive to generate chances for upside gains of high magnitude. Thus directed, a group of managers certainly would be more disposed to high risk strategies. It should be noted, however, that stock option-based incentives tend to operate in the long term. To effect a tie between compensation and Enron's managers' obsession with short-term numbers, we need to look to Enron's performance-based bonus scheme. These awards grew as Enron's stock price performed better relative to the market as a whole and as managers met performance criteria in respect of factors like funds flow, return on equity, and earnings per share. Amounts paid in 2001 based on 2000's numbers were substantial: $9.6 million for Lay; $7.52 million for Skilling, $3.295 million for Jeffrey MacMahon, $3.036 million for Fastow, and $2.3 million for Kopper.

But bonuses and options do not, taken alone, provide a plausible explanation for the Enron disaster. For one thing, performance-based bonuses and lavish option plans now are ubiquitous among American firms. If compensation schemes explain the behavior of Enron's managers, we should be seeing their behavior pattern replicated everywhere. As yet, however, they remain outliers. For another thing, Enron's managers gambled with more than other people's money. As they crossed the line to fraud, they staked their personal liberty. One requires more than cupidity and the behavioral skews of option pricing fully to explain such behavior.

For an alternative rational expectations explanation of the behavior of Enron's managers, we can turn to the "end period problem." In this scenario, an ordinarily risk averse rational actor finds her firm in distress due to business reverses. Bankruptcy being the most negative outcome possible, the actor rationally becomes risk prone, gambling everything in one last play to avoid destruction. Concealment comes with the territory. This explanation would make sense for Enron if either the foregoing story of conventional business reverses turns out to be much more severe than presently known or the allegations of a derivatives-based disaster turn out to be true. On either scenario, Enron's principals stumbled into distress and rationally started manufacturing income and concealing obligations as a way of buying time to turn things around and avert disaster.

If, on the other hand, Enron's business was sound but troubled, we need to tell a longer story. This was a firm where concealment became a way of life long before the start of the end period. Enron's principals did not just wake up to find themselves in trouble. They created much of the trouble themselves, voluntarily and unnecessarily driving the firm into an end period. They did so in pursuit of projects and returns that their business plan could not support. Arguably, rational, risk-averse actors would have moderated the pace of expansion, reporting negative numbers to extent necessary to an accurate portrayal of the firm's financial condition. To tell a compelling causation story on this scenario, then, we must look to Enron's organizational culture as well as its principals' economic incentives.

Enron fell because it pursued winning to excess. At Enron, winning was everything and everything became a tournament. Its business plan took unbundling to its logical conclusion, projecting a competitive victory over not only other firms but vertical industrial organization itself. Enron's top managers wanted to be surrounded exclusively by winners. So they made their workplace a tournament without end. They created a space that, unlike the outside world of regulation protecting losers, valued above all winning and the risk taking which necessarily precedes it. Winning also meant stunning earnings numbers: Where the tournament is ongoing, what counts is the most recent score. So important was winning at Enron that it became conflated with value maximization.

Labor economics holds out a formal model of a "superstar" actor. Inspired by the distribution of returns in show business, this describes situations where the size of personal rewards grows in lockstep with the size of the market and both market size and reward are skewed to the most talented people in the activity. To apply the description by analogy to firms in a market, for a "superstar firm," small advantages in capability vis-à-vis the top firm's competitors would result in the firm's disproportionately dominating its market. No doubt Enron saw itself in this light—as the Tiger Woods of energy trading. Its problem was that given ease of entry into energy trading and shrinking margins